Dedicated to

Charles L. Brewer

teacher, colleague, and friend

Handbook of Demonstrations and Activities in the Teaching of Psychology

Volume I

Introductory, Statistics, Research Methods, and History

edited by

Mark E. Ware
Creighton University

David E. Johnson
John Brown University

LEA LAWRENCE ERLBAUM ASSOCIATES, PUBLISHERS
1996   Mahwah, New Jersey

Lawrence Erlbaum Associates, Inc., Publishers
10 Industrial Avenue
Mahwah, New Jersey 07430

Library of Congress Cataloging-in-Publication Data

Handbook of demonstrations and activities in the teaching of psychology /
    edited by Mark E. Ware, David E. Johnson.
        p.   cm.
    Includes bibliographical references and index.
    Contents: v. 1. Introductory, statistics, research methods, and
history -- v. 2. Physiological-comparative, perception, learning, cognitive,
and developmental -- v. 3. Personality, abnormal, clinical-counseling, and social.
    ISBN 0-8058-1793-X (set : alk. paper). -- ISBN 0-8058-1790-5 (v. 1
: paper : alk paper). -- ISBN 0-8058-1791-3 (v. 2 : paper : alk.
paper). -- ISBN 0-8058-1792-1 (v. 3 : paper : alk. paper)
    1. Psychology--Study and teaching (Higher) 2. Psychology--Study
and teaching--Activity programs. 3. Psychology--Study and teaching-
-Simulation methods. 4. Psychology--Study and teaching--Audio
-visual methods. I. Ware, Mark E. II. Johnson, David E., 1953-
. III. Teaching of psychology (Columbia, MO)
BF77.H265 1996
150'.71'1--dc20   95-42447
                                                         CIP

Printed in the United States of America

10 9 8 7 6 5 4 3 2

Table of Contents

2. Making Statistics Relevant

3. Generating Data

4. Teaching Specific Concepts

5. Combining Statistics and Research Methods

Section III: Research Methods

1. Reviewing the Literature

2. Teaching Experimental Design and Methods of Observation

3. Teaching Research Ethics

4. Teaching Principles, Concepts, and Skills

5. Using Computers

6. Using Popular Media and Scholarly Publications

Section IV: History

Preface

The history of teaching psychology is as old and as new as psychology in the United States. G. Stanley Hall, one of modern psychology's promoters, devoted considerable attention to the teaching-learning processes including the founding of the journal, *Pedagogical Seminary*, in 1891. In addition Hall (1905) examined the meaning of pedagogy and concluded that pedagogy aimed to "unfold all the powers of the individual to their maximal maturity and strength" (p. 375). In earlier writing about pedagogy, Hall (1881) commented that "reverence of knowledge for its own sake is superstitious. Ignorance is preferable to knowledge which does not affect life, and the object of discipline is to make it practical" (p. 321).

More recently, one committee at the National Conference on Enhancing the Quality of Undergraduate Education in Psychology discussed the use of pedagogical techniques authorities refer to as active learning. The committee's observation (Mathie, 1993) that pedagogy should "include strategies that foster critical thinking and problem-solving skills" (p. 184) seemed to reiterate and operationalize Hall's conclusion. Members of the committee also observed that "there is too much information being offered to students and too little attention being paid to the strategies for learning, inquiry, and problem solving" (p. 184). Thus for over 100 years, psychologists have recognized that effective teaching and learning consist of developing and applying students' skills. Because effective teaching strategies are never out of vogue, this book consists of a collection of tried and tested teaching demonstrations and activities.

Teaching of Psychology (ToP), the official journal of Division Two of the American Psychological Association, previously published all of the articles in this book. Since its inception in 1974, *ToP* has become increasingly respected as a journal devoted to improving teaching and learning at all educational levels. An article (Weimer, 1993) in an issue of *Change* featured three from among almost 50 pedagogical journals; *ToP* was one of those three. The year 1993 also marked the completion of two decades of publishing *ToP*. Those interested in a history of the journal will find the founding editor's (Daniel, 1992) personal account both stimulating and informative.

We organized 291 articles into three volumes. Volume 1 consists of 91 articles about teaching strategies for courses that make up the core of most psychology curricula; introductory psychology, statistics, research methods, and history of psychology. The topical headings in Volumes 2 and 3 reflect the order of topics in many introductory psychology texts. Volume 2 consists of 104 articles about teaching physiological-comparative, perception, learning, cognitive, and developmental psychology. Volume 3 consists of 96 articles about teaching personality, abnormal, clinical-counseling, and social psychology.

In general we assigned articles to courses in which authors developed the demonstration or activity. A table at the end of each volume identifies the primary course in which readers can use each demonstration. In many instances, we also identified other, secondary, courses in which readers might use demonstrations.

The percent of articles representing each of the 13 topical areas was about evenly distributed. Noteworthy exceptions with more than 10% of the total number of articles were developmental (14%), research methods (13%), and social (12%).

Curious readers might speculate about trends in publishing demonstrations and activities during each of *ToP*'s two decades. Inspection revealed that 62% of the total number of articles appeared during the second decade. The number of articles for developmental and social psychology showed the most dramatic increases. History and statistics were the only topics that showed a decrease in the number of articles. We can offer no unequivocal explanation for such trends.

We would like to acknowledge the assistance of several individuals who contributed to this book. Marianne Haindfield, Sergio deLourenco, and Paul Marchio from Creighton University and Beth Magallon and Blaine Hubbard from John Brown University provided dedicated and persistent assistance.

Mark E. Ware
David E. Johnson

References

Daniel, R. S. (1992). *Teaching of Psychology*, the journal. In A. E. Puente, J. R. Matthews, & C. L. Brewer (Eds.), *Teaching psychology in America: A history* (pp. 433-452). Washington, DC: American Psychological Association.

Hall, G. S. (1881). American and German methods of teaching. *The Harvard Register, 3,* 319-321.

Hall, G. S. (1905). What is pedagogy? *Pedagogical Seminary, 12,* 375-383.

Mathie, V. A. (with Beins, B., Benjamin, Jr., L. T., Ewing, M. M., Hall, C. C. I., Henderson, B., McAdam, D. W., & Smith, R A.). (1993). Promoting active learning in psychology courses. In T. V. McGovern (Ed.). *Handbook for enhancing undergraduate education in psychology* (pp. 183-214). Washington, DC: American Psychological Association.

Weimer, M. (1993, November-December). The disciplinary journals on pedagogy. *Change,* 44-51.

SECTION I:
INTRODUCTORY

Promoting Active Participation

To promote critical thinking and rational debate among students, Michael Gorman, and his colleagues organized their introductory courses into three global perspectives (biological, environmental, and humanistic). The instructors discussed and defended the perspectives using *Walden Two* by Skinner and *The Eden Express* by Vonnegut. Students joined a group charged with supporting one of the positions in an in-class presentation followed by class discussion. Students gained valuable insights into the nature of the three perspectives and learned that the three perspectives were neither mutually exclusive nor completely adequate to explain all of the content of psychology.

Believing that biographical information on famous figures in psychology is lacking in most introductory texts and that students find this information interesting, Richard Kellogg developed a set of mini-biographies on major contributors to the field. The author presented the mini-biographies, which included photographs, to his students throughout the semester.

In an attempt to involve students actively in learning, Richard Wesp asked groups of students in upper-division courses to design and implement an out-of-class activity or demonstration for the introductory class. The advanced students implemented their projects in small groups of introductory students. The instructor distributed the introductory students' reactions to the advanced students. Both groups of students reaped benefits from the exercise.

Introducing Research Methods

This introductory psychology instructor, John Bates, told his students that he had telepathic powers. He demonstrated these "psychic" abilities by transmitting various images into the minds of the students and a confederate. Students generated alternative hypotheses to account for the phenomena and designed methods to test their hypotheses. By having students experience firsthand the importance of the rules of science, this instructional method may encourage greater scientific skepticism than simply teaching that the pseudosciences are false.

Using concepts and principles from a basketball game, James Polyson and Kenneth Blick taught their students about the fundamentals of the experimental method. The basketball game provided a context for illustrating an hypothesis, independent and dependent variables, and controls. The authors expressed delight at the quality of classroom discussion using this technique.

Art Kohn and Max Brill developed a method for exposing introductory students to laboratory demonstrations by enlisting the services of advanced psychology majors as instructors and administrators. Upper-level students volunteered to develop and implement sessions, and introductory students chose to experience the demonstrations in a cafeteria-choice format. Demonstration labs were developed for eight different content areas (e.g., sensation and perception, learning, social). Both the students who implemented the demonstrations and those who attended them derived numerous benefits. The authors identified suggestions for improving their original procedure.

Neil Lutsky promoted active learning among his students by having them develop a research idea from computerized analyses of previously collected data. After developing a research idea, students identified the basic statistical procedures required to analyze data, performed the data analysis according to a script using a computer statistical package, wrote summaries of the project, and critically evaluated the results. In addition to experiencing the research process first-hand, students gained a greater appreciation for the intricacies of doing research.

Roger Ward and Anthony Grasha employed astrology as a vehicle to teach valuable lessons about research methods. Students chose the personality profile that they believed most closely matched their own from a set of descriptions corresponding to the purported characteristics of persons born under the signs of the zodiac. The students' success in selecting their personality profiles provided an engaging method to introduce research issues such as hypotheses development, statistical significance, and social desirability.

Judith Larkin and her colleagues took a common student behavior (comparing grades on returned exams) and introduced the systematic study of that behavior into an introductory psychology class. The authors and students used Festinger's theory of social comparison and generated and tested hypotheses about the origins of students' exam-comparing behavior. The class discussed data collected from other introductory courses and related them to the theory. The discussions produced several questions for future research.

Using Computers

Thomas Brothen added computers to instruction in methodology by developing a set of exercises to give students experience with experimentally derived data. Students began the exercises as subjects in a data collection session that included studies on interpersonal attraction, personality, and conformity. Students tabulated the data and compared their individual data to the group data. This exercise is an effective method for introducing students to computer data collection.

Thomas Brothen and Janet Schneider developed computer software that introductory psychology students used to study for their final exam. Brothen and Schneider modified previously published Top 100 terms or concepts in psychology to match the presentation in their textbook. Students tested the efficacy of their study by attempting to match the terms or concepts with the definitions in their text. Preliminary data suggested that this exercise enhanced students" learning of the material.

John Bare developed techniques to use computers to demonstrate some of the classic methods and studies in psychology. Computers controlled the presentation of stimuli and collected data in simple short-term memory and sensory memory experiments. The author highlighted aspects of hypothesis testing and drawing inferences.

Integrating Supplementary Literature

Drew Appleby identified over 400 articles from *Psychology Today* that had relevance to a wide variety of undergraduate majors and careens. He organized the articles into categories that represented the diversity of students in his introductory psychology course (e.g., premed and theology) and allowed them to write extra credit reports on the articles they read. Students not only responded well to the articles but also found the list to be useful for projects in courses outside of psychology.

Lita Schwartz devised a way to introduce a theme of interest to her and of relevance to introductory psychology students. Schwartz used Ehrlich's novel, *The Cult.* and her research on conversion techniques as foci. The students' written reports about the novel explicitly applied previously discussed psychological concepts to cult situations.

David and Marilyn Winzenz offered their students a way to integrate literature and psychology in their introductory courses. They compiled a list of books (e.g., *One Flew Over the Cuckoo's Nest)* illustrating psychological concepts. Students chose five books to read during the semester and had short conferences with the instructor to assist them in making salient connections between the books and class material.

Employing Introductory Laboratories

Thomas Fish and Ian Fraser asked introductory students to complete a science fair project. Students had considerable latitude in choice of topic and presented their projects to their classmates for practice. Subsequently, students presented their projects in a fair atmosphere attended by over 1,000 people, including high school and university students and faculty. The authors surveyed upper level students who completed science fair projects and students who did not complete a project. Science fair participants believed that the experience prepared them for future course work and increased their learning of the material.

Albert Katz outlined how he avoided the expense of animal learning exercises and was able to give students significant laboratory experiences in introductory psychology. The article described the development of conditioning chambers for planaria and the implementation of conditioning labs. The use of planaria versus more traditional subjects (e.g., rats) for learning laboratories proved to be cost-effective and useful for introducing a wide range of concepts.

1 . PROMOTING ACTIVE PARTICIPATION

Making Students Take a Stand: Active Learning In Introductory Psychology

Michael E. Gorman, Anne Law
and Tina Lindegren
University of New Hampshire

One of the major goals of education is to foster critical thinking. The information we teach our students in psychology classes may be out of date in twenty years, but not the ability to think and argue. If students can be taught to critically evaluate new ideas, then they will be better prepared to continue learning long after they leave the classroom. To encourage this kind of active learning, we designed a new teaching technique for introductory psychology classes. Specifically, we built into our course a requirement that students take a stand on a major perspective in psychology and then actively defend this position against alternative views. The goal of this technique was threefold: (a) to stimulate critical thinking and evaluate skills in psychology and other areas; (b) to provide an overall framework and organizing structure from which to present basic ideas, empirical research and concepts from the varied topical areas in psychology; and (c) to encourage discussion and student participation in the classroom.

In three sections of introductory psychology (up to fifty students in each class), one taught by each of the authors, we presented three perspectives as representative of the dominant and prevailing approaches to understanding psychological phenomena. The first was termed the biological position, the idea that human behavior is primarily the result of genetic and evolutionary mechanisms. The second was defined as the environmental position, the idea that human behavior is primarily the result of environmental influences. The third perspective was referred to as the humanistic position, the idea that people are free to choose how they will behave. None of these positions alone is adequate to explain "human nature," nor are the three positions necessarily mutually exclusive. But rather than explaining this to students, the goal was for them to discover it for themselves.

These perspectives were discussed and defended in relation to two books selected by the instructors, *Walden Two* by B. F. Skinner and *The Eden Express* by Mark Vonnegut. *Walden Two* was chosen because it is a forceful and controversial statement of the environmental position. In Skinner's utopia, human beings are easily modified by manipulation of their environment. Skinner seems to ignore biological constraints on learning and dismisses the idea that people are in some way free to choose how they will behave and think. As a novel, this book provides no counter-arguments and thus it is an ideal catalyst—it forces students to generate their own criticisms.

In *The Eden Express*, Mark Vonnegut tells the story of his own descent into, and return from, schizophrenia. Because the effective therapy for Mark involved the use of tranquilizers and megavitamins, he believed the root of his madness was biological. However, the book also shows how Mark was caught up in existential dilemmas, family problems, troubles with his girl-friend, etc. There is ammunition for other perspectives: humanists could focus on the tension between Mark's real and ideal selves and environmentalists could focus on changes in his living situation, the way other people treated him, and the hospital environment in which he finally recovered.

At the beginning of the semester, the details of this teaching technique were explained to the students. Each instructor spent the first week of class discussing how each of the three perspectives could be applied to an understanding of aggression. From this, students were able to gain an initial appreciation of each perspective's approach and basic philosophy, *and* had some basis for choosing a position to defend in the subsequent discussions. Students either signed up for a group espousing one of the three positions (biological, humanistic, or environmental), or served as members of a separate evaluation group.

The position groups met several times, both in and outside of class, to prepare 10-15 minute presentations of their positions on each of the books. One class period was set aside for presentations with the next class reserved for discussion of all three perspectives. Evaluators listened to each position group's presentation on both books. Their role was to compare and evaluate, in writing, the perspectives and presentations. The *Walden Two* discussion was held approximately one month into the semester; *The Eden Express* discussion was conducted near the end of the semester.

The grading procedures were defined as the following: (a) position groups would receive a group grade based on each of their presentations; (b) members of each position group would write an individual paper describing his/her group's position on each book, encompassing both the pros and cons of their perspective; (c) evaluation group members would write a paper after each group presentation and the following discussion. These evaluation papers were to contain individuals' reactions to the three presentations, the positions they espoused, and the relation of these views to the important issues in each book. (In order to balance the workload, evaluators were also required to write a critique of a book selected from a prepared reading list.)

Evaluation. To assess the effects of this teaching technique, we distributed questionnaires at several times during the semester. It was our belief that small group discussions would facilitate individual student participation in the generating of ideas to defend their group's position and criticize other positions. After each in-class discussion, all position group members were given a questionnaire designed to assess the students' perception of the usefulness of this position group technique. One question asked students to rate, on a scale from 1 to 7, the extent to which their understanding of their own position has been increased by this group experience. A second question asked students to rate, again on a scale from 1 to 7, their impression of the combined effects of the group presentations and class discussion on understanding all three perspectives. For each question, mean ratings were combined across the three classes (n=76). Results of the questions from the *Walden Two* and *Eden Express* questionnaires are presented in Table 1. Results from the first question suggest that participation in a small group does lead students to perceive an understanding of their own position in relation to the books discussed. Results from the second question show that, overall, students felt this was an important learning experience. These results support our general hypothesis that small group participation is a useful technique to encourage critical thinking and increase general understanding of the issues at hand.

In general, we were pleased with our attempt to induce an appreciation for the complexity of psychology. We feel that we encouraged students to think critically about issues as opposed to (or in addition to) learning the "content" of introductory psychology. The three perspectives served as three themes that ran through the course. They provided the cohesion that is often lacking in introductory psychology courses, where the instructor feels as though he/she is teaching five courses instead of one.

This technique complements a wide range of teaching styles and approaches. Each of us taught the course somewhat differently, and emphasized different topics. Although we made an attempt to relate each topic to the perspectives, we often found that students were making the connections on their own. This reinforced our observation that the discussion groups were effective.

Many large sections of introductory psychology employ teaching assistants. This technique would lend itself well to that situation, as teaching assistants could run small sections for presentations and discussions. This could be a substantial improvement over traditional discussion sections that often degenerate into arguments over trivial points, or where students end up not knowing what is expected and contribute little to the discussion.

Students in large classes often feel stifled and anonymous. Splitting the class for discussion and assigning each student an active role may relieve some of the lost feeling of being only one of two or three hundred students. Presenting, arguing and questioning are important skills and this technique forces students to go beyond just learning information, to thinking critically about major issues in psychology.

Table 1. Mean Ratings by Combined Classes on Two Evaluation Scales

Position groups	Scale Item	
	Understanding of position due to group experience	Understanding of all positions due to presentations and discussion
Biological		
Walden Two	5.62	5.90
Eden Express	5.68	5.67
Humanistic		
Walden Two	5.38	5.33
Eden Express	4.40	5.74
Environmental		
Walden Two	5.48	5.30
Eden Express	5.26	5.57

N = 76. Rating of 7 = strongest effect.

The Mini-Biographical Approach to Psychology Instruction

Richard L. Kellogg
SUNY Agricultural and Technical College

It has been my experience in teaching that students often express greater interest about the personal lives of famous psychologists than about their research and theories. They ask questions about such topics as Freud's childhood, Piaget's relationship with his children, and the reasons why Watson was forced to terminate his academic career. Since most introductory textbooks present little material on the lives of noted psychologists, I have developed a set of "mini-biographies" which are incorporated into my lectures.

Although my selection of psychologists is subjective and based on a specific course outline, I have assembled photographs and biographical data on Francis Galton, Sigmund Freud, John Watson, Jean Piaget, and B. F. Skinner. Other instructors, of course, can develop brief biographies of those psychologists who receive the most emphasis in their courses.

To demonstrate this approach, I would like to summarize some of the material included in the mini-biography of the British psychologist, Sir Francis Galton (1822-1911). Students are impressed with the idea that a gifted amateur in field of psychology could make such major contributions to the discipline. Galton also serves as an excellent example of the attitudes, concepts, and values which prevailed in England during the last half of the nineteenth century.

As a pioneer in the study of individual differences, Galton tried to form an alliance between scientific methodology and the theory of evolution. He had a genius for creating tests of mental ability and developing several pieces of apparatus for laboratory research. What were some of the factors in Galton's experience which led to his versatility as a scientist?

First of all, it is significant that Galton descended from an illustrious and wealthy family. The seventh and final child to be born, Galton's father was a successful banker and his mother was half-sister of Charles Darwin's father. He inherited a large fortune in his youth which enabled him to pursue his hobbies and interests throughout adult life. This privileged background allowed him to become an amateur in the sciences, and completely independent of the universities.

English boarding school provided him an educational foundation. Galton attended until the age of sixteen but the stern emphasis on rote learning was not to his liking. Despite his unpleasant introduction to school, his later life indicates a profound respect for the value of academic preparation.

An interest in medicine persisted throughout the career of the psychologist. Galton initiated his medical studies at Birmingham General Hospital and displayed a disturbing tendency to perform medical experiments on himself. He completed subsequent study at the medical school of King's College in London but did not complete requirements for a medical degree. He did, however, receive an arts degree in 1843 from Cambridge University.

Galton was afflicted several times with emotional problems which threatened to destroy his career. Perhaps because of the intense academic competition, he suffered an emotional breakdown during his third year at Cambridge. Upon the death of his beloved father in 1844, Galton suffered another emotional collapse and relinquished all hopes of attaining a medical degree. These emotional conflicts may have motivated the young Galton to delve more deeply into the complexities of human psychology.

Like many Victorians of the upper class, Galton was a man of the world who was fascinated with travel and exploration. He traveled throughout Egypt, the Sudan, and the Middle East during the 1840s. His reputation as an explorer was established through an expedition which he led to Africa in 1850. He was later involved, as an officer of the Royal Geographic Society, in planning other expeditions to remote corners of the world.

Probably as a result of his travels, Galton became interested in creating new methods for the prediction of weather patterns. He developed a system for collecting weather information from numerous places in the world and then plotting it on maps. The important relationships he discovered between high and low pressure systems are still employed in reporting weather conditions.

Another characteristic of Galton was his concern with problems of human evolution. He was strongly influenced by his cousin Charles Darwin's *On the Origin of Species*, a work which postulated a process of natural selection as the basic mechanism for the evolution of different species. Galton, in his book

Hereditary Genius (1869), speculated that psychological traits could be inherited in the same way as biological characteristics. He contended that the human race could be improved through eugenics, the science of selective breeding.

This focus on Darwinian thinking was accompanied with a degree of anti-religious sentiment. Galton's attitude was typical of a general antagonism between evolutionists and organized religion during this era. He felt that evolutionary principles exposed the dogmatism and simplistic nature of traditional religious beliefs.

Along with an anti-theological stance, Galton believed in the inherent inferiority of women. Fancher (1979, p. 252) has commented that Galton "Like most Victorian males, was certain that women were intellectually inferior to men." This notion, based on the incorrect logic of correlating intelligence and sensory acuity, stemmed partially from results obtained at the first mental-testing center that he established in 1882. Galton also concluded that the most intelligent people were those with the most accurate senses.

As to the nature-nurture controversy, he asserted that heredity was the major agent for transmission of intellectual abilities. By the use of statistical techniques, Galton demonstrated in *Hereditary Genius* that eminent men tended to have eminent offspring. He concluded, incorrectly, that any environmental effects on intelligence were negligible.

To support his views on heredity, Galton developed the twin-study method to determine the relative contributions of genetics and environment on human development. He calculated statistical correlations of identical and fraternal twins to find whether specific traits were inherited or acquired. This method is still used to determine the genetic component of psychological characteristics.

Francis Galton was also the inventor of the word association test. His test was a predecessor to the free association method later used by Sigmund Freud in psychoanalytic therapy. Galton found, much to his surprise, that many of his associations went back to childhood and some of them were rather embarrassing. He may have suspected something similar to the unconscious mind lurking behind the peculiar associative processes.

One interesting innovation of Galton is found in the area of fingerprinting. He created the first reliable system for classifying and identifying fingerprints in 1892. Scotland Yard adopted his procedure in 1901 and it soon spread to police agencies around the globe. Boring (1929, p. 453) has said of Galton that he "initiated experimental psychology in England as he introduced so many other things." Francis Galton was knighted in 1909 for his unique contributions to scientific advancement.

To conclude, it is apparent that a mini-biography of Galton can readily lead to a discussion of exploration, meteorology, statistics, genetics, evolution, and eugenics. As students learn about the life of Galton, they develop a curiosity to discover more about his amazing scientific legacy. This approach can help students to realize that Sir Francis Galton demonstrated a sophisticated understanding of human psychology which was unparalleled in England during the late nineteenth century.

References

Boring, E. G. *A history of experimental psychology.* New York: Appleton-Century Company, 1929.

Fancher, R. E. *Pioneers of psychology.* New York: Norton, 1979.

Conducting Introductory Psychology Activity Modules as a Requirement in Advanced Undergraduate Courses

Richard Wesp
Elmira College

Small-group activities provide more personalized attention in large introductory psychology classes but require considerable instructor time. Small groups of students in three upper level undergraduate courses were required to design, implement, and evaluate projects that would actively involve introductory students in a topic related to one that the upper level students were studying. Students in Introductory Psychology classes selected and participated in two activities. Advanced and introductory students said that involvement in these activities was a valuable experience and should be required in subsequent terms. This method allows upper level undergraduates the opportunity to apply what they have learned by requiring them to teach, and it increases the amount of individual attention provided students in the introductory class.

One way of providing more personalized attention in large introductory psychology classes is through small-group activities, such as lab exercises or discussion groups (Benjamin, 1991). Typically, undergraduate teaching assistants (TAs) conduct these sessions. For example, Kohn and Brill (1981) described a low-cost, introductory level psychology lab run by students.

Kohn and Brill's approach was unusual in having minimal faculty involvement, but the authors identified this as one of the weak points of their procedure. More typically, faculty take an active role in training TAs and coordinating the small-group activities, requiring more of the instructor's time (Benjamin, 1991). Mendenhall and Burr (1983) required weekly meetings with TAs who served as small-group discussion leaders. In my experience, weekly meetings are the minimum required to ensure course quality, consistency, and coherence. When more diverse activities are offered, additional individual meetings are likely required.

Thus, instructor time is a limiting factor in using TAs. The time can be reduced, however, if students from an instructor's advanced courses serve as TAs. Because TAs benefit from their teaching experience (Mendenhall & Burr, 1983), students in advanced courses should see similar benefits, justifying their participation.

Cooperative arrangements between classes have been used before. For example, Anderson, Gundersen, Banken, Halvorson, and Schmutte (1989) had undergraduate students in abnormal psychology serve as "clients" for graduate counseling students and reported that the experience was beneficial to both groups. Wagor (1990) required students in a Sensation and Perception course to construct a demonstration of a sensory or perceptual phenomenon. Students donated their projects for use in other classes. The technique described herein extends Wagor's idea by having the advanced students conduct their demonstrations for introductory students and grade the introductory students' papers.

Method

Small groups of 2 to 5 students in three upper level courses designed, implemented, and evaluated projects that actively involved introductory students in a topic related to one that the upper level students were studying. This project was in addition to other required activities in these otherwise traditionally taught courses. Twenty-three students in Experimental

Methods and 21 students in Biofeedback and Self-Control worked with 33 students in one Introductory Psychology class during one semester. In a second semester, 29 students in Behavior Therapy worked with two introductory classes of 36 students each.

On introducing the assignment to the upper level students, I described several possible activities, such as a field trip to a local psychiatric center and computer simulations. I told students that projects should engage 5 to 15 introductory students, take about 1 hr outside of participants' scheduled class, have no significant costs, and require a written assignment in which the introductory students would summarize and react to the activity. Each group submitted a description and a critical evaluation of its project. These teaching projects were worth 5% of each upper level student's grade.

Students in the Introductory Psychology classes were required to participate in two of the available activities. I described each activity, announced when it would be scheduled, and circulated a sign-up sheet. After participating, introductory students wrote their papers, which I collected and passed on to the upper level students who graded them and provided written comments. Each activity was worth 5% of the course grade and was evaluated on a pass-fail basis.

Results and Conclusions

The upper level students developed activities for progressive relaxation, simple lie detection, basic biofeedback, a field trip to a local psychiatric center, a research study on alcohol use, operant conditioning with rats, and systematic desensitization. Students spent from 1 to 2 weeks identifying and planning their activity. Although some activities required more than 1 hr, the remaining criteria (active participation, small groups, low cost, and a written assignment) were met for all of the projects.

In evaluating their projects, all groups of upper level students suggested that the assignment was a valuable experi-ence and should be required in the future. Comments included that introductory students seemed to react well to seeing other undergraduates teach, that projects should be worth a larger portion of the course grade, and that they learned course material better because they were required to apply it. Their written descriptions of the projects suggested that the students had developed a good understanding of the concepts they presented.

In two of the introductory classes, 81% of enrolled students completed written evaluations. Of these respondents, 86% indicated that having out-of-class activities was valuable and should be done again, and 90% reported that they liked having other students teach them. Students also rated how much each project increased their understanding of the material covered. On a scale ranging from *very little* (1) to *very much* (7), the mean ratings ranged from 3.5 for the relaxation exercise to 5.8 for the biofeedback project; the overall average was 4.1. These ratings seemed low, considering that 86% of the students suggested that projects be offered in future introductory courses. Ratings may have been lower than expected because the projects offered new information that did not relate directly to the exam questions.

Although the procedure took slightly more time than I typically spend on individual activities in the introductory class, there were several benefits. One was that the time I spent helping advanced students design their projects I would normally have spent in meetings with TAs or conducting the demonstrations. Given that the introductory students enjoyed having upper level students teach them, it seems that little was lost in not having me conduct the projects. Possibly the most valuable outcome was that the upper level students were able to apply some of the skills and knowledge they had learned in their courses. Moreover, many students in the upper level classes might never have had the time or inclination to serve as TAs. Requiring students to work in groups allowed the less self-confident and less skillful students to conduct successful projects. Finally, the procedure provided introductory students with a wider variety of options as well as several new activities that I had never offered.

References

Anderson, D. D., Gundersen, C. B., Banken, D. M., Halvorson, J. V., & Schmutte, D. (1989). Undergraduate role players as "clients" for graduate counseling students. *Teaching of Psychology, 16*, 141-142.

Benjamin, L. T., Jr. (1991). Personalization and active learning in the large introductory psychology class. *Teaching of Psychology, 18*, 68-74.

Kohn, A., & Brill, M. (1981). An introductory demonstration laboratory produced entirely by undergraduates. *Teaching of Psychology, 8*, 133-138.

Mendenhall, M., & Burr, W. R. (1983). Enlarging the role of the undergraduate teaching assistant. *Teaching of Psychology, 10,* 184-185.

Wagor, W. F. (1990). Using student projects to acquire demonstrations for the classroom and laboratory. *Teaching of Psychology, 17,* 253-255.

Note

I gratefully acknowledge suggestions made by Ruth Ault and three anonymous reviewers.

2. INTRODUCING RESEARCH METHODS

Teaching Hypothesis Testing by Debunking a Demonstration of Telepathy

John A. Bates
Department of Educational Foundations & Curriculum
Georgia Southern University

Introductory psychology students were told that their instructor had telepathic powers. The instructor demonstrated these "psychic" abilities by transmitting various images into the minds of the students and a confederate. Students generated alternative hypotheses to account for the phenomena and designed methods to test their hypotheses. This article describes the methods used to perform the psychic acts and outlines the structure of the hypothesis-testing activity. By allowing students to experience firsthand the importance of the rules of science, this instructional method may encourage greater scientific skepticism than does the direct teaching of the falseness of pseudoscientific claims.

Many postsecondary educators are concerned about the rising tide of pseudoscientific, fundamentally anti-intellectual belief among otherwise well educated Americans. Bates (1987) reported that nearly half of a large sample of teacher education students believed that the full moon causes violent behavior. Feder (1986) found that more than one third of the students at a northeastern state university believed that ghosts are real. Miller (1987) conducted a national survey indicating that nearly two fifths of college graduates believe that the earth has been visited by aliens from other planets.

Educators combat student misbeliefs by debunking pseudoscientific claims specific to their own disciplines (e.g., Eve & Harrold, 1986; Harrold & Eve, 1986; Hoffmaster, 1986). These efforts have met with modest success: Some have demonstrated increased factual knowledge about reality without much corresponding decrease in pseudoscientific beliefs (Harrold & Eve, 1986); others have reported significant gains in scientific skepticism, but only for students with a neutral position on pseudoscientific claims (Banziger, 1983). Only a few reported attempts (notably, Gray, 1984) have demonstrated significant long-term changes in students' beliefs across a broad range of paranormal and irrational claims.

The classroom exercise described here holds some promise as a technique to debunk a specific pseudoscientific claim and to promote critical, scientific inquiry into psychological phenomena in general. An important goal of this exercise was to capture and hold students' attention. As Hoffmaster (1986) noted, "one of the driest subjects on earth to try to teach is the scientific method" (p. 432). The key to this goal, I believed, was to be found in the application of some basic principles of psychological arousal theory and of stage magic.

Format of the Activity

The Students

The activity was conducted in two different classrooms of introductory psychology. Both classrooms included about 35 students, all first-semester freshmen, about two thirds of whom were women.

The Lesson

All aspects of the activity were identical for both classrooms and proceeded in four stages.

Introductory information. The first 30 min of a class meeting was used to discuss some basic concepts of science. Initial consideration was given to the scientific belief in a physical reality that is independent of any observer. Special emphasis was given to the formulation of empirical hypotheses, in contrast to other sorts of answers to questions. Finally, it was pointed out that scientific hypotheses must be stated in such a way that evidence could be obtained to demonstrate that they are false, if they really are false. The lecture component of the presentation concluded with the assertion that all scientific endeavors, including scientific psychology, are not attempts to establish absolute truth, but rather are attempts to expose and eliminate false claims about the nature of reality.

Demonstration of psychic ability. After completing the lecture component, I announced that I had discovered a talent for transferring my thoughts

13

telepathically into the minds of other people. I offered to demonstrate my talent, but said that it was not yet refined, so I could not guarantee that everyone would receive exactly the right thought.

I told the class that I would think of a two-digit number from 1 to 50, such that both numbers would be odd and different from each other. As examples, I told them that the number could not be something like 11, but that 15 would be okay. After a moment, I wrote a number on my tablet, drew a line through it, wrote another, and commented that the second number seemed to be a better choice. Next, I stared at the number and announced that I was transmitting it to the class. Each student was to write down the first number that came to mind and that fit my description.

As soon as all students had written a number, I asked if any of them had chosen 37. To their surprise, about one third of the students had thought of that number. I looked disappointed, then asked whether any had chosen 35. I showed them my tablet and explained that I had written 35 first, then crossed it out. Some of the class thus might have picked up the wrong signal. I asked how many of them had thought of either 35 or 37, and more than half the class raised their hands.

I suggested that numbers do not always work for everyone; sometimes, a picture is better. Therefore, I told them that I would think of two simple geometric shapes, one inside the other. At this point, I drew something quickly on the tablet, grumbled about being sloppy, tore off the page, and drew something else. I informed the class that I was sending the image of the two shapes, and I asked them to draw what first came to their minds. After a moment, I held up the tablet for all to see the shapes of a triangle completely circumscribed by a circle. Again, about one third of the class indicated that they had drawn the same picture.

I asked whether any had drawn a circle inside a triangle, explaining that the images sometimes become reversed in the transmission. Another third raised their hands. I then showed them the drawing that I had rejected—one of a square not fully surrounded by a circle—and asked if anyone inadvertently had picked up a stray signal of it. Several more hands went up. Then, one student volunteered that she had put a triangle inside a square. I asked whether anyone else had received parts of both signals. By now, nearly everyone had raised a hand.

Finally, I told them we had with us a guest who shared with me an almost perfect psychic link. The guest, another member of my department, was introduced. I explained that our special mental relationship was best demonstrated by a simple playing-card guessing game. A volunteer shuffled a standard deck of cards and dealt three rows of five cards each, face up, on the table at the front of the room. My partner faced the back of the room, and I asked one of the students to point to one of the cards. When the student did, my partner turned around, and I proceeded to point to an apparently random sequence

of the cards, saying after each, "Is it this one?" or "Is it that one?" Each time I did not point to the target card, my partner replied negatively. When, after five or six repetitions of this procedure, I finally pointed at the target, my partner quickly responded affirmatively.

Small-group generation of hypotheses. Several repetitions yielded successful detection of the target card. Students who were still skeptical of my ability were challenged to develop a more parsimonious account of what they had observed. Students organized into groups of three or four and tried to produce at least two different testable hypotheses that could answer the question, "How did he do that?"

Hypothesis testing/revision. At the beginning of the next class meeting, students again organized into their groups, and a single, one-page worksheet requiring several categories of responses was distributed to each group. Students first were asked to summarize their observations of the psychic phenomena, to generate at least two alternative empirical hypotheses to account for their observations, and to design a test that could falsify each hypothesis. Thirty min were allotted for this part of the activity.

Next, my colleague and I made ourselves available for hypothesis testing. The groups took turns specifying a set of conditions under which the playing card "thought transfer" should occur. To ensure all groups sufficient time to test their hypotheses, I informed the class that if I knew it would be impossible to perform the transfer under a given set of conditions, then I would tell them so, rather than taking the time to demonstrate it.

The most common hypotheses involved either some prearranged number of cards to which I would point before reaching the target card or some mathematical formula involving the numerical values of the target and other cards. These were quickly rejected when the groups discovered that they could specify when in a sequence I should point to the target, and my colleague still would be able to identify it. The next most common hypotheses involved where on a card my finger was when I pointed to it. These were rejected when I varied the part touched or when I was not permitted to touch the card, which had no effect on the outcome.

Once all groups had tested both hypotheses once, they were given the opportunity either to retest what seemed to be the better of the two or to test a modified or new hypothesis. Most groups rejected all versions of numerical or positional hypotheses and focused on the modification of what I said to my partner or the tone or volume of my voice.

Within about 20 min., one or two groups were certain that they had determined the correct explanation for the phenomena, so I invited one of the members to take the place of my partner to see if the outcome could be duplicated. It was to their considerable delight, as well as to the consternation of some of their classmates, when these students were able to identify the target card.

Hypothesis testing, revision, and retesting continued until 15 min remained in the class period. Time was provided for the completion of the worksheet, including discussions of test outcomes, modifications of hypotheses, and final conclusions regarding my "special ability." As the students turned in their assignments and filed out, many of them looked at me with knowing smiles, some appeared less than sure of themselves, but nearly all were commenting to each other about what had occurred, using words like *falsified, replicate,* and *empirical.*

Postscript: How the Psychic Deeds Were Done

There were three components to the psychic demonstration, all supposedly involving the transference of thoughts from one mind into one or more other minds. The first two—transference of a number and transference of a shape—are illusions commonly performed by stage mentalists like Kreskin and may be thought of as the hook to capture student attention. Procedures for performing these feats are discussed in detail by Marks and Kammann (1980) in their critical analysis of claims of psychic ability.

Number transference and shape transference rely on poorly understood but documented and reliable population stereotypes in the construction of various categories of thought. As you recall, the demonstration involved the mental transference of a two-digit number between 1 and 50, such that both digits were odd and different from each other. Generally, few people realize that the qualifications placed on number selection have severely reduced the possible choices. There are only eight numbers that satisfy all the criteria: 13, 15, 17, 19, 31, 35, 37, and 39. Furthermore, the instructions were clarified by adding that the number could not be 11, but that something like 15 would be acceptable. Using 15 as an example of an acceptable target guarantees that virtually no one will select it, thus reducing the number of likely choices to seven. Marks and Kammann (1980) found that about 33% of a sample of adults think of 37 as the target number and that another 25% select 35. Thus, by claiming to have chosen first one then the other of these numbers as I was performing the thought transference, I was able to include nearly 60% of the class in my set of successes.

Most college students probably could discover that the limited number of possible targets made the outcome far less dramatic than it first appeared. It is important, therefore, to move on immediately to another, different demonstration of psychic ability—the transfer of an image of two simple geometric shapes, one inside the other. Population stereotypes for shape selection are as strong as those for number selection. Marks and Kammann reported that 33% will draw a combination of a triangle and a circle, 25% will draw a combination of a square and a circle, and 11% will combine triangle with square. With a little showmanship, I demonstrated to about 70% of my students that I had indeed transferred my thoughts into their minds.

The central component of the entire demonstration was the card-selection routine that my colleague and I enacted. To perform this illusion, cards are arranged randomly in three rows; the number of cards in each row is irrelevant. The confederate for this task needs only to remember that the top and bottom rows will be the *this* rows and the middle row will be the *that* row. If the "mentalist" points to a card and uses the correct adjective for that row of cards, then it is not the target card. The mentalist is pointing to the target only when the incorrect modifier is used.

For example, assume that the target card was in the middle row. I might point successively to cards in the top row, the middle row, and the bottom row, before pointing to the target. I would ask, "Is it this one?," "Is it that one?," and "Is it this one?," respectively. My partner would respond, with varying degrees of apparent certainty, that none of those was the target. Finally, I would point to the target and ask, "Is it *this* one?" My partner quickly would be able to respond correctly.

This routine has several advantages as an event for which students must generate empirical hypotheses. First, it is easy to do: My colleague only had about 1 min of instruction before we entered the classroom for our performance, and he never made a mistake. Second, very few students are likely to be familiar with it. Third, the trick behind the event seems to be obvious but it is not. The unexpected difficulty that students experience in trying to explain what they have observed tends to arouse and maintain their curiosity. Most important, for its use in a classroom, the demonstration and its underlying causes are empirical events. Students can directly manipulate the variables of the demonstration and observe a variety of outcomes. Hypotheses can be tested quickly, modified, or rejected, without special equipment or training. Best of all, when students uncover the solution to their problem and are able to replicate the event as evidence of their success, they experience the same sort of satisfaction felt by scientific psychologists in their systematic study of human behavior.

An important goal of this activity is to capture student attention. I have been teaching undergraduate students the basic principles of science for about 12 years and do not recall ever having achieved the enthusiastic class participation that is maintained throughout the demonstration of my psychic powers. Whether this enthusiasm is due entirely to the mode of presentation of the lesson or to some combination of environmental and student factors, I cannot say. My experience suggests that incorporating novel, surprising, and varied (i.e., psychologically arousing) stimuli is essential if students are going to pay attention to the abstract concepts and philosophical issues central to scientific inquiry. This lesson incorporates such stimuli and captures student attention.

References

Banziger, G. (1983). Normalizing the paranormal Short-term and long-term change in belief in the paranormal among older learners during a short course. *Teaching of Psychology, 10,* 212-214.

Bates, J. A. (1987). Degrees of scientific literacy and intellectualism among students in a college of education. *The Foundations Monthly Newsletter, 4,* 7-9.

Eve, R. A., & Harrold, F. B. (1986). Creationism, cult archaeology, and other pseudoscientific beliefs A study of college students. *Youth and Society, 17,* 396-421.

Feder, K. L. (1986). The challenge of pseudoscience. *Journal of College Science Teaching, 26,* 180-186.

Gray, T. (1984). University course reduces belief in paranormal. *The Skeptical Inquirer, 8,* 247-251.

Harrold, F. B., & Eve, R. A. (1986). Noah's ark and ancient astronauts: Pseudoscientific beliefs about the past among a sample of college students. *The Skeptical Inquirer, 11,* 61-75.

Hoffmaster, S. (1986). Pseudoscience: Teaching by counterexample. *Journal of College Science Teaching, 26,* 432-436.

Marks, D., & Kammann, R. (1980). *The psychology of the psychic.* Buffalo: Prometheus Books.

Miller, J. D. (1987, June). The scientifically illiterate. *American Demographics,* pp. 26-31.

Note

I thank Leigh Culpepper for his help in preparing this article.

Basketball Game as Psychology Experiment

James A. Polyson
Kenneth A. Blick
University of Richmond

Helping students understand basic concepts in experimental method can be quite a challenge for the introductory psychology teacher. Some students find the topic difficult or boring, leading one teacher (Gleitman, 1984) to recommend covering methodology only where it is necessary in order to understand some other topic. Even if one agrees with Gleitman, that still leaves a lot of methodology to be taught in introductory psychology.

It has been suggested (Vandervert, 1980) that the learning of psychological concepts is facilitated when the material is presented in relation to topics that are meaningful to students. One strategy for making psychological knowledge more relevant to students' real-world interests has been the use of popular culture in the classroom (Hughes, 1984; Polyson, 1983; Solomon, 1979). Using a similar approach, we have found that it is possible to introduce new methodo-

logical concepts and illustrate previously defined concepts using a basketball game.

It should first be noted that using basketball examples might be more effective at a school with a high level of enthusiasm for the intercollegiate basketball program. Such was the case at the University of Richmond this past season. The Spiders had their best season ever, winning two games in the NCAA tournament before losing to perennial power Indiana. Basketball was a popular topic of conversation on campus, and it was during such a discussion that the present authors discovered their mutual interest in using basketball to illustrate basic experimental method.

A basketball game can be construed as a psychology experiment. For example:

Hypothesis. A basketball game is the testing of a hypothesis regarding which of two teams is "better" in the wide array of mental ad psychomotor skills called basketball. Some observers, such as a loyal fan or bettor, would predict a winner. That is a one-tailed hypothesis. An impartial observer, such as a TV commentator, might decline to say which team will win, thus making a two-tailed hypothesis.

Independent Variable. The independent variable is simply the two teams, the groups that are being compared. The experimenter in psychology often tries to compose the two groups in a random fashion so they are as equal as possible at the outset. Random assignment is impossible in basketball, although the pro draft is an attempt to introduce some "fairness" into the team selection process at that level.

Dependent Variable. The behavior that is being compared must be defined in a measurable way. The measure of skill in a basketball game is the number of points scored; the "better" team is the one scoring higher on that measure. That is the operational definition. We must also define "higher." How much higher? When psychologists compare the scores of two or more groups, they use statistical analysis to decide what difference is necessary in order to say that the outcome was not just luck or chance. In basketball, the necessary difference is 1 point, except for some neighborhood pick-up games in which a team must win by 2 points.

Control. The basic reason a basketball game is an experiment and not just a "guess" is that the designers of the game have attempted to minimize any explanations for the game's outcome other than basketball skill ("to keep the losers from making excuses," as one student put it after our big upset win over Auburn). That is why the number of players on the court is kept even and irrelevant skills such as judo are ruled out by calling fouls. The home court advantage can be ruled out by doing the experiment twice in a home-and-away series (replication). A loose rim provides no advantage for either team because the teams switch goals at halftime (counterbalanced design). This is essentially what a psychology experiment attempts to do: Define the relevant variables and control for as many irrelevant ones as possible. For example, basketball did not adopt the 12-foot goal proposed during the dominant college career of Lew Alcindor (now Kareem Jabbar), presumably because it was decided that a player's height is relevant to the game and should not be counteracted with that rule.

These and other basketball examples were presented during lecture in three introductory classes and one experimental psychology class. In the introductory classes, the lecture and discussion were presented in conjunction with a 30-minute film, "Methodology: The Psychologist and the Experiment" (produced by McGraw-Hill), and in both courses the same concepts were brought up throughout the semester whenever a topic involved experimental research.

Unfortunately, we have no direct evidence for the effectiveness of the basketball analogy as a learning device. However, we were impressed by the quality of class discussion generated by the basketball lecture. (For instance, how would you design a rule in basketball to eliminate coaching as an influence on the outcome?) Also, in the second author's experimental psychology course, there was a final exam question asking students to illustrate experimental concepts using another sport of their choice. Students chose a variety of team and individual sports and most of their answers were thoughtful and well-written. It is possible that any unifying theme around which students can organize a number of related concepts could be helpful in promoting students' understanding of those concepts. Perhaps the basketball analogy just caught their attention.

Sort of like a good slam dunk.

References

Gleitman, H. (1984). Introducing psychology. *American Psychologist, 39,* 421-427.

Hughes, R. L. (1984). Teaching concepts of personal adjustment using popular music. *Teaching of Psychology, 11,* 115.

Polyson, J. A. (1983). Student essays about TV characters: A tool for understanding personality theories. *Teaching of Psychology, 10,* 103-105.

Solomon, P. R. (1979). Science and television commercials Adding relevance to the research methodology course. *Teaching of Psychology, 6,* 26-30.

Vandervert, L. R. (1980). Operational definitions made simple lasting, and useful. *Teaching of Psychology, 7,* 57-59

An Introductory Demonstration Laboratory Produced Entirely by Undergraduates

Art Kohn and
Max Brill
Oakland University

This hands-on program features no-cost, use by several courses, and enthusiastic student involvement in organization and administration.

In the Winter Semester of the 1978-79 school year, an Introductory Demonstration Laboratory (IDL), for the introductory psychology courses, was planned and produced almost entirely by undergraduate students. We discuss the situation which inspired the IDL, and the plan as it was developed, with six major features characteristic of the IDL (with at least some of these features being, we believe, unique), how it worked out, and the results as indicated by the students who attended IDL sessions and the student-staff who put them on. We conclude with some suggestions as to how we think IDLs of this sort might be produced at other universities, with fewer problems, and with more positive features than we were able to realize in this first attempt.

The Situation

Introductory Demonstration Laboratories (IDL) have not been conspicuously successful as adjuncts to introductory psychology courses. At least they have not been successful enough to inspire any large number of psychology departments to insist on including them in their programs. None of the best known universities in our state (University of Michigan, Michigan State, and Wayne State) produce IDL's nor has our own Oakland University since ". . . back in the sixties" (according to the vague memories of two senior faculty members). Western Michigan has the rather famous Skinnerian lab attached to its gigantic introductory course, but it is not really one of the type that is being referred to here; it is not a *general* psychology lab as most of us would think of one. Some of the other universities in Michigan do produce IDLs, most do not. Michigan universities, in this regard, are probably more like those of the other 49 states than not.

Oakland University is a medium sized university (11,000 students) located in a suburb north of Detroit. During the typical Winter Semester, there are about 400 students enrolled in the three introductory psychology courses. These courses have been taught almost entirely in the traditional lecture style. There has been little opportunity for the students to profit from individual or small group instruction except where there have been special teaching-assistant-run meetings. Generally, these have been concerned with priming students to pass imminent quizzes.

The project started among several undergraduate psychology majors (including A. K., then a student, since graduated) who had been teaching assistants during the preceding Fall Semester, in one of the introductory psychology courses (that of M. B.).[1] They were interested in psychology, and in teaching, and they felt that Oakland's introductory psychology courses would be improved if IDL's were added.

With undergraduate enthusiasm, the originating group of students decided to enlist peer help and themselves produce an IDL that would be available to all students enrolled in any of the introductory psychology courses, or, for that matter, in any other lower level courses where there might be interest.

Their goals were not particularly novel. They wanted to provide additional learning opportunities for themselves, to have a chance to teach, and to have fun doing it. More altruistically, they wanted to help their fellow students to a better understanding of some of the basic concepts of psychology, and thereby to encourage in them a more active interest in course material and in the field itself.

The Plan

If the student goals were ordinary, the IDL plan arrived at had several features which were probably unique, or at least worth additional comment. Features. (a) The IDL was to be student-planned, student-staffed, and student-run; (b) It was to be put on essentially without funding; (c) It was to be available on a voluntary attendance basis to students who were enrolled in any of several courses, each taught by a different regular faculty member; (d) It was to be an IDL with different multiple "sessions" for each major psychological topic and multiple "stations" in each session, giving it cafeteria-choice features; (e) There was to be a prefab statement of the points being made and post-lab quizzes covering these points; and (f) It was to be evaluated purely in terms of what the students thought about what was important and what had gone on; not in terms of what faculty thought or might have measured.

It did not all turn out as planned, but it worked out remarkably well for a first effort. It is worth looking at each of these planned features, and at what happened when the plan was realized.

Feature #1: Student-Planned, Student-Staffed, and Student-Run. The entire project was indeed planned and pulled off by undergraduate students. We think that this is a unique (and wondrous?) feature of what was done.

Before anything more than talk and planning could be accomplished, departmental permission to proceed had to be obtained. This proved to be surprisingly easy, as the idea was supported by the chairman of the department and by the three faculty members who were teaching the introductory psychology courses that semester. It helped that virtually nothing was added to the faculty teaching burden. It also helped that some preliminary laboratory demonstrations had been successfully produced during the preceding semester, for the students of one of the courses (that of M. B.) Not only was permission granted, but the student-staff members were reinforced by being given upper-level Psychology credits for their semester's work on the project.

The faculty's only role, besides approving credit for the student-staff members, was to offer an extra credit grade point or two to those of their students who attended the IDL sessions, to give clearance to proposed lab demonstrations which might in some way be controversial or unethical, and to offer occasional suggestions for additional interesting demonstrations.

A "student-staff" was recruited. It was composed of 16 undergraduate students. Of these, five were upper-class psychology majors, seven others were beginning psychology majors but had previously taken only an introductory psychology course, and four were non-psychology majors who had taken introductory psychology plus a variety of other psychology courses. They met regularly to plan and discuss the project and to assure that assigned responsibilities were being carried out.

Feature #2: Produced Without Funding. The IDL for the semester was not, as we had hoped, produced for nothing, But the entire IDL cost was less than $100.00, which is about as close to nothing as one can get these days.

Because the lab added little to the faculty teaching load, and the student-staff worked for love and for course credit, there were no salaries to pay. There were only a few miscellaneous clerical and supply costs. The major expense was for the purchase and keep of six albino rats which were used in some of the

lab demonstrations. The necessary demonstration equipment was acquired through the "beg, borrow, and fix-up" method. As many departments must, ours had a messy storeroom full of equipment that had been long ignored. Much of this was put into reasonable working order, and used. Other pieces of equipment (e.g., finger mazes, reaction times measures, photographs, cognitive devices, etc.) were produced from scraps and ingenuity.

Feature #3: Available on a Voluntary Basis to Students in Different Courses. The IDLs were administratively independent of any of the regular Psychology Department courses. They were designed to serve all of the students in any course where the professor was interested. The professors teaching the three *Introductory Psychology* courses showed interest as did the professor teaching *Introduction to Social Psychology,* and the one teaching *Introduction to Research Design.* The students who attended the IDLs ("student-attendees"), therefore, came from five different courses. They came voluntarily, after having signed up the week before.

Feature #4: A Multiple Station IDL. The student-staff decided to produce a number of IDL "sessions," each of which would be devoted to a different psychological topic, and each of which would be composed of a number of demonstration "stations. "

A different topic was covered in each week's sessions, eight different topics in all. They were, in order of presentation, Sensation and Perception, Learning, Memory, Motivation, Emotion, Cognitive/Develop-mental, Abnormal/Personality, and Social. This was an order which, with a few compro-mises, was a reasonable approximation of that which the three faculty members were using in their introductory courses. The student-staff also produced some lab sessions which they called "IDL's Greatest Hits," the title hinting at the varied content.

Each IDL session was composed of seven to ten stations. Each station was meant to feature an experiment or demonstration that exemplified an area of research within the week's IDL topic. It was in coming up with plausible, interesting, and informative stations that the student-staff was most taxed. Special efforts were made to design the stations in a way which would require active student attendee participation wherever possible. As it turned out, better than two thirds of them involved the active collection of data for treatment and analysis.

Some of the stations produced were "old chestnuts." Others were original and showed a pleasant ingenuity. Typical of the more popular stations used are these five:

(1) *Classically conditioned eye blink.* A wooden panel was mounted on a table. The student-attendee looked through an opening in the panel at a fixation point on the wall several feet away. A small diameter

plastic hose was mounted on the wooden panel, on the side away from the student, so that one end was available to the experimenter and the other end opened toward the subject's eye. The experimenter snapped a toy "cricket" (the conditioned stimulus) and immediately blew a puff of air through the hose at the subject's eye (unconditioned stimulus) Classical conditioning of the eye blink to the cricket noise was easily and dramatically demonstrated. With some student-attendees, the eye blink response was "extinguished" by sounding the cricket a number of times without the puff of air. Other student-attendees were not directly extinguished but were allowed to 'forget' the CR. They attended other stations of the IDL directly after having been conditioned. At the end of the session, al l of the students were tested again and none of them still showed the CR. The two reasons for the loss of the conditioned response, extinction and forgetting, were compared

(2) *Weber's Law*. This was demonstrated with a weight discrimination task. Student-attendees tried to place in the correct order *20* little Kodak film canisters, each of which contained a measured weight of BBs, and which formed an ascending scale of weights. The weights differed, one from the other, by exactly equal increments. Student-attendees were presented with the canisters in a random order and attempted to arrange them correctly. It was easy to show that the difficulty of the discriminations, as measured by the number of errors. increased markedly as the canisters got heavier. Weber's Law was discussed in its historical context, and was offered as an explanation of the results obtained

(3) *Developing cognitive strategies*. A *set* of *24* drawings was available on 1½" X 1½" pieces of paper. These were sketches which could easily be put into four categories: "transportation," "animals," "home furnishings," and "clothing." Student-attendees were shown the drawings one at a time, each one being placed face up on the table in a random arrangement. Subjects were allowed three minutes to attempt to memorize them. Some of the students physically rearranged the drawings on the table according to the categories, some did not. The students who grouped them according to the categories were shown to remember more of the drawings correctly than those who had not done so. Organization aids memory.

(4) *Lie detection*. Student-attendees selected a playing card and attempted to conceal its suit by lying when questioned about it. Both an old GSR apparatus and a new Hagar Voice Analyzer were used in the lie detection.

(5) *Halo effect*. Student-attendees were shown six photographs of persons of the opposite sex. Unknown to the student-attendees, these photographed persons had previously been rated, by the student-staff, as either "unattractive," "moderately attractive," or "very attractive." The student-attendees

rated each of the six persons on a number of perceived characteristics. The "very attractive" persons were seen as highest on "kindness," "sociability" and "bisexual responsiveness" but lowest on "future prospects as a spouse" or "as a parent." The "unattractive" persons were rated differently. The "moderately attractive" were rated somewhere in between.

Each student-staff was made a co-chief responsible for one of the IDL topics that was covered. The co-chiefs working with the student-staff leaders determined the content of the lab. They gathered the required equipment, found space, scheduled the IDL sessions and handled the promotion necessary to induce introductory students to attend these sessions.

Each IDL session was scheduled to last two hours and to be repeated 11 times during the week, Saturdays included. Most were given for just one week. Student-attendees signed up the week before for one of the upcoming sessions. Each session was open to a maximum of ten students. Ordinarily, 12 or 13 signees had to be obtained in order to have 9-11 actually attend. Once that discovery was made, the student-staff played to full houses thenceforth. Several of the sessions were repeated at odd times to accommodate students who were unable to attend the labs as they were originally scheduled.

The stations were physically scattered within a large classroom or a lounge, or whatever room was available at the scheduled time. As it worked out, the IDL was as "floating" as any crap game. The stations were managed by student-staff members who were expected to be physically present at at least five IDL sessions per week. An attempt was made to give all of the student-staff members experience managing each of the many stations through the semester.

The typical session was introduced by a student-staff member who explained how this week's topic fell within the overall field of Psychology, and what was to be found at each of the stations. They also mentioned some of the major points which the IDL was designed to get across, and it was explained that a post-lab quiz would be given and that it would have to be passed for IDL credit to be given.

After the opening remarks, the student-staff members took charge of the stations which were assigned to them. They introduced the station to the student-attendees, directed the activities there, and answered questions. Student attendees were expected to go to each of the available stations and to take part in the activities. In actuality they tended to prefer some stations to others, lingered at these, and sometimes returned to them after having done the circuit. At any particular station, the student-attendee might take the role of passive observers subjects or experimenter. Often, as it worked outs they added the role of student-staff member. The regular staff member did no more than explain the station to the first student-attendee who approached it. Then that student-attendee explained the station and discussed it with those who came after.

About 90 minutes were allowed for the students to attend all of the stations. The entire group was then reconvened for the "wrap-up." This was designed to help the student attendees to develop some kind of encompassing picture, and to fit what they had observed into that picture. Each student-staff member was given a short time to review and explain what had gone on at his or her station. Where data had been collected at a station, the results were looked at and explained. Open discussions were encouraged, and these usually turned out to be lively and long.

At the close of the sessions which was almost always determined by the pressures of time rather than by the lack of interest or sense that all that could be said had been said, the student-attendees were read a list of questions from which the post-lab quiz, given later, was selected.

Feature #5: **Pre-Lab Statements and Post-Lab Quizzes.** The post-lab quizzes were, of course, intended to measure whether anything that had been "taught" had been "learned." The student-staff made special attempts to be clear in all of their statements of the principle points being made. A list of seven or eight short-essay questions had been read to the student-attendees as the last act of each session. They were reasonably demanding questions and to answer them correctly required some genuine understanding of what the IDL session had been about.

The quiz itself was, whenever possible given immediately following the next meeting of the students' regular class. This was usually within three or four days after the IDL session they had attended. The quiz consisted of two or three questions selected from the list that had been read to the students at the close of the IDL session. The quiz rarely took more than five minutes to complete and it was graded by staff members on an S/N basis. All student-attendees were required to take and pass the appropriate post-lab quiz before they were given extra credit by the professors involved .

Feature #6: **Effectiveness Measured in Terms of What Students Thought.** The effectiveness of the lab was measured in three ways; (a) by the performance on the post-lab quizzes (b) by a questionnaire survey of the student attendees and (c) by a questionnaire filled out by the student-staff. We would like to have some kind of measure of the IDL as seen by faculty, but frankly, no one thought of it at the time. The student-staff was, as they say, "student oriented."

Results

Post-Lab Quiz Performance. Over 98% of the post-lab quizzes were graded "satisfactory." Such a satisfactory pass rate indicated we believed that something worthwhile had happened in the IDL sessions. Casual observations of students who took one or more of the quizzes have reinforced our idea that something was well learned. One student attendee, for example, four months after he attended the IDL Memory session, was able to state the main point for six of the seven stations he had encountered.

Student-Attendee Survey. A student-attendee survey was distributed at the end of the semester to all of the introducto psychology students who were available (about 350); those who had attended the IDL sessions and those who had not. Of these questionnaires, 220 were returned, 129 of which were from students who had attended at least one IDL session. Twenty-one had attended only one, 85 had been to two, 19 had been to three, and four had been to four or more. A check was made of some of the more obvious variables, (age, sex, introductory professor, G.P.A., etc.) and those who attended the sessions were not found to be noticeably different from those who had not. It was clear, from what they wrote, that most of those who had not attended any of the sessions had other time obligations, such as outside jobs, families waiting with baby-sitters, etc., which precluded attendance.

Seven questions were asked, all using a one to seven scale, with one being very positive and seven very negative. The actual labels used varied: One was either "very much" or "strongly agree," while seven was either "not at all" or "strongly disagree." (Whatever subtle differences there appeared to be in this phrasing at that time do not seem to be there now.) The questions and the tabulated answers are in Table 1A. It is obvious that everything is clearly skewed in the desirable direction.

The student-attendees also indicated, in their free comments, their approval or disapproval of various aspects of the IDL. As Table 1 results would lead us to predict, mostly it was approval. For example: "The staff was closer to the students in the lab. I never felt intimidated by anyone and, as a result, I was more willing to get involved in the experiments." "I like this way of learning; superior to lectures." ("Perhaps," says M. B.) "I was always eager to discuss any questions with the students running the lab . . . the discussion gave me a much better understanding of the course material and an overall better liking for the course." It is interesting to note that 18 of our respondees after attending IDL sessions expressed great interest in

Table 1. Frequency of Survey Responses by Scale Value

Item	Scale Value						
	1	2	3	4	5	6	7
A. Student Attendees (N = 129)							
The labs increased my interest in Psychology.	18	31	36	21	12	6	5
The labs increased my understanding of the course material.	19	33	38	17	10	8	4
The lab increased my interest in the course material.	23	22	40	22	9	9	4
I found the lab to be informative and interesting.	42	43	29	8	2	4	1
The "station" approach is a good way to organize the lab.	41	51	16	13	2	5	1
I enjoyed the lab.	58	38	17	8	4	3	1
I enjoyed having an undergraduate as a teacher.	68	32	11	12	1	4	1
B. Student-Staff (N=10)							
The lab increased my understanding of Psychology.	6	2	2	0	0	0	0
The lab increased my interest in Psychology.	3	5	2	0	0	0	0
The lab caused me to want to study more Psychology.	3	4	1	2	0	0	0
As a result of the lab, my teaching skills have improved.	3	5	2	0	0	0	0
Compared to other Social Science classes, I retained more from the IDL.	4	4	1	0	1	0	0
The lab gave me a broader perspective on Psychology.	7	3	0	0	0	0	0
I enjoyed working in the IDL.	10	0	0	0	0	0	0

becoming members of the student-staff. And about one-fifth of the students attended more than two sessions even though there was no extra grade credit for going beyond two. If the student survey is to be credited, it is clear that the IDL was a happy success.

Student-Staff Survey: A student-staff survey (anonymous) was distributed at the end of the semester to the 14 (of our 16) staff members who could be reached. Ten of the 14 questionnaires were returned.

Seven questions were asked, all using a one to seven scale, with one being either "very much," or "strongly agree" and seven being either "not at all" or "strongly disagree.66" The questions and the tabulated answers appear in Table 1B. It also clearly shows that everything is skewed in the desirable direction.

The only question where the responses were not markedly skewed in the good direction was an eighth question which asked about the "degree of organization" of the IDL itself. The one to seven scale ranged from "very organized" to "very disorganized." The modal response ($N = 5$) was three. Evidently, the student-staff perceived the IDL as lacking something in the way of administrative organization.

There were also some free comments which conveyed the same positive attitude that the rating scales indicated. One student-staff member wrote: "The lab gave me a view of all of Psychology. I finally see where different kinds of research fit in." Another wrote: "I enjoyed working with the staff and I got a big thrill when the students got involved in the labs." Another: "The IDL gave me a way to discuss with others what I am interested in. I don't just mean with students either. I mean with friends, relatives, etc. If my statements were questioned, I could back them up." And another: "The staff got along very well and worked well together. If there had been an easier way

to learn the stations (a project booklet), then the lab would have run smoother. But for a first year staff, things went pretty well." Finally] one student-staff member expressed it best: "I learned that it is possible to develop an atmosphere which not only aids in the learning of psychology but that can make it enjoyable as well . . . I feel that it was a tremendous opportunity for undergraduates to staff the IDL and I believe that we proved that it could be done effectively. Right on undergraduates! "

Suggestions

It is always a pleasure to make suggestions to those who might follow; giving advice is easy. The student staff went through the IDL semester aware of many things that might have been better. They spent many hours discussing what was wrong and why, and how it might have been improved. Since then we have given the matter additional thought In capsule form the suggestions are: (a) Better administration, (b) Better preparation of the student-staff, (c) More and better stations, (d) More student-attendees at more sessions, (e) Better distribution of station explanatory information to the student-attendees, and (f) A permanent location.

Better Administration. There were clearly recognized problems in the way the whole thing was run. Student-staff members often yearned for faculty guidance, but there was little available. The direction within the student-staff itself was based almost entirely upon the personality interactions among its members. Some were explicitly or implicitly recognized as leaders, others regularly and willingly followed, others balked at times. Some handled every responsibility, but others let too much slide. Some were frequently unprepared, some came late to too many sessions, etc. The student-staff leaders had no way to assure the performance of the others of the student-staff, except persuasion. This sometimes failed.

Having a faculty member directly involved would almost certainly help. An interested faculty member might assume overall responsibility for the lab, and offer a regular course called something like "IDL Staff Participation." Faculty administrative involvement would probably go far toward reducing student-staff "goof-offs." As a bonus, it would probably make information gathering, student-staff recruiting, equipment purchasing, room scheduling, etc. much easier.

We are thinking of some sort of faculty-student-staff hierarchy, and a semester-to-semester continuity. New groups of interested students might be invited to join the IDL student-staff and to move upward in the hierarchy. The first semester student-staff members would spend most of their time studying and running stations. Second semester student-staff members would study and run stations, but would also be in charge of designing IDL topic sessions and seeing that it all came off well. One or two of the most capable students, who had already had one or two semesters in the IDL, and perhaps some TA experience, would then be made student-staff leaders with overall IDL supervision, subject to guidance by the faculty member involved.

We think it important that the IDL still be mostly student planned and student run. Faculty skill would be tested in giving just the right amount of guidance and leeway to the student-staff.

The semester to semester continuity would be the basis for an accumulation of interesting stations and for the development of improved techniques for getting things across. This leads to our second suggestion.

Better Preparation of the Student-Staff. Student-staff members were often inadequately prepared for running the stations; the time and the means for instructing them were simply not available. Some of the student-staff members felt acutely their lack of relevant background knowledge. It is revealing, however, that few of the student-attendees perceived the student-staff to be unprepared. ("You can fool some of the people, some of the time . . .").

The problem of preparation is one that something positive can be done about. We think that it is important that information notebooks be prepared for the student-staff to study. These notebooks should contain introductory discussions of the various session topics, plus descriptions and explanations of each of the stations. They might also contain references for suggested further reading. Student-staff accounts of their experiences running stations might also be added from semester to semester. This would make the notebooks more entertaining to read, and have

motivational and informational value as well. New station ideas would be added to the notebooks as they were thought of, and pertinent information would be developed over time. The notebooks might be reviewed periodically by the faculty member in charge, or by other faculty members who might have special relevant knowledge or information. Part of the semester's grading of student-staff members might be based on their demonstrated knowledge of the contents of these notebooks, and on their contributions to the notebook itself.

More and Better Stations. A greater variety of stations should be developed. The suggestions made above (better administration, and information notebooks) would almost certainly open the IDL sessions, and the stations themselves, to continuing critical review. We feel that this review would lead to the development of more interesting and challenging stations. Some of those of the first attempt turned out to hold little interest for some of the student-attendees, some held little challenge. Designing a few of the stations for competition and others for cooperative student performances might help. We also see that the student-attendee should be made into the "experimenter" more often. And some kind of "write-up" experience might well be incorporated into the IDL's. It could start with very simple partial write-ups and gradually work toward a final full scale one. This suggestion assumes, of course, that the student-attendee would be coming to each of the labs during the semester. As you might have guessed, this leads to another suggestion.

More Attendees at More Sessions. It is the nature of projects, when they are perceived by those involved as having been successful, to expand. We must admit that we have had speculations in that direction. Our introductory students attended purely on a voluntary basis. Most student attendees came to one or two sessions. A dream would be to have all of the potential attendees attend a session for every topic. Whether the logistics of the situation (facilities, time, energy, etc.) would allow for such an enlarged project is a problem that each department contemplating an IDL would have to tackle. A suggestion that we have played with is to make the lab sessions day long and continuous. Studentattendees could then attend any time that they wished during the week of a particular topic. Quizzing would then be done more formally, with the introductory professors adding a selection of the handout questions to their regular quizzes, or quizzing in some other way as they saw fit.

Better Information to Student-Attendees. Handouts should be prepared and distributed to each student-attendee at every station. These handouts should contain the obvious descriptions and explanations. They might also contain blank charts and tables of the type generally found in laboratory workbooks. Finally, the handouts should contain three or four questions about the station. The post-lab quizzes would then, of course, consist of a selection of these questions taken from all of the handouts of a given IDL session.

Permanent Location. It would be nice, and it would make things easier, if there were a permanent lab room set aside for the IDL. Permanently set up stations, with self-explanatory directions, could be part of the lab. This might help to de-emphasize the role of the student-staff members as operatives of stations; student-attendees could work many of the stations themselves with minimal student-staff guidance

Conclusion

It is clear that something of value was added to the teaching of our introductory psychology students by other students working pretty much on their own initiative, and with few funds expended. The added value was to the student attendees who came as consumers to the Introductory Demonstration Laboratory sessions, and especially to the student-staff who put on the whole thing. What was added for both groups seems to have been a better understanding of the realities involved in the accumulation and development of the facts and theories which go to make up psychology. Among the student-staff in particular, there was added some appreciation of the problems involved in getting material across, and much enthusiasm and self-confidence derived from the fact that they had individually and collectively created something so obviously worthwhile.

We believe that any psychology department which would institutionalize an IDL of the type described and suggested would accumulate a corps of highly enthusiastic and involved psychology students—that would, in this world of so much talk of apathy, be nice.

Notes

1. M.B. has become involved in this write up as a second author The fact is that he contributed relatively little to the actual production of the IDL. This makes it, at times, somewhat awkward for us to use the term "we" while telling the story. It is a bit awkward, but we are doing it in lieu of a better idea.
2. The authors want to offer a special thank you to the following people who helped to make the I.D.L. possible: Bill Dobreff, Jean Crews, Robyn Stevens, Kathy Soditch, Michelle Scheuern, Bohdan Hrecznyj, and Lynn Yadach. We also thank the other members of the student staff; Gary Forbes, Rene Hinkle, Bob Kreigh, Tina MacKintosh, Sue Parka, Katie Royce, Alison Spear, Kevin Takacs, Nina Warrick, Jodi Wolozynski, and Gary Wylin - we did it!

Undergraduate Research Experience Through the Analysis of Data Sets in Psychology Courses

Neil Lutsky
Carleton College

A method for involving large numbers of introductory psychology students as active researchers is described and evaluated. Students are assigned a project requiring them to develop research questions and to answer those questions by means of a computerized analysis of previously collected data. Results of a study of the project's effects on attitudes toward research in psychology indicate that students reported valuing research more, understanding statistical procedures better, and feeling less anxious about statistics and computers. These and other findings are taken to suggest that this assignment may be an effective way to introduce introductory students to research activities and values in psychology.

An effective way to involve introductory psychology students as active participants in research is to assign a course project requiring the analysis of previously collected data. I have regularly given classes access via computer to large data sets and required students to develop an original research question, analyze relevant data using a statistical package, and complete a research report. In this article, I discuss the goals of such an assignment, describe the project in detail, report evidence of its effects on students' attitudes toward research in psychology, and consider some of the benefits and difficulties associated with its use.

Projects designed to give introductory psychology students hands-on research experience include research simulations (e.g., Hartley, Fisher, & Hartley, 1977), laboratory experiments (e.g., Bare, 1982; Brothen, 1984), and data analysis assignments. These projects have several educational goals. One is to increase student familiarity with the phenomena, theories, and findings under investigation. A second goal is to expose students to the tasks that normally constitute research in psychology (e.g., manipulating equipment, using statistics, interpreting results). Participation in research may allow students to appreciate the importance of these tasks, learn some of the technical skills required by research, and test their proclivities for doing research. A third and more complex goal is to influence students' attitudes toward the research claims of psychology.

Research experience may affect attitudes toward psychological research in a variety of ways. Students who obtain expected results when they test basic predictions may become more confident about the validity of other research claims. A failure to replicate a basic finding, however, may have the opposite effect. Both experiences, although probably the latter more than the former, may also make students more sensitive to the choices that psychologists make when conducting research—choices about what might be examined, how information about certain objects or processes can be collected and analyzed, and how findings can be interpreted and presented. Any experience that encourages students to recognize these choices, understand their justifications, and think critically about their features may contribute to a deeper understanding of psychology and its research foundation.

The value of active research experience is clearly recognized in the training of psychology majors (Cole & Van Krevelen, 1977). For example, students in core methodology courses typically assist in the design and completion of research (e.g., Kerber, 1983; Yoder, 1979). Students in upper-level psychology courses often conduct laboratory work (Cole & Van Krevelen, 1977), and selected students may have the opportunity to develop individual research projects (e.g., Kierniesky, 1984; Palladino, Carsrud, Hulicka, & Benjamin, 1982).

Introductory psychology students, however, are less likely to be given an opportunity to conduct research. Faculty members may find it difficult to supervise and support the work of a large number of novices. Moreover, introductory psychology students may not be able to complete or appreciate a research project, given their limited understanding of research techniques (e.g., statistics) and inexperience with research decisions. On the other hand, Medawar (1979) strongly encouraged young scientists to become involved in research and confront results even before they are fully prepared to understand what they have done. He believed that such experiences give students a sense of pride in their work and may motivate continued learning about research.

An assignment to analyze previously collected data may provide a research experience well suited to the abilities and interests of introductory psychology students. Such a project offers students the freedom to pursue individual research questions in an original data base but gives them concrete research variables to help organize their thinking about possible research questions. The project spares students the necessity of collecting data but does require them to master some rudiments of statistical analysis and computer usage. In general, the project exploits the potential for computers to stimulate active student thinking about psychological issues (Collyer, 1984) and to serve education by allowing large numbers of students opportunities that might not be feasible otherwise.

The Research Project

Data Sets

I have used several data sets for projects in my introductory and middle-level courses, courses likely to include a high percentage of students without previous research experience. For example, one data set used in the introductory psychology course, provides subjects' background information (e.g., gender and class year) and test results from the Eysenck Personality Questionnaire, the Bem Sex Role Inventory, the Self-Monitoring Scale, and the Act Report measure of gregarious behavior. This data set is relevant to course discussions of personality theory, personality assessment, and sex roles. Another data set, used in a middle level social psychology course, allows students to explore the Ajzen and Fishbein (1980) model of attitude-action relationships through individual records of attendance at voluntary weekly college convocations and earlier measures of theoretically related attitudes, intentions, social norms, and personality variables (e.g., self-monitoring). All of these data sets are based on previous research with students at Carleton College.

The Research Assignment

Students are given a five-page handout that describes the project and its data base. (The handout and other materials referred to in this article are available from the author.) The handout summarizes the purposes and methodology of the original study and provides references to sections of the course text that discuss the specific procedures, instruments, and issues the handout introduces. A codebook listing variable names and scoring information is included.

The handout leads the student through the steps of the project. The first step requires each student to define an individual research topic (e.g., "Sex Differences in Extraversion as Measured by the EPQ" or "Self-Monitoring as a Moderator of Intention-Action Relationships"). Second, students must identify the basic statistical procedures needed to answer their research questions. The handout describes simple possibilities (correlations, t tests, frequencies) and encourages the student to review the statistics appendix in the text. The third step describes procedures needed to edit and run a command file in the statistical package used ($SPSS^X$).

Students must write a short paper (usually 3 to 5 pages) that summarizes the project and its findings, critically evaluates the results obtained, and relates the research question to material covered in the course. An appendix to the handout describes a word processing program that students can use to write papers on the computer.

Comment

This assignment poses a difficult challenge to students. Because each step of the project is logically dependent on prior ones, students must approach their work in a systematic manner. The project is usually assigned 2 weeks before it is due, and students are encouraged to complete the early steps soon after receiving the assignment. For many students, especially those in the introductory course, the project represents a first encounter with the computer and with the manipulation of statistics. Thus, it is important to have specific and easy-to-follow instructions in the handout. Students are also strongly encouraged to seek guidance from their instructor and teaching assistants (advanced psychology majors) as they work through the assignment.

The project challenges students to use statistical techniques and computer technology in the service of definite and intelligent ends. When confronted with the project, students are usually concerned about their abilities to use the computer and to complete an appropriate data analysis. They are initially less attentive to issues involved in conceptualizing interesting and meaningful research questions, and in evaluating findings in a thoughtful and critical manner. The instructor and teaching assistants counsel students to help them avoid completing technically competent but uninteresting projects and papers.

Project Evaluation

Student reactions to these projects have been assessed in several ways. As part of a standard course evaluation, students were asked to rate the computer project and comment on it. When asked to indicate how valuable the project was, students in an introductory course ($N = 75$) and a middle-level social psychology course ($N = 38$) rated the project positively ($M = 2.9$ and $M = 2.8$, respectively, on 6-point scales where 1 = *excellent* and 6 = *poor*). Positive comments lauded the creativity allowed in the project and the fact that the project helped clarify course material. Some students indicated a desire to continue a more active involvement in research. Negative comments centered on student confusion concerning statistical and computer procedures and the lack of definitive answers found for some project questions.

Recently, a more formal evaluation of student responses was completed in a large introductory psychology course. Eighty students, primarily freshmen, completed a questionnaire on "Attitudes toward Research in Psychology" after receiving a brief description of the research project they were about to be assigned. (The project had also been mentioned previously on the course syllabus.) This questionnaire was administered before students received the full assignment handout midway through the course. The questionnaire consisted of 20 questions designed to assess general attitudes toward research in psychology and student expectations about the project. An example of the questions concerning attitudes toward research is: "I think research studies in psychology have led me to think about issues in psychology in a more precise way." Student beliefs about the project were assessed through questions about their abilities (e.g., "I believe that I can successfully complete the computer-based project in this course"), anxieties (e.g., "I am anxious about the prospect of having to use and interpret statistics"), and expectations (e.g., "I expect that the computer-based project in this course will be valuable and interesting").

Shortly after the papers from the projects were submitted, approximately 3 weeks after the first questionnaires had been completed, a second attitude questionnaire was administered. In it, students were asked to estimate the amount of time they spent on various project tasks (e.g., reviewing notes for the project, working at the computer) and the number of times they sought help from their peers and instructor. Students were also asked whether they found the project valuable and interesting, whether they believed they understood statistical procedures better after completing the project, whether they would be anxious about the prospect of having to complete a similar project in the future, and a number of other questions designed to match pretest items (see Table 1). All attitude answers were rated on 7-point scales ranging from *strongly disagree* (1) to *strongly agree* (7). In addition, background data (sex, class, intended major) and project grades were available for the students in this study.

Results of the initial belief and attitude assessments showed that students expected the project to be valuable and interesting, but that they were generally anxious about the project and its computer and statistics components (see Table 1). Students anticipated that the project would be difficult ($M = 4.7$) and that they would have to spend a considerable amount of time on it ($M = 5.3$), but they were confident that they could complete the project successfully ($M = 5.4$).

In fact, almost all students completed the project successfully. After spending, on average, over 8 hr on their work (1.9 hr planning the research, 2.1 hr using the computer, 1.4 hr interpreting results, and 3.3 hr writing papers) and consulting the instructor and peers a number of times (on average, 1.6 and 3.1 times, respectively), students submitted projects they believed to be successful ($M = 5.4$). In addition, students reported understanding statistical procedures and using the computer better ($M = 5.0$ and $M = 5.2$, respectively) as a result of having completed the project. The results of paired t tests (summarized in Table 1) also show that students reported significantly less anxiety about projects of this kind and about using statistics and computers following their research experiences. The final grades students received on their papers were not significantly related to these attitude and time measures, but were associated with the initial measure of self-assessed efficacy ("I believe that I can successfully complete the com-puter-based project in this course"), $r = .23$, $p < .05$.

Students' attitudes toward research in psychology were also apparently influenced by their research experience. As Table 1 indicates, after completing their work, students were more likely to label research

results in psychology as imprecise and difficult to interpret but also indicated an increased appreciation of the ability of research to challenge preconceptions and stimulate precise thinking. Students also held the belief that researchers can easily influence research findings through decisions about data analysis without significant change over the course of the study ($M = 5.71$ and $M = 5.83$ for the pretest and posttest assessments, respectively).

Sex differences were also assessed. Males reported feeling less anxious about using and interpreting statistics than females did before the assignment ($M = 3.38$ and $M = 4.43$ for males and females, respectively), $t(63) = 2.55$, $p < .05$, and also expected to spend less time completing the project, $t(63) = 2.84$, $p < .01$. This sex difference in initial anxiety about statistics remained even after controlling for previous exposure to statistics. However, no corresponding posttest differences were obtained in anxiety ratings concerning computer usage or in measures of time actually spent on the project.

Discussion

The thesis of this article is that an assignment to analyze a data set allows students to become actively involved in research in a way that contributes to their interest in and understanding of the field. The results appear to support this claim. Students viewed the project as a challenge and responded to it positively. Following their work, they reported less anxiety about a project of this kind and a greater understanding of the use of statistics and computers. In addition, students reported becoming more aware of the complexities and ambiguities inherent in research and of the potential contributions of research to their thinking about psychological issues. Thus, participation in the project may have raised students' sensitivity to the uncertainties of their own ideas and those advanced in research as they grappled with the interplay of the two.

There are reasons to be cautious about these findings, however. All that can be claimed is that students reported these attitudes; no confirmation of supposed effects on understandings of research was attempted. Moreover, it was easier for students to be less anxious about an abstract assignment during the posttest questionnaire than about one due 2 weeks after the pretest. It is also possible that demand characteristics in the research or additional course experiences may have influenced reported attitudes.

The results are consistent, however, with my observations of the project and its effects. Students appeared to have been highly involved in their work and engaged by the conceptual, methodological, and statistical problems they faced. Students seemed to benefit from the fact that they were required to use statistics and not simply to read about them. Similarly, students appeared to develop positive attitudes toward the computer, perhaps because they were using

Table 1. Attitudes Before and After Completion of the Reasearch Project

	Pretest M	Posttest M
Attitudes Toward Project and Project Tasks		
Project valuable and interesting	4.76	4.84
Anxious about computer-based project	4.34	3.43**
Anxious about using and interpreting statistics	4.22	3.57**
Confident about using the computer	3.78	4.64**
Attitudes Toward Research in Psychology		
Research studies imprecise	4.17	4.93**
Research plays vital role in psychology	5.84	5.97
Research studies difficult to understand	4.00	4.67**
Research often challenges preconceptions	5.09	5.48*
Research findings easily influenced by decisions researcher makes about data analysis	5.71	5.87
Research in psychology led me to think about issues more precisely	4.88	5.29*

Note. Ratings have been coded on a scale ranging from *strongly disagree* (1) to *strongly agree* (7).
*$p < .05$, **$p < .001$; correlated t tests.

computers to serve their own specific purposes and did not feel under the control of an impersonal electronic regimen. Another valuable feature of the project is that students were encouraged to interact with their instructor in individual, task-oriented meetings. Finally, there was ample evidence in students' papers that they were thinking carefully about methodological issues in their own work and in the literature related to it in light of questions raised by their concrete findings.

The use of a project of this kind is not without its disadvantages and pitfalls. It requires the instructional staff to spend considerable time helping students during their work on the project, although it has been used in introductory classes of over 90 students. The success of the project also depends on the quality of the data set available. Data sets that do not include a number of theoretically related variables may not allow room for meaningful variation in the questions students choose to ask. Data sets that result in few interesting and reliable findings may also fail to reinforce the students' sense of accomplishment. Finally, there are other sources of frustration that the students and instructor may experience (notably, unanticipated problems in the computer system).

The overall results of this study suggest that undergraduates may benefit greatly from a research project involving the analysis of previously collected data. If certain resources (a data set, an open computer system, a statistical package) are available, teachers might consider offering their students this opportunity to participate actively in the research process in psychology and to learn more directly about the values, decisions, and operations that comprise psychology's research foundation.

References

Ajzen, I., & Fishbein, M. (1980). *Understanding attitudes and predicting social behavior.* Englewood Cliffs, NJ: Prentice-Hall.

Bare, J . K. (1982) . Microcomputers in the introductory laboratory. *Teaching of Psychology, 9,* 236-237.

Brothen, T. (1984). Three computer-assisted laboratory exercises for introductory psychology. *Teaching of Psychology, 11,* 105-107.

Cole, D., & Van Krevelen, A. (1977). Psychology departments in small liberal arts colleges: Results of a survey. *Teaching of Psychology, 4,* 163-167.

Collyer, C. E. (1984). Using computers in the teaching of psychology: Five things that seem to work. *Teaching of Psychology, 11,* 206-209.

Hartley, A. A.,Fisher, L. A., & Hartley, J. T. (1977). Teaching the arts of psychological research. *Teaching of Psychology, 4,* 202-204.

Kerber, K. W. (1983). Beyond experimentation: Research projects for a laboratory course in psychology. *Teaching of Psychology, 10,* 236-239.

Kierniesky, N. C. (1984). Undergraduate research in small psychology departments. *Teaching of Psychology, 11,* 15-18.

Medawar, P. B. (1979). *Advice to a young scientist.* New York: Harper & Row.

Palladino, J. J., Carsrud, A. L., Hulicka, I. M., & Benjamin, L. T., Jr. (1982). Undergraduate research in psychology: Assessment and directions. *Teaching of Psychology, 9,* 71-74.

Yoder, J. (1979). Teaching students to do research. *Teaching of Psychology, 6,* 85-88.

Notes

1. Portions of this article were presented at the annual convention of the American Psychological Association, August, 1984, Toronto, Canada.
2. Preparation of these projects was supported by NSF Cause Grant SER77-06304 to Carleton College. I thank Perry Ferguson for his contributions to the evaluation study.

Using Astrology to Teach Research Methods to Introductory Psychology Students

Roger A. Ward
Anthony F. Grasha
University of Cincinnati

A classroom demonstration designed to test an astrological hypothesis can help teach introductory psychology students about research design and data interpretation. The activity illustrates differences between science and nonscience, the role of theory in developing and testing hypotheses, making comparisons among groups, probability and statistical significance, and the complications involved in interpreting research data.

Teaching the principles of research methodology to introductory psychology students is not an easy task. Such students are interested in learning about human behavior but are seldom enthusiastic about learning research methodology. We use a classroom exercise to test several assumptions of astrology in order to capture their interest and to introduce them to concerns psychologists face in doing research. The following activity is based on a "quasi-experimental" design and can be used to illustrate several concepts: differences between science and nonscience, the scientific method, the role of theory in developing and testing hypotheses, making comparisons among groups, probability and statistical significance, biases in self-report data, the identification of the dependent variable, and how empirical research leads to accurate information about the world.

Flow of Classroom Activity

Introduction to Activity

Students are asked whether they know anything about astrology and if they know their astrological sign. An informal poll of the class is taken. Individuals who do not know their zodiac sign are given a copy of the morning newspaper to refer to. Those individuals in class who are familiar with astrology are asked to suggest the assumptions they think astrologists make about human behavior. Student comments are listed on the blackboard. Student responses generally focus on how astrologists believe that the position of the stars and planets help to determine our personalities and behavior. This introduction usually takes about 10 min.

Generating a Hypothesis

A brief (10 to 15 min) explanation of the nature of science, nonscience, and the scientific method is presented. In particular, the role of theory and hypothesis testing in scientific research is emphasized. Students are then placed in small groups for 10 min and asked to generate a hypothesis based on an assumption they believe astrologists make about human behavior. The class is polled and ideas for hypotheses are listed on the blackboard. The student responses give the instructor an opportunity to mention that hypotheses should be testable and that a research study should allow them to be disconfirmed. Problems with a couple of the hypotheses that students generate are mentioned.

If students have not suggested it, we raise a hypothesis based on an assumption of astrologists that our personalities are associated with certain zodiac signs. The class is then asked to accept the challenge of testing whether this is accurate, and in the process, to learn a little more about gathering and interpreting data.

The Personality Profiles

Students receive a set of six personality profiles based on personality traits that astrologers believe people with certain zodiac signs possess (cf. March & McEvans, 1982). Each set of profiles was formed by dividing the astrological year in half. Thus, students born between March 21 and September 22 receive the six sets of traits appropriate for that period and those born after September 22 and before March 21 receive the second set of profiles. Students are given 6 instead of 12 profiles to save time, to make the task more manageable, and to illustrate a potential flaw in the design when the data are later analyzed. A sample of two of the personality descriptions appear in Table 1 (and a complete list can be obtained from the authors upon request).

Table 1. Two Examples of Personality Profiles

Profile for Aries	
Impulsive	Intolerant
Courageous	Quick-tempered
Independent	Arrogant
Domineering	Blunt
Profile for Taurus	
Patient	Self-indulgent
Conservative	Stubborn
Domestic	Possessive
Sensual	Materialistic

Instructions Given to Students

Students are asked to select the personality profile that best describes them and to mark the letter code corresponding to that profile on a separate sheet of paper. They are told to read each profile carefully and not to accept or reject a particular profile on the basis of one or two traits. Instead, they are asked to concentrate on the overall personality pattern when making a decision.

Data Analysis

After students make their choices, the correct zodiac signs for each letter code are placed on the board. Students are asked to indicate whether they correctly or incorrectly chose their zodiac sign. The number of correct and incorrect choices for each zodiac sign is then listed. We examine the data in several ways to illustrate points about data analysis and interpretation.

We note that the number of correct and incorrect responses are the dependent variable and mention that if the hypothesis is accurate, then the number of correct choices should exceed the number of incorrect choices. We explain that under ideal conditions there should be no incorrect responses.

Next, we begin to modify this simplistic way of examining the data by introducing the concepts of chance responding, probability, and statistical significance. Because everyone responded to six personality profiles, we explain that people have a one in six chance of selecting a correct profile on the basis of chance. Thus, on the basis of chance, correct choices should account for 16.6% and incorrect choices for 83.4% of the choices. The extent to which the observed data differ from these figures is noted. At this point we mention that giving everyone only 6 profiles from which to select is a potential flaw in the procedure, and that having 12 profiles would make it more difficult to select the correct profile by chance.

In addition, the concept of statistical significance is raised by having students focus on the number of correct zodiac identifications and those we expected to see occur by chance. We explain that it is important to

be sure that any differences favoring astrology are not due to chance. We then note that certain statistical procedures can help us to do this. To illustrate the latter point, we use the chi-square test to analyze the overall number of correct and incorrect responses against what one would expect based on chance. Chi-square is quickly computed using a calculator programmed to do the test. A brief explanation of what it suggests is given. It is important to note that we do not teach students the intricate details of the chi-square test. The test is only used as an example of how a statistical procedure can help determine whether an event exceeds chance expectancy.

After testing for statistical significance, additional complications in interpreting research data are raised. For example, students are told that our procedure assumes people know what they are like and can accurately select personality profiles that describe themselves. We suggest that this is not always the case and is one of the reasons psychologists use objective personality inventories to determine differences among people. We also point out that individuals may select a given personality profile because it is much more flattering and/or socially acceptable, or because they are familiar with astrology and thus know what profile they should pick. Thus, the biases in self-report data like social acceptability, personal validation, and self-fulfilling prophecies can be pointed out.

We also indicate that if certain personality profiles are more popular, and if the subject pool is composed mainly of people who were born under those zodiac signs, an incorrect conclusion about the validity of astrology can be drawn. The latter point is a good way to introduce students to the idea that the level of chance responding may underestimate the popularity of each zodiac sign. This latter point allows a discussion of how such problems are handled by random selection of subjects or by randomly selecting as participants an equal number of people with each zodiac sign.

Specific biases present in selecting zodiac signs in the activity are shown by counting how many people correctly and incorrectly selected a particular zodiac sign as most like them. Our data analyses reveal that certain profiles are more socially acceptable than others. Profiles for Taurus, Leo, Libra, Pisces, and Sagittarius are selected 2 to 3 times more often than those of other zodiac signs. As one would expect, more people correctly selected the popular zodiac signs. We use the latter data to show students that correct selections are due to the popularity of certain personality descriptions and are not evidence for the validity of astrology. The latter analysis is beneficial because there have been times when the mix of birthdates in the class produced results that suggested people were selecting correct zodiac signs at a rate that was statistically significant.

Depending upon how much time is allocated to each of the phases, the activity as previously outlined takes about 75 min to complete. We have run it in a 50-min session by shortening the introduction to the activity, not mentioning the distinction between science and nonscience, and not placing students in small groups to generate hypotheses. In the latter case, we have introduced astrology, indicated several of the assumptions it makes, and suggested a hypothesis that could be tested in class. The general manner in which a hypothesis is tested is noted and the other phases of the demonstration are conducted as already presented.

Prior Preparation of Students

What to emphasize and how much time to spend depends in part on what information students have had in previous class sessions and textbook assignments. We typically use this activity after the students have had a textbook assignment and an 80-min classroom session on the nature of research in psychology and the types of research methods psychologists employ (e.g., controlled experiment, case study, surveys). Thus, they are generally familiar with concepts like independent and dependent variables, hypotheses, control and experimental groups, correlational research, random sampling, statistical significance, and related terms.

Evaluation of Activity

During the current academic year, 147 students have participated in the activity. An overall indication of how much students liked and disliked the activity was assessed on a 7-point rating scale. A rating of 1 represented the worst classroom activity they had ever participated in and a rating of 7 represented the best classroom activity they had ever participated in. The mean rating was 5.46. When asked to list 2 or 3 things they liked about the activity, the most frequent responses (i.e., endorsed by at least 5 students) included: (a) the ability of the activity to hold their interest on potentially boring material, (b) seeing results from a research project immediately, (c) recognizing how deceptive research findings sometimes could be, and (d) learning that there were different ways to look at research findings. When asked to list 2 or 3 things they disliked, frequent responses (i.e., endorsed by at least 5 students) included: (a) it was somewhat long, (b) the activity tended to oversimplify astrology, (c) it was boring in places, and (d) there was nothing they disliked. Overall, evaluations suggested that the advantages of the exercise outweigh the disadvantages.

We recommend that teachers pilot test this activity with a small group of students before using it in a large class. Timing is important in order to complete the activity in a reasonable amount of time. Teachers vary in how much additional information they prefer to present and which parts of the activity to emphasize. A trial run will help to resolve these issues.

Reference

March, M. D., & McEvans, J. *(1982). The only way to learn astrology.* San Diego: Astro Computer Services.

Science, Psychology and Self: A Demonstration Experiment for Introductory Psychology

Judith Candib Larkin and Harvey A. Pines
Canisius College
James W. Julian
State University of New York

It's a wonder more students are not turned off after their first week in psychology. At the beginning of every science course from grammar school on, our students have read and heard lectures about The Scientific Method. At last in psychology where they are finally expecting to learn about themselves, the first thing they hear is one more definition of a hypothesis, a theory, and the four (or is it five?) steps in the Scientific Method.

Teachers can do something to liven up the methodology section of their course. Although we know that the tenets of science are the foundation of psychology, the student who seeks self-insight and better understanding of others needs more than a lecture to tune in to the relationship between science, psychology, and self. The answer we propose is to capitalize on students' interest in themselves by involving them at the beginning in an experimental study of their own behavior.

The demonstration described in this paper is a student oriented introduction to psychology as science. The behavior we investigated, and later discussed with our students, is social comparison—in particular, what goes on in the classroom when the teacher returns the graded exam. Getting back one's own exam and finding out how others did may be the most universal of all classroom activities. How much comparing of grades actually does take place? Why does it occur? Where? When? By whom? Even in the largest of lecture sessions, students will involve themselves in discussing this widely shared experience.

From Observation to Theory. The starting point of many a research project is a simple observation—in this case, that students compare grades. However, when we ask *why* the behavior occurs, we are looking for explanations, and this is where a ready-made theory is helpful. For our purposes, Festinger's (1954) theory of social comparison[1] is not only appropriate, it is clear, easily understood, and handily facilitates the demonstration of scientific thinking. According to this theory, people have a need to evaluate their abilities (and beliefs); to find out how good they are. Although some abilities are tested against a recognizable physical standard, many can only be evaluated by comparing with other people. When there are no absolute standards or when we don't have enough information, we look to others to find out how we're doing. Festinger goes on to theorize that we will compare with others who are similar to us in ability, and that the more similar they are to us, the more accurate and stable our self-evaluations will be.

From Theory to Hypotheses. With no more theory than is given above, we can demonstrate the scientific thinking of a research psychologist. Using the theory as a starting point, we discussed in class how to make hypotheses and predictions about behavior and test them out in an experiment. We decided to investigate how, when and where social comparison occurs. Our first hypothesis was that the *less* information students have about their test performance, the *greater* will be their need to compare, and consequently they should find out more grades of other students. On the other hand, if provided with rather complete information about their performance, students will be better able to

evaluate it, will have less need to find out how others performed and, we predict, would do less comparing of grades.

The first hypothesis helps us understand how high or low information about performance affects social comparison. Our second hypothesis was concerned with the opportunity for social comparison. There should be more opportunity for comparing when exams are returned at the beginning rather than the end of the class. We hypothesized, then, that when the corrected exam was returned early in the period, there would be a greater amount of comparison behavior and, consequently, students would know more of their classmates' grades.[2]

Gathering Data. We solicited the cooperation of the teachers of eight sections[3] of introductory psychology (other than our own) who agreed to return their next exam at a time determined by us and provide students (a total of 442) with a greater or lesser than usual amount of information about their performance. The amount of *opportunity for social comparison* in the classroom was varied by returning the exams either at the beginning of the class period (high opportunity) or just before the end (low opportunity). The *amount of performance information* was varied by giving subjects in the low information condition only their raw score, but subjects in the high information sections received their raw score, a letter grade, and the class distribution of scores which was written on the blackboard.

We collected the data at the first class meeting following return of the exams. The students in the experimental sections filled out a one-page form- to provide detailed information about social comparison: they were asked to list everyone whose grade they knew, the location of the person, relationship to the person, as well as how, when, and where they learned the grades.[4]

Presenting the Results. To increase student involvement in the presentation of data, we asked our students to predict the results and then presented those that we actually obtained. Summarizing the results provides a high interest opportunity for demonstrating the purpose and calculation of descriptive statistics. Teachers who do this study may want to compare their students' results with ours.

Results. First of all, how much comparison really goes on in the classroom? We found that on the average in our classes (size 40-50 students), a student knows the grades of 3.24 other students. If a professor returns an exam at the beginning of class, students on the average know markedly more scores (3.99) than if exams are returned at the end of class (2.50). It appears that there is more opportunity to compare when the exam is given back early in the period.

Comparison does appear to be affected by the amount of information one knows about one's score.

For example, if students know their score, letter grade and the distribution of scores, there is apparently less motivation to find out other people's grades. (Mean number of comparisons = 2.66.) If only the score is known, and not the other information, there is apparently more motivation to find out other's grades. (Mean number of comparisons = 4.17.)

Whom do students compare with? Is sheer distance an important factor? Apparently so because 60% of the comparisons were made with people sitting in adjoining seats (front, back and side); only 30% of comparisons were made with students who did not sit nearby. The remaining 10% of comparisons were with students in other class sections.

Is one more likely to know the grades of friends than of people who are slight acquaintances? Forty-two percent of the people whose grades students knew were friends, but 33% were people known only by sight or name (seldom interacted with). The remaining comparisons were made with people who were acquaintances.

When does comparison take place? An average of 67% of the comparisons were made during the class period in which the exam was returned. The remaining 33% were divided fairly evenly among the following categories: 1 hour after class; from then until midnight; the next day; and later.

How does the comparison actually take place? Students typically learned another's grade in three different ways: by directly asking the person (35%); seeing the person's grade (28%); and the person volunteering the grade without being asked (25%). Only 8% of the scores were found out second hand, i.e., by someone else passing on the information.

Discussion and Conclusion. The final step in an experiment is to "discuss" its findings: to relate them back to theory and to show how the results raise questions for further research. In our case it appeared, at first, that we had obtained clear support for Festinger's theory. But, through discussion, we discovered that pre-existing experimental group differences raised some question about the opportunity and information manipulations and made evident the need for a better controlled replication. This observation, as well as questions like "Would the results be the same in a smaller class?" provided a good opportunity for showing the importance of skeptical and critical evaluation in the scientific process.

References

Festinger, L. A theory of social comparison processes. *Human Relations,* 1954, 7, 117-140.

Latane, B. (Ed.). Studies in social comparison. *Journal of Experimental Social Psychology,* 1966, Suppl. 1.

Suls, J. M. & Miller, R. L. (Eds.). *Social comparison processes: Theoretical and empirical perspectives.* Washington: Hemisphere, 1977.

Wheeler, L, Shaver, K. G., Jones, R. A., Goethals, G. R., Cooper, J., Robinson, J. E., Gruder, C. L., & Butzine, K. W. Factors determining choice of a comparison other. *Journal of Experimental Social Psychology,* 1969, 5, 219-232.

Notes

1. Recent empirical studies based on the theory are included in the references, although not all are cited.
2. For the more advanced students, teachers may discuss experimental design in greater detail. This demonstration is a 2 x 2 factorial design, with two levels of opportunity for comparison, and two levels of information. Using this design, one can demonstrate main effects and the difficult concept of interaction.
3. We want to thank Drs. Dewey Bayer Clifford Mahler, Frank Merigold, Donald Tollefson, and Richard Weisman for their cooperation and allowing the use of their class time for this project.
4. Sample data collection forms may be obtained from the first author.

3 . USING COMPUTERS

Three Computer-Assisted Laboratory Exercises for Introductory Psychology

Thomas Brothen
University of Minnesota

A growing trend in the past few years has been the adaptation of computer technology for individual use. The availability of home computers for everything from stock market forecasting to video games is changing our society. Small children are becoming familiar with computers in video arcades, their homes, and their schools. Many children now in elementary school are gold hands" at using computers and both they and their parents expect computers to play an important role in their elementary, secondary, and college education (Williams & McDonald, 1982).

Of course, recognizing and utilizing the advantages of computers in our psychology classes is not an easy task. Basic models to guide development of computer-assisted instruction are needed. This paper describes such a model and three instructional packages derived from it.

In the summer of 1981 a University of Minnesota Graduate School research grant to the author supported development of a model for computer-assisted instructional packages. The resulting packages were put into computer language and tested with students the following year. During the summer of 1982 a grant from the University of Minnesota Educational Development Program supported revision of the computer programs and completion of the ancillary materials for use during 1982-83.

Examination of the *Index to computer-based learning* (5th ed.) (University of Wisconsin, Milwaukee) and the *Directory of teaching innovations in psychology* (Maas & Kleiber, 1976) revealed that less than half of the twenty-seven catalogued packages were designed for introductory psychology, and most of those taught basic material. Only three included exercises for students to complete. It was apparent both that computer-assisted instruction was not widely available to introductory psychology students and that what was available used the computer primarily for routine drill.

The Model. The computer-assisted instructional packages described here were designed to meet three goals. First, the packages complement course objectives. A primary objective of my introductory

psychology course is to help students understand the method of experiment in drawing conclusions about human behavior and the packages were designed to teach the experimental method. Second, the packages do not do things that might be done more efficiently by textbooks, standard programmed learning materials, or other less expensive means. To achieve this, the computer programs are interactive. Through simple branching techniques they provide information, and then we make certain that students can verbalize what they are supposed to know. Third, the packages are hybrid in nature. That is, they make use of written materials as well as the computer. They require students to make written responses while working on the computer and later when drawing conclusions about their experience.

The three instructional packages described in this paper were designed to give students experience dealing with experimentally derived data and they are assigned after students complete a unit on psychological methods. This unit also contains a computer-assisted instructional package that drills students on the important elements of a psychological experiment they are assigned to read. At this point, then, students are prepared to record and interpret experimental data.

The instructional packages all have the same basic structure. First, students go to a computer terminal in the role of experimental subjects and the computer asks them to respond to stimuli it generates. The computer then explains the structure of the experiment and questions students in an interactive format intended to make certain they understand how the experiment was designed. Students cannot proceed until they work their way through this branching program. Once students have demonstrated that they understand the experiment, the computer directs them to tabulate their data on a worksheet. When this is completed, students leave the terminal with their print-out and worksheet.

The final step utilizes groups of six to eight students in their laboratory section. They are given laboratory worksheets that show them how to tabulate their individual data into group data. They then

37

respond to worksheet questions that ask them to compare their individual data to the group data.

The Three Packages. The three packages differ slightly in what they ask students to do. The second requires more complex tabulation than the first and the third more than the second. The first contains a 2x2 experiment with both variables determined by the computer. The second contains a 2x3 experiment with one variable determined by the computer and one variable determined by students' scores on a personality test administered by the computer. The third contains a 3x2 experiment with one variable determined by the computer and one variable determined by a median split of group members scores on a behavioral measure of conformity.

The first package asks students to rate people on a one-to-five liking scale. Twelve hypothetical individuals are described with three trait adjectives taken from Anderson's (1968) list. Half of the individuals described have male names and half female. When they finish the rating task, students are told that they rated two different types of males and females to test the question in social psychological research of whether three moderately positive traits (e.g., gentle, serious, convincing) elicit more liking than two very positive traits and one somewhat negative trait (e.g., warmhearted, opinionated, quick-witted). They are told that each individual has been described with the same total amount of positivity so that the two competing theories can be tested against each other. Next, they are asked what their data show and, as an illustration of the need for researchers to be open to other things their data might show, they are asked if sex of the individual made a difference. Students enter their "liking scores" into the computer and are asked whether their data support either of the competing theories. Through a branching procedure the computer tells them whether they have drawn the correct conclusion. The group worksheet handed out in laboratory asks them to tabulate group data, compare them to the individual data, and determine which theory was supported.

The second package asks students to provide two types of data. First, it asks them to rate ten hypothetical stimulus persons on a five-point liking scale from statements they are purported to have made. The statements were adapted from "power and toughness" items of the F-Scale (Adorno, et al., 1950) and were designed to portray the stimulus person as high or low on the "power motive." Second, students are asked to respond to items on the "Shortened F for Political Surveys" (Janowitz & Marvick, 1953)—an authoritarianism scale. Scores on this test serve as students' "power motive" scores.

Students are told that the experiment is designed to test two hypotheses: that people like others with similar "power motives" and that people with low power motives are liked best. Students enter their liking

scores and their own "power motive" scores into the computer and are given feedback on what their scores mean and whether they were correct in saying their data did or did not support the hypotheses.

In the laboratory session, students are given a worksheet which directs them to tabulate the data according to group members' "power motive" scores (high, intermediate, or low). Questions about whether the group data support the hypotheses are also asked.

The third package asks students to play a "word game." Students are given a stimulus word and two accompanying words from which they are to choose a synonym. The students (mostly freshmen) find the task difficult because the words are not in common usage (e.g., induration, accretion). Students are told that to be "helpful" the computer will report how many previous students from their class picked each word.

After students finish the "game" they are told that they took part in an experiment on conformity. Because the words were so difficult they weren't expected to score at levels higher than chance. They were exposed to three levels of social influence in that the supposed percentage of students choosing a word was fabricated and always in a majority of about 55%, 75%, or 100% for the incorrect word. Students are asked to enter the number they got wrong into the computer. Below chance responding (i.e. more than 50% incorrect) is interpreted by the computer as evidence of conformity. Students also indicate whether they responded differently to the three levels of influence (55% vs. 75% vs. 100%) and whether their data support the hypothesis that higher levels of influence cause more conformity. The computer then gives them feedback on their responses.

The laboratory worksheet requires students to separate the group into high and low conformers (by median split of students' total incorrect responses) and tabulate the group data. Students are asked whether the group data support the hypothesis and how high and low conformers responded differently to different levels of influence.

Evaluation. The packages were evaluated with three methods during their first year of class use. First, the worksheet grades were reviewed to determine whether the questions posed on the worksheet were answered adequately. Students did a better than adequate job—demonstrating by and large that they understood the assignments and were able to complete them satisfactorily. Seventy-five percent of the laboratory groups got perfect scores on the laboratory worksheet which means they tabulated the data correctly and drew the correct conclusions about whether the data supported the hypotheses. Almost all of the other groups missed only one point of a possible five.

Second, the individual worksheets students brought to the computer terminal included an evaluation question. It asked them to indicate which of five statements described how much they enjoyed completing the computer part of the package. Statements were: "I didn't like it at all" (scored one), "I liked it some" (two), "I liked it quite a bit" (three), "I liked it very much" (four), and "I liked it better than anything else I've done in college" (five). Over all three projects, 3% of students selected the first alternative, 35% the second alternative, 35% the third, 22% the fourth, and 5% the most positive. The mean response of 2.92 *(SD= 0.93)* was quite positive.

Third, at the end of each term students completed a course evaluation instrument. It contained an item that measured students' assessment of the laboratory projects. Students were asked whether they disagreed strongly (scored one), disagreed moderately (two), agreed moderately (three), agreed strongly (four), or agreed totally (five) with the statement: "The laboratory projects were a beneficial learning experience for me." Only one student (less than 1%) disagreed strongly, 9% disagreed moderately, 36% agreed moderately, 32% agreed strongly, and 22% agreed totally. Once again, evaluation of the packages was positive with a mean response equal to 3.64 *(SD=0.95)*.

In summary, students are able to complete the packages satisfactorily, find them interesting, and find them to be a beneficial learning experience. Thus, the three packages met the goals set for them. They fit the course objective of giving students more experience dealing with the experimental method; they add a new dimension to the learning resources available to students; and they integrate computer and written work. And now that they are in place and being used by large numbers of students, other questions about student learning and computer-assisted instruction can be addressed by future research.

References

Adorno, T., et al. *The authoritarian personality,* New York: Harper, 1950.

Anderson, N. Likableness ratings of 555 personality-trait words. *Journal of Personality and Social Psychology,* 1968, *9,* 272-279.

Index to computer-based learning (5th ed.). Milwaukee: University of Wisconsin.

Janowitz, M., & Marvick, D. Authoritarianism and political behavior. *Public Opinion* Quarterly, 1953, *17,* 185-201.

Maas, J., & Kleiber, D. *Directory of teaching innovations in psychology,* Washington, DC: American Psychological Association, 1976.

Williams, D., & McDonald, D. H. The great computer frenzy. *Newsweek,* December 27, 1982.

Note

An earlier version of this paper was presented at the Ninth International Conference on Improving University Teaching, Dublin, Ireland, July 1983.

A Computerized Application of Psychology's Top 100

Thomas Brothen
Janet Schneider
University of Minnesota

This article describes a computer-assisted study exercise for introductory psychology classes adapted from Boneau's (1990) list of the top 100 terms and concepts. We discuss alternative uses for the list, computer program development, and student use of the program in studying for the final examination. Preliminary evaluation suggests that the exercise increases student knowledge of introductory psychology.

Boneau (1990) asked 250 psychology textbook authors to indicate which terms were most important in each of 10 subareas of psychology. The responses from 159 authors produced 10 lists of 100 terms. In addition, the most highly rated items formed what Boneau referred to as psychology's Top 100 terms and concepts. Boneau suggested that all "literate" psychology students should know them, but he emphasized the tentative nature of his work and asked "Where do we go from here?" (p. 900).

Alternative Uses

The Top 100 list can serve various purposes. First, it could be used to evaluate psychology instruction. If students are not being taught the Top 100 terms and concepts, course content or textbooks could be adjusted. Second, the list could be used by instructors to judge how closely their course content matches what other psychologists consider crucial in an area of study. Third, the list could be used to help students learn psychology (e.g., instructors could incorporate it into a statement of learning objectives, or students could use it as a summary of what they should know for the final examination).

The latter purpose motivated us to adapt the Top 100 list as a computer exercise for students studying for the final examination in introductory psychology. The need for the exercise arose from our observations that students have difficulty simply remembering and understanding a basic core of psychological knowledge by the end of a 10-week quarter. Our approach deals primarily with a basic stage in the learning process (see Gronlund, 1970); however, students need this type of review to achieve higher cognitive levels. Our evaluation is preliminary because our immediate goal was to create software that stimulated studying behavior.

Program Development

For our purposes, Boneau's (1990) list required editing because several of the terms and concepts were not in the course textbook (Gerow, 1989) or were presented in a slightly different form. Thus, we adapted the list in two ways to create our own Top 100 list.

First, 19 terms were replaced with the next highest rated term from the same subarea list if the replacement terms were not already used and if they were covered in our textbook. Terms were replaced because they simply were not covered (e.g., *visual angle* was replaced with *cone)* or, in our judgment, overlapped too much with other terms on the list. For example, we kept *binocular depth cues* but replaced *depth perception* and *visual depth perception.*

Second, minor wording changes were made in 13 terms to reflect textbook usage. For example, *avoidance learning* was changed to *avoidance conditioning, associationism* to *behaviorism,* and *longitudinal research* to *longitudinal method.*

After compiling a final list, we abstracted each term. We avoided using only definitions by capturing the text's main point about the term. We used phrasing directly from the text wherever possible to create descriptions similar to multiple choice questions. For example, we created the following descriptions. For the term *behaviorism:* "A study of what people do; Skinner followed Watson's lead and studied the relationships between responses and consequences."

For *hypothesis:* "A scientist formulates this tentative proposition and then tests it in a way which leads to its confirmation or rejection. "

Then we developed a computer exercise to give students feedback on their knowledge of the Top 100 terms. We incorporated it into existing practice exercises programmed in Pilot, a programming language similar to BASIC (Barker, 1987). The resulting package enabled students to take practice quizzes on individual chapters, take a practice final examination consisting of 100 items similar to those in the actual final examination, or complete the Top 100 exercise.

Student Use

Students used the program in the classroom in which they take their introductory psychology course on a computer network (Brothen, 1991). The classroom contains 40 networked computers on which students do all their in-class work. We handed out the Top 100 list (available from the authors) during the last week of classes and told students that 159 textbook authors rated those terms as the 100 most important to know. We also stressed that knowing the terms would not guarantee a high final exam grade but would give them a good knowledge base in psychology.

The computer classroom was open for students to do any of the three practice exercises during final examination week. All students had at least three "open lab" days available for study before their final exam. The practice quizzes and practice final simply presented items in random order and reported the number correct to students once they finished. The Top 100 exercise randomly presented our 100 abstracted descriptions one at a time without replacement. After reading each description, students examined the list of 100 terms, selected the correct match, and then entered it. After typing an answer, they were told if it was correct and had the options of continuing, seeing the textbook page number for the term before trying again (after an incorrect answer), or quitting. When they quit, the computer told them how many terms they attempted, how many tries they took to answer them, and how many they got correct overall. Their goal was to repeat the exercise until they answered all 100 terms correctly in one try each (i.e., when scores equal 100 terms, 100 total tries, 100 correct).

Evaluation

Of 124 students who finished the course, 92 used the Top 100 exercise at least once. We and our classroom assistants informally observed and talked with students doing the exercise. Students said that the exercise was difficult, but they agreed that the list contained information that they should know and that the computer provided valuable feedback on their study progress.

We also explored whether there were any differences between those who used the exercise and those who did not. Students using the Top 100 exercise at least once scored higher on the 100-point final examination *(M* = 57.5) than students not using the exercise *(M* = 54.9), but the difference was not statistically significant, $t(122) = 1.21$, $p = .22$. There was, however, a statistically significant relation between the number of times they used the exercise *(M* = 1.08) and their final exam scores, $r = .23$, $p = .011$. This was not true for the number of times 103 students used the practice final *(M* = 1.24), $r = .10$, n.s.

Partialing out the relation between the practice final and final exam score in a multivariate analysis helps clarify these relations. We used the number of times students took the practice final in a multiple regression analysis to predict final exam scores. Then we added the number of times students did the Top 100 exercise to the regression equation. We found no effect for the practice final, $F(2, 121) = .006$, n.s., but a significant effect for the Top 100 exercise, $F(2, 121) = 5.22$, $p = .024$, was discovered.

These analyses suggest that use of the Top 100 exercise promoted learning (as reflected by final exam scores). An alternative explanation that students with higher motivation used the exercise but got higher scores for other reasons is mitigated by the lack of relation between practice final use and final exam scores.

We cannot say with certainty that the Top 100 exercise contributes significantly to learning about psychology. Nevertheless, individual students indicated to us that it helped them. They reported that the exercise was more difficult than practice exams because it required them to study the material more in order to do well on it. Also, tentative data indicate that students who used the exercise benefited from it. From an instructional perspective, we know that the content of the exercise is important and that feedback is crucial to learning. Our observations indicate that the exercise promotes active learning (Schomberg, 1986) by forcing students to consult their books and think before answering. These are useful student behaviors; any exercise that increases them is beneficial.

References

Barker, P. (1987). *Authoring languages for CAL.* London: Macmillan

Boneau, C. A. (1990). Psychological literacy: A first approximation. *American Psychologist, 45,* 891-900.

Brothen, T. (1991). Implementing a computer-assisted cooperative learning model for introductory psychology. *Teaching of Psychology, 18,* 183-185.

Gerow, I. (1989). *Psychology: An introduction* (2nd ed.). Glenview, IL Scott-Foresman.

Gronlund, N. (1970). *Stating behavioral objectives for classroom instruction.* London Collier-Macmillan.

Schomberg, S. (1986). *Strategies for active teaching and learning in university classrooms.* Minneapolis: University of Minnesota Communication Services.

Note

An earlier version of this article was presented at the annual meeting of the American Psychological Association, San Francisco, August 1991.

Microcomputers in the Introductory Laboratory

John K. Bare
Carleton College

The use of microcomputers is growing and there have appeared on the market the necessary interfaces for use with laboratory equipment; together these components may very well replace much of the current timing, recording, and equipment control devices used in teaching laboratories as well as in research. The purpose of this paper is to describe two successful uses of such a computer system in the laboratory for the first course.

The study of cognitive processes has emphasized one of psychology's earliest measures—reaction time. The computer system employed had the capacity for measuring reaction time on sixteen separate inputs, storing the values for 32 trials, and giving hard copy of the data. For a number of pedagogical reasons we chose to use that capacity to replicate, in slightly modified form, Sternberg's 1966 study of retrieval from short term memory. We used memory sets of one, three, and six digits and a single probe. Five "yes" and five "no" trials were conducted for each memory set length, and thus the design was a three-by-two factorial for three set lengths and two conditions (yes/no).

Each subject had two push button switches labeled "yes" and "no". The sets and probes were put onto slides and projected on a screen at the front of the room. A trial consisted of a "'ready" slide followed by the memory set and then the probe. The position of the probe in sets of three and six digits was distributed throughout the set. Reaction times were recorded in a virtual array file in the buffer and then called up from that file.

The statistic employed was the factorial design with repeated measures on both factors, and the analysis was performed by the computer when the data had been collected. The results of the analysis were thus immediately available.

Two hypotheses can be tested, one by each of the factors: Retrieval is by serial search rather than by parallel search; and if one uses a serial search, the process is self-terminating rather than exhaustive. We point out to the students that even if we have no awareness of this rapid search, it would be counter-intuitive for it to be exhaustive in the "yes" case. The data from 13 subjects are displayed in Figure 1.

Memory set size had a significant effect $F_{(2,12)}$ = 36.91 ($p < .001$), and neither the difference between the "yes" and "no" means nor the interaction was significant. We could conclude that the retrieval process appeared to be serial and not parallel, and the students are always tempted to conclude that it is exhaustive rather than self-terminating because of the similarities of the reaction time values for the "yes" and "no'" trials at all set lengths.

At this point we always examine the question of whether the failure to reject the null hypothesis can support an hypothesis. We then raise the question of whether an experiment can ever prove an hypothesis or only disprove one. The discussion is very likely to lead to the decision to test the self-terminating hypothesis.

Logic and a little friendly persuasion lead us to a second test patterned after the study of Wingfield and Bolt (1970), in which memory sets were three and six digits long but *three* probes were provided. The students were instructed to respond with "yes" if any *one* of the three probes were in the memory set. The data, presented in Figure 2, can only be described as very satisfying.

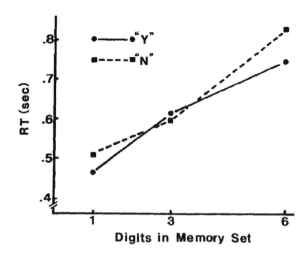

Figure 1. Reaction time as a function of the number of digits in the memory set for a single probe.

The same kind of analysis of variance shows set size to be a significant variable, $F_{(1,12)} = 39.01$ ($p < .001$), the reaction time to be longer for "no" than for "yes" cases, $F_{(1,12)} = 22.42$ ($p < .001$), and the interaction between the two variables is also significant, $F_{(1,12)} = 4.97$ ($p < .05$). A comparison of the ordinates of Figures 1 and 2 shows that the reaction times are longer in the second study, as might be expected. The hypothesis that the search is exhaustive is not supported, but one finds no reason for rejecting the conclusion that it is self-terminating. The significance of the interaction serves as a springboard for further class discussion.

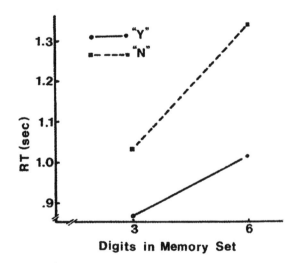

Figure 2. Reaction time as a function of the number of digits in the memory set for a three-digit probe.

A second experiment exploited the computer's capability for precise timing in the control of equipment. The study chosen was a replication of one of those in the now classic paper by Sperling (1960) on sensory (or iconic) memory.

Slides of three-by-three matrices of consonants were prepared and presented by a projector and a photo-cell operated shutter. The exposure duration was 100 msec. For the uncued trials, the subjects were provided an answer sheet with blank matrices for each trial and were instructed to put the consonants in their proper position. In the partially cued trials, the computer was programmed to pause after sending the "operate" signal to the projector, that pause of such a length that the "operate" signal to the three sound sources occurred 50 msec after the slide had disappeared. For the cued trials, the subjects were provided answer sheets with rows of three cells in which they were to put the consonants in their proper places. With 30 uncued trials designated the "A" condition and 30 cued trials the "B" condition 120 trials in an ABBA order were presented.

With an N of eight, the demonstration appears to be almost fail-proof. Because the subjects are unpracticed compared with those of Sperling, the recall is somewhat less under both conditions than he reports, but for a related measures t, the p values range in the various sections of the laboratory between .05 and .01. For an N of 25, $t(24) = 9.45$ ($p < .001$, two-tailed test).

The uses of microcomputers in the future in laboratories for the first course may be limited only by our imaginations and by our ability to convince colleagues in our departments that microcomputers are not only for research.

References

Sperling, G. The information available in brief visual presentations. *Psychological Monographs,* 1960, *74* (Whole No. 498)

Sternberg, S. High speed scanning in human memory. *Science,* 1966, *153*, 652-654.

Wingfield, A. & Bolt, R. A. Memory search for multiple targets. *Journal of Experimental Psychology,* 1970, *85*, 45-50.

Note

The purchase of the computer was made possible by NSF Cause Grant SER77-06304 to Carleton College.

4. INTEGRATING SUPPLEMENTARY LITERATURE

Using *Psychology Today* Articles to Increase The Perceived Relevance of the Introductory Course

Drew C. Appleby
Marian College

This article describes the purpose, construction, and use of a bibliography of Psychology Today *articles that have been categorized according to their relevance to various academic majors and career areas. Its use in the introductory course increases students' awareness that a knowledge of psychology can help them to accomplish their academic and career goals.*

One goal of the introductory course is to help students realize that psychology is a relevant field of study (i.e., it can contribute positively to their lives, and is not something to be merely memorized, regurgitated on tests, and then forgotten). Several authors have reported their attempts to increase students' perception of the relevance of psychology courses. Some attempts involve the opportunity to read popular books (Benel, 1975; LeUnes, 1974; McCollom, 1971) and articles (Wortman & Hillis, 1975) dealing with compelling psychological topics. Others concentrate on the application of psychological principles to explain or deal with everyday life incidences or problems (Brender, 1982; Grasha, 1974). Students have even replicated the "scientific" studies cited to lend validity to the claims made on television commercials (Solomon, 1979).

The concept of relevance has changed in the past 15 years. What was relevant to students in the past may seem irrelevant today. A question that occupies the minds of many contemporary students is: Will my undergraduate education provide me with the skills I need to get a good job after graduation? One way to capitalize on the motivation resulting from this question is to give students an opportunity to discover that a knowledge of psychological principles can benefit them in their academic majors and future careers. Students form strong loyalties to their academic majors and are ego-involved with their career choices. They perceive information that can help them to succeed in these areas to be highly relevant.

Students' eagerness to learn can be increased by an opportunity to improve their grade in the introductory course with extra credit projects. Such projects can facilitate learning more about psychology and about students' own academic major or career choices. Students are more highly motivated when they are allowed to write extra credit reports on articles related to their major and/or career choices, but their enthusiasm wanes if they are unable to locate such materials. This article includes a bibliography designed to alleviate this problem. It provides introductory students with a large amount of well organized and accessible literature that can simplify their search for relevant psychological information.

The first step in producing this bibliography was to assemble a list of the 27 academic majors and career areas offered by Marian College. Because there is a great deal of overlap in the subject matter in many of these areas, several list items were combined into single categories (e.g., Allied Health, Nursing, and PreMed), reducing the total number of categories to 18. The next step was to peruse the table of contents of each issue of *Psychology Today* published since 1967 to locate articles that contain information related to one or more of these categories. This exhaustive search produced 407 articles. The mean number of articles per category was 22.6 and the range was 34 (7 to 41). Some areas were surprisingly well represented (e.g., theology-36 articles, English-31, and home economics—30); other areas were less popular (e.g., foreign languages—7 and computer science and math-8).

The response to this bibliography has been very positive. The number and quality of extra credit reports have increased. Students say that they enjoyed writing the reports because the articles they reviewed contained information that was personally relevant. An unexpected benefit was that many students used the list to find references for term papers and speeches in courses outside psychology. When copies of this bibliography and a memo explaining its purpose were distributed to the chairpersons of other academic departments, the response was very gratifying. Several stated that they had not realized how much their majors could learn about their own disciplines in the introductory psychology course. This bibliography is well suited to the introductory course in which students first encounter the diversity of psychological literature. Because most introductory psychology students never take another psychology course, it is important to expose them to as much relevant information as possible during their brief encounter with our discipline. This technique would not be appropriate for more advanced psychology courses in which the development of library research skills is valued, and students are expected to identify and find articles on their own.

The following list of *Psychology Today* articles and their publication dates is a sample from the complete bibliography. Two articles were chosen from each of the 18 major and/or career categories on the basis of their high level of interest for introductory students and the recency of their publication dates.

Allied Health, Nursing, and PreMed
  "Stress and Health" (8/85)
  "The Mystery of Alzheimer's" (1/84)
Art and Art Therapy
  "Stalking the Mental Image" (5/85)
  "How the Mind Draws" (5/86)
Biology
  "Crime in the Family Tree" (3/85)
  "Genes, Personality, and Alcoholism" (1/85)
Business, Accounting, and Economics
  "What Makes a Top Executive?" (2/83)
  "To File, Perchance to Cheat" (4/85)
Chemistry
  "Alcohol, Marijuana, and Memory" (3/80)
  "The Chemistry of Craving" (10/83)
Computer Science and Mathematics
  "The Human-Computer Connection" (3/84)
  "Computer Games, Let the Kids Play" (8/85)
Education
  "Challenging the Brightest" (6/84)
  "Who's Intelligent?" (4/82)
English
  "When is a Word a Word?" (11/85)
  "A Conversation With Isaac Asimov" (1/83)
Foreign Languages
  "Fear of Foreign Languages" (8/81)
  "The International Language of Gestures" (5/84)
History and Political Science
  "Reagan and the National Psyche" (1/82)
  "Psychology and Armageddon" (5/82)
Home Economics, Dietetics, and Fashion Merchandising
  "Clothes Power" (12/82)
  "The Funk Food Syndrome" (1/82)
Music

"Music, the Beautiful Disturber" (12/85)
  "The Music of the Hemispheres" (6/82)
Philosophy
  "A Sense of Control" (12/84)
  "Is it Right?" (6/81)
Physical Education
  "Beating Slumps at Their Own Game" (7/84)
  "The Playing Field of the Mind" (7/84)
PreLaw
  "Beat That Lie Detector" (6/85)
  "Mind Control in the Courtroom" (5/82)
Sociology
  "Arresting Delinquency" (3/85)
  "Marriages Made to Last" (6/85)
Theater and Speech
  "The Language of Persuasion" (4/85)
  "The Psychologist as TV Guide" (8/86)
Theology
  "The Children's God" (12/85)
  "Stages of Faith" (11/83)

References

Benel, R. A. (1975). Psychological thrillers: Thrilling to whom? *Teaching of Psychology*, *2*, 176-177.

Brender, M. (1982). The relevance connection: Relating academic psychology to everyday life. *Teaching of Psychology*, *9*, 222-224.

Grasha, A. F. (1974). "Giving psychology away": Some experiences teaching undergraduates practical psychology. *Teaching of Psychology*, *1*, 21-24.

LeUnes, A. (1974). Psychological thrillers revisited: A tentative list of "master thrillers." *American Psychologist*, *29*, 211-213.

McCollom, I. N. (1971). Psychological thrillers: Psychology books students read when given freedom of choice. *American Psychologist*, *26*, 921-927.

Solomon, P. R. (1979). Science and television commercials: Adding relevance to the research methodology course. *Teaching of Psychology*, *6*, 26-30.

Wortman, C. B., & Hillis, J. W. (1975). Some "thrilling" short articles for use in an introductory psychology class. *Teaching of Psychology*, *2*, 134-135.

Tying it All Together: Research, Concepts, and Fiction In an Introductory Psychology Course

Lita Linzer Schwartz
Pennsylvania State University,
Ogontz Campus

After I was assigned to teach the Introductory Psychology course for the first time in ten years, I sought ways to make it an experience that would have lasting impact on the students. The goal was not original, nor were many of the supplemental aids such as films, handouts, paper-andpencil activities, and discussions (in a class that began with more than one hundred freshmen and sophomores). Concurrent with the course planning, however, I was (and continue to be) involved in a study of conversion techniques, particularly as they have been used by contemporary cult groups. The possibility of tying this research to the course seemed to be an effective yet low-key method of uniting instructor interest and course content. It also offered an opportunity to make students aware of some of the characteristics of cult groups without preaching to them. The specific mechanism to be used was a report on Ehrlich's novel, *The Cult* (1979).

A traditional introductory text was assigned as basic reading for the course (Belkin/Skydell, 1979), with students encouraged to use the accompanying Study Guide as well. Four quizzes, each based on three chapters of the book, were scheduled. A report on *The Cult* was the fifth component to be considered in determining the student's grade.The report was focused on identifying the application of a number of psychological concepts in the novel . Although students were aware from the opening day of the course that they would have the report to write, specific instructions for the paper were not distributed until half-way through the 10-week course. I thought that by then the students would be less anxious about the terminology used. The instructions read:

In Psy 2, we have studied many principles and concepts that are demonstrated in this novel. From the list below, select a minimum of five (5) principles or concepts, and write a brief paragraph or two for each describing how it is applied in the cult situation. Cite specific examples and page references from Ehrlich's book.

Altered states of consciousness
Attitude change and cognitive dissonance theory
Behavioral modification
Conformity: compliance and internalization
Deindividuation
Effects of sleep and diet deprivation
Leadership and leader-follower relations
Motives for becoming involved with groups such as "the cult" (i.e., what needs are satisfied in this type of group?)

Students were referred to the text for definitions of the terms, particularly those not yet discussed in class.

Every student was able to select appropriate applications of at least four concepts, most found one or more examples for five concepts, and a few reached for six concepts. Verification of the knowledge gained from reading the novel as well as the text was sought in the error rate on the dozen final quiz questions (out of 50) that dealt with several of these same ideas.

The last three chapters of the Belkin/Skydell text, on which the final quiz was based, included psychotherapies, social behavior, and group processes. Principal ideas of each chapter were discussed in lecture, supplemented by a film. The only differences between the content of 38 of the questions and the remaining dozen, which were scattered throughout the quiz, were that the latter had also been involved in the novel and the paper based on it. To determine whether this activity had any effect on reinforcing certain concepts, analysis of error rates for the two groups of questions was made.

An initial inspection of the data revealed that students made 1-27 errors on the total quiz, with both the median and mode at 11 errors, or a 22% error rate. The mean was 11.58 errors, or a 23% error rate. The number of errors on the 12 questions relevant to the concepts emphasized in *The Cult* ranged from one to 9, with nine of the 81 students (11%) making more than three errors, or an error rate in excess of 25 percent. On the remaining 38 questions, the number of errors ranged from one to 18. Ten or more errors would exceed the expected 25% error rate. Forty students of the 81, or almost 50%, had error rates above what was expected. The significance of the difference in error rates was analyzed using the Wilcoxon matched-pairs signed-ranks test formula for large samples, for which $z = -5.94$, which is significant beyond any tabled value. This statistically significant result suggests that learning was enhanced for those concepts demonstrated in the additional reading assignment.

As noted earlier, there was another goal in the assignment. As a result of the author's research and discussions with cult-involved young adults and their families, there was genuine concern that these students, most of whom have not been away from home independently, should have enough information about cult-type groups to be able to make an informed decision on whether or not to accept an invitation to visit such a group. That the goal was attained was apparent in many verbal comments even before the reports were submitted . In the papers themselves, there were also several comments that reflected the hoped-for awareness:

> Personally I would like to add that I found reading *The Cult* to be an eye-opening experience. I had been in some doubt about cults in general. However, after reading Ehrlich's book I regard them in a new light It is my opinion that cults are not true religions or churches and they are mentally harmful to those people who choose to join them.

> I feel this book was very informative. I have been interested in fraudulent cults for two years, realizing the increasing international problem. I have come in contact with many devotees in the city collecting "for orphanages and old age homes" (I have never contributed a cent). I truly hope more young people become informed on this evilness than just the 106 people in this class.

> Ehrlich's book has left me with a sharpened awareness of a fascinating yet petrifying phenomenon. *The Cult* has brought me to realize that in this world people must be wary with whom they associate. While reading the book, it induced me to think about all the people I come in contact with and question how well I really know them. *The Cult* shows how belief in an authority figure, such as Rev. Hodges of the SFJ, can be carried to a frightening extreme.

> I liked this book very much. It was intriguing to read, and very unsettling at times. My advice to anyone who comes in contact with one of those groups is to just keep walking. Don't stop to talk or buy a pamphlet. Pretend that they are not there.

(Note: Class members were also sharing their information and opinions with other students on campus, a "bonus" as far as I was concerned, because students in my other courses told me that they'd heard about or even borrowed the book to read. Although this feedback was rewarding, there was an allied reaction that was also very unexpected. In common with many other colleges and universities, we have a student body that rarely reads for pleasure. That fact made the following comment all the more gratifying: "I read the book from cover to cover without once putting it down. For me that's probably the first time.")

Although the choice of novel in this instance was dictated by the instructor's research activities, it would seem that there are at least two other novels that might be equally effective as teaching instruments. These are Huxley's *Brave New World* (1932) and Orwell's *1984* (1949). Both demonstrate the use of psychological principles in manipulating human behavior and life-styles. Although they lack the timeliness of *The Cult* in terms of a current problem, there are aspects of each that can be tied to contemporary events. That the use of the novel as part of the required reading for the introductory course is worthwhile is evident from the reinforcement of information as determined by the significantly lower error rate on novel-related questions.

References

Belkin, G. S., & Skydell, R. H. *Foundations* of *psychology.* Boston: Houghton Mifflin, 1979.

Ehrlich, M. *The cult*. New York: Bantam Books, 1979.

Huxley, A. *Brave new world*. New York: Harper, 1932.

Orwell, G. *1984*. New York: Harcourt, Brace, 1949.

Note

Appreciation is extended to Diane Winnemore for performing the calculations for the Wilcoxon test, and to Dr. Jeanne L. Smith of the Ogontz Campus, Pennsylvania State University, for her assistance.

Individualized Reading for Introductory Psychology

David Winzenz
Marilyn Winzenz
California State University

Over the years, reading research has investigated the nature of certain relationships between reader interest and reading comprehension. According to Shnayer (1969) and Estes and Vaughan (1973) strong relationships can exist between reader interest and reading comprehension at various reading levels. Fader and McNeil (1975) have developed an educational program based on a saturation of the student's environment with high interest materials which they report enhances student attitude, interest, and reading comprehension. A university level approach to capitalizing on student interests was developed by McCollom (1971) who presented students with a list of "psychological thrillers" from which to select books for their course reading in introductory psychology.

Using a revision of McCollom's reading list and a modification of his instructional technique, we also offered individualized reading opportunities for introductory psychology students. During the first class meeting each student was given a detailed outline of the semester's lectures with notations regarding which books correlated with each day's lectures. Each student chose five selections from the list to be read during the semester and, using the outline, could choose to read a given book during the time that related discussion was occurring in class.

Before reading each selection, students were encouraged to (a) skim the book, (b) predict what the book would be about, (c) formulate a variety of written comprehension questions of their own to guide their reading, and (d) predict the relationship of the book to the corresponding lecture. After reading each book the students then prepared for individual conferences by jotting down on a file card salient information of a psychological nature that they felt they had learned from the book. Each conference was ten minutes long, was graded credit/no credit, and was an opportunity to discuss psychology in a relaxed, one-to-one context where the student and instructor could share insights on the book.

Each conference was structured in part by the student's notations on the file card and in part by the instructor's questions, which were intended to relate the book to other course material. For example, two concepts were stressed in the discussion of *The Oxbow Incident* by W. Clark. First, the behavior of the mob and its influences on individuals both before and after the lynching was considered in relation to studies of obedience and conformity. In addition, students analyzed the level of moral development of several main characters in the book, using Kohlberg's (1968) theory of moral development. The paired selections, *I Never Promised You a Rose Garden* by H. Green and *One Flew Over the Cuckoo's Nest* by K. Kesey were used to expose students to the experience of madness and the experience of mental institutions. Schizophrenic language was oftentimes singled out for discussion and both books provided a background for a lively discussion of Rosenhan's (1973) research on being sane in insane places. Each selection on the list was carefully considered in this way for its topical integration into the course material.

A record of reading interests and ease of comprehension was established for each student to allow the instructor to aid in the selection of readings and in the formulation of appropriate goals in the reading program. The records were also useful in planning instruction to develop such reading, thinking skills as the abilities to compare and contrast, to generalize, and to apply a theoretical notion to a specific situation .

In these ways the reading list with individual conferences has been used both with a standard course text and as sole reading material for the course with equal success. Variations on this approach to individualize reading for introductory psychology are certainly possible to provide for individual differences in learning styles, interests, and abilities.

References

Estes, T., & Vaughan, J. Reading interest and comprehension: Implications. *The Reading Teacher,* 1973, 27, 149-153

Fader, D., & McNeil, E. *Hooked on books.* New York: Berkeley Publishing Corporation, 1975.

Kohlberg, L. The child as a moral philosopher. *Psychology Today*, 1968, *2*(4), 25-30.

McCollom, I. Psychological thrillers: Psychology books students read when given freedom of choice. *American Psychologist,* 1971, *26*, 921 -927

Rosenhan, D. On being sane in insane places. *Science*, 1973, *179*, 250-258.

Shnayer, S. Relationships between reading interest and reading comprehension. In J. A. Figurel (Ed.). *Reading and realism.* Newark: International Reading Association, 1969, 698-702.

5. EMPLOYING INTRODUCTORY LABORATORIES

The Science Fair: A Supplement to the Lecture Technique

Thomas A. Fish
Ian H. Fraser
St. Thomas University

From 1984 to 1990, more than 400 students, taught by four different instructors, participated in psychology science fairs as part of their introductory psychology course. A sample of 110 students in upper level psychology courses responded anonymously to a questionnaire assessing their retrospective impressions about their introductory psychology course, current course selections and performance, and future academic plans. Students who had participated in a science fair (n = 30) gave significantly higher ratings than students in other introductory psychology courses (n = 80) to understanding basic principles and their application to everyday life, learning from the instructor and textbook, being prepared for other psychology courses, and having an opportunity to explore topics of interest. Science fair participants also reported exerting more effort in their coursework and being more likely to have taken another course from their introductory psychology instructor. Results suggested that a science fair can provide a unique, valuable, and memorable experience for students.

Poster sessions and science fairs have been used as substitutes for undergraduate seminar courses (Chute & Bank, 1983) and as devices to educate the public (Benjamin, Fawl, & Klein, 1977) . Chute and Bank (1983) found that students responded favorably to poster sessions, indicating that they had learned a great deal from the experience. Benjamin et al. (1977) advocated that the science fair be used as a mechanism to deal with public misconceptions of psychology as a scientific discipline. They pointed out, however, that fairs do not compensate for the lack of appropriate instruction.

Science fairs and poster sessions have two major benefits. First, these organized events, if open to the public, can be an educational experience. Second, they can be an effective learning medium for advanced undergraduate students.

We were interested in studying the possible benefits of the fair for undergraduates in an introductory psychology course. Such benefits might include allowing the student to explore in depth a topic of interest; promoting cooperation and discourse among students, as well as between students and instructors; motivating students to exert more effort in their course work; and allowing for the practical and theoretical exploration of a topic (Fish, 1988). We compared the retrospective impressions of introductory psychology courses for students who did and students who did not experience a fair component.

Description of Science Fair Component

During the first week of classes, students were informed that they would be required to do a major project suitable for presentation at a science fair to be held near the end of the second semester. Their science fair contributions would be worth 30% of their final grade and be based on the quality of individual projects and on contributions to various science fair student committees. The remainder of their course grade would be based on test and final exam performance. From one to three classes (each with approximately 60 students) have participated in the event in any given year.

Individual Projects

To encourage creative expression, we gave students little direction regarding their projects. All topics and formats were welcomed as long as the topic was relevant to psychology and the format involved the active participation of science fair visitors.

After all topics had been approved (by the 6th week of the first semester), classes participating in the science fair attended an information meeting that included a narrated slide presentation focusing on previous science fairs. The meeting was designed to stimulate enthusiasm for the event, give students a clear understanding of the type of space that would be available for individual projects, and provide specific examples of projects that have received both high and low grades.

Committees

Students volunteered to serve on one or more committees. Committee activities included designing a program for visitors, promoting the event, fund-raising, and coordinating procedures for setting up and taking down projects.

Class Presentation

Approximately 2 weeks before the science fair, students presented their projects to classmates. This format allowed students to practice their oral presentations and receive suggestions for improving them. They also had a chance to learn about the work of their peers.

The Science Fair

More than 1,000 people have attended the science fair each year. Visitors have included university and high school students, community groups, and the general public. Each student describes his or her project to approximately 100 visitors.

Grading Procedures

A few days after the science fair, students met with instructors to discuss the strengths and weaknesses of their individual efforts and to negotiate a grade.

Examples of Projects

Projects have covered many facets of psychology. One student with a spinal cord injury gave fair visitors an opportunity to negotiate access to campus buildings in a wheelchair. Another student demonstrated a biofeedback machine. Others have built their own tachistoscopes, mazes, and perceptual illusions. Still others chose to share the experience of staying at a shelter for the homeless.

Evaluation Study

Participants

Participants were 3rd- and 4th-year students in upper level psychology classes. Thirty had conducted a science fair project in the previous 3 years, and 80 had experienced other introductory formats.

Materials

Students anonymously reported their retrospective impressions of their introductory psychology course by responding to 14 questionnaire items using a 5-point Likert scale ranging from *not at all (1)* to *to a great degree (5)*. They also answered four questions about their pursuit of a major.

Results

Table 1 indicates the mean student ratings for each questionnaire item and the *t* values comparing the science fair students to the students with other course formats. In addition to these findings, 65% of the science fair participants (vs. 41% of other format students) were also more likely to have taken other courses from their introductory psychology instructor, χ^2 (1, N = 30) = 5.56, p < .05. However, science fair and other format students did not differ in their (a) grade point average (GPA) in psychology, (b) desire to major or to achieve honors in psychology, and (c) desire to pursue a graduate degree or career in psychology.

Discussion

Results indicated that ratings of introductory courses with a science fair component compared favorably with ratings for courses with other formats. Although students missed some regular classes to plan

Table 1. Mean Student Evaluation Ratings for Science Fair and Other Formats

Item	Science Fair	Other Formats	t
Opportunity to explore interests	3.62	3.14	2.02*ᵃ
Prepared for other courses	4.03	3.49	2.23*ᵇ
Understood basic principles	4.00	3.57	1.80*ᵇ
Principles applied to everyday life	3.97	3.59	1.87*ᵇ
Course effort	4.20	3.72	2.12*ᵇ
Learned from text	4.40	3.94	1.83*ᵃ
Learned from instructor	3.97	3.30	2.05*ᵃ
Improved oral skills	2.77	2.64	n.s.ᵇ
Improved written skills	2.57	2.43	n.s.ᵇ
Discussed with those not enrolled	3.14	2.99	n.s.ᵃ
Understood research	3.41	3.46	n.s.ᵃ
Enjoyed class	4.13	3.87	n.s.ᵇ
Learned from classmates	2.35	2.48	n.s.ᵃ
Learned from research	3.17	2.74	n.s.ᵇ

ᵃ107 *df*. ᵇ108 *df*.
*p < .05.

for a science fair, this lost time did not appear to detract from ratings of their learning experience. Science fair participants actually reported a better understanding of psychological principles and their application, as well as better preparation for subsequent psychology courses.

Results also indicated that students gave comparable ratings for improving oral and written skills and providing discussion opportunities. Furthermore, no differences were detected in student ratings of how much they learned from their classmates or from personal research. It is important to note that science fair ratings were compared with combined ratings of collaborative research (Reither & Vipond, 1989) and self-paced (Bourque & Hughes, 1991) courses specifically designed to encourage small-group research and discussion and to provide opportunities for improvement of oral and written skills. Thus, the science fair appears to be a valuable alternative for instructors.

Science fair participants reported exerting more effort and learning more from their textbook and instructor than did students experiencing other formats. They were also more likely to take additional courses from their introductory psychology instructors. Because up to three different instructors have coordinated the science fair in any given year, these results are not likely due to particular instructor characteristics. It appears, therefore, that positive regard for the unique qualities of the science fair generalizes to the instructors involved.

It is important to remember that the results represent differences in student beliefs about the quality of their learning experience and do not necessarily translate into demonstrable learning benefits. Moreover, the sample included no introductory students who did not take more psychology courses. Although science fair courses received higher ratings on a number of indices, science fair participants did not differ from other format students in GPA for subsequent psychology courses or in their desire to pursue further studies. Despite these caveats, results indicate that the science fair is a useful pedagogical tool that can be successfully adapted for introductory courses with a lecture format. It provides a unique and valuable learning experience for students and instructors.

References

Benjamin, L. T., Jr., Fawl, C. L., & Klien, J. (1977). The fair: Experimental psychology for high school students. *American Psychologist, 32,* 1097-1098.

Bourque, W. L., & Hughes, G. R. (1991, June) . *The Keller plan still works.* Paper presented at the Annual Conference of the Society for Teaching and Learning in Higher Education, Halifax, Nova Scotia.

Chute, D. L., & Bank, B. (1983). Undergraduate seminars: The poster session solution. *Teaching of Psychology, 10,* 99-100.

Fish, T. A. (1988, June). *Begged, borrowed, and stolen: Nontraditional approaches to teaching.* Paper presented at the Enhancement of University Teaching Conference, Sackville, New Brunswick.

Reither, J. A., & Vipond, D. (1989). Writing as collaboration. *College English, 51,* 855-867.

Note

We gratefully acknowledge the editorial assistance of Daizal Samad and Ruth L. Ault.

Inexpensive Animal Learning Exercises for Huge Introductory Laboratory Classes

Albert N. Katz
University of Western Ontario

In the psychology department at the University of Western Ontario, the introductory course consists of 12 laboratory exercises in addition to the traditional lecture experience. In order to accommodate the 2300 or so students who annually take the course, 76 laboratory sections are scheduled, each meeting every other week for two hours. The laboratories cover a wide range of experimental topics, such as physiological (brain asymmetry), perception (psychophysical techniques), memory (effect of filled delay on the serial position effect), behaviour modification (building a hierarchy for use in systematic desensitization) and group processes (the risky shift phenomenon). The sheer number of people taking the laboratories has forced us to depend to a large extent on paper-and-pencil tasks. Such an option was not deemed advisable for the teaching of basic learning principles inasmuch as such tasks are not representative of the techniques used in learning research and would not allow the student to observe or interact with animals.

The option of using animals in traditional classical or instrumental learning tasks is, however, prohibitively expensive. Consider the cost of employing rats in the cheapest of learning chambers for the 2300 students we must serve. We estimated a minimum of $10,000 initial investment and $3000 per year operating expenses. We have overcome the problems of expense, space and maintenance by employing the planaria *Dugesia Dorotocephala* as our experimental subjects, and by building a cheap, yet effective, learning chamber. The net economic saving has been considerable. The capital outlay in building the chambers was only $375.00, and the operating costs (for 1500 organisms) was under $200.00. Furthermore, employing planaria in our learning chambers has proved to be a useful introduction to selected topics in learning theory, experimental control, ethology, psychobiology and behavioral approaches to mental "illness."

Dugesia Dorotocephala and the Conditioning Apparatus. We have found that the planarian *D. Dorotocephala* can be successfully employed in both classical and instrumental conditioning paradigms. This animal is small (20 mm), easy to caretake, harmless and inexpensive (approximately 10 cents each).[1] In addition the animal is placed in a unique position in the evolutionary scale—it is the first bilaterally symmetrical animal, it is the first animal to have *true* synaptic nerve conduction and it also has a protobrain (a mass of ganglia located in the anterior region). Thus the demonstration that this animal is capable of true learning not only is fascinating in its own right but permits the instructor to introduce questions about the minimal physiological properties needed to produce learning, and how this learning might be represented in the nervous system.

The conditioning chambers which we constructed[2] for the learning laboratories serves for both classical and instrumental conditioning, is inexpensive, flexible and solid. The chamber consists of a clear plastic petri dish which rests within a hole cut in a wooden base. The petri dish can thus be easily removed for cleaning and for the transport of the planaria. When testing occurs the dish is filled 2/3 with water. The base supports a 25-watt light which is mounted 6 inches above the petri dish, as well as two electrodes which extend into the petri dish. Electricity is provided from a regular wall socket, which is connected to a power box (schematically depicted in Figure 1). When one switch is closed the light (conditioned stimulus) is turned on; the closure of the second switch powers the electrodes after having passed through a transformer and bridge. The resultant unconditioned stimulus is 40-volts of

direct current with an intensity of 1 to 2 milliamps. This intensity was found to be the minimum level that elicited a vigorous turning response (unconditioned response), and is of a much lower level than typically employed in such experiments. The cost of the whole unit, including transformer, switches, bridge and plugs was about $15.00.

This apparatus is used for both classical and instrumental conditioning exercises. The classical

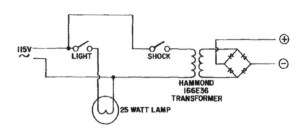

Figure 1. Circuitry of Conditioning Apparatus.

conditioning followed closely from the original Thompson and McConnell (1955) experiment, and consists of pairing the onset of light with electric shock until light onset alone can produce the turning response. The instrumental conditioning exercise employed a punishment training procedure and, although not based on a specific experiment, was suggested by the work of Best and Rubinstein (1962), Corning (1964) and Crawford (1968). The following procedure was used (see Katz, 1976, pp.39-48). A cardboard was placed underneath the petri dish; half the cardboard was painted black while the other half was white. Directly in the middle of the cardboard a circle was drawn to represent a start box. The planaria was placed in the petri dish so that it was located in the start box and the number of times it moved into the black (and white) side was recorded for 10 two-minute periods. After each period the animal was replaced in the start box. Following these 10 baseline periods, the same procedure was followed excepting now a shock was delivered every time the animal entered the side which, according to baseline, it preferred. The task was to see if the animal learned to avoid the punished side. Avoidance invariably occurred within 30 minutes.

Whereas the laboratories "worked," from a purely technical perspective, we were worried that the students might not find them enjoyable, relative to our other laboratory exercises. These worries were elicited by the dislike some students appeared to take to the planaria (which are, after all, neither furry nor huggable) and to the hesitations expressed about shocking the animals. Finally, we were worried that the relatively more detailed coverage given learning in the textbook may have made the conditioning labs more redundant and less informative than the other labs. Evaluative data on these concerns were obtained from a questionnaire made available to students at end of term. The survey addressed questions about the course in general, the text, performance of lab assistants, etc. There was a voluntary supplementary section in which the students were asked to rank-order the 12 laboratory exercises in terms of how enjoyable they were, and in terms of how much they felt they learned from each. Not unexpectedly, the rankings differed considerably. For example the lab on methodology and statistics was overwhelmingly ranked the least enjoyable but was considered to be among the most informative; the lab on systematic desensitization was generally enjoyed but was felt to have taught little. The two learning labs were above the median on both rankings (N = 227 voluntary returns). The classical conditioning lab was ranked between fourth and fifth in both hierarchies (mean enjoyability = 4.6, mean learning = 4.9) while the instrumental conditioning lab was ranked slightly lower (mean = 4.9 and 5.4 respectively). On the basis of unsolicited written comments by some students on their questionnaire it appears that the major factors affecting the enjoyment ranking positively were use of animals and of the equipment, while the major negative contributors were use of worms, use of shock, and the repetitive nature of the procedure.

The factors which underlie the learning-value rankings also appear to be complex, with some students commenting that the exercise helped them better understand the concepts and procedures discussed in the text, but others thought the labs too redundant with the text material. Finally, in an attempt to get a rough index of the effectiveness of the conditioning labs, I examined test performance for questions pertaining to conditioning relative to other topics, for both of the sections which I taught (total N = 500). In both sections students' performance was about one SD above the mean for questions related to classical conditioning (z scores = +0.94, and +1.2) and just at the mean for those questions dealing with instrumental conditioning (z scores = + 0.16, and -0.04). In summary then, relative to their other labs, the exercises on conditioning were perceived as relatively enjoyable and informative and, as measured in a subsequent test, were as well or better learned than the other lab materials.

Some Limitations and Some Further Didactic Uses of the Planaria and Learning Chamber. It must be emphasized that use of the chamber, and of planaria, have definite financial gain for only certain learning conditions and that they should not be considered omnifarious tools. For example, the chamber does not allow manipulation of shock intensity nor have the capability to present a substantially different form of conditioned stimulus. Thus exercises dealing with discrimination learning or higher-order conditioning can not be performed on the equipment. Some of these limitations can doubtless be overcome with additional expenditures (for example, by setting the

dish on a bell and using vibration as a second conditioned stimulus), but the very nature of the apparatus and organism probably make other limitations insurmountable. The apparatus has no capability to provide a non-aversive stimulus and thus labs to demonstrate positive reinforcement and schedules of reinforcement appear to be eliminated. Moreover, the simple repertoire of the organism does not readily permit demonstration of common phenomena like shaping, and precludes more complex phenomena like chaining.

Despite these shortcomings, the apparatus and organism can still be used to demonstrate selected phenomena of general interest. Some of the more useful applications are listed below.

To demonstrate general principles of experimental control. It is often somewhat difficult to ascertain whether the planaria has contracted or not, i.e., whether it exhibited the conditioned response. Thus at least two independent observers are required to rate the animals performance. This procedure is an ideal lead-in to questions regarding the construction of rating scales, to reliability, and to doubleblind procedures.

The use of planaria also has special relevance to control questions pertinent to the study of learning inasmuch as the demonstration of classical conditioning in planaria (Thompson & McConnell, 1955) has been questioned on methodological grounds (James & Halas, 1964). The controversy permits the introduction of the problem of pseudoconditioning and of sensitization, and the need to control for procedure artifacts in order to demonstrate true learning.

To demonstrate general questions of psychology and ethology. Observation of the planaria swimming in the petri dishes can be used to demonstrate some ethological concepts such as phototropic and geotropic movements. Such observations were built into the instrumental learning laboratory in that data were collected concerning whether the dark or light side of the dish was preferred by the planaria. (Because planaria are negatively phototropic a dark side preference can be expected).

The demonstration of true learning in planaria is especially exciting since this learning occurs in such a simple organism. The question arises as to how learning is physiologically represented. The presence of true synaptic transmission in these animals permits an ideal introduction to theories of learning which depend on changes at the synapse (Hebb, 1972). Finally, the classical conditioning of planaria has been used as the first step in studying the biochemistry of memory (McConnell, 1962; McConnell, Jacobson, & Kimble, 1959). The laboratory demonstration can thus be extended in that direction, especially if the introductory text being used is biologically oriented (e.g., Krech, Crutchfield & Livson, 1974, pp. 416-442; McConnell, 1977, pp. 368-383).

To demonstrate the behavioral approach to maladaptive activities. When shocked repeatedly the animal becomes lethargic, an effect which Best (1 963) discussed in terms of an emotional, frustration response. The manifestation of this phenomenon has proven to be a useful introduction to learned helplessness, and hence to one learning explanation of depression. It also serves as a peg for questions related to consciousness, the need to postulate inner mental states, and to behaviourism.

References

Best, J B. Protopsychology. *Scientific American,* February 1963, *208,* 54-62.

Best J., & Rubinstein I. Maze learning and associated behavior in planaria. *Journal of Comparative and Physiological Psychology,* 1962, *55,* 560-566.

Corning, W. Evidence of right-left discrimination in planaria. *Journal of Psychology,* 1964, *58,* 131-139.

Crawford, F. T. Operant rate of planarians as a function of photic stimulation. *Psychonomic Science*, 1968, *11,* 257-258.

Hebb, D. O. *Textbook of psychology* (3rd ed.). Philadelphia: Saunders, 1972.

James, R., & Halas, E. No difference in extinction behavior in planaria following various types and amounts of training. *Psychological Record,* 1964, *14,* 1-11.

Katz, A. *N.* (Ed.). *A laboratory manual for an introduction to psychology* (Volume 1) London, Ontario: University of Western Ontario, 1976, pp. 39-48.

Krech, D., Crutchfield, R., & Livson, N. *Elements of psychology,* New York: Knopf, 1974.

McConnell, J. Memory transfer through cannibalism in planarians. *Journal of Neuropsychiatry,* 1962, *3,* supplement 1, S42-S-48.

McConnell, J. *Understanding human behavior.* New York: Holt, Rinehart and Winston, 1977

McConnell, J., Jacobson, A., & Kimble, D. The effects of regeneration upon retention of a conditioned response in the planarian. *Journal of Comparative and Physiological Psychology,* 1959, *52,* 1-5.

Thompson, R., & McConnell, J. Classical conditioning in the planarian, Dugesia dorotocephala. *Journal of Comparative and Physiological Psychology,* 1955, *48,* 65-68.

Notes

1. The planaria were obtained from Boreal Laboratories, 1820 Mattawa Avenue, Mississauga, Ontario, Canada. The care of the animals is best outlined in a special edition of the *Journal of Biological Psychology,* January 1967.

2. The person most responsible for translating my descriptions into a working model was D. Pulham. Thanks are also due J. Orphan and D. Garrod.

SECTION II:
STATISTICS

Starting the Semester

Kathleen Dillon described an exercise that she used in the first statistics class of the semester. Students wrote their anonymous responses to how they felt about taking statistics and about a formula for the *t*-test. Students learned that their concerns and worries were shared by most of their classmates. The article also provided suggestions for reducing students' statistics anxiety.

Marcus Hastings described several strategies he used to introduce his statistics course. He emphasized the use of statistics as a tool, instructing students to learn the language of statistics (definition of terms), directing students to generate data and visualize results, encouraging daily study, and answering questions when they arose.

Keith Jacobs used a variety of techniques for reducing his students' statistics anxiety. One of the most effective techniques used the data acquired from a questionnaire that he developed. After displaying data on the chalkboard, he illustrated statistical concepts (e.g., scales of measurement). Careful selection of items for the questionnaire can provide teachers and students with a data pool to use throughout the semester.

Making Statistics Relevant

Some instructors combine methods for reducing statistics anxiety with ways to "bring the statistics course to life. " Bernard Beins developed an approach to overcome students' anxiety about or boredom with statistics. The author directed students to write and ask manufacturers for further information supporting researched-based advertising claims. The article detailed the results of students' inquiries and the pedagogical advantages of the approach.

Mark Shatz followed a similar thread by using a simulated labor-management dispute to teach students some fundamental concepts of descriptive statistics, including measures of central tendency and characteristics of distributions. Students used comparable data sets to prepare a statistical presentation that supported their position in the dispute. From the principles underlying this technique, readers can develop their own simulations and add relevance to teaching statistics.

Ken Weaver used familiar experiences and situations (e.g., falling leaves and common exclamations) to help students better understand statistical concepts such as variability and confidence intervals. A particularly interesting approach to testing the null hypothesis involved students' knowledge of persons' characteristics who fall into the categories "normal," "rare," or "abnormal." The author reported that students were amazed at the extent to which their daily experiences could be related to the more technical aspects of statistical thinking.

This article from Michael Dillbeck examined the role of situation variables in teaching statistics. The article described a classroom activity designed to lead students to discover statistical principles. The author viewed the discovery process as instrumental for understanding and retention.

Generating Data

Generating data sets for students to use throughout the statistics course can be a challenge. Leslie Cake and Roy Hostetter reported on the use of DATAGEN for generating unique and independent or correlated data samples. Instructors can specify the population parameters for the samples. The program also provides summary statistics for each sample and results from statistical analyses.

Paul Hettich developed a technique using student-generated data and student-centered examples. On the first day of class, he instructed students to provide information about themselves and to complete two paper and pencil inventories. Students used the resulting data to illustrate levels of measurement, frequency distributions, shapes of distributions, percentile ranks, standard scores, central tendency and dispersion, correlation, sampling techniques, sampling distributions, and the central limit theorem.

W. P. McGowan and Boyd Spencer developed a table of numerical values having integer means and standard deviations for sample sizes of five, six, and seven. The authors produced the table to provide students with sets of data for computing statistics easily and quickly. The authors pointed out how instructions can convert the values in the table into many other sets of data.

Frank Dudek expanded on the approach in the preceding article by providing a systematic technique for generating data sets for larger samples. The article outlined a simple but versatile procedure to construct data sets for homework or exam problems.

Teaching Specific Concepts

John Duke developed tables to help students become aware of size differences in correlations and of the frequency of exceptions to relationships implied by various correlation coefficients. The author included technical assumptions for using the tables.

Schuyler Huck and his colleagues devised a method using standard decks of playing cards to demonstrate how variability relates to the magnitude of the Pearson r statistic. Students used the cards to draw samples that represented IQ scores. After sampling, students performed several analyses that demonstrated the effects of restriction of range and reduction of measurement error on the Pearson r. Students learned that changes in variability have differential effects on the correlation coefficient. Significantly, the authors verified the reliability of the demonstration by running Monte Carlo simulations on the sample data generated in class.

The article by David Johnson described a simple but effective demonstration for illustrating the central limit theorem. The author generated three or four equal-sized random samples, consisting of the numbers 1, 2, and 3, for each student in his statistics class. After the students calculated the sum of each random sample, the teacher constructed a distribution of the results on an overhead projector. He then discussed the finer points of the central limit theorem and probability.

Jerzy Karylowski reported a demonstration illustrating regression toward the mean using a psychological context. The demonstration can be used in small and large groups, and it does not require that students have any previous statistical background.

Joel Levin developed two modifications for overcoming some limitations of an earlier demonstration of regression toward the mean. The author reported that students' reactions were enthusiastic, and he described additional distinctive characteristics of his demonstration.

A "bag of tricks" was proposed by Dominic Zerbolio to enhance students' understanding of sampling distributions. Students imagined a bag of marbles that served as a population of raw scores. The instructor used this imaginary bag of marbles to draw imaginary samples. By using this imaginary sampling technique, the instructor demonstrated a variety of sampling phenomena, including the distribution of sample means and the distribution of differences between sample means. As the author pointed out, the only requirements for this demonstration are a good imagination and a flair for the dramatic.

Michael Moore developed a technique to demonstrate the concepts of true score, true variance, and standard error of the mean and to prepare students for the concept of reliability. The task required students to measure and report the lengths of 50 lines. The resulting data also permitted calculation of parallel-forms reliability coefficients. Students responded favorably to the demonstration.

Analysis of variance frequently poses problems for introductory statistics students who have difficulty understanding how covariation between within- and between-groups variance relates to the F statistic. David Johnson used a technique that held within-groups variance constant while varying between-groups variance in a succession of simple data sets. Within-groups variance was then introduced in a similar fashion. Even students who take a concrete perspective toward statistics seemed to benefit from this technique.

The article by Richard Williams pointed out that many textbooks for graduate students use instructional procedures that may encourage rote memorization instead of intuitive understanding. The author's alternative approach consisted of an algorithm for computing regression weights in a multiple regression scheme. The author also described the instructional steps that students followed after exposure to this algorithm.

Concepts such as measurement error and reliability were made more concrete by Jane Buck in a simple, in-class activity. Students responded randomly to multiple-choice items on machine scored answer sheets. These "tests" were then "scored" according to a "key." Because the students had no knowledge of the correct scores, their true score was zero; any score above zero was attributable to chance. The activity related the concepts of chance scores and reliability to the standard error of measurement.

Gordon Allen described a technique that he used to help students understand the χ^2 statistic by pointing out its similarities to Weber's Law. Allen proposed that just as the value of χ^2 is a function of the difference between the observed and expected frequencies relative to the expected frequency, Weber's Law demonstrates that judgments of differences between stimuli are relative to the magnitude of the standard stimulus.

Combining Statistics and Research Methods

Joseph Rossi gave his graduate and undergraduate students a valuable lesson in data analysis and presentation by asking them to recompute the statistical tests from summary data in published journal articles. The alarmingly large number of mistakes emphasized to the students the need for more careful data analysis and presentation, as well as a healthy skepticism when reading the literature.

Kathleen Dillon reported her surprise that only a few students recognized the lack of psychological significance associated with a satirical article from *Worm Runners Digest*. The author's comments on educating students about the difference between statistical and psychological significance is a worthwhile reminder for those who teach statistics.

1. STARTING THE SEMESTER

Statisticophobia

Kathleen M. Dillon
Western New England College

The first year I taught Statistics, I asked the class if anyone was *anxious* about taking this course in Statistics and everyone said "no." I was surprised to hear that answer, but felt I could proceed "full speed ahead." I soon realized we were using two different definitions of the word *anxious.* I was using the psychological definition, meaning "having a diffuse fear or feeling nervous" about something. The class was using the popular definition of *anxious,* meaning "eager." What they were saying to me was that they were not eager to take this course. Why? Because they were afraid of taking a math course.

I now begin my first statistics lecture by asking students to complete, anonymously and honestly, the following two sentences on a piece of paper:

When I think of taking this course in Statistics, I feel _____.

When I look at this equation:
(Display here the
formula for *t*.)

I feel _____.

About 2% of the time I get responses like: 'I feel confident and the equation seems relatively surmountable given more information." Usually these few students are Engineering majors who have already taken Engineering Statistics and have wandered into my class by mistake or thinking they have found an easy "A" elective.

More typically, I get the following responses which I read aloud to the class: I feel "unsure," "nauseous," "panicky," "uneasy," "sick," "worried," "like running over to the registrar's office to change my major," "frustrated," "angry that I have to take a math course," "doomed," "overwhelmed," "lost," "terrible," "confused," and so forth.

By doing this exercise, I confirm for myself what has become very obvious, but I also let students know that I hear them expressing their fears, and the students let each other know that their feelings are shared. Then I give a lecture on math anxiety—where it comes from and what can be done to cope with it. (I recommend Tobias, S. *Overcoming math anxiety.* New York: Norton, 1978, for some ideas for this lecture.)

At the end of the semester I repeat the exercise, modifying the tense of the first sentence. Usually the feelings are now those of confidence and self-assuredness. Students recognize the formula and talk about it in an informed manner. Repeating this exercise appears to give them an awareness of mastery and progress; they have mastered their fears and have progressed to a point where they can intelligently discuss something that was once quite foreign and formidable to them.

Statistics: Challenge for Students and the Professor

Marcus W. Hastings
Keene State College

Many psychology majors approach courses in statistics beset by math anxiety and unrealistic expectations about the nature of the course. Thus, statistics (often referred to as sadistics) not only represents a challenge to the student, but also to the professor. This challenge must be met successfully because of the importance of statistics in a psychology curriculum (Lux & Daniel, 1978; Bartz, 1981). If the professor can reduce math anxiety and provide a realistic framework to aid the student's approach to the course, most students discover that the course is not nearly as difficult as anticipated and they perform well. In the following paragraphs, I will outline some of the procedures that I have found successful in meeting the challenge of teaching statistics.

Statistics should be introduced to students as a means to an end, a tool to be used to answer questions rather than as a math course. I often tell students that if they can balance their checkbooks, solve equations like $8 = 32/x$, and understand notations like $(X)^2$ and (X^2), they have the basic skills necessary to do well in statistics. With the rapid growth in the use of calculators and computers, a conceptual understanding is a much more important goal to achieve than computational skills. If students acquire a sound conceptual understanding of statistical theory and procedures, then competence in computational skills is easy to achieve. However, good computational skills are of little value if the student does not have the conceptual basis to understand the procedures and conclusions.

To help students acquire a sound conceptual understanding, I instruct them to approach the course like a language course rather than a math course. It is important for students to be able to define terms like the mean, variance, and to be able to explain verbally concepts like sampling, random sampling distribution of the mean, and statistical significance. Not only is this verbal expression critical for a sound understanding of statistics, but many students are less intimidated by verbalizing than computing. By the time most students have reached their sophomore or junior year, they have developed good verbal memory skills and need to be encouraged to use them to acquire the basic vocabulary. Many students do not like to "memorize" terms and feel that it is not a sound

educational procedure, but the simple fact remains that it is hard to understand what a random sampling distribution of the mean is if you cannot define the concept. My experience teaching statistics has convinced me that students who say "I understand the material, but I cannot put it into words to explain it to you," are far less likely to understand the material than students who can verbalize. I actually encourage students to talk out loud to themselves to learn the terminology, as well as emphasizing verbalizing concepts in class lectures.

In addition to verbalizing concepts, I have students generate data and visualize the procedures and end results. For example, concepts like the random sampling distribution of means, which is troublesome for many students, can be made "real" for them by having them take a number of random samples ($n = 5$) from a large population of scores, compute the mean for each sample, and then plot in a frequency distribution the means that they derived. This activity does not consume a great deal of time and the process of doing the exercise makes it much easier for students to visualize a sampling distribution of means and to use the concept meaningfully in the context of future statistical thinking. Thus, verbalizing and visualizing are important steps in acquiring a good conceptual understanding of statistics. Too many textbook writers have counted on computation exercises to teach students statistics, but this approach is not always effective. Computation exercises can be of value to students only if they already possess some conceptual understanding of the statistical concepts involved.

Two additional strategies that I encourage students to employ are to study statistics everyday, and to ask questions when they arise, if possible. Working on statistics everyday helps to insure that they never get behind schedule (a critical error in a cumulative course like statistics). This approach is consistent with the massive literature on the nature of learning and memory, or as I often tell my students, "a little rain everyday seeps slowly into the ground and yields a good crop, so a little statistics everyday will seep into your cortex and yield a good conceptual understanding of statistics as well as an A in the course!". Lastly, I encourage students never to let a question go unasked or to say to themselves "I'll figure it out later." Both of these avoidance strategies can be very detrimental to effective learning, and often puts the student behind schedule, which eventually results in cramming. I often warn students that they may have crammed successfully in other courses, but it is very difficult to do so successfully in statistics. Knowing that many students feel reluctant to ask questions unless they sound sophisticated, I encourage students to simply say "I do not understand," "Please, repeat what you said" or "Clarify and give an example." When I first started teaching statistics, I soon discovered that some well structured and delivered lectures were very ineffective because I failed to realize that students were confused and they did not tell me. Now, I take nothing for granted and work hard from the first day of class to build rapport with the students so they will ask questions indicating where they are having problems. This also begins to reduce their anxieties about the course and their performance. Students quickly learn and feel comfortable with my basic philosophy concerning the course, "What you don't know, I can teach you; what you don't ask about, I can't teach you."

In summary, the success that I have achieved in meeting the challenge is accounted for by (a) presenting statistics as learning a new language to emphasize the conceptual as opposed to the computational understanding, (b) reducing math anxiety and presenting realistic expectations for the course, (c) developing rapport with the students to facilitate a good learning environment, and (d) helping students develop good study skills. I have derived a tremendous amount of satisfaction from teaching statistics (my colleagues like it, too). Students enter the course with a variety of anxieties, unrealistic expectations, and very little knowledge of statistics. After 15 weeks of hard work on their part and mine, they leave the course knowing a great deal more about statistics, having improved their study skills and knowing themselves a little better because they, too, have met the challenge.

References

Bartz, A E. The statistics course as a departmental offering and major requirement. *Teaching of Psychology.* 1981, *8*, 106.

Lux, D. F. & Daniel, R. S. Which courses are most frequently listed by psychology departments? *Teaching of Psychology,* 1978, *5*, 13-16.

Instructional Techniques in the Introductory Statistics Course: The First Class Meeting

Keith W. Jacobs
Loyola University

Experience from several semesters of introductory statistics courses suggests that students usually approach the course with a mixed set of fears. During the past semester students were asked during the first class meeting to introduce themselves and mention "either the best or worst thing that could happen during the semester." This was intended to help students become acquainted with each other and begin to neutralize some of the students apprehension about the course. Although possibly successful in that respect it also served to remind the instructor about the high anxiety conditions under which students approach the class.

In an attempt to deal with that anxiety, "statistics," were defined by the course instructor as "tools used to make sense out of research data." To introduce this concept, the instructor showed a series of common tools to the class (pliers, scissors, stethoscope, reflex hammer, etc.), students were asked to name each, the names were written on the board, and the class was asked to decide what characteristic these all had in common. After the set of objects was identified as "tools," several simple statistics were added to the list on the board (e.g.,the formula for the mean), with the assertion that these are also tools. The discussion proceeded to the point that the correct use of tools requires practice and feedback regarding success. Members of the class agreed that they had already learned to use some of the tools on the list; the argument was advanced that they could also learn to use other tools, including statistics.

The specific tools displayed can easily be adapted by the instructor to the students in the course: for example, including a stethoscope and blood pressure cuff when Nursing majors are in the course. This seems to be a graphic way for the instructor to make a point, as well as an opportunity to create a student expectation of success.

The technique during the first class meeting which seems to have been most useful is to distribute a brief questionnaire and show how statistics are used to make sense out of the data obtained. This approach is very similar to, but somewhat shorter than, an approach suggested by Hettich (1974), in which students complete a questionnaire and several short psychometric instruments.

The present form of the shorter instrument is a one page form asking students to: indicate their sex, how many brothers they have, how many sisters they have, how many children they would like to have, to pick a number from zero to ten, and then to enter a zero if it was an even number and a one if it was an odd number. A question asking them to indicate their birth order has also been used some semesters. These unsigned questionnaires are then collected by the instructor and used for class discussion.

The data are immediately displayed on the blackboard as a "data matrix" and one variable is selected to be converted to a "frequency distribution." This distribution is then used to show measures of central value and variability, with the students told that they will soon learn to calculate these statistics themselves. The questionnaire items can be discussed in terms of "scales of measurement" and the definition of "measurement" can easily be introduced at this point. Additional research hypotheses can also be posed from these data (e.g., is there a relationship between size of the students' families and the size of the families they want to have?); the role of statistics can be clearly shown in terms of questions which they can use statistics to answer. This data set and the original questions are later reproduced for the students and used throughout the course to provide a continuity across various statistical techniques (descriptive, correlational, t-test, and nonparametric statistics). In this way students are given an overview of the course while working with a personally meaningful data set which can be used throughout the semester to supplement problems available in the text.

The first class meeting is assumed to set the mood for the remainder of the semester; careful attention needs to be paid at this time to reduction of student anxiety, motivation for future performance, and an introduction of the course. These techniques seem to contribute to those goals and will probably remain in some form in future courses, where more formal evaluation of them is likely to become a part of the second class meeting.

Reference

Hettich, P. The student as data generator. *Teaching* of *Psychology,* 1974, *1*, 35-36.

2. MAKING STATISTICS RELEVANT

Teaching the Relevance of Statistics Through Consumer-Oriented Research

Bernard Beins
Thomas More College

Students in a small experimental design class obtained information about statistical and research applications concerning a variety of products advertised by different companies. The resulting data were perceived to have several advantages for the students: (a) it made collecting and interpreting data more interesting and less mysterious, (b) it helped them to understand how research design and statistics are used in real-life situations, and (c) it helped them to make more discerning judgments about advertisers' claims for their products.

Everybody who teaches statistics and experimental psychology courses faces students who are either overcome with anxiety ("I've never been good in math") or terminally bored with the apparent lack of relevance of the course to their lives. Many students are bound to fall into one or both of these categories, given the large numbers of undergraduate psychology departments that require or recommend a course in statistics. From 147 college and university catalogs sampled by Bartz (1981), all but 12 either required or recommended a statistics course. Further, informing students that even graduate programs in clinical psychology require statistics and experimental courses is not highly motivating. The continuing battle to make the courses more palatable to undergraduates is reflected in the efforts by psychologists to alter and update their statistics/experimental courses. To this end, *Teaching of Psychology* has published regular articles dealing with these areas (e.g., Bartz, 1981; Dillbeck, 1983; Hastings, 1982).

One of the most obvious ways to overcome the anxiety associated with statistics is to focus students' attention on various kinds of information they already have. Jacobs (1980) suggests that statistics is simply another kind of tool used for achieving some goal, no different in principle from a hammer or screwdriver; students are shown these mundane implements and consequently, a new set of tools, namely simple statistical formulas, are derived. According to Jacobs, "Members of the class agreed that they had already learned to use some of the tools on the list; the argument was advanced that they could also learn to use other tools, including statistics" (p. 241). In a slightly different procedure, Hastings (1983) suggests to his students that they approach statistics as they would any other language they are likely to encounter. Allen (1981) tries to relate the statistics to information that students already know from other classes and, presumably, with which they are already familiar.

In a small experimental design course (6 students), I attempted to decrease anxiety and bring relevance to the classroom by having the students go out and find instances of statistical and research applications. I directed them to the myriad of claims proffered on television and in magazines. Their task was to isolate specific instances in which manufacturers made claims based on research and then to write the companies for further information.

The point I was trying to make was that many people actually use statistics in the real world. I also wanted the students to encounter statistics and research formats that were of interest to them and that they would be able to evaluate on their own. The students were free to communicate with any company on any kind of product, as long as some research claims were made. They reported to the class as they received each response.

Students contacted a wide variety of companies, including the makers of soft drinks, cereal, infants' vitamins, and automobiles. It was apparent that students' interests determined, in part, what information they requested. For instance, the biology students tended to request information on medical products (e.g., Anacin, Childrens' Tylenol, sugarless gum, salt content of margarine); one varsity athlete requested information on bicycle helmets; one student interested in auto mechanics requested data on mufflers, another on auto batteries. Thus, it seems that the students took their assignments seriously enough to seek information in areas in which they were knowledgeable and interested.

The students' responses to the replies fell into three overall categories: increased skepticism; increased respect for marketing research; and a renewed awareness that, in commercials, things are not always what they seem.

The skepticism arose because, in some cases, the students (as consumers) were treated with suspicion in phone conversations and were queried by company personnel as to what consumer group or company they represented. In other instances, the students were promised information that they had not received by the end of the term (about 10 weeks after their initial contact with the company).

On the other hand, most students came to the realization that some marketing research is extensively planned and well conducted. The most compelling example involved a response to an inquiry about bicycle helmet safety: The manufacturer sent a complete technical report run by an independent cyclists' group in Washington, DC. When students discussed the report, they could find no flaws in design or interpretation. In fact, whenever companies had sent complete information, students tended to be more positively impressed.

The third type of response was that it is easy to be misled by advertising claims because the advertisers are very good at setting the stage for specious inferences by consumers. One example was given in a letter from Union Carbide Corporation, the manufacturer of Energizer batteries. The student had interpreted the claim that "Of all leading brands, nothing outlasts the Energizer from Eveready" as a statement that the battery "outlasts them all." The company noted that "you have read something into these ads which is not there. We have never used the phrase 'outlasts them all,' or any other words to that effect." This example was all the more compelling because the student had listened to the commercial and then written down the claim immediately, and had still drawn an erroneous inference.

Students in the class uniformly approved of the assignment when questioned at the end of the term. I asked them to comment on "whether future classes should be asked to do this project or whether it was more trouble than it was worth." I also asked them what they learned, if anything, from this assignment.

According to a questionnaire, everyone claimed to derive some benefit from the exercise. Although I cannot eliminate the possibility of demand characteristics, the responses appeared candid, as with one student who commented that, at first, the assignment "may sound stupid, but students will find it worthwhile when they get the replies."

Another benefit from the assignment was that the students learned that research is not an "ivory-tower" exercise. One student commented on the large number of marketing companies and suggested that it was "amazing to discover that many of the concepts and tests discussed in class are used in the real world."

This project seemed to have its intended effect in relaxing the students in their approach to statistics and research design. The assignment also seemed to have taken some of the mystery away from the process of collecting and interpreting data. Finally, our real-life exercise gave the students some indication of the relevance of statistics and research.

References

Allen, G. A. (1981). The χ^2 statistic and Weber's law. *Teaching of Psychology, 8,* 179-180.

Bartz, A. E. (1981). The statistics course as a departmental offering and major requirement. *Teaching of Psychology, 8,* 106.

Dillbeck, M. C. (1983). Teaching statistics in terms of the knower. *Teaching of Psychology, 10,* 18-20.

Hastings, M. W. (1982). Statistics: Challenge for students and the professor. *Teaching of Psychology, 9,* 221-222.

Jacobs, K. W. (1980). Instructional techniques in the introductory statistics course: The first class meeting. *Teaching of Psychology, 7,* 241-242.

The Greyhound Strike: Using a Labor Dispute to Teach Descriptive Statistics

Mark A. Shatz
Ohio University—Zanesville

A simulation exercise of a labor-management dispute is used to teach students some of the basics of descriptive statistics, such as measures of central tendency and the nature of distributions. Using comparable data sets generated by the instructor, students work in small groups to develop a statistical presentation that supports their particular position in the dispute.

Students enrolled in statistics classes frequently have difficulty understanding the relevance of statistics for everyday events. The strike by the Greyhound bus drivers last year provided me with the opportunity to develop a classroom activity that illustrated the various ways data can be manipulated with descriptive statistics.

To begin the activity, the class was divided into two groups. The first group of students represented the position of labor (i.e., against a salary cut) and the second group represented the position of management (i.e., for a salary cut). To facilitate the computational aspects of the activity, the students were directed to work in groups of four.

The students were presented with factitious data based on the circumstances of the Greyhound strike. The first part of the data included the individual salaries of the striking employees (n = 50) and the average fringe benefits of the employees. Several of the salaries were noted as the salaries of trainee drivers. The second group of data focused on the salaries earned by drivers at three rival companies. For each company, the following information was presented: the number of employees, the average employee benefits, and descriptive measures of the drivers' salaries (mean, median, mode, and standard deviation). The salary data for the three companies were designed to illustrate normal and skewed distributions.

After the students were presented the data, they were instructed to focus on the salary data of the striking employees and then to consider comparisons with the other companies. The stated goal was for the students to manipulate the data in order to provide the best defense for their respective positions. When the students completed their computations, the two groups debated the salary issue and I served as the arbitrator. The activity was evaluated by the students at the completion of the arbitration period.

The activity had several specific objectives. The first objective was to illustrate how the definition of a construct (i.e., salary) can affect its measurement. This was accomplished by requiring the students to specify the data (e.g., trainees' salaries, fringe benefits) that were used in the computation of salary statistics. The second objective was to demonstrate how the size of a class interval can affect the appearance of a frequency distribution. To achieve this objective, students were required to experiment with class intervals of different sizes until they developed a frequency distribution table that best illustrated their position. The third objective was to provide practice in generating visual representations of data. The students had to identify the visual medium (e.g., bar graph, frequency polygon) that best supported their argument. The fourth objective was to demonstrate the effects of skewed data on the measures of central tendency. The students were required to select the measures of central tendency of each company that were most generous to their position (and for instructional purposes, to identify the most appropriate measures).

The activity took approximately 1 hour to complete. During that time, the students had an opportunity to compute and interpret most of the descriptive statistics that are typically taught in the first unit of a statistics course. Also, students were able to use the various techniques that are used to manipulate data.

Several major themes were identified in the students' written evaluations of the activity. First, the students said that the activity helped them to understand the role of descriptive statistics. Second, the students indicated that they had gained an appreciation of how descriptive statistics can be used to alter the appearance of a data set. And finally, the most frequently mentioned benefit was that the debate format of the activity provided an opportunity for the students to use their statistical skills by defending an argument with statistics. As one student commented about the activity, "It helped by allowing us to talk about the stuff that we just learned and not just compute statistics."

Although this activity was illustrated with a nonpsychological topic, the debate format of the activity could be adapted for research-oriented problems. For example, an instructor could generate data for a study that investigated the efficacy of a new treatment program. The types of data needed would be similar to the data used in the above activity; that is, individual scores for the subjects in the new treatment program and descriptive measures of several existing programs. The students would be directed to defend the relative merits of the new procedure or the existing programs. By using a research example, the activity would provide an excellent review of descriptive statistics and would be an ideal introduction to inferential statistics.

The main benefit of this activity was that the debate format provided students with an opportunity to use the statistical skills that they had acquired. The positive student response has encouraged me to make greater use of issues that students are aware of, and to design activities that allow students to verbalize the course material. Although this type of activity requires an instructor to spend time generating data, the resulting instructional benefits are well worth effort.

Elaborating Selected Statistical Concepts With Common Experience

Kenneth A. Weaver
Emporia State University

Most statistics teachers strive to make the course material meaningful. This article presents specific examples for elaborating the statistical concepts of variability, null hypothesis testing and confidence interval with common experience.

Introductory statistics textbooks usually describe statistics as a "new way of thinking about and learning about the world" (Glenberg, 1988, p. v). By including news items and cartoons; textbook authors use well-known information to illustrate new concepts. In this article, I show how exclamations, circus and cartoon characters, and falling leaves can be used to elaborate statistical concepts, such as variability, null hypothesis testing, and confidence interval.

Variability

After demonstrating how to compute the standard deviation, I present an exclamation and ask students to evaluate the statistical information it contains. For example, a visiting grandmother remarks, "My, how you've grown!" Understanding this exclamation requires comparing one's sense of a child's average growth with the amount of growth since grandmother's last visit. The greater the difference, the more unusual is the amount of growth, and the louder is the exclamation. Familiar exclamations include Jackie Gleason's refrain "How sweet it is!" and the line from the opening song of the play *Oklahoma* (Rodgers & Hammerstein, 1942), "Oh, what a beautiful morning!"

As a class exercise, students generate their own exclamations. After learning about z scores, students convert their exclamations to an approximate z score. Selected students present their z scores to class members, who evaluate the sign and size.

I also suggest that one's intuition about averageness and difference can be intentionally manipulated for a dramatic effect. Dr. Jekyll and Mr. Hyde and Popeye before and after eating spinach exemplify obvious and extreme variation. In contrast, more subtle is the variation of selected behaviors by the same character, such as the ferocity of King Kong except for its gentleness with Ann Redman.

Testing the Null Hypothesis

After lecturing about probability, the critical region, and the null hypothesis, I talk about circus or cartoon characters that have unusual characteristics corresponding to measures in the tails of the appropriate distribution. These unusual scores (and unusual characters) can help teach students about the statistical (and social) rejection associated with such deviations from the norm.

I rhetorically ask the class: What makes circus attractions like the bearded lady or a midget so popular? My answer is that these individuals are so unusual, relative to the rest of the population, that they belong in the extremes of the distribution for that attribute. I remind students that the extreme area of the distribution is labeled the critical or *alpha* region and contains cases so different that they are not accepted as part of the group.

Adjectives such as *rare, abnormal,* and *bizarre* describe cases in the critical area. Not being accepted as a member of a particular distribution becomes increasingly likely the more unusual the individual. For example, Pinnochio's nose length, Flash's speed, and a witch's beauty (or lack of it) produce measurements that fall in the critical area and are thus rejected as members of the "regular" group.

I use the single sample *t* test to connect the logic of rejecting extremes with making statistical decisions. If the sampling error converted to standard deviations falls in the t distribution's critical region, then the error is not accepted as belonging to the population of "normal"-sized errors, and the null hypothesis is rejected.

Students have previously been told that *alpha* specifies the degree to which chance can be an explanation for the results. They also have been warned that *alpha is* not a measure of effect size. Thus, characterizing a result as being "highly" or "very" or "marginally" significant, based on the value of *alpha, is* inappropriate (Harcum, 1989).

Confidence Interval

For this exercise, I describe the following scene:

Imagine a wind-sheltered orchard of trees during autumn. As the trees shed their leaves, piles form around the trunks. Each pile is tallest next to the tree and decreases in height farther away from the tree. Note the similarity between the shape of each pile and the outline of the standard normal distribution. Imagine standing next to a tree's trunk and picking up a leaf from the pile. How sure are you that the particular leaf fell from the tree under which you are standing? Now imagine moving 60 ft away and picking up a leaf from the same pile. How sure are you that this leaf came from the same tree and not a neighboring one?

Invariably, students respond that they are much more confident that the leaf near the trunk belongs to that tree. I continue the discussion by saying that as distance from the tree increases, a point is ultimately reached beyond which any leaf on the ground would more confidently be considered as coming from another tree. Then I associate the trunk with the estimated population mean, the leaves with sample means, and the confidence points with 1–*alpha* and say that the confidence points form the interval's two endpoints within which the population mean has a 1–*alpha* probability of being located.

Conclusion

This article describes how common experiences can be used to elaborate selected statistical concepts. Students have been intrigued by the notion that the thinking they use during the exercises overlaps with the technical principles being presented in the course. They generally indicate that the exercises increase their comprehension of the related text material or, if not, provide a perspective from which to ask meaningful questions. I would appreciate knowing how other statistics instructors use commonplace experiences in their courses.

References

Glenberg, A. M. (1988). *Learning from data: An introduction to statistical reasoning.* New York: Harcourt Brace Jovanovich.

Harcum, E. R. (1989). The highly inappropriate calibrations of statistical significance. *American Psychologist, 44,* 964.

Rodgers, R., Hammerstein, O., II. (1942). *Oklahoma.* New York: Williamson Music Corporation.

Note

I thank Charles L. Brewer and three anonymous reviewers for their comments on an earlier draft.

Teaching Statistics in Terms of the Knower

Michael C. Dillbeck
Maharishi International University

The classroom activity described here is a structured problem series developed for students to discover concepts themselves.

Among psychology students, introductory statistics is a course which often is less appealing than other courses. As a result, one of the major challenges in teaching it to undergraduates is making the material both interesting and relevant to the student's personal experience. This is particularly true in relation to other courses in the major, where the self-referential nature of the content insures at least some degree of relevance.

During the past three years, I have taught introductory statistics courses to classes which included not only psychology majors but also education and biology students. The success of these courses and feedback from students[1] has convinced me that a few key features of the course structure and manner of presentation of the material are primarily responsible for making the courses effective and enjoyable. These features all relate the material to the direct experience of the students. This approach has a strong justification both from educational theory (e.g., Dewey, 1938) and from psychological research (e.g., Craik & Lockhart, 1972); material made meaningful in this way is more likely to be assimilated and retained.

In particular, the aspect of individual experience to which the statistical material is conceptually related is the manner in which knowledge is gained. This will be elaborated later in the article; the justification of this approach can be made in terms of the nature of the discipline as well as pedagogically. Statistical inference is directly concerned with specifying principles by which scientific knowledge is gained; by relating the content of statistics to one's own experience of gaining knowledge, one sees more clearly the core of the discipline.

This paper first describes the classroom activities which have been features of this approach; it then reviews the manner in which statistical principles have been conceptually related to the students' experience of gaining knowledge.

Class Structures and Activities. The primary principle at the basis of the classroom activities was *discovery,* operating within a highly structured context. It was felt that if the students could discover the statistical principles and techniques for themselves, then they would "own" the material and this would best insure understanding and retention. In order to do this, I structured for each lesson a series of problems which led them to discover for themselves the main concept or technique of the lesson.

This problem set, and the direct experience of discovery it created, was the basis of the lesson. The problem set was preceded by only a few introductory remarks to define the general context of the lesson. After working the problems, a lecture followed to conceptualize and clarify the topic. Only after this did the students read the text chapter on the topic and work further example problems. In this way, ideally, the students always gained intellectual clarification of something which they had discovered for themselves. In addition, the problem sets were always solved by working in small groups. This allowed students to progress more quickly and to have peer tutorial help on any unclear points. It also built a good collective feeling within the class. Teaching assistants and the teacher circulated among the groups while they worked on the problem sets, answering questions and prompting where necessary.

In the best of these problem sets, the questions led students sequentially through a process of reasoning which arrived at the goal of the lesson and which, at each step, allowed the students to experience an "aha" of figuring out a point. For example, in the lesson on single-factor analysis of variance, the sequence of problems followed this outline:

1. The students created the F distribution as a basis for further work. In answering questions they deduced the shape of this distribution formed by the ratio of the variances of two samples drawn from the same population.

2. The need for the ANOVA was established. The students were presented with a problem in which they wanted to test for differences among the means of seven groups. Students were asked to calculate how many t tests that would take, and how firm their conclusions would be if only one pair reached significance at the .05 level. The problem also asked how many group differences at the .05 level would be expected among seven groups of random numbers. Students then reflected on the caution against running multiple comparisons.

3. In order to test simultaneously for differences among group means, the idea was presented that it should be possible to test whether the variance among group means would be large enough to reject the hypothesis that all were samples from the same population. Students were asked how they would compute the variance among group means, and how this would be used as an estimate of the population variance. They then performed these calculations for a data set for which sample means and variances were given.

4. It was pointed out that under the null hypothesis of samples from the same population, this unbiased estimate of population variance should approximately equal any other independent estimate of the population variance. Students were then asked to create such an independent estimate which would not be affected by differences among group means, given the hint that the sample variance of each group is an estimate of population variance.

5. Students were then asked how the ratio of these two estimates would be distributed, assuming the null hypothesis were true and the experiment performed many times. They were asked for the expected value of the ratio and asked where they would draw a rejection region for their test of this null hypothesis, given that the first estimate calculated was the numerator. Students were then told that this test they created is called the analysis of variance.

Other problem sets simply gave an experiential appreciation of the point of the lesson without such a great degree of sequential reasoning. An example of the latter type of problem set was on the central limit theorem and its ancillary theorems, for which the groups of students actually took samples from a population and compared the means and standard deviations of the population and sampling distribution.

The sequence of group insight problems, then lecture, reading, and example problems was very effective. The group problems were frequently mentioned in evaluations as the most enjoyable part of the sequence. These group problems effectively gave the student a direct experiential grasp of the context and reasoning behind a particular method; on that foundation the lecture and text reading were immediately familiar.

Adaptability of the Class Structure. There are several points that must be considered in adopting the features of this course structure to another statistics class. The most important is how to fit this sequence into a semester or quarter teaching schedule. These courses were taught on the block system[2], wherein the student takes one course full time each month, covering a semester's worth of material. In that context, the usual sequence was to have the morning group problem session followed by a lecture. In the afternoon the students worked problems on prepared computer programs and read the text; evenings were devoted to homework. For a typical semester-long course a suggested format might be to cover one topic in two class periods. The first could consist of a group problem session followed by reading the text at home. The second class period would be a lecture, followed by homework problems. Computer work could be fit in where appropriate. The other alternative would be to have group problem session and lecture in one period; however, my experience would be that this would be much too rushed for a substantial and useful problem set.

A second issue relating to the block system in contrast to other systems is that the effectiveness of the group problem sessions is aided by the fact that on the block system the students are together daily for a month, which increases cohesion. Nonetheless, even when the students see each other for only two or three hours a week such small group problems should help create a cooperative emotional environment that contributes to the enjoyment of the problem sessions and the class as a whole. Another point to note in adopting this method is that the problem sets should ideally be written around the approach taken in the text. This plan provides a coherence that allows the students to assimilate the material most easily.

Relating Statistics to the Knower. In addition to the classroom activities, which spontaneously brought the material closer to the students, the statistical content was also related conceptually to the students' own experience of gaining knowledge. As stated before, this approach not only makes the material more relevant, but also allows the students to see more clearly the inferential statistical principles used in the scientific method as formalizations that both extend and correct the individual experience of gaining knowledge (Fisher, 1935/1971, pp. 7-8). The use of statistical models in psychology is commonplace, e.g., signal detection theory and some mathematical learning theories. The present approach is the converse—to use mental functioning to "model" statistical principles.[2]

To illustrate the generality of this approach in the context of teaching statistics I will give two examples of general principles which relate statistical topics to the process of gaining individual knowledge. One example of a principle of the knower that applied to introductory statistical topics is that decreased variability of perception or internal functioning leads to greater discrimination. This principle is easily related to everyday experience, whether the source of variability is external and can be reduced by turning on windshield wipers, or is internal, such as text anxiety. Among the statistical concepts that express this principle are: the expansion of sample size to reduce variability and increase power; the use of matching to reduce variability and the resulting difference in power of the t test for dependent means in contrast to that for independent means; and the effect of reducing within-groups variability on the magnitude of the F ratio.

An example from psychological research that relates to this principle is, of course, signal detection theory, for which perceptual "noise" is a central concept (Swets, 1964). Another example is that stability of the autonomic nervous system and field independence are positively related to each other (Silverman, Cohen, Shmavonian, & Greenberg, 1961). Yet another example is from the study of behavioral and cognitive skill; as a task becomes highly skilled, anxiety and behavioral variability decrease, and the performer begins to discriminate the more subtle and flexible aspects of task performance (Lindsay & Norman, 1977, p. 674).

Another example of a general principle of the knower which can be related to several statistical areas is that knowledge of an item of information is most meaningful in the perspective of its whole context; it is this connection of part and whole that supports veridical knowledge. Many examples of misperception of the context of a message could be used as illustrations. A number of statistical concepts express this principle. For instance, the central limit theorem allows one to create the whole distribution of possible samples in the light of which a single sample provides knowledge relevant to one's hypothesis; on this basis rests the whole logic of hypothesis testing. Similarly, when using ANOVA techniques it is the analysis of the whole of the data configuration that gives meaning to the smaller parts. That is, in the presence of a significant interaction between factors, the interactions between subsets of these factors and main effects of those factors do not provide meaningful information; for this reason simple interactions or simple main effects are examined. Related to the same point, one sets up an overall ANOVA design rather than looking at sections of the data separately in order to avoid the inflation of type-one error which would compromise the meaningfulness of the results.

In terms of the knower, this general principle of the part gaining meaning from its whole context may be illustrated by a variety of research topics from cognitive psychology. One example is the importance of context on pattern recognition and the idea of "top-down" or conceptually driven processing (Lindsay & Norman, 1977, p. 13). Other examples are the use of schemata to organize knowledge, the effectiveness of an organizational framework in assisting later recall,

and the dependence of reading comprehension on the identification of higher order organizational text structures (Anderson, 1980, pp. 128, 192, 401). Similarly, the study of cognitive development suggests that as the child gains access to more abstract mental structures, knowledge is able to be assimilated into a broader, more abstract and veridical context (Piaget, 1954). Each of these research areas provides useful concrete examples in the life of the student.

In summary, both classroom activity and the conceptual approach may be used to make statistical material more relevant to the experience of the student. In particular, viewing statistical procedures as formalizations of the processes of gaining knowledge is a conceptual approach that both provides such relevance and is consistent with the nature of the discipline. This allows one to teach statistics with reference to the daily experience of the students and with reference to psychological processes.

References

Anderson, J. R. Cognitive psychology and its implications. San Francisco: Freeman 1980.

Craik, F. I., & Lockhart, R. S. Levels of processing: A framework for memory research. Journal of Verbal Learning and Verbal Behavior, 1972, 11, 671-684.

Dewey, J. Experience and education. New York: Collier, 1938.

Fisher R. A. The design of experiments. New York: Hafner, 1971. (Originally published, 1935).

Lindsay, P. H., & Norman, D. A. Human information processing: An introduction to psychology (2nd Ed.). New York: Academic Press, 1977.

Piaget, J. The construction of reality in the child. New York: Basic Books, 1954.

Silverman A. J. Cohen, S. I., Shmavonian B. M., & Greenberg, G. Psychophysiological investigations in sensory deprivation: The body-field dimension. Psychosomatic Medicine, 1961, 23, 48-61.

Swets, J. A. (Ed.). Signal detection and recognition by human observers. New York: Wiley, 1964.

Notes

1. The average overall rating on the courses has been approximately 4.75 on a scale ranging from one ("Not at all descriptive") to five ("Very descriptive") in response to the statement: "Overall, this was an excellent course."

2. The motivation for structuring a statistics course from this perspective was that at MIU, where the course originated, all courses are taught from an interdisciplinary framework of principles termed the "Science of Creative Intelligence," which relates the academic material to the students direct experience. These principles are said to describe the experience of the student during the

Transcendental Meditation (TM) technique (practiced by all MIU students), to describe longitudinal development predicted to occur from its practice, and to describe the functioning of natural processes more generally.

3. The format of classroom activities suggested here developed from discussions with Susan Levin Dillbeck. Her assistance is gratefully acknowledged.

3. GENERATING DATA

DATAGEN: A BASIC Program for Generating and Analyzing Data for Use in Statistics Courses

Leslie J. Cake
Roy C. Hostetter
Sir Wilfred Grenfell College
Memorial University of Newfoundland

A BASIC program (DATAGEN) for use by instructors of statistics courses is described. DATAGEN generates unique data samples (independent or correlated) for each student from populations with parameters specified by the instructor. The program also provides the instructor with summary statistics for each generated sample. In addition, for independent data, a one-factor, completely randomized ANOVA is available. For correlated data, the program calculates prediction equations and t values for the significance of the difference between means and for the significance of the obtained correlation coefficient. DATAGEN facilitates the demonstration of some fundamental statistical concepts and encourages students to work independently.

In many undergraduate statistics courses, students are provided with a common set of data to analyze. The reason for using common data is often one of convenience; the instructor need only look up the answer or perform one set of analyses for purposes of correction. However, the use of common data may be undesirable for several reasons. Common data allow for the possibility of copying calculations and results, thereby reducing the need for careful, independent work by each student. In addition, common data sets do not provide the student with a feeling for the variable nature of repeated sampling from a common population. Thus, the opportunity to teach a basic reason for the existence of statistical procedures can be missed. The BASIC program described in this article permits instructors to present each student with unique sets of data while eliminating the need for tedious repeated analyses. That is, DATAGEN is a program that generates data samples from a population with specified parameters and provides the instructor with some basic statistical calculations and analyses for these data.

Program Description and Use

An initial menu offers the instructor the choice of independent or correlated data samples; these options are described in turn.

Independent Data Samples

Initially, the number of samples and the *N* for each sample are specified. The mean and standard deviation for the population from which each data sample was drawn are entered next. If desired, the instructor may also provide a label for each of the samples and request that a completely randomized, one-factor analysis of variance (ANOVA) be calculated for each student's data. Also, if desired, the instructor can provide text (e.g., a description of a study and/or instructions for analysis) that will be printed out with each student's unique data set.

The program then proceeds to generate and print out unique data samples for each student. An algorithm (Hansen, 1985), using the central limit theorem, repeatedly generates normally distributed random numbers from a population with mean of 0 and standard deviation of 1. For each random number, the corresponding sample data point is then calculated using the following formula.

$$\text{data point} = \text{input M} + (\text{input } SD \times \text{random number})$$

The result is a sample of data randomly chosen from a population with specified mean and standard deviation. This procedure is repeated for each sample for each student.

Table 1. Sample Independent Output for One Student

Output for the Student

NAME: Leslie J. Cake

Thirty skilled typists were randomly assigned to 1 of 3 groups that received different dosages of alcohol (0 mg / 25 mg / or 50 mg per 100 ml BAL). Typing speed was then measured in words per minute using a standard typing test. Calculate the mean and standard deviation for each alcohol group and a one-factor, completely randomized ANOVA. What would you conclude about the effect that alcohol has on typing speed?

DATA:

0 mg alcohol (Control)

| 61 | 76 | 46 | 60 | 67 | 60 | 59 | 64 | 66 | 48 |

25 mg alcohol

| 63 | 61 | 57 | 45 | 74 | 56 | 56 | 52 | 38 | 45 |

50 mg alcohol

| 29 | 30 | 50 | 42 | 48 | 36 | 25 | 34 | 46 | 49 |

Output for the Instructor

* Input values *

0 mg alcohol (Control) input N = 10
input M = 60   input SD = 8
25 mg alcohol   input N = 10
input M = 50   input SD = 10
50 mg alcohol   input N = 10
input M = 40   input SD = 9

Summary statistics for Leslie J. Cake

0 mg alcohol (Control) N = 10

| M = 60.7 | Variance = 77.12223 | SD = 8.781926 |
| Sum X = 607 | (Sum X)^2 = 368449 | Sum X^2 = 37539 |

25 mg alcohol N = 10

| M = 54.7 | Variance = 107.1222 | SD = 10.34999 |
| Sum X = 547 | (Sum X)^2 = 299209 | Sum X^2 = 30885 |

50 mg alcohol N = 10

| M = 38.9 | Variance = 85.65556 | SD = 9.255029 |
| Sum X = 389 | (Sum X)^2 = 151321 | Sum X^2 = 15903 |

ANOVA Summary Table

Source	SS	df	MS	F
Between	2536.266	2	1268.133	14.096
Within	2429.102	27	89.967	
Total	4965.367	29		

The algorithm for generating normally distributed random numbers was tested with three replications each for sample sizes 10, 100, 1,000, and 10,000. The average means and standard deviations obtained were, respectively, -0.012 and 1.187 (N = 10), 0.060 and 0.999 (N = 100), 0.000 and 1.012 (N = 1,000), and 0.0004 and 0.994 (N = 10,000). These results suggest that the algorithm is generating an appropriate distribution.

Output of the data samples may be directed to the printer or the screen. If printer output is selected, the student's name, the text (if provided), and unique data are printed on separate pages for each student. Next, summary statistics for each student are printed, again on separate pages, for the instructor. Sample statistics provided are N, mean, variance, standard deviation, sum X, (sum X)^2, and sum X^2. If requested, an ANOVA summary table for a one-factor, completely randomized design (equal or unequal N) is also calculated and printed. A sample output for independent data is presented in Table 1.

Table 2. Sample Correlated Data Output for One Student

Output for the Student

NAME: Roy C. Hostetter

An investigator is interested in the relationship between age and memory. She has information from a previous experiment on the number of words recalled (out of 100) by people of varying ages. These data are reproduced below. Calculate the mean and standard deviation for each variable and the correlation coefficient. Test the significance of this correlation coefficient. What would you conclude about the relationship between age and memory? Calculate the regression equation for predicting memory score from age. Given an age of 45, what memory score would you predict?

DATA:

Age	Words recalled (/100)
37	73
58	44
56	48
47	60
39	76
63	32
66	50
51	73
53	39
31	75
36	69
36	86
59	42
53	51
52	55
57	60
56	55
57	63
44	62
62	62

Output for the Instructor

N for samples = 20
Input M_x = 45   Input SD_x = 10
Input M_y = 60   Input SD_y = 15
Input correlation coefficient = $-.7$

Summary Statistics for Roy C. Hostetter

M_x = 50.65   Variance X = 104.5553 SD_x = 10.22523
M_y = 58.75   Variance Y = 196.9342 SD_y = 14.03333
Correlation of X vs. Y = $-.7606226$
Prediction of Y from X Y' = $-1.043895\ X$ + 111.6233
Prediction of X from Y X' = $-.5542193\ Y$ + 83.21038
Sum X = 1013   (Sum X)^2 = 1026169   Sum X^2 = 53295
Sum Y = 1175   (Sum Y)^2 = 1380625   Sum Y^2 = 72773
Sum of cross products = 57440
Standard error of difference = 5.097936
t for difference between means = -1.588878
df = 19
t for significance of correlation coefficient = -4.970852
df = 18

Correlated Data Samples

Initially, the instructor enters the N for the two samples and the means and standard deviations for the populations from which the samples were drawn. The desired correlation between the two populations is also entered. The program then presents the standard error of estimate based on the entered information and continues in the same manner as the independent data case, up to the point of generating unique data points for the two samples.

For each pair of data points, two random numbers are generated using the random number algorithm (Hansen, 1985). The first random number is used to derive the X value using the same formula as in the independent data case. The Y member of the pair is derived using the standard prediction equation, the standard error of estimate, and the second random number. This process is repeated until all data points for both samples for all students have been generated. Student samples (and text if provided) are then printed out.

In addition to the sample statistics presented for the independent data case, the sum of cross products, the actual Pearson product-moment correlation coefficient, and the regression equations for predicting X from Y and Y from X are calculated. The *t* values for the difference between sample means and for the significance of the correlation coefficient, along with the appropriate degrees of freedom, are also provided. A sample output for correlated data is presented in Table 2.

General Comments on Program Use

We have used versions of DATAGEN with undergraduate statistics classes and noticed several benefits. When the program is used for generating laboratory exercises, the students appear to concentrate on the way various analyses should be carried out rather than on obtaining the "correct" answer as often occurs with common data. A second benefit relates to the ease of demonstrating various statistical concepts. The variability found in repeated sampling from a common population can be demonstrated by having students compare their data and results. The effect that sample size has on the standard error of test statistics is easily demonstrated by specifying samples of different sizes. The nature of the confidence interval can be demonstrated when each student has different samples. The use of carefully selected means and/or standard deviations can be used to demonstrate the probabilistic nature of hypothesis-testing statistics.

In summary, we believe that demonstrations of various statistical concepts are more dramatic, and that understanding occurs more rapidly, by using DATAGEN to generate unique data sets for student exercises. Although the program provides various analyses, using this program can be slightly more time-consuming than merely assigning certain exercises from a textbook. This extra effort is offset, however, by the program's advantages; it offers a closer approximation to analyzing "real" data.

Reference

Hansen, A. G. (1985). Simulating the normal distribution. *Byte, 10,* 137-138.

Notes

1. The authors acknowledge the assistance of Connie Gibbons and Daniel Stewart in the preparation of this article and the program.
2. The program was written in "standard" Microsoft BASIC. Hence, the program should be easily ported to a number of microcomputers. We have versions available for the Tandy 1000 and compatibles including the IBM PC, and for the Commodore PET and compatibles.

The Student as Data Generator

Paul Hettich
Barat College

Among the leading concerns of Statistics teachers is the creation or location of examples, problems and exercises which generate student interest above the level of "learn-it-or-else." Wanted is not just any problem or example which is valid, but rather ones which spark a student's enthusiasm for learning. Many statistics texts do contain problems extracted from actual behavioral science research; however, "real" research examples are frequently remote from the student's immediate frame of reference. For instance, the calculation of standard scores derived from an eighth grade science test represents an actual problems but what *immediate* meaning does the problem contain for the statistics students unless the student expects to teach?

The writer certainly is not assuming that such "immediacy" is a necessary criterion for selecting problems, but it *is* an aid to learning. The following details a technique which integrates the student with the subject matter: the utilization of student produced data and student centered examples.

On the first day of class students are given 3 x 5 cards on which they print their names (on the top line) and class (sophomore, junior, etc.), academic majors number of psychology courses completed, and height on subsequent lines. In additions students are administered Pressey's survey of study habits (Morgan & Deese 1969) and the Test Anxiety Scale (TAS) described in Sarason and Ganzer (1962). The completed 3 x 5 cards are assembled to form 8½ x 11 sheets (student names are covered) and then Xeroxed. Students' scores on the two questionnaires are paired on a master summary sheet. Finally, a copy of the card and questionnaire data along with the original questionnaires are returned to the students. Besides supplying the students with data and the teacher with information about his class, the cards function as a ready reference for student advisement.

Statistics Generation. How does the student generated data become incorporated into statistics?

1. The variables which formed the data (e.g., class, majors questionnaire scores) are introduced as examples in discussions of the four *levels of measurement* (nominal, ordinal, interval, ratio).
2. Class, academic major and questionnaire data areused in exercises requiring the preparation of *frequency distributions*.
3. To recognize that the type of graph employed in a particular situation depends on the corresponding level of measurement and that various *shapes of distributions* (e.g., mesokurtic, skewed, normal) occur, students are instructed to construct graphs for the variables of class, academic major and test anxiety.
4. Concepts and problems pertaining to percentile *ranks* and *standard scores* utilize the study habits and TAS scores.
5. The measures of *central tendency* and *dispersion* and the relation of each to the levels of measurement can be illustrated using card and questionnaire data.
6. Comparisons of student performance on the study habits and test anxiety measures provide an excellent opportunity for presenting concepts, techniques and questions related to *correlation* (e.g. Which coefficient of correlation is best suited for these data? How do Pearson and Spearman coefficients differ on the same data?). Discussions of the relationship between study habits and test anxiety illustrate the concepts of correlation in a manner that can be personally meaningful and potentially useful to students. For the past two classes low

negative correlations between these measures were obtained, providing an opportunity to critically examine the underlying behaviors and the instruments used to measure them.
7. When classes are too large to realistically permit the use of all student scores in calculations of correlation coefficients, 10, 15, or 20 pairs can be selected from the population, a procedure that can open an examination of *sampling techniques.*
8. After the concepts of *sampling distribution* and the *central limit theorem* are explained, students are instructed to cut the height data from their Xeroxed sheets, mix it in a container, and draw samples of $N=2$, $N=5$ and $N=10$. Means and grand means are calculated and subsequently related to these concepts.

By now you may have identified additional concepts or problems suitable for the employment of student produced data; the examples summarized here are not exhaustive.

Values. What are the effects of using student generated data? Because statistics is taught annually at this school to only one section it has not yet been possible to collect "outcome" data on learning effectiveness of comparison groups. However, tutor assistants and students frequently remark that reading statistics and completing homework assignments are more interesting when student centered problems are used than when text examples or exercises are given.

Additional advantages accrue using this teaching technique. Because student generated data is not contrived it possesses characteristics of actual data: occasional ambiguity and complexity. For instance, when constructing a frequency distribution, in what category of "major" would an "Art-Psychology" student be assigned? Or, what is done with illegible or confusing data (student cards are Xeroxed)? Also, means and standard deviations seldom occur in easily calculated whole numbers when using actual data: decimals do exist. Furthermore, students can ponder why so-called normally distributed variables (e.g., height) may occasionally produce a skewed distribution for a given group. Or, as happened last semester when three students obtained a closer approximation to the population mean using sample sizes of two than with sample sizes of five and ten, a particular concept may not hold true for a particular instance.

Besides developing interest and critical thinking, students can begin to realize that the use of statistics and scientific methodology is not restricted to textbooks and laboratories. On one occasion when the writer was describing pretest-posttest designs, student attention increased markedly when it was mentioned that many seniors were participating in a school-wide pretest-posttest questionnaire attitude study. Many students are surprised to learn that questions regarding their likes or gripes about student life can be translated into testable hypotheses capable of producing data which can be analyzed by tests of significance.

When the teacher presents statistical concepts in a meaningful manner, students are likely to become interested in this traditionally abstract area of psychology. If principles relating motivation to learning hold true in the statistics classroom, it is reasonable to expect that the use of student generated data and student centered problems can result in an increment of learning.

References

Morgan, C. T. & Deese, J. *How to study* (2nd ed.). New York: McGraw-Hill, 1969.

Sarason, I. G. & Ganzer, W. J. Anxiety reinforcement, and experimental instructions in a free verbalization situation, *Journal of Abnormal and Social Psychology,* 1962, *65,* 300-307.

For Statistics Classes: Data Sets With Integer Means and Standard Deviations

W. P. McGown
W. Boyd Spencer
Eastern Illinois University

One problem associated with test construction in introductory statistics is developing sets of data for which statistics can be computed quickly and (if correct) easily. One way of dealing with the problem is to generate sets of data having integer means and standard deviations. Presented in Table 1 are representative samples of data sets with different means and standard deviations for sample sizes of five, six, and seven.

It should be noted that the samples presented above can easily be converted into many different sets of data. Adding a constant to each score will change the mean but not the standard deviation. Multiplying each score by a constant will change both measures. A complete list of data sets is available from the authors.

Table 1
Data Sets With Means and Standard Deviations

Sample						M	SD
2	4	5	6	8		5	2
1	3	4	5	7		4	2
1	7	9	10	13		8	4
6	8	9	10	12		9	2
1	3	5	9	12		6	4
1	3	3	12	16	19	9	7
1	7	11	11	13	17	10	5
1	11	13	14	17	28	14	8
1	15	15	16	22	27	16	8
1	19	21	25	27	27	20	9
1	3	7	8	10	14	27	10	8
1	7	10	14	24	27	29	16	10
1	11	12	12	20	22	27	15	8
1	14	15	16	21	26	26	17	8
1	18	18	20	25	25	26	19	8

Data Sets Having Integer Means and Standard Deviations

Frank J. Dudek
University of Nebraska

McGown and Spencer (1980) suggested that construction of tests for introductory statistics is facilitated if data sets have means and standard deviations that are integers. They presented several sets for samples of n = 5, 6, and 7. It is fairly easy to devise data sets with integer means and standard deviations for larger samples. One advantage of data sets with larger n's is that they look realistic when plotted as histograms or frequency polygons. Such frequency distributions are also typical of tabulations where data have been grouped into class intervals for computational purposes.

The procedure is to devise several sets with unit variance and zero mean; and then any combination of these also results in another set with unit variance and zero mean. A set with any desired mean (M_T) and standard deviation(s) can be achieved by employing the transformation $T = s(x) + M_T$; here T represents

Table 1. Data Sets with Zero Mean and Unit Standard Deviation from Which Other Data Sets Having any Desired Mean and Standard Deviation Can Be Generated

x	f_A	f_B	f_C	$f_{A'}$	$f_{B'}$	$f_{C'}$	f_A+f_C	$2f_A+f_B$	T_1	T_2	T_3
2.0	1	1	1	0	1	2	2	3	44	62	45
1.5	1	1	2	1	2	1	3	3	43	59	40
1.0	2	2	3	3	1	1	5	6	42	56	35
.5	2	5	3	4	4	6	5	9	41	53	30
0	1	3	6	1	3	6	7	5	40	50	25
− .5	4	4	6	2	5	3	10	12	39	47	20
−1.0	3	1	1	2	2	3	4	7	38	44	15
−1.5	1	2	1	1	1	2	2	4	37	41	10
−2.0	0	1	2	1	1	1	2	1	36	38	5
n	15	20	25	15	20	25	40	50			
mean	0	0	0	0	0	0	0	0	40	50	25
s.d.	1	1	1	1	1	1	1	1	2	6	10

the reported measures or scores. Table 1 presents values of x in the first column and frequency distribu-

tions in the next three columns for data sets A, B, and C with n's = 15, 20, and 25 respectively. Each distribution has unit standard deviation and a mean of zero. From the three frequency distributions it is possible to generate many other distributions all having mean = 0 and standard deviation = 1. So, for example, in columns 5, 6 and 7 each of the original sets is simply inverted or transposed by interchanging frequencies in the highest interval with those of the lowest, those from the next to the top interval with the interval next to the bottom, etc. If a distribution where n = 30 is desired, the frequencies in distribution A can be multiplied by 2; or the frequencies in distributions A and A' can be added. To obtain a frequency distribution with n = 35, the frequencies of distribution A and distribution B can be added; or frequencies of distribution B can be added to those of A'. Shown in the seventh column of Table 1 is the distribution with n = 40 resulting when distributions A and C are combined, and in the next column a distribution of n = 50 that results from doubling the frequencies in A and then adding the frequencies from B.

Values of the measures or scores, T, can be determined by utilizing the transformation noted above to achieve any desired mean and standard deviation. The last three columns of Table 1 show three different transformations: $T_1 = 2(x) + 40$; $T_2 = 6(x) + 50$; and $T_3 = 10(x) + 25$. Any of the frequency distributions related to T_1 scores would have a mean = 40 with standard deviation = 2, while T_2 scores would result in a mean = 50 with standard deviation = 6, etc.

Reference

McGown, W. P., & Spencer, W. B. For statistics classes: Data sets with integer means and standard deviations. *Teaching of Psychology*, 1980, 7, 63.

4. TEACHING SPECIFIC CONCEPTS

Tables to Help Students Grasp Size Differences in Simple Correlations

John Daniel Duke
Appalachian State University

When the writer was enrolled in a beginning psychology class back near mid-century, his instructor tried to explain what simple correlations measure. After describing direct and inverse relationships, he made the usual cautions. Correlations are not percentages. The sign indicates the kind of association between X and Y, and a minus sign certainly does not indicate a low or an absent or deficient relationship. Correlations neither imply nor preclude causal relationships. On scatter diagrams, straight lines of dots indicate perfect relationships, circular clusters indicate zero relationships, while elliptical clusters indicate some degree of linear association. Even verbal labels were applied: 0.00 to 0.25 indicated from no to a very low relationship; 0.25 to 0.50 indicated from a low to a moderate relationship; 0.50 to 0.75 indicated from a moderate to a high relationship; and 0.75 to 1.00 indicated from a high to a perfect relationship.

Although the instructor did not mention that the amount of the covariation between X and Y was approximately the square of the correlation coefficient, he did all he reasonably could to give beginning students an intuitive appreciation of what correlations measure. Despite his efforts, however, subsequent tests showed that he attained limited success. The statistics items had the highest rate of failure then, and they still do today.

Later that quarter a generation ago, the instructor mentioned IQ scores and their correlates. Among other generalizations, he mentioned that there was a small but significant correlation (about +.20) between IQ scores and ratings of physical attractiveness. The attractive male and female students forgot the early qualifications. Here was a discipline suggesting not only that they were attractive and bright, but psychologists said that the relationship was "significant" (garbled in their minds to mean "important" or "impressive"). The less attractive students also failed to comprehend. Aware that some of their attractive peers were definitely not very bright, many of these not so attractive students decided that class content had little or any reference to events in the real world. Of course, some of the students had a reasonable understanding of the many exceptions to a generalization implied by a low correlation, but not many. Then and now, instructors have difficulty teaching students to appreciate size differences in correlation. Today and then, students overestimate how often relationship generalizations will apply, and underestimate how many exceptions there will be.

Based upon a brief discussion of tetrachoric correlations found in Edwards (1960) and a table itself originally published by Davidoff and Goheen (1953) and reproduced in Edwards, the writer derived a table which might help students become both aware of size differences in correlations and of frequency of exceptions implied by various correlation coefficients. Given 2 x 2 cell entries on dichotomized variables X and Y, the Davidoff and Goheen table uses the larger ratio of diagonal cell products, one to the other, for rapid estimation of the tetrachoric correlation. Working backward from the Davidoff and Goheen table, Table 1 derived the expected percentages of "fits" and "exceptions" to relationships defined by correlations varying from 0.00 to 1.00.

Now consider the correlation of +0.20 between IQs and attractiveness. Table 1 reveals that for all those above the median in IQ, *only 56% are at the same time above the median in rated attractiveness.* The remaining 44% are below the median in rated attractiveness. Conversely, for those below median in IQ, 44% are above the median in rated attractiveness, and 56% are below the median. Thus for correlations as low as + 0.20, Table 1 shows that there will be about 44 "exceptions" (less attractive bright people) per 100 people for all those above the median level of intelligence, and another 44 "exceptions" (attractive dull people) per 100 people among all those below the median level of intelligence. The expected percentage of exceptions to a generalization relating X to Y is a concrete analysis of correlational data that most college students can digest.

Here is another example. Suppose a correlation of +.69 is found between height and weight. Table 1 entries show us that for all those people above the median on one variable, 74%, approximately, are expected to be above the median on the other variable. Or 26% of all people would be exceptional cases (below median on one variable while above median on the other).

If the correlation is negative, column percentage entries are reversed for all tables recorded in this paper. Suppose in the open field test using rat subjects,

Table 1
Minimum Probable Percentages of Above and Below Median Cases on a Second Variable of All Cases Above the Median on the First Variable (Assuming True Correlations From 0.00 to 1.00)

True Correlation	% Expected on 2nd Variable*		True Correlation	% Expected on 2nd Variable*	
	Above Med	Below Med		Above Med	Below Med
0.00	50.0	50.0	0.51	66.9	33.1
0.01	50.2	49.8	0.52	67.3	32.7
0.02	50.5	49.5	0.53	67.6	32.4
0.03	50.8	49.2	0.54	68.0	32.0
0.04	51.1	48.9	0.55	68.4	31.6
0.05	51.4	48.6	0.56	68.8	31.2
0.06	51.7	48.3	0.57	69.1	30.9
0.07	52.1	47.9	0.58	69.5	30.5
0.08	52.4	47.6	0.59	69.9	30.1
0.09	52.7	47.3	0.60	70.3	29.7
0.10	53.1	46.9	0.61	70.7	29.3
0.11	53.4	46.6	0.62	71.1	28.9
0.12	53.7	46.3	0.63	71.5	28.5
0.13	54.0	46.0	0.64	71.9	28.1
0.14	54.3	45.7	0.65	72.4	27.6
0.15	54.6	45.4	0.66	72.8	27.2
0.16	55.0	45.0	0.67	73.2	26.8
0.17	55.3	44.7	0.68	73.6	26.4
0.18	55.6	44.4	0.69	74.1	25.9
0.19	55.9	44.1	0.70	74.5	25.5
0.20	56.2	43.8	0.71	75.0	25.0
0.21	56.6	43.4	0.72	75.4	24.6
0.22	56.9	43.1	0.73	75.9	24.1
0.23	57.2	42.8	0.74	76.3	23.7
0.24	57.6	42.4	0.75	76.8	23.2
0.25	57.9	42.1	0.76	77.3	22.7
0.26	58.2	41.8	0.77	77.8	22.2
0.27	58.5	41.5	0.78	78.3	21.7
0.28	58.9	41.1	0.79	78.8	21.2
0.29	59.2	40.8	0.80	79.3	20.7
0.30	59.5	40.5	0.81	79.8	20.2
0.31	59.9	40.1	0.82	80.4	19.6
0.32	60.2	39.8	0.83	80.9	19.1
0.33	60.5	39.5	0.84	81.5	18.5
0.34	60.9	39.1	0.85	82.1	17.9
0.35	61.2	38.8	0.86	82.7	17.3
0.36	61.6	38.4	0.87	83.3	16.7
0.37	61.9	38.1	0.88	84.0	16.0
0.38	62.3	37.7	0.89	84.6	15.4
0.39	62.6	37.4	0.90	85.3	14.7
0.40	63.0	37.0	0.91	86.1	13.9
0.41	63.3	36.7	0.92	86.8	13.2
0.42	63.7	36.3	0.93	87.6	12.4
0.43	64.0	36.0	0.94	88.5	11.5
0.44	64.4	35.6	0.95	89.4	10.6
0.45	64.7	35.3	0.96	90.5	9.5
0.46	65.1	34.9	0.97	91.6	8.4
0.47	65.4	34.6	0.98	92.9	7.1
0.48	65.8	34.2	0.990	94.5	5.5
0.49	66.2	33.8	0.995	96.9	3.1
0.50	66.5	33.5	1.000	100.0	0.0

*For negative correlations, column entries are reversed.

an experimenter found a correlation of -0.88 between activity level (number of grids crossed per unit time) and number of boluses defecated per unit time. Table 1 now shows that for all rats with an above median level of activity, 84% are expected to defecate a below median number of boluses. Since the correlation describes an inverse relationship as the general trend in the association between X and Y, those rats above or below median on both variables at the same time are

the exceptions. With a correlation of -0.88, only 16% of the rats behave exceptionally.

Table 1 is overly long but is included for those who might want to reproduce it for a set of statistical tables. For pedagogical purposes, and perhaps for reproduction in introductory text discussions, Table 2 will suit the purposes of most users. Table 2 uses only correlation coefficients round to tenths or twentieths (left side), and correlations to hundredths which produces multiples of 5 in the percentage splits of fitting and nonfitting cases (right side). Table 2 shows that with a correlation of 0.10, 0.40, and 0.95, for example, that

Table 2
Given All Cases Above the Median on Variable 1, Concurrent Percentages of Above and Below Median Cases on Variable 2 for Selected Values

Correlation Intervals			Percent Intervals		
True Correlation	% Expected on 2nd Variable*		True Correlation	% Expected on 2nd Variable*	
	Above Med	Below Med		Above Med	Below Med
0.10	52.7	47.3	0.00	50	50
0.20	56.2	43.8	0.16	55	45
0.30	59.5	40.5	0.31	60	40
0.40	63.0	37.0	0.46	65	35
0.50	66.5	33.5	0.59	70	30
0.60	70.3	29.7	0.71	75	25
0.70	74.5	25.5	0.81	80	20
0.80	79.3	20.7	0.90	85	15
0.85	82.1	17.9	0.96	90	10
0.90	85.3	14.7	0.99	95	5
0.95	89.4	10.6	1.00	100	0

*For negative correlations, column entries are reversed.

there are, respectively, 47%, 37%, and 11% of the cases expected to be exceptions, and that it takes a correlation of +0.16 to hold down the percentage of exceptions to 45%, a correlation of +0.31 to reduce the exceptions to 40%, etc.

Most correlations are estimates based on limited observations, not parameter values. Table estimates assume parameter correlations. The tables are still useful with nonparameter estimates, however, provided only that the user remember that the "true" correlation may vary somewhat from the estimated value. Advanced students can obtain confidence limits for their statistics. Suppose on a limited sample size, a negative correlation is found between husbands' incomes and wives' waist lines, measured in inches. Suppose the 99 percent confidence interval places the true correlation somewhere between -0.28 and -0.46. From Table 1, one could estimate that for all husbands earning above median incomes, between 35 and 41 percent would expect to have wives with above median waist lines.

Assumptions and Cautions in Use of the Tables.
Technical assumptions for use of all tables in this paper are that the dichotomized variables be essentially continuous and normally distributed. Percentages ap-

ply only if both variables have been divided at their medians and if the correlation is "true," that is, without any error of measurement.

But even if the assumptions are only approximately met, and even if nonparameter estimates are used, the tabled data should still provide "ballpark estimates" which should give students some idea of the percentages of fitting and nonfitting cases suggested by different sized correlations. These rough estimates should improve on the uninformed and usually exaggerated estimates of fitting cases now guessed at by students.

The caution should be made, however, that there are quite technical analyses of what correlations measure, and that the tables presented offer only beginning insight into understanding of relationships between paired variables. When appropriate, students should be exposed to technical discussions about regression, and they should learn how r and r^2 relate to the slope of, and variability around, the regression line. Usually, however, complex analyses of the meaning of correlation measures will be reserved for a second or third course in statistics.

How the Tables were Derived. As already noted, the tables were derived by working backward from the Davidoff and Goheen table to estimate tetrachoric correlations. A 2 x 2 cell matrix is created by dividing two variables at the median. Cell a stands for being below the median on both variables. Cell b stands for being above the median on the second variable but below the median on the first. Cell c stands for being above the median on the first variable, but below on the second. Cell d stands for being above the median on both variables. Davidoff and Goheen instruct readers to take the ratio of bc/ad, or its reciprocal (whichever is larger), and to look up in their table to find what correlations are associated with what ratios.

By varying a from 0 to 1000, while making c the result of subtracting a from 1000, and by reversing b and d systematically with changes in a and c, Table 1 can be created. Beside the correlation of +0.38 in Table 1, for example, the percentages cited are 62.3% ("fits") and 37.7%("exceptions"). In a 2 x 2 matrix with a total frequency of 1000, a and d would both be 623 and b and c would both be 377. The ratio of ad/bc is larger than the ratio of bc/ad, and from the Davidoff and Goheen table, the resulting ratio is best associated with a correlation of 0.38. It took 1000 calculations to produce the 102 sets of entries in Table 1. Table 2, of course, was directly abstracted from Table 1 entries.

Summary. Two tables are presented to help students and others better understand size differences in correlations. The tables were independently developed by the author who does not know if they have been created or presented by others. The pedagogical value of the tables was illustrated and stressed. Technical assumptions and cautions in use of the tables were noted, and a brief explanation was given of how the tables were derived.

References

Davidoff, M. D., & Goheen, M. W. A table for the rapid determination of the tetrachoric correlation coefficient. *Psychometrics*, 1953, *18*, 115-121.

Edwards, A. L. *Statistical methods for the behavioral sciences*. New York: Rinehart, 1960.

Pearson's *r* and Spread: A Classroom Demonstration

Schuyler W. Huck
S. Paul Wright
Soohee Park
College of Education
University of Tennessee (Knoxville)

For many students, the connection between spread and Pearson's r is elusive. Confusion arises because different factors that increase score variability do not have the same effect on r. To help students understand that increases in σ may lead to an increase or a decrease in r or to no change whatsoever, we devised a simple and enjoyable classroom exercise. Using standard decks of playing cards, students generate hypothetical data on two well-known variables (IQ and GPA). Once analyzed, the data make clear the point that changes in score variability influence r in different ways—or not at all—depending on the reason why σ_x (or σ_y) increases or decreases.

Of the many things that students learn about Pearson's *r*, one of the most troublesome involves the relation between spread and the magnitude of Pearson's *r*. The connection between these two concepts is often perplexing because of apparent inconsistencies in what students read (or hear) as their formal academic training unfolds. Over time, students typically confront three seemingly incompatible claims: (a) variability and *r* are directly related, (b) variability and *r* are inversely related, and (c) variability and *r* are unrelated. These claims lead students to wonder how dispersion can be related to Pearson's *r* in three different ways.

The answer to this question is tied to the meaning of dispersion—or stated differently, why variability is high or low. If the measured spread on *X* and/or *Y* is decreased because errors of measurement are reduced, then the correlation between *X* and *Y* will increase. If, on the other hand, the variability of *X* and/or *Y* is decreased because we focus on a subgroup with restricted range, then the correlation of *X* and *Y* will decrease. A third case exists when the metric of *X* and/or *Y* is changed by multiplying all observed values by a constant; here, the computed variance changes without a concomitant change in *r*.

To help students understand that changes in variability affect *r* in different ways, depending on the reason why the spread of scores has increased or decreased, we developed a simple but powerful exercise. This exercise involves (a) using playing cards to generate hypothetical scores on two well-known variables and (b) computing and comparing various standard deviations and correlation coefficients. As a supplement to textbook discussions and lectures on the topic of Pearson's *r*, this exercise is easy to conduct and helps students understand the multifaceted relation between spread and *r*.

Data Generation

Data generation requires approximately 10 min of class time and a standard deck of playing cards for each student. By following an explicit set of instructions, each student generates two sets of self-descriptive (though hypothetical) numbers: true and fallible IQ scores as well as true and fallible grade point averages (GPA).

To generate the IQ and GPA scores, each student takes a deck of 52 cards and divides it into two parts referred to here as HIGH and LOW. The 28 highest cards (7s, 8s, 9s, 10s, Jacks, Queens, and Kings) are assigned to HIGH; the remaining 24 cards (Aces, 2s, 3s, 4s, 5s, and 6s) are assigned to LOW. After forming HIGH and LOW, students shuffle each stack and then place HIGH and LOW face down.

After setting up HIGH and LOW, each student takes the top two cards off HIGH and turns them over to reveal their values. (If selected, a Jack, Queen, or King is valued at 11, 12, or 13, respectively.) These two cards are designated H_1 and H_2.

Once H_1 and H_2 are selected, each student takes the top two LOW cards and turns them over to determine their values. (If selected, an Ace is worth 1 point.) These two cards are designated L_1 and L_2; order of selection is noted. After the values of L_1 and L_2 are recorded, these two cards are returned to LOW, LOW is reshuffled, and then two new cards from LOW are selected as before. The values of this next pair of cards are designated L_3 and L_4, again order of selection is noted. Finally, L_3 and L_4 are returned to LOW, LOW is reshuffled one last time, and then a third pair of cards is selected from LOW. The values of these final two cards are designated L_5 and L_6; again, order of selection is noted.

After two cards from HIGH and six cards from LOW have been selected, students compute their "true" IQ and "true" GPA scores (hereafter referred to as IQ_T and GPA_T) as follows:

$$IQ_T = 5(H_1 + H_2)$$
$$GPA_T = .1(H_1 + H_2) + .08(L_1 - L_2)$$

Students are told that (a) $70 \leq IQ_T \leq 130$ and $1.00 \leq GPA_T \leq 3.00$, (b) IQ_T represents the hypothetical IQ score each of them would earn if given a fully valid intelligence test, and (c) GPA_T represents the hypothetical GPA each of them would have after 4 years of college under the assumption that one's grades are influenced by only two factors: native intelligence and individual decisions to do extra work, to goof off, and so on. (If any student's L_2 is higher than L_1, this means that he or she worked less than average, goofed off more than average, etc.)

After computing IQ_T and GPA_T, students are told that no test is perfectly accurate; test content is sometimes biased, students sometimes select their answers by random guessing, students sometimes take tests when ill or emotionally upset, and so forth. Consequently, "fallible" IQ and "fallible" GPA scores (hereafter referred to as IQ_F and GPA_F) must be generated to match the realism of actual IQ and GPA scores. The procedure for obtaining these two fallible scores is:

$$IQ_F = IQ_T + 6(L_3 - L_4)$$
$$GPA_F = GPA_T + .2 (L_5 - L_6)$$

The quantities $6(L_3 - L_4)$ and $.2 (L_5 - L_6)$ represent errors of measurement. Once this measurement error is added to the true scores, $40 \leq IQ_F \leq 160$ and $0.00 \leq GPA_F \leq 4.00$.

Before turning to the data analysis, a comment about class size is in order. This exercise works better if many pairs of IQ and GPA scores are produced. Having $N \geq 40$ generally provides sufficient data. If the class size is smaller than 40, each student should generate two (or more) sets of paired IQ and GPA scores.

Data Analysis

After students generate the data, four specific analyses should be performed. These analyses correspond to four sets of questions:

1. Using the data generated by your class, what value does r assume when IQ_T is correlated with GPA_T? How large is the standard deviation for the data collected on each variable?

2. If we introduce measurement error (by looking at the IQ_F and GPA_F scores), how large are the two stan-

dard deviations and what value does r assume? Comparing these findings with those of Question 1, what inference can be drawn about the impact of measurement error on standard deviations and on Pearson's r?

3. If we focus on only those cases in which $IQ_T > 100$, how large are the two standard deviations (of IQ_T and of GPA_T) and how large is r when computed on the true scores from this "bright" subgroup? Comparing these findings with those of Question 1, what conclusion can be drawn about the impact of restriction of range on score variability and on Pearson's r?

4. If we double all GPA_F scores to produce a scale that extends from 0 to 8 (rather than 0 to 4), how large will the new GPA standard deviation be? And what value will r assume if computed on IQ_F and the rescaled GPA_F scores? Comparing these findings with those of Question 2, what conclusion can be drawn about the impact of linear data transformations on standard deviations and on r?

By answering the first set of questions, one obtains baseline figures with which subsequent results can be compared. The results obtained by answering the final three sets of questions illustrate that (a) an increase in spread, if brought about by the intrusion of measurement errors, causes r to *decrease;* (b) a decrease in spread, if brought about by restriction in range, causes r to decrease; and (c) a change in σ, if brought about by altering the metric of X and/or Y; has no effect on r.

Expected Results

Because the data generated by students for this exercise involve sampling, one cannot predict with certainty the values that the two standard deviations and the one r will assume in the first, second, or third parts of the data analysis. Nevertheless, the instructor can be confident that the results will allow the desired points to be made. Evidence to support this claim comes from a computer simulation of the full demonstration.

Using SAS/IML, all possible pairs of IQ and GPA scores from the data generation phase of the demonstration were specified, along with their corresponding probability of occurrence. Then this population of values was sampled, with 40 cases extracted ranomly. From the resulting pairs of IQ and GPA scores, sample standard deviations and correlations were computed (first using true data, then a second time using fallible scores). These results were then examined to see whether the introduction of measurement errors caused an increase in the IQ and GPA standard deviations and a decrease in the correlation between IQ and GPA.

This first set of 40 sample values also was analyzed to determine the effects of range restriction. To accomplish this objective, cases for which the true IQ was ≤ 100 were deleted, with the remaining cases used as a basis for computing the true standard deviations and the correlation. Results were examined to determine whether the imposed restriction of range caused not only the standard deviations but also the correlation to decrease, as compared with the values computed on the basis of the full 40-person sample.

The full Monte Carlo simulation was based on 1,000 random samples, each analyzed in the same fashion. Outcomes indicated the high probability that results obtained from any group of students will be as desired. For example, when measurement error was introduced, all 1,000 replications were identical in that (a) the computed standard deviation for IQ_F was greater than that for IQ_T, (b) the computed standard deviation for GPA_F was greater than that for GPA_T, and (c) the correlation between IQ_F and GPA_F was lower than the correlation between IQ_T and GPA_T.

The Monte Carlo simulation revealed that this exercise also is highly likely to work well in illustrating the relation between spread and r when the range is restricted. In 975 out of the 1,000 sets of data examined, the correlation between IQ_T and GPA_T was smaller for the "bright" subgroup of the sample than it was for the full sample.

The issue of sampling, of course, has no bearing on the results generated by any group of students to answer Question 4 (i.e., the question dealing with the way a linear transformation of GPA affects spread and r). Here, there is a full guarantee that the variability of the rescaled GPA scores will increase while r changes not a whit.

Demonstrating the Central Limit Theorem

David E. Johnson
John Brown University

Explaining abstract, theoretical distributions to beginning students is sometimes difficult. This article describes a demonstration that helps to make the central limit theorem for generating sampling distributions concrete and understandable.

As any teacher of introductory statistics knows, it is often difficult for students to achieve a full understanding of theoretical distributions. Students frequently complain about the abstract nature of these distributions. In the past, I have experienced particular difficulty explaining the nature and properties of distributions that result from the use of the central limit theorem.

Simply stated, the central limit theorem suggests that the sums or means of a large number of equal-sized random samples can be combined to form an approximately normal distribution if the size of these samples is large enough. Furthermore, this relationship holds regardless of the shape of the original distribution. Invariably, I encounter resistance and confusion on the part of students at this point in the course. With a little prodding I can convince some students of the accuracy and usefulness of the theorem. Other students, however, express a need for a concrete demonstration.

To satisfy these students and to reduce the amount of verbal explanation of the central limit theorem, I have adapted a demonstration from an example presented by Weinberg, Schumaker, and Oltman (1981). In their example, Weinberg et al. ask the reader to imagine a very large box that contains a large number of slips of paper. These slips of paper have either 0, 1, or 2 printed on them in approximately equal numbers, yielding a rectangular distribution. If equal-sized random samples are taken from this population and their sums or means are combined, the resulting distribution approaches normality.

My demonstration is a direct extension of this example. Before the class meeting I prepare approximately three or four equal-sized random samples for each student. These random samples are generated by a microcomputer using a standard program. Because my software will not generate zeros as random numbers, I specify the population to be comprised of values 1, 2, and 3. Thirty random samples are selected. These samples are then printed.

In class, I announce that we will be using the central limit theorem to begin building our own distribution of sample sums and sample means. The random samples are distributed to the students and I explain the process of random selection. Students are asked to determine the possible limits of our distribution if *N*

= 30. They quickly respond that 30 is the lowest possible value (a sample of ones), and that 90 is the highest value (a sample of threes). I then place a pre-drawn scale ranging from 30 to 90 on an overhead projector.

The students then obtain the sum of each of their random samples. When they have finished, the students, in turn, call out their sample sums and I place an X on the prepared number line to represent each one. As we proceed with the exercise, it becomes apparent that the Xs are accumulating in the middle of the scale; clustering around the theoretical center of the distribution (the value 60). When all responses have been recorded we examine our distribution and discuss its properties. For example, we discuss the fact that the distribution of sample means would look exactly like our distribution of sample sums except for the numerical range. The distribution of sample means would have a lower range of one and an upper range of three. We also reemphasize the fact that our sampling distribution would eventually approximate the normal distribution even though our original population was obviously not normally distributed but, in this case, rectangular.

This demonstration has been helpful to many students, judging from the numerous positive comments that I have received in the past. Students seem more readily to accept the presentation of theoretical distributions in later stages of the course because of this demonstration.

This demonstration is also useful when we discuss certain aspects of probability. For example, students know that, theoretically, the most frequent observation in our demonstration should be the midpoint of the distribution (60 in this case). However, with our limited number of samples, 60 is rarely the most frequent observation. The resulting discussion helps students to understand the difference between theoretical outcomes in the long run and actual short-term outcomes in practice.

Finally, an enhancement of this demonstration might involve selecting random samples from other nonnormal parent populations and building sample distributions from them. Constructing sample distributions from highly skewed or multimodal parent distributions would further reinforce students' acceptance of the utility of the central limit theorem.

Reference

Weinberg, G. H., Schumaker, J. A., & Oltman, D. (1981). *Statistics: An intuitive approach* (4th ed.). Monterey, CA: Brooks/Cole.

Regression Toward the Mean Effect: No Statistical Background Required

Jerzy Karylowski
University of North Florida

A new classroom demonstration of the regression toward the mean effect is proposed. The demonstration is highly concrete and strictly psychological in nature. It may be used in both small and large classes. It does not assume any statistical background. Although some assumptions about the nature of the measurement process are explictly made, these assumptions are highly intuitive and are easily accepted even by students who are not familiar with measurement theory.

One source of bias in assessing the effects of any intervention or manipulation preceded by an initial screening procedure is regression toward the mean effect. Unfortunately, this phenomenon is difficult to understand for students who lack statistical background.

Several years ago, Cutter (1976) developed a classroom demonstration of the regression toward the mean effect. His demonstration, which is based on dice sums, provides an accurate model of the phenomenon. However, the way in which the effect is produced in that demonstration is often perceived by the students as highly artificial and lacking psychological content. The lack of clear psychological relevance greatly diminishes the effectiveness of Cutter's demonstration for the less abstractly minded students. The same criticism applies to the recent modification of the regression toward the mean demonstration (Levin, 1982), in which two decks of playing cards are used instead of dice.

The present demonstration is not only highly concrete, it is strictly psychological in content. It engages the students and may be used in both small and large classes. It does not assume any statistical background. Although some assumptions about the nature of the measurement process (inevitability of measurement error and the random nature of such an error) are explicitly made, these assumptions are highly intuitive and are easily accepted even by students who are not familiar with measurement theory.

PROCEDURE

Announce to the students that you are going to simulate a study on the level of aspiration and that they will be asked to serve as your research assistants. Introduce briefly the concept of the level of aspiration as a relatively stable personality trait (Rotter, 1954). Explain that both very low and very high aspiration levels are maladaptive. Tell them you believe that you possess a special psychic power, which has a therapeutic influence on people with too low or too high aspiration levels.

Discuss briefly some potential measures of aspiration level as a trait. Make it clear that there is no such thing as a perfect measure. Suggest that a score on any measure will always be a function of at least two components: (a) true score, and (b) contribution of transient factors (error score). Give some examples of transient factors (e.g., subject had a particularly good or a particularly bad day, subject misunderstood some items, there were clerical errors). Ask each student to think of three or four people the student knows well. These people will constitute an initial pool of subjects in your simulated study.

Instruct the students to "test" their subjects. Explain that the scale is a 6-point scale with scores 1 and 2 indicating a tendency for aspirations to be lower than the ability level, scores 3 and 4 indicating an appropriate aspiration level, and scores 5 and 6 indicating unrealistically high aspirations. The "testing" is done in the following way:

1. Each subject is assigned a true score. In making these judgments the students should use any information or intuitions they have about their subjects.

2. Each subject is assigned a transient factors score. This is done on the basis of dice tossing.
3. A test score is computed for each subject. I usually assume an equal contribution of true scores and transient factors scores and use an average of the two as a simulated test score.

On the basis of the "testing scores" select from the initial pool two extreme groups: a low aspirations group and a high aspirations group (upper and lower, 10% or 25%). Tell the students that you believe that both groups will benefit from your psychic treatment.

Announce that 1 day has passed during which the psychic power treatment was provided and ask the students to "retest" their subjects. Tell your students that unless they believe in your psychic power (the chances are they don't), they should reassign the same true scores. Transient factors scores are assigned on the basis of a new round of dice tossing and new test scores are computed.

Tabulate the pretreatment and the posttreatment results for both the low aspirations and the high aspirations groups. The students will immediately notice a decrease in the test scores for the high aspirations group and an increase for the low aspirations group!

You may, if you wish, change your assumptions concerning the contribution of transient factors (error) and repeat the demonstration using a modified formula for computing the test scores. For instance, if you assume a 25%, rather than a 50% contribution (i.e., a more reliable measure), the regression toward the mean effect will become smaller. If you assume a 75% contribution (i.e., very low reliability), the effect will increase. The demonstration extended like this will provide a good vehicle for discussing the concept of reliability and the relationship between reliability and the regression toward the mean effect.

References

Cutter, G. R. (1976). Some examples for teaching regression toward the mean from a sampling viewpoint. *American Statistician*, *30*, 194-197.

Levin, J. R. (1982). Modifications of regression-toward-the-mean demonstration. *Teaching of Psychology*, *9*, 237-238.

Rotter, J. B. (1954). *Social learning and clinical psychology*. Englewood Cliffs, NJ: Prentice-Hall.

Modifications of a Regression-Toward-the-Mean Demonstration

Joel R. Levin
University of Wisconsin, Madison

A few years ago, Cutter (1976) provided a demonstration of the statistical phenomenon, regression toward the mean. His demonstration, based on dice sums, is very concrete and thus is a valuable pedagogical device for students in introductory statistics and research methodology courses. The article stimulated me to devise two modifications, which I believe remedy a few problems in the original deomonstration. With Cutter's procedure, outcomes on the first set of dice rolls are not individually paired with those on the second and, as a result, students are liable to view the connection between the two as somewhat arbitrary. Moreover, the manner in which the concept of correlation is induced (by having the two sets of outcomes share a die face) may seem somewhat artificial. My first modification was to make the connection between the two sets of outcomes (Variables 1 and 2, or Times 1 and 2) more explicit. My second modification framed the regression problem in terms of a commonly desired real-world comparison, namely that involving extreme groups.

The procedure is as follows: Two standard decks of playing cards are designated A and B. Remove all 7s from deck A to form partial decks A_1 (composed of all Aces, 2s, 3s, 4s, 5s, and 6s) and A_2 (all 8s, 9s, 10s, Jacks, Queens, and Kings), but keep deck B intact. Allow n students (5 or so seems to work well) each to select three cards from A_1, and another n students each to select three cards from A_2. Record the sums of all the n students' cards within each group (counting Ace = 1 . . . King = 13). These "low" (A_1) and "high" (A_2) groups should have means close to the theoretical values of 10.5 and 31.5 respectively, with a mean difference of 21. This difference constitutes the "classification" measure to be used in each demonstration. It is readily apparent that there is no overlap between the two groups.

Demonstration 1. Next, take measurements on Variable 2 or at Time 2. The same students (classified as "highs" and "lows") participate, but this time they select only two cards from their respective A decks and the third card from deck B. Following a tabulation of the resulting sums, the students will immediately notice a reduction in the original mean difference (theoretical means are 14 and 28, for a difference of 14).

Demonstration 2. Repeat the process, having the students now draw one card from their respective A decks and two from B. Now the mean difference will shrink to about seven.

Demonstration 3. Finally, with students in both groups drawing three cards apiece for Deck B, the mean difference will have all but vanished—as should be the case when regression is completed (i.e., when the two measurements are completely uncorrrelated).

The demonstration is easily related to real-world analogs such as: (a) measuring mathematics achievement on two different occasions; (b) measuring reading achievement on one occasion and mathematics achievement on the other; and (c) measuring height on one occasion and mathematics achievement on the other. These can be used, respectively to illustrate what would be expected to happen to extreme-group differences if highly correlated (Demonstration 1), moderately correlated (Demonstration 2), and uncorrelated (Demonstration 3) measurements are taken on the same students.

Informal feedback from students indicates that they are quite enthusiastic about demonstrations such as this that are based on concrete analogies. In the present context, the playing cards serve as an analogical device to help the more abstract concept of regression toward the mean "come alive." Such demonstrations would be expected not just to heighten students' interest and attention; the available empirical data suggest that they will improve students' actual comprehension and recall of the concept being taught (e.g., Mayer & Bromage, 1980; Royer & Cable, 1976). Similar demonstrations involving playing cards have been used successfully by the present author to concretize other abstract statistical concepts, such as the sampling distribution of a statistic and the Central Limit Theorem. Indeed, an entire introductory course can be taught using this approach (Knappl 1979)

Three other distinctive characteristics of this demonstration should be noted. First, there is active ongoing student participation during the process, ranging from students drawing the cards to those recording the outcomes to those calculating the means.Related to this is the fact that real data collection is accompanied by instantaneous data analysis—something not often experienced in a research context. Finally, the important distinction between expected and actual outcomes iswell communicated through a comparison of the theoretical and obtained mean differences. Certainly the closeness of the match varies from one demonstration to the next. Nonetheless, each individual demonstration never fails to reveal that despite their fickleness, statistics based on adequately sized randon samples really do a commendable job of estimating unknown population parameters.

References

Cutter, G. R. Some examples for teaching regression toward the mean from a sampling viewpoint. *American Statistician,* 1976, *30,* 194-197.

Knapp, T. R. *Statistics through playing cards.* Unpublished manuscript, Graduate School Education and Human Development, University of Rochester, 1979.

Mayer, R. E., & Bromage, B. K. Different recall protocols for technical texts due to advance organizers. *Journal of Educational Psychology,* 1980, *72,* 209-225.

Royer, J. M., & Cable, G. W. Illustrations, analogies, and facilitative transfer in prose learning. *Journal of Educational Psychology,* 1976, *68,* 205-209.

A "Bag of Tricks" for Teaching About Sampling Distributions

Dominic J. Zerbolio, Jr.
University of Missouri-St. Louis

This classroom technique uses imaginary marbles, chips, and bags to create distributions of sample means, differences between independent sample means, mean difference scores, and raw score populations. With this technique, students more easily grasp the distinctions between raw score populations and sampling distributions. With these distinctions established, the need for different measures of variability for each distribution becomes apparent. Then, solutions for the probabilities of specific observations for each sampling distribution are easily generalized from the raw score model. Once students learn to answer probability questions for each sampling distribution, generalizing to hypothesis testing procedures is facilitated. The technique requires only the instructor's flair for the dramatic and the students' imagination to make it work.

To solve statistical problems, one uses more logic than math skills. Unfortunately, many students believe statistics is mathematics, and their beliefs restrict how they approach learning statistics. Too often, this means students adopt a *plug and chug approach* (i. e., fill in the numbers and arrive at a correct numerical answer), which works and provides the correct answer, as long as someone tells them what numbers to plug into what formulas. With the plug and chug approach,

students typically fail to grasp the meaning and logic behind statistical procedures and, therefore, rapidly forget what they have been taught. If students could see and understand some of the key concepts and distributions, they might not so readily adopt and restrict themselves to plug and chug.

A key concept in understanding how statistics work is the notion of sampling distributions, an idea that seems to escape many students. Students grasp the idea of measures of central tendency, variability, and probability with raw score distributions, but often have difficulty generalizing these concepts to sampling distributions. Because understanding sampling distributions is central to understanding hypothesis testing, a little extra effort to help students conceptualize sampling distributions seems reasonable.

For several terms, I have been using a lecture procedure that helps students understand and differentiate sampling distributions. The procedure involves teaching students to imagine marbles and chips as various kinds of theoretical distributions and relies only on the instructor's flair for the dramatic. Once the various distributions are depicted as bags of marbles and/or bags of chips, students more easily grasp not only the plug and chug mechanics but also the underlying nature of statistical distributions. This grasp aids teaching both the logic and generality of statistical procedures.

The first step is teaching students to visualize raw score distributions. Referring to a commonly recognized distribution, like the Stanford-Binet IQ distribution, helps because most students know the average IQ is 100, and some even know its standard deviation is 16. Depicting the distribution involves describing each score in it as a "marble with a number on it." The population of raw scores becomes a "bag containing all the marbles." During the presentation, the imaginary bag is held high with one hand while the other hand points to the bag. Using marbles and bags to demonstrate the probabilities of scores in a distribution provides repetition and facilitates visualization.

Probabilities are taught by reaching into the bag (with appropriate hand and body gestures) and drawing a marble. With the imaginary marble held high in the free hand, students are asked, "What is the probability that this marble has a 120 or higher on it?" Calculating z scores for marbles (scores) and translating the z scores into probability statements quickly become routine. After a few draws, students readily accept the bag and marbles as a population of raw scores. Once the marbles and bag are established, the generation of sampling distributions becomes fairly easy.

The One-Sample Case Sampling Distribution

The one-sample case sampling distribution is the distribution of means of equal-sized samples. Two steps are required to establish this sampling distribution and distinguish it from the raw score population. In Step 1, students are asked to visualize a large number of drinking glasses. With appropriate motions, a glassful of marbles is scooped out of the raw score population bag. Each glassful of marbles represents a random sample of marbles and, by implication, is a random sample of raw scores. Additional glasses are filled with the same number of marbles as the first until the population of marbles (raw scores) is exhausted. This procedure creates a population of glassfuls, each containing the same number of marbles.

Step 2 is to create the distribution of sample means. A mean is calculated for each glass and written on a chip. All of the chips are gathered into a new or second bag. Once all the chips are put into the second bag, the new bag is held aloft and students are asked, "What's in this new bag?"

Most students recognize that the bag of chips is different from the original bag of marbles, which establishes a distinction between the raw score population and a distribution of sample means. This distinction can be enhanced by pouring all the marbles back into their own bag and holding the bag of chips in one hand and a bag of marbles in the other. I taught students earlier that they need two parameters to describe any normal distribution (a mean and a measure

of variability), so a classroom discussion of the mean and standard error necessary to describe the bag of chips can be initiated. As an option, the normal shape of the chip distribution can be defended by introducing the central limit theorem at this point.

With the mean and standard error of the bag of chips established, a single chip can be drawn from the bag of chips, and students are asked, "What is the probability that the value on the chip is 105 or higher?" Most students realize the solution requires the calculation of a z score. The contrast between the proper error terms (standard deviation for the bag of marbles and standard error for the bag of chips) becomes obvious. With the proper mean and standard error term for the bag of chips understood, students easily see how to calculate z scores for chips and, using a z table, translate their z values into probability statements. With the z-score procedure for a distribution of sample means in hand, the probability of a mean (or chip) being drawn from a distribution of means (or chips) with a specific population average can be established. At this point, it is a relatively short step to the one-sample hypothesis testing procedure.

The Difference Between Independent Sample Means Case

The distribution of the differences between independent sample means seems to cause problems because students initially confuse it with the difference between the means of two independent distributions of sample means. The distribution of differences between independent sample means has an infinite number of values whereas the difference between the means of two independent sampling distributions of means has only one value. Demonstrating the distribution of differences between independent sample means to students requires a two-step process.

Step 1 is to have students visualize two glasses, one red and one blue. Each glass is filled from a bag of marbles (or population), and then the two glasses are taped together. Additional pairs are filled and taped, with the same number of marbles as in the first pair, until the original marble population is exhausted. Once all possible pairs of red and blue glasses are filled, the second step can begin.

In Step 2, the means for each pair of red and blue glasses are calculated, and the difference between the means (red mean—blue mean) is determined. Each difference is written on a chip, and the chip is placed in another bag. When the population of paired red and blue glasses is exhausted, the bag of chips, which represents the distribution of differences between sample means, can be dealt with.

A chip is drawn from the bag and students are asked, "What's on the chip?" Of course, each chip represents a difference between independent sample means and has no relation to the original sample means. Emphasizing the chip contains no information about the original means can be accomplished by asking what original means led to the number on the chip. Most students see that chips have no information about the original sample means, but represent a different kind of population, a difference between populations.

Once the difference between distribution is established, students see that describing it requires a measure of central tendency and variability. An explanation of the mean and standard error of the distribution of differences between independent sample means ensues. With the mean and standard error in hand, one can draw a single chip from the "bag of differences between" and ask about the probability of its occurrence.

Note that I referred to the distribution as the "difference between" rather than the "difference between two sample means." My experience suggests that omitting the words *sample means* enhances students' grasp of the distinction between distributions of sample means and distributions of differences between sample means. Presented this way, more students see that the "difference between" is what is important and that the actual values of the sample means are incidental. As before, once the mean, standard error, and probability characteristics of the "difference between" distribution are established, generalizing to the hypothesis testing procedure is easier. Note that red and blue glasses can be used later to denote different treatment conditions.

The Difference Between Correlated Sample Means Case

Analyzing the distribution of the differences between correlated sample means requires all the work in analyzing the distribution of differences between independent samples means plus the computation of a correlation coefficient. To reduce the computational burden, most texts use an alternative, the *direct difference method.* The direct difference method's sampling distribution is the distribution of mean differences between paired scores, known as the *bar D*-distribution, which can be demonstrated with a three-step procedure.

Step 1 uses a chip to represent both the X and Y values of a pair of raw scores. With an X value on one side and a Y value on the other, the population of paired X,Y scores becomes immediately obvious to most students. With the bag (population) of chips established, the second step begins.

In Step 2, a chip, marked with its X and Y scores, is drawn. The difference between its X and Y scores is written on a marble. This procedure is repeated for all chips, and all the marbles are put in another bag. Then, the bag of marbles, which is the difference score distribution, can be held aloft and distinguished from the original bag of chips.

Step 3 is filling glasses with marbles. As in the one-sample case, each glass has the same number of marbles. A mean is calculated for the marbles in each glass, each mean is written on a chip, and the chips placed in another bag. However, this second bag of chips is different from the first because only one value, the mean of a sample of difference scores (or bar D), appears on each chip. As before, students are asked how to describe the bag of mean difference scores. By this point, most students realize that they need a specific mean and standard error term to characterize the bar-D distribution and often ask for them before they are presented. Once the mean and standard error term for the bar-D distribution are specified, single chips can be drawn from the bag and questions about the probability of specific bar-D values asked. Students typically generalize the entire z-score procedure immediately. Once the mechanism for determining probabilities is established, it is a short step to the hypothesis testing procedure.

Some students see the similarity between the bar-D distribution and the one-sample mean distribution. When they do, it is easy to show that the only mechanical (plug and chug) difference between the two statistical procedures is using a difference score (D) in place of a raw score (X). Noting the similarity helps some students see the generality of the statistical procedure. For the remainder, it probably means one less formula to learn. If and when the similarity is shown, the instructor must be careful to maintain a clear distinction between what the D and X scores represent.

The value of these procedures depends on the way the instructor presents the bags of marbles and chips. If bags are presented with panache, students not only seem to grasp the distinctions between various distributions more quickly, but learn the nature of the underlying sampling distributions as well. Once sampling distributions are clearly differentiated from raw score distributions, the generality of the procedures for determining probabilities can be seen, and the entire hypothesis testing procedure is much easier to show. Further, by depicting sampling distributions, students begin to see the conceptual logic and generality of statistical procedures, rather than restricting themselves to learning a series of superstitiously performed plug and chug procedures. Student reaction to the technique is good. Many find the presentation amusing, which also serves to hold their attention. More important, more students have commented that they understand sampling distributions with the bag procedure than with any other lecture technique I have tried. This understanding is often seen in our Statistics Lab sections wherein students ask more questions about sampling distributions than about plug and chug mechanics. Even more reassuring, when the same students take my Research Methods course, many see the application of the statistics and sampling distributions to research data more readily than students taught with other procedures. I have even seen Research Methods students instructing their less knowledgeable classmates about statistical comparisons using the "bag" analogy.

As a closing remark, I would not recommend using real bags, marbles, or chips, because that necessarily implies a finite limit to theoretical populations. It is important for students to see populations and sampling distributions as logical or abstract entities. The procedure works well without real props.

An Empirical Investigation and a Classroom Demonstration of Reliability Concepts

Michael Moore
Technion, Israel Institute of Technology

Many of the concepts of classical reliability theory (e.g. Nunnally, 1978) are highly abstract notions, difficult both to teach and to learn in lower level measurement courses. The concepts of *true score, true variance, standard error of measurement* undoubtedly fit this description. The classroom experiment described below is an attempt to provide an instructive demonstration of such concepts. A further purpose of the experiment is to demonstrate to students the fallibility of a simple measurement procedure in a highly objective situation, thereby preparing them for the consideration of reliability problems in psychological and educational measurement.

Method. Sixty-five freshmen enrolled in an Introductory Statistics and Measurement course at the School of Education of the University of Haifa, Israel, participated in the experiment.

Fifty straight, vertical lines, ranging from 21 to 99 mm (M= 66.9; SD= 20.01), were randomly distributed on a 33 x 21 cm sheet. The 50 lines consisted of 25 different lengths, each length being represented by two lines. Lines of equal length did not appear adjacent. The lines were consecutively numbered from 1 to 50. On the right margin the numerals 1 through 50 appeared below one another with enough space left to fill in measured lengths. Instructions on the top of the sheet read: "Measure each line and record its length in the appropriate space on the right side of the page." This sheet was then reproduced. Lengths of the lines were remeasured on a typical reproduced copy.

Copies of the above described sheet were given to students as an obligatory take-home assignment. They were told to follow instructions and to return the assignment in one week. After the data had been received, they were analyzed and the results were presented to and discussed with the students.

Results. Most students recorded their responses with an accuracy of 0.1 cm. When greater accuracy was attempted, responses were rounded off to the nearest mm. Frequency distributions were then obtained for each line. Illustrative distributions and some descriptive statistics appear in Table 1.

For each line, three measures of central tendency were compared to its *true* length. Both the *mode* and the *median* (rounded off to an integer) were equal to the true value in 83% of the cases; they both overestimated the true value by one mm in the remaining 17%. The *arithmetic mean* (rounded off to an integer) was equal to the true length of the line in 53% of the cases; in the remaining 47% it overestimated the true length by 1 mm. The range of the standard deviations for each line was between 1.312 and 7.945, with a median value of 1.843.

In addition to the above analysis, reliability coefficients were computed as follows. Since each length appeared twice[1], *parallel-forms* reliability coefficients could be computed for each student participating in the experiment. These correlation coefficients ranged between 0.8587 and 0.9997, with a median value of 0.9982. To obtain *interjudge* reliability coefficients, the responses of pairs of students to each line had to be correlated. Only 30 randomly selected pairs of the $\binom{62}{2}$ = 2080 possible pairs were formed. These coefficients, each based on 50 pairs of observations, ranged between 0.8027 and 0.9994, with a median value of 0.9952.

The standard deviation obtained for each distribution may be treated as a *standard error of measurement* (or standard error of an obtained score). As indicated above, these SEs have a median value of 1.843. This actual computation of an SE enables us to compare it with its value as estimated from an independently obtained reliability coefficient; conversely,

Table 1. Distribution of Errors in Line Measurements

Line #	Error in mm Under 60//26//20//	6	5//	2	1	0	Over 1	2	3	4	5	6//10	11	12//15	True Length	Mean	Mode	Mdn	SD
1			1		4	37	19	3					1		96	96.2	96	96.2	2.9
47	1		1		7	42	10		1			1		2	96	95.6	96	96.1	7.9
2					5	38	16	1		2	1	1		1	93	93.7	93	93.2	2.2
16					2	18	30	8		3		3	1		93	94.3	94	93.9	1.9
3	2		1	2	1	36	22					1			39	38.5	39	39.2	4.8
38			1		3	33	24	1				1		2	39	39.8	39	39.4	2.4

// = gaps in continuity: no responses occurred in these intervals for lines shown in the table.

the reliability coefficient may also be estimated from the computed value of the standard error of measurement. Table 2 presents these comparisons.

Discussion. The relatively small and finite number of participants in this experiment is not sufficient for a rigorous test of classical reliability theory; nevertheless it is gratifying to see that measures of central tendency converge upon the true score even with N = 65. The distributions of observed scores are definitely skewed; this finding, however, is not due to the finite sample size but rather to an element of bias in the measurement procedure. (The measurement of length with rulers is subject to overestimation, owing to the wrong placement of the ruler.) In line with the goal of this study, namely the demonstration of measurement principles to students, it should be pointed out that this bias (i.e., a constant rather than random error) is equivalent in its operation to the *leniency error* (Guilford, 1954, p. 278).

Table 2. A Comparison of Calculated vs Estimated Values of Reliability Coefficients and Standard Errors of Measurement

Statistic	Lower limit	Median	Upper limit
Parallel forms:			
Calculated r_{tt}	.8587	.9982	.9997
Estimated SE_{meas}	7.5217	0.8489	0.3465
Interjudge:			
Calculated r_{tt}	.8027	.9952	.9994
Estimated SE_{meas}	8.8881	1.3863	0.4901
Estimated r_{tt}	.8424	.9917	.9958
Calculated SE_{meas}	7.945	1.843	1.312

The comparison of obtained statistics with their estimated value reveals a rather close correspondence at the lower limit of the reliability coefficients, with an increasing divergence occurring toward their upper limit[2] (Both reliabilities and standard errors are *under*estimated.) The reason for the lack of numerical equivalence is obvious: Whereas calculated SE_{meas} values are associated with each *line,* the calculated reliability coefficients "belong"' to each *student,* or each *pair of students.*

In addition to providing some empirical evidence that demonstrates the meaning of the standard error of measurement, this experiment also illustrates the problem of reliability. In spite of median reliability coefficients surpassing 0.99, individual obtained scores sometimes seriously deviate from true scores (see Table 1). The range of scores in this study has on purpose been selected to resemble scholastic grades. It is instructive to contemplate that even if a classroom examination could be graded as objectively as the length of a line can be measured, the 95% confidence range around a true score would be 1.96 x 1.84 = ± 3.61 points.

Since this experiment was but one of several classroom demonstrations in a regularly scheduled undergraduate course in statistics and measurement, it was not formally evaluated as a separate project. The instructor's subjective impressions, however, were extremely favorable: The demonstration appeared to have both interest and surprise value. Students were intrigued by the task and amazed at the dispersion of obtained values. Thanks to its applied and immediate character, this method of teaching reliability concepts appeared to the instructor to be both more efficient and more through than conventional techniques.

References

Guilford, J. P. *Psychometric methods.* New York: McGraw-Hill, 1954.

Lord, F. M. Tests of the same length do have the same standard error of measurement. *Educational and Psychological Measurement,* 1959, *19,* 233-239.

McMorris, R. F. Evidence on the quality of several approximations for commonly used measurement statistics. *Journal of Educational Measurement,* 1972, *9,* 113-122.

Nunnally, J. C. *Psychometric theory* (2nd ed.). New York: McGraw Hill, 1978.

Notes

1. Because of difficulties in reproduction, four lines had slightly doubtful lengths and had to be omitted from this analysis. Therefore, here n = 21, rather than 50/2 or 25.

2. For the sake of comparison, the standard error of measurement approximation by Lord (1959; see also McMorris, 1972) would result in 3/7(50) = 3.03.

An Intuitive Approach to Teaching Analysis of Variance

David E. Johnson
John Brown University

A significant number of students in introductory statistics courses may function at Piaget's concrete operational level of thought. These students may find it difficult to understand the complex correlations and interactions between variables that typify many statistical procedures. A technique for introducing analysis of variance (ANOVA) in a concrete fashion is presented. This technique leads students to an intuitive understanding of the concepts of between- and within-groups variance and their relationship to each other.

Instructors of introductory statistics know that students approach their course with considerable anxiety (Dillon, 1982; Hastings, 1982). Many students complain about the mathematical nature of the course and their inadequate preparation for it.

Evidence also suggests that a significant number of students in the introductory statistics course may operate at a concrete-operational level of thought, as defined by Piaget (1952). Some researchers have estimated that up to 50% of the adult population functions at this level (Kuhn, Langer, Kohlberg, & Haan, 1917; McKinnon & Renner, 1971). Others have demonstrated that it is common for college students to operate at a concrete level or to be transitional between concrete and formal levels of cognitive development. (Allen, Walker, Schroeder, &Johnson, 1987). According to Piaget, persons at the formal-operational level are capable of abstract thought and reasoning. They can understand hypothetical situations, combine information from several sources, and comprehend correlations and interactions between variables. These capabilities are necessary for understanding the problems students encounter in their first statistics course.

Students who function at a concrete-operational level are unprepared to comprehend the fundamental operations required for complete understanding of basic statistical concepts. The anxiety that students experience may aggravate this situation by causing them to narrow their attention to fewer details of these statistical concepts (Easterbrook, 1959). Instructors could use an effective, concrete demonstration to communicate some of these complex statistical concepts to their students.

The ANOVA appears to be one of those procedures that requires a concrete presentation. A technique I use for teaching ANOVA involves manipulating between- and within-groups variance and observing the resulting changes in the ANOVA summary table. A description of that technique follows.

Method

My introduction to ANOVA is fairly standard: Students are informed of the reasons for using ANOVA (as compared to the more familiar *t* test for independent groups), the concepts of between- and within-groups variance are introduced, the computational techniques for obtaining the *F* ratio for a one-way ANOVA are explained, and the conceptual relationship of between- and within-groups variance is described.

At that point, I describe a hypothetical experiment in which three independent groups of subjects (labeled A1, A2, and A3, with each group containing five subjects) are exposed to one of three levels of an independent variable. The range of possible responses on the dependent variable is 0 through 4. Students are then given a data set that contains scores for the 15 subjects.

In the initial data set, the values are identical (i.e., each subject recorded a value of 1). The students recognize that this outcome is highly unlikely. They also realize that there is no variability in the data. One of two methods can then be used to continue the presentation. In the first approach, a copy of the data and the outline of an ANOVA summary table are presented on a screen using an overhead projector. The computations are then completed for the students. Another approach involves projecting the data and the completed summary table. This approach takes less time but does not expose students to the actual computational procedures. Regardless of the method used, students observe that the absence of between- and within-groups variability leads to mean squares of 0 in the summary table.

Students are then given a second data set which is identical to the first with one notable exception: Between-groups variance is introduced by increasing all five values in Group A3 to 3. The between-groups variance now indicates the possible effect of the independent variable manipulation. It is obvious to the students that Group A3 is different from the other two groups (mean square A = 6.65); however, there is no within-groups variability (mean square S/A = 0).

Students are given a third data set that incorporates within-groups variance into Group A1 (see Table 1). This data set contains the same amount of between-groups variance as the previous one (i.e., the means are unchanged). Students are encouraged to compare the results of the second and third data sets and to observe the absence of change in the between-subjects values represented by the mean square of 6.65 for both data sets. They are encouraged to notice how the introduction of dissimilar scores into Group A1 increased the value of the mean square for within-groups variance. The students are asked to note the value of the F ratio, which is 39.12 in this case.

Subsequently, students are given a fourth data set,

Table 1. Data Set Number 2

	Group		
	A1	A2	A3
	0	1	3
	1	1	3
	1	1	3
	1	1	3
	2	1	3
Group Mean	1	1	3

Summary of ANOVA				
Source	Sum of Squares	df	Mean Square	F
A	13.3	2	6.65	39.12
S/A	2.0	12	.17	

which differs from the previous one in only one way: Additional within-groups variance has been added by changing the values in Group A2 to match those in Group A1. The students' attention is directed to the fact that the means for each group are identical to those in the previous data set. The computed values reveal that, compared to the previous data set, the between-groups mean square remains unchanged, but the within-groups mean square is larger. As a result, the F ratio is smaller.

At this point, students begin to understand the relationship of between- and within-groups variance and how this relationship affects the magnitude of the F ratio. To reinforce this emerging understanding, a final data set is presented. This data set continues the trend of the previous two data sets in which additional within-groups variance is introduced while the group means remain unchanged. One value in Group A3 is reduced by 1 and another value is increased by 1, thereby maintaining a mean of 3 for that group. Again, students are told to note the unchanged between-groups mean square and the increased within-groups mean square, as compared to the previous data set. As a result, the F ratio is smaller.

The final step in the presentation depends on the class in which it is used. In a statistics class where limited information about research design is presented, I briefly review the procedure and determine the level of students' understanding. Discussion of the functional relationship between the F and t statistics (e.g., $F = t^2$) is useful.

In a research methods course, however, I spend additional time discussing topics that directly relate to the nature of ANOVA and its relationship to practical aspects of experimental procedure and design. The significance of previously discussed issues, such as the importance of controlling sources of variance and developing strong independent variable manipulations, is reinforced.

Results and Discussion

Students in a research design course (N = 10) were asked to rate the usefulness of this technique in facilitating their understanding of ANOVA. The ratings were made on a 7 point scale ranging from *not at all* (1) to *considerable* (7). Students were also asked to indicate if they would recommend using this technique in future classes. The mean rating for the usefulness of the technique was positive, but not overwhelmingly so *(M = 4.9, SD* = 1.85). When asked whether the technique should be used in future classes, however, 9 out of 10 students answered yes. Because of the variability in their usefulness ratings, students were asked to comment on the procedure. Several students indicated that they believed the procedure is very useful, but that they had doubts as to whether their understanding of ANOVA would ever be "considerable." Apparently, some of the students confused the assessment of usefulness of the procedure with an estimation of their eventual understanding of ANOVA.

I believe that this technique is useful, especially for students who operate at a preformal level of thought.

Systematic manipulation of a small range of numerical values seems to alleviate the math anxiety that some students experience. The technique is particularly helpful for students who are intimidated by the dynamic relationship of between- and within-groups variance in determining the F ratio.

References

Allen, J. L, Walker, L. D., Schroeder, D. A., & Johnson, D. E. (1987). Attributions and attribution-behavior relations The effect of level of cognitive development. *Journal of Personality and Social Psychology, 52,* 1099-1109.

Dillon, K M. (1982). Statisticophobia. *Teaching of Psychology, 9,* 117.

Easterbrook, J . A. (1959). The effect of emotion on cue utilization and the organization of behavior. *Psychological Review, 66,* 183-201.

Hastings, M. W. (1982). Statistics: Challenge for students and the professor. *Teaching of Psychology, 9,* 221-222.

Kuhn, D., Langer, J., Kohlberg, L., & Haan, N. F. (1977). The development of formal operations in logical and moral judgment. *Genetic Psychology Monograph, 95,* 97-288.

McKinnon, J. W., & Renner, J. W. (1971). Are colleges concerned with intellectual development? *American Journal of Personality, 39,* 1047-1052.

Piaget, J. (1952). *The origins of intelligence in children.* New York: Harcourt, Brace. (Original work published 1936)

Note

I thank Joseph Palladino and four anonymous reviewers for their helpful comments on an earlier draft of this article.

A New Method for Teaching Multiple Regression to Behavioral Science Students

Richard H. Williams
University of Miami

Describing a computing algorithm which promotes intuitive understanding rather than memorization for students in statistics.

The required course in statistical inference is viewed with trepidation by many graduate students in the behavioral sciences. Yet these students realize that an adequate knowledge of statistical methodology is necessary to make intelligible their reading of published research in psychology. One factor which may contribute to the great amount of student anxiety often associated with quantitive psychology courses is to be found in the course textbooks. Some of the widely adopted statistical textbooks designed for graduate students in the behavioral sciences employ pedagogical devices which may lead the student to resort to rote memorization rather than to intuitive understanding.

As an example of this, consider the problem of teaching students to compute regression weights in a multiple regression scheme. In many textbooks treating this topic a computing algorithm is given without any mention of the mathematical rationale underlying the algorithm. As a case in point, Baggaley (1964) applies Aitken's pivotal condensation method to some "real" scholastic prediction data which appear in a paper authored by Franz, Davis, and Garcia (1958). A second example is provided by McNemar (1969), who applies the Doolittle method to data from the Minnesota study of mechanical ability (Patterson, 1930). Further examples could be cited. Although these authors do not present the: rationale for the computing algorithms introduced, they do include references which make it possible for the reader to locate the original publications which contain the rationale. Nevertheless, it is unlikely that a student will bother to seek out such sources. This makes it likely that the learning of these statistical techniques by graduate students may depend on mechanisms similar to those underlying the rote memorization of nonsense syllables. This kind of learning is not well retained and will not facilitate transfer.

In Walker and Lev's *Statistical Inference* (1953) the problem of determining the regression weights is approached in a dual manner.

> Two explanations will now be offered. Explanation A should be helpful for persons who have studied matrix algebra and incomprehensible to others. The latter need not look at it but may go on at once to explanation B. Persons who can read explanation A will not need explanation B. Those who cannot read explanation A will probably have to take the routine more or less on faith and need not strain to understand the underlying rationale (p. 332).

One problem here is that Walker and Let's explanation A assumes a knowledge of matrix algebra but their text contains no instruction on matrix algebra. Furthermore, students who have studied matrix algebra may possess the mathematical maturity needed to profit from the general linear hypothesis approach to statistical inference (Bock, 1975; Morrison, 1967).

Hays (1973) chooses to exclude any presentation of a general algorithm for computing multiple regression weights, contending that "all signs point to such problems being handled by electronic computers in the future" (p. 706.). His book, however, contains no information about electronic computers in general or about suitable canned statistical computer programs in particular, and thus the student may feel a lack of closure.

An Alternative Procedure for Computing Multiple Regression Weights. This section of the paper is devoted to presenting a brief sketch of an alternative computing algorithm, together with a rationale for the algorithm which presupposes knowledge of only a modicum of matrix algebra. In the Department of Educational Psychology at the University of Miami, CAI materials written in the conversational language BASIC (Kemeny & Kurtz, 1971) are used to teach our students the necessary matrix algebra. Students sit at teletypes, call the desired computer programs, and interact with these programs. The four matrix lessons currently available on the UNIVAC 1106 at the University of Miami are: (1) Matrix Algebra: Definitions and Operations, (2) Determinants, (3) Simultaneous Linear Equations, and (4) Vectors.[1] Although the CAI matrix lessons are completed by the students without instructor intervention, this experience is immediately followed up by a question and answer session.

When standard score regression equations are to be solved, the system of equations, which contains as many unknowns as there are equations in the system, can be written as follows:

$$r_{11}\beta_1 + r_{12}\beta_2 + \ldots + r_{1n}\beta_n = r_{1c}$$
$$r_{21}\beta_1 + r_{22}\beta_2 + \ldots + r_{2n}\beta_n = r_{2c}$$
$$\vdots$$
$$r_{n1}\beta_1 + r_{n2}\beta_2 + \ldots + r_{nn}\beta_n = r_{nc}$$

The r's in these equations are ordinary zero order Pearson product moment correlation coefficients and the B's are standardized multiple regression coefficients. The correlation coefficients to the right of the equals signs can be regarded as validity coefficients and those to the left are the intercorrelations among the predictors. The above system can also be expressed as a matrix equation

$$AX = B, \tag{1}$$

where

$$A = \begin{bmatrix} r_{11} & r_{12} \cdots r_{1n} \\ r_{21} & r_{22} \cdots r_{2n} \\ \cdot & \cdot \\ \cdot & \cdot \\ \cdot & \cdot \\ r_{n1} & r_{n2} \quad r_{nn} \end{bmatrix}, X = \begin{bmatrix} \beta_1 \\ \beta_2 \\ \cdot \\ \cdot \\ \cdot \\ \beta_n \end{bmatrix}, \text{ and } B = \begin{bmatrix} r_{1c} \\ r_{2c} \\ \cdot \\ \cdot \\ \cdot \\ r_{nc} \end{bmatrix}$$

Since the object of the algorithm is to solve for the unknown beta weights, it is necessary to solve equation (1) for the vector X. Multiplying through equation (1) (on the left) by the inverse of the coefficient matrix A gives

$$X = A^{-1}B. \tag{2}$$

This suggests that if a method is provided for finding the inverse of A, then the original set of equations can be solved. The method of inverting a square matrix to be presented here depends on the celebrated Cayley-Hamilton theorem (Birkhoff & MacLane, 1965), which simply states that: Every *square matrix satisfies its characteristic equation.*

Every square matrix A satisfies an equation of the form

$$A^n + a_{n-1}A^{n-1} + \ldots + a_0 I = 0. \tag{3}$$

where n is the size of the matrix A, I is the unit matrix and 0 is the zero matrix. The inverse of A exists if and only if $a_0 \neq 0$. In fact if $a_0 \neq 0$, then,

$$A^{-1} = \frac{1}{a_0}(A^{n-1} + a_{n-1}A^{n-2} + \ldots + a_1 I). \tag{4}$$

The results presented thus far are now summarized. If the equation satisfied by the matrix A can be constructed, then A^{-1} can be determined, and knowledge of the inverse of A enables one to solve the system of linear equations for the desired beta weights.

Let λ be a real number and let A denote a square matrix. if $|A - \lambda I| = 0$, λ is said to be a *characteristic value* or *eigenvalue* of A. In this context the symbol "| |" denotes the determinant of a matrix. The equation $|A - \lambda I| = 0$, is called the *characteristic equation* of the matrix A. Solving this equation for λ will yield all of the eigenvalues of A. Although it is not necessary to compute these values to solve the problem at hand, the computation of the eigenvalues of a matrix is important to many kinds of problems. The basic problem in factor analysis, for example, is the determination of the eigenvalues of a matrix containing the intercorrelations among scores on psychological tests. At this point the Cayley–Hamilton theorem is employed to get from the characteristic equation to equation (3).

A summary[2] of the results which have been presented thus far reveals the following method for finding the multiple regression coefficients:

(1) Given a system of regression equations, first determine the coefficient matrix A.
(2) Next find the characteristic equation of A, $F(\lambda) = |A - \lambda I| = 0$.
(3) Now replace λ by A to obtain $F(A) = 0$
(4) Use the equation $F(A) = 0$ to get an expression for A^{-1}.
(5) Compute A^{-1} by making the appropriate substitutions.
(6) Use A^{-1} to solve equation (1) for X.

The determined beta weights can then be used to compute the multiple correlation coefficient, the multiple standard error of estimate, and other related statistical quantities. A standard score prediction scheme can also be constructed. By using the means and the standard deviations of the variables in the configuration, together with the known relations among raw score regression weights and the corresponding standard score weights, a raw score prediction equation can be generated.

Concluding Comments. After students have developed some intuitive understanding of the rationale underlying the computational algorithm, they can be taught to call available computer programs. At the University of Miami our students are first required to complete a three predictor regression problem using the method given in this paper or some alternative method which they understand. Since the calculations are to be done by hand or with the aid of a desk calculator, the number of data points is typically small (say $n = 20$). Then the students learn to call the stepwise multiple regression program (BMD02R) of the Biomedical Computer Programs of UCLA (Dixon, 1 973) and apply it to a set of "real" data provided by the in-structor or generated by the students. Here any number of predictors can be included in the configuration. It is this writer's contention that there is little point in teaching students to call canned computer programs until the underlying mathematical models and the algorithms developed within the mathematical models are understood by the students.

It would appear that a method such as the one outlined above would lead to greater retention and to greater transfer of training than the "cookbook" procedures given in many of the standard texts. A student exposed to this method, for example, should be more ready to assimilate material in subsequent quantitative psychology courses such as test score theory and multivariate statistical analysis.

References

Baggaley, A. R. *Intermediate correlational methods*. New York: Wiley, 1964.

Birkhoff, G., & MacLane, S. *A survey of modern algebra* (3rd ed.). New York: Macmillan, 1965.

Bock, R. D. *Multivariate statistical methods in behavioral research*. New York: McGraw-Hill, 1975.

Dixon, W. J. (ed.). *BMD: Biomedical computer programs* (3rd ed.). Berkeley, California: University of California Press, 1973.

Franz, G., Davis, J. A., & Garcia, D. Prediction of grades from pre-admissions indices in Georgia tax supported colleges. *Educational and Psychological Measurement*, 1958, *18*, 841 -844

Hays, W. L. *Statistics for the social sciences* (2nd ed.). New York: Holt, Rinehart, & Winston, 1973.

Kemeny, J. G., & Kurtz, T. E. *Basic programming* (2nd ed.). New York: Wiley, 1971.

McNemar, Q. *Psychological statistics* (4th ed.). New York: Wiley 1969.

Morrison D. F. *Multivariate statistical methods*. New York: McGraw-Hill, 1967.

Paterson, D. G., et al. *Minnesota mechanical ability tests*. Minneapolis: University of Minnesota Press, 1930.

Walker, H. M., & Lev, J. *Statistical inference*. New York: Holt, Rinehart, & Winston, 1953.

Notes

1. These programs were written by Dr. Patricia Gaynor, Computing Center, Appalachian State University, Boone, North Carolina 28608.
2. A copy of the author's class handout containing the application of this method to the scholastic prediction data presented in the paper by Franz, Davis, and Garcia (1958) can be obtained by writing to: Miss Dot Lamp'l, Department of Educational Psychology; School of Education, University of Miami, Coral Gables, Florida 33124.

A Demonstration of Measurement Error and Reliability

Jane L. Buck
Delaware State College

The related concepts of reliability and measurement error are often difficult for students to understand. This article describes a simple and inexpensive demonstration of several underlying notions necessary to understanding these concepts: chance score, true score, error variance, true score variance, and their relation to each other and to reliability.

Two related concepts that often cause difficulty for students in tests and measurement courses are the standard error of measurement and reliability. Fundamental to an understanding of both concepts is the definition of an *individual obtained score* as the sum of an error component and a true score. It follows from this definition that the variance of a test is equal to the sum of true score variance and error variance (Sax, 1980).

If a test is perfectly reliable, its error variance is zero. Hence, the variance of the test is equal to true score variance, and the correlation between two administrations of the test is 1.00. If a test is totally unreliable, the variance of the test equals the error variance. In this case, the expected value of the correlation between two administrations of the test is zero, because the correlation is between error scores, which are assumed to be randomly distributed (Sax, 1980).

Even if students have a fairly good working knowledge of measures of central tendency, variability, and correlation, some concepts are not always intuitively obvious. Students may not understand why the expected mean chance score for a given test is equal to the probability of correctly guessing the answer to an item multiplied by the number of items, with a standard deviation equal to the standard error of measurement (Sax, 1980). Equally difficult are the notions of error scores, true scores, and obtained scores as components of reliability.

I developed a simple, inexpensive, and easily administered device that demonstrates these concepts and their interrelations as well as factors that tend to lower reliability. I have used both test-retest and equivalent forms reliability on different occasions. This article describes a demonstration using equivalent forms as the model.

Method

Materials

The only materials required are five-position, machine-scorable answer sheets and pencils. Prepare two answer sheets as keys for the two forms of the test by randomly choosing one of the answer positions as the correct answer for each item.

Procedure

Demonstration of position preference set. Begin the exercise with a demonstration of position preference set. Once students are aware of the nature of randomness, they consciously attempt to avoid displaying their sets. However, if you have not discussed the notion of randomness, instructions to answer each question randomly should produce results that will demonstrate position preference set.
Distribute answer sheets to students, instructing them to choose, at random, one of five options for each of 100 questions. After they fill out their answer sheets, have students count the number of times they chose each option. Point out that if they chose certain options more often than the theoretically expected 20% of the time, they exhibited a position preference set.

Demonstration of chance score. Distribute new answer sheets to students. In small classes, distribute more than one answer sheet to each student in order to obtain a total of approximately 100 answer sheets. Tell students to randomize their answers on this trial by means of a table of random numbers or by blindly drawing slips of paper marked with option positions, replacing the slips after each draw.
Score the test twice using the prepared keys to provide scores on the two forms of the test. Calculate the means, standard deviations, and variances of the test scores. It is important to emphasize to students several logical points that are essential to an understanding of the demonstration. An obtained test score has two components: true score and error. A *true score* is a measure of actual knowledge; *error* repre-

sents chance factors (Sax, 1980). In this case, an individual's true score is zero, because a correct answer is based entirely on chance, not knowledge. Thus, any obtained score greater than zero is attributable to chance or error (plus a true score of zero). This point is crucial to understanding the rest of the demonstration. Students usually see quite readily that answering test questions randomly produces scores that are composed entirely of error and that their true scores are zero.

Explain hat on any given item the probability of obtaining a correct answer by chance alone is .2. Thus, the expected value of an individual chance score is 20 (100 Items x .2 per Item). However, deviations from the expected value because of sampling error are not unusual.

The relation between chance scores and the standard error of measurement. Because each true score is zero on both forms of the test, the means, variances, and standard deviations of the obtained chance scores are actually measures of error. The means for both forms should be very close to the expected value of 20, with minor deviations attributable to sampling error. The variance of the obtained, chance scores is the error variance; the standard deviation is the standard error of measurement.

Demonstration of the relation between reliability and the standard error of measurement. Calculate the index of reliability (i.e., the correlation between obtained and true scores for each form of the test). The value will be zero for both forms of the test, because the true score for each individual is zero. The reliability coefficient or the square of the index of reliability will, of course, also be zero (Hopkins, Stanley, & Hopkins, 1990). This is true despite the fact that calculating the

reliability coefficient from the obtained chance scores might yield a value greater than zero because of sampling error. Keep in mind that one advantage of this demonstration is that, unlike a real-life situation, the true scores are known, allowing the direct calculation of the population correlation coefficient (the index of reliability), a value that by definition is zero when all true scores are zero.

In summary, in the extreme case of zero reliability, this demonstration illustrates that the standard error of measurement is equal to the standard deviation of obtained chance scores. Hence, the reliability coefficient and the index of reliability are zero.

I have successfully used this demonstration for several years. Students enjoy generating the data and report that doing so clarifies difficult concepts and facilitates their integration.

References

Hopkins, K. D., Stanley, J. C., & Hopkins, B. R. (1990). *Educational and psychological measurement and evaluation* (7th ed.) . Englewood Cliffs, NJ: Prentice Hall.

Sax, G. (1980). *Principles of educational and psychological measurement and evaluation.* Belmont, CA: Wadsworth.

Note

I thank Ludy T. Benjamin, Jr., Charles L. Brewer, and three anonymous reviewers for their comments on an earlier draft of this article.

The χ^2 Statistic and Weber's Law

Gordon A. Allen
Miami University

When introducing my students, primarily psychology majors, to the Pearson χ^2 statistic for testing goodness-of-fit, I point out the similarity of this statistic to Weber's Law, a concept that many remember from their introductory psychology course. This discussion serves to illustrate the notion that many ideas, particu-

larly mathematical ideas, appear in seemingly unrelated areas. In addition, the discussion serves as the basis for emphasizing several features of the χ^2 statistic.

Weber's Law, first proposed by the physiologist E. H. Weber but named in honor of him by Gustav Fechner in 1860, was the foundation of Fechner's approach to psychophysical scaling. Fechner is considered to be the founder of psychophysics, that branch of psychology concerned with relating the magnitude of a sensory experience to the intensity of the physical stimulus. A central concept in classical psychophysics is the idea of a threshold, a concept Fechner borrowed from physiology. There are two types of thresholds—absolute and difference. Although Weber's Law is not concerned with the absolute threshold, it serves as a useful starting point.

The absolute threshold of a particular sense is the minimum amount of stimulus energy needed to elicit a sensation. For example, even though the diaphragm of a loudspeaker is vibrating, the amplitude may be so low that an observer does not report hearing a tone. As the amplitude of the vibration increases, a point is reached when the observer does report hearing the tone; this point is the absolute threshold for loudness. Unfortunately, the value of the absolute threshold is not a constant; it fluctuates from moment to moment so that the threshold must be defined statistically. The usual definition is that stimulus value that gives rise to a sensation fifty percent of the time, although a sample mean is frequently used to estimate the value. One technique for determining the absolute threshold is called the Method of Adjustment. In this technique the observer is given control of the intensity of the stimulus, e.g., a variable resistor that controls the loudness of a tone. The observer is instructed to adjust the control so that the tone is just audible. The observer repeats this procedure ten times, five times starting at an intensity well above threshold and five times at an intensity well below threshold. The absolute threshold is the mean of the ten values. Most people are familiar with the audiogram, the figure used to summarize the results of a hearing test. It is nothing other than a plot of the absolute threshold for each of many different frequencies of tones. Almost any experimental psychology text, such as Matlin (1979), may be consulted for further information about the various psychophysical techniques used to estimate thresholds.

Weber's Law is concerned with the difference threshold, which is defined to be the minimum increase in stimulus energy needed to elicit the sensation of a different stimulus; this value is frequently called the just noticeable difference or jnd. For example, suppose our observer is holding a 60 gm weight in one hand, a weight that is well above the absolute threshold. How much heavier does another weight have to be before the observer notices a difference between the two? If it is the case that our observer reports no difference between the standard and 61 gm weight but identifies a 62gm weight as being heavier, then the difference threshold is 2gm. As is the case of the absolute threshold, the difference threshold is usually defined statistically and is most accurately estimated using one of the psychophysical methods (see Matlin, 1979).

Weber's Law states that the ratio of the difference threshold to the value of the standard stimulus is a constant, that is:

$$\frac{\Delta I}{I} = k \qquad (1)$$

where ΔI is the difference between the test and the standard stimulus, I is the value of the standard stimulus, and k is the value of the constant. In our example, the constant would be estimated to be equal to 1/30. When a 120gm weight serves as a standard, Weber's Law predicts that our observer would not be able to detect the difference between it and a 122gm weight, a 2gm difference that was detectable before. The weight would have to be 124gm before the difference could be detected. It is not the absolute but the relative difference that is important for sensation. An everyday example of this phenomenon is that at night a car's headlights illuminate the road for yards; however, during the day headlights are frequently left on since the driver cannot detect the light added to the sunlight. Another example is that although a nickel, a quarter and a Susan B. Anthony dollar differ in diameter by almost the same amount, the coins are not equally distinguishable. The nickel and the quarter are easily discriminated, but the quarter and the dollar are not, leading to the controversy surrounding the new coin.

Instead of detecting differences in magnitude among stimuli, investigators using the Pearson χ^2 statistic are attempting to detect a difference between a set of observed event frequencies and a hypothesized model for those events. For each category of event, there is an expected frequency of occurrence and an observed frequency of occurrence, f_e and f_o respectively. The Pearson statistic is given by

$$\chi^2 = \sum \frac{(f_o - f_e)^2}{f_e} \qquad (2)$$

where the sum is taken over the set of events. The statistic becomes large, providing evidence for the rejection of the null hypothesis, as the discrepancy between observed and expected frequencies grows large. However, the statistic is not based solely upon the absolute difference (or difference squared), but rather each difference is weighted by the magnitude of the difference relative to the expected frequency. The expected frequency serves the function of a standard stimulus. Thus Weber's Law and the Pearson statistic are similar in that a difference is more salient when the standard is small.

Another similarity between Weber's Law and the χ^2 statistic is that both are approximations of underlying relationships so that care must be exercised when using them. In the case of Weber's Law, the law seems to hold for stimuli in the middle range of values but not for extreme values. In addition, the rule does not hold for all stimulus dimensions, e.g., pain, so that the law cannot be applied without thought. In the case of the χ^2 statistic, the statistic is an approximation to the multinomial distribution that would be applicable in the situation. It is a satisfactory approximation as long as the sample size is reasonably large, where the specification of large is provided in terms of the expected frequencies. In addition, all of the assumptions of the multinomial distribution must be met, namely having mutually exclusive categories and random independent sampling.

Weber's Law and the Pearson statistic do share some features, but it is possible to place too much emphasis on the similarities. The two equations are not identical in form, so there exists some possibility that students will confuse the two, although I have found that knowing one equation helps one to memorize the other. The two relations arise from quite different theoretical backgrounds. Weber's Law is a rule that was developed to describe an empirical relationship, whereas the Pearson statistic is an approximation to a likelihood ratio test. Given these disclaimers, however, a brief discussion of the similarities does serve a useful purpose. Students too often compartmentalize their knowledge so that information learned in a psychology course is viewed as irrelevant to statistics and vice versa. This discussion serves to break down these artificial barriers in addition to adding to the process of understanding the chi-square statistic.

Reference

Matlin, M. W. *Human experimental psychology.* Monterey, CA: Brooks/Cole, 1979.

5. COMBINING STATISTICS AND RESEARCH METHODS

How Often Are Our Statistics Wrong? A Statistics Class Exercise

Joseph S. Rossi
University of Rhode Island

Using this exercise, students recompute the values of statistical tests published in journal articles, and the recomputed values are compared to the published results. My experience with one undergraduate and one graduate class suggests that errors in statistical results published in professional journals may be more common than is generally believed. Recalculations indicated that approximately 13% of the results reported as statistically significant were not. Some possible reasons for the discrepancies between published and recomputed values are discussed, as are students' reactions to the exercise.

Several years ago, Rosenthal (1978) published an article with the provocative title, "How Often are Our Numbers Wrong?" The point of his study was to determine the frequency of data recording errors, and the extent to which such errors were likely to be biased in favor of the experimenter's hypothesis. His results were encouraging, because only about 1% of all observations were found to be erroneous. However, about two thirds of the errors were biased in favor of the experimenter's hypothesis. In this article, I describe an out-of-class exercise, similar to one first outlined by Barnwell (1984), for a course in statistics or research methodology that examines a question similar to that posed by Rosenthal: How often are our statistical test results wrong?

Exercise

Students are asked to find examples in the journal literature of one or two statistical tests that have been covered in class. Chi-square, *t* tests, and one-way ANOVA are the most frequently assigned tests, because they are among the most commonly used statistical techniques, and more important, they can be recomputed from summary statistics. The number of tests assigned to each student depends on a variety of factors, such as the level of instruction (graduate or undergraduate) and which techniques have been discussed in class. For undergraduate classes, students are usually permitted to choose either chi-square or *t* tests. For graduate classes, I usually assign both *t* and *F* tests to each student.

Each journal article containing the appropriate statistical test must be checked to verify that sufficient information is reported to enable the student to recompute its value. Raw data are rarely reported, but usually there are sufficient summary data to permit recalculation. For example, recomputation of a chi-square test requires cell frequencies. Independent groups *t* tests and ANOVA require sample sizes, means, and standard deviations for all groups. Correlation coefficients and repeated measures analyses (both *t* and *F)* cannot be included in this exercise, because they cannot be recomputed from summary statistics.

Formulas to recompute chi-square and *t* values from summary data are available in most introductory statistics texts. Formulas for computing *F* ratios from summary statistics are not widely known and must be presented to the class. Gordon (1973) and Rossi (in press) have provided such formulas for one-way ANOVA, and Huck and Malgady (1978) for two-way ANOVA. Not all journal articles provide sufficient summary data to recompute statistical tests. Students were asked to record the number of articles searched that had to be rejected for incomplete reporting of data.

Study 1

For the first study, an undergraduate class was assigned the task of locating and recomputing either a *t* test or a chi-square test. Each student recorded the number of journal articles rejected because of insufficient summary data. When a suitable journal article was located, the student recomputed the value of the statistical test. Degrees of freedom *(df)* were also computed and compared to the author's report.

Results

The number of articles searched and rejected by each student ranged from 1 to 50 (median = 8). Sufficient summary data appeared to be more frequently available for chisquare tests (median rejections = 4.5) than for *t* tests (median rejections = 10). This difference was significant by the Wilcoxon rank-sum test, p < .05.

Several students inadvertently selected the same journal articles for analysis. When duplicates were omitted, the number of t tests selected for recomputation was 12; the number of chi-square tests was 9. (One student selected and recomputed results based on a one-way ANOVA. This test will be included among the t-test results.) Discrepancies between the value of the test statistic reported by the author and the value recomputed by the student were apparent for 3 of the t tests (25%) and 2 of the chi-square tests (22.2%). In all, 5 of 21 test values (23.8%) appeared to be inaccurate. No specific criterion (e.g., percentage of discrepancy) was given to students to aid their classification of a result as "in error" or "not in error." However, I checked all student computations, and none of the five discrepancies could be attributed to only minor deviations, which are inevitable due to the rounding of values in reported summary statistics.

Table 1 shows the reported and recomputed values, as well as the percentage of discrepancy[1], for each of the five statistical tests. The average discrepancy was 23.5% (median = 23.3%). Percentage of discrepancy was also determined for all remaining statistical tests reported in the five journal articles containing the inaccurate results. Average discrepancy for these "nondiscrepant" results was 1.5% (median = 1.3%). Thus, all five discrepancies appeared substantial. In addition, there was one incorrectly reported df for a t test (reported df = 10; recomputed df = 5).

Study 2

My original purpose in developing this exercise was to point out to students that the statistical tests taught in class really are used by professional scientists. In addition, I wanted to demonstrate that, using relatively simple computations, the students would be able to achieve the same results as obtained by the authors. At first, I expected only a very small error rate (cf. Rosenthal, 1978). Because the results of the first study yielded a much greater error rate than assumed, I planned a more elaborate exercise for a graduate class in statistics. Each student was instructed to recompute the value of a t test and of a one-way ANOVA F test. The number of rejected articles was

---

[1] Percentage of discrepancy was computed using the following formula:

$$100 \times \frac{|A - R|}{R},$$

where A is the value of the test statistic reported by the author, and R is the recomputed value. Thus, it is a measure of the extent to which the published value is discrepant from the recomputed value.

Table 1. Discrepant Test Results for Study 1

Test	Reported Value	Recomputed Value	% Discrepancy
x^2	2.223	2.904	23.5
x^2	41.5	48.2	13.9
t	1.25	1.63	23.3
t	2.27	2.95	23.1
F	3.91	5.88	33.5

again recorded, as were the reported and recomputed test values and degrees of freedom. Some additional data were also tabulated: the percentage of discrepancy (see Footnote 1) between the author's value and the recomputed results, and the significance levels attained by the reported statistical test results and by the recomputed test results.

Results

The number of articles rejected for insufficient data was much lower for the graduate class (range = 0 to 13; median = 2) than for the undergraduate class in Study 1. Rejections for t tests (median = 1) and for F tests (median = 3) did not differ significantly.

The much lower rejection rate for the graduate class was not unexpected. Graduate student search strategies should be more efficient than those of undergraduates, many of whom may be dealing with the journal literature for the first time. In addition, my experience with the first class led me to recommend some journals and to discourage others. For example, APA journals were not recommended, because complete summary data often appear to be missing in APA journal reports (standard deviations are frequently not reported). *Psychological Reports, Perceptual and Motor Skills,* and several other journals were recommended because the editorial policy seems to encourage complete reporting of summary data. Furthermore, these journals include a large number of articles in each issue, often running no more than two or three pages in length, and with a decidedly empirical (rather than theoretical) basis, resulting in relatively simple statistical analyses. Such journals are thus wellsuited for this exercise, especially for undergraduates. Nevertheless, 14 different journals were selected by students in Study 2.

A total of 46 statistical tests were examined (23 t tests and 23 F tests). Discrepancies between reported and recomputed values of less than 5%—about what might be expected as a result of rounding errors—were obtained for less than 60% of the tests. Discrepancies greater than 20% occurred for almost 25% of the statistical tests, and discrepancies greater than 50% were obtained for about 7% of the statistical tests (see Table 2). Table 3 displays the reported and recomputed values of the statistical tests for which discrepancies greater than 30% were obtained. Errors

Table 2. Cumulative Frequency Distribution of Discrepant Results

Discrepancy	% of Tests
≤ 5%	56.5
> 5%	43.5
> 10%	30.4
> 20%	23.9
> 30%	15.2
> 40%	13.0
> 50%	6.5
>100%	4.3

Table 3. Discrepancies Greater Than 30%

Test	Reported Value	Recomputed Value	% Discrepancy
t	7.66	5.89	30.1
F	1.01	0.72	40.3
t	1.80	3.05	41.0
t	1.70	1.20	41.7
F	4.25	9.47	55.1
F	46.85	21.62	116.7
t	1.70	0.39	335.9

were almost three times as likely to favor the experimenter's hypothesis than not.

Approximately 13% of the tests published as "significant," $p < .05$, were not significant, $p > .05$, after recomputation. Table 4 shows the reported and recomputed values as well as the percentage of discrepancy for these statistical tests. The discrepancies are quite low for two of the tests, because the reported values are very near the critical (.05) values. Note, however, that for one of the two, even the reported value was not significant, because it did not exceed the critical value! And for the second "low discrepancy" test, the degrees of freedom were also incorrectly reported. In all, there were four cases of incorrectly reported df, all for F tests. These are displayed in Table 5.

General Discussion

The results of these two exercises are surprising and worrisome. Results are consistent with those reported by Rosenthal (1978) concerning the proportion of errors that favor the author's hypothesis, but frequency of errors seems to be much greater than reported by Rosenthal. Of course, the context of Rosenthal's study was different. Nevertheless, the frequency of errors in the reporting of statistical test results requires further explanation.

The most optimistic possibility is that some students deliberately sought out instances of discrepant results. Although both classes were explicitly asked not to do this, the possibility cannot be ruled out. Because students in Study 2 turned in copies of their journal articles with their reports, a check of sorts is possible. I analyzed all of the remaining statistical tests in the selected articles, a total of 114 additional tests. Re-

sults were not quite as extreme as for the student-selected tests, but in general, the essential character of the results remained the same.

A second possibility is that the reported summary statistics (Ms and SDs) are in error, and not the reported test values. The situation is essentially indeterminate in this respect, and at any rate, it would not be much of a consolation if it were the summary

Table 4. Tests Incorrectly Reported as "Significant!"

Test (df)	Critical Value	Reported Value	Recomputed Value	% Discrepancy
t(21)	2.08	2.07	2.03	2.0
F(3, 67)	2.75	2.78	2.67	4.1
t(22)	2.07	2.19	1.73	26.6
t(25)	2.06	1.70	1.20	41.7
t(25)	2.06	1.70	0.39	335.9

Table 5. Incorrectly Reported df for Study 2

Test	Reported df	Recomputed df
F	7, 80	7, 40
F	3, 188	3, 88
F	2, 66	2, 69
F	3, 76	3, 67

statistics that were incorrectly reported. A third possibility—typographical errors—seems implausible, and would again not be saying much for the journal editorial and review process, nor for the author's responsibility to proofread the galleys.

The impact of these results on students is hard to overestimate. The point of the exercise is to emphasize the need for the student to evaluate critically even the numbers that appear in a journal article. Students may be accustomed to evaluating logical arguments in journal articles, especially by the time they are graduate students. Unfortunately, the data that appear in such articles often seem to be authoritative to students: "It's hard to argue with the numbers." This exercise is extremely successful in dispelling such attitudes.

One cautionary note is in order, however. It is important for the instructor to guard against the establishment of overly critical student attitudes. The goal of the exercise is not to make students mistrust statistical arguments in general, but to generate a detective-like attitude toward reading journal articles. "Statistician as sleuth" would be a good description of my intentions for this exercise.

Therefore, it is important to plan carefully the presentation of the collective results of the exercise to the class. I have found it useful to present the exercise in the context of more general methodological techniques, such as metaanalysis or secondary data analysis. Unfortunately, these are relatively advanced topics that are more appropriate for graduate-level courses. Furthermore, discussion of these issues is not yet common in most methods and statistics textbooks, though reasonably priced paperbound editions on these topics have begun to appear, especially for metaanalysis (Cooper, 1984; Fienberg, Martin, & Straf, 1985; Hunter, Schmidt, & Jackson, 1982; Jacob, 1984; Kielcolt & Nathan, 1985; Light & Pillemer, 1984; Rosenthal, 1984; Wolf, 1986).

For undergraduate classes, the results of the exercise may be described in connection with the general problem of conducting a thorough literature review (i.e., verifying the statistical computations in a journal article should be a routine part of conducting a literature review). It is convenient to present this material toward the end of the semester, because it then leads naturally to a discussion of the literature reviews the students will conduct as part of their laboratory research projects in our experimental methods course, which most of our undergraduate majors take in the semester immediately following statistics.

Finally, it is worth noting that several students (both graduates and undergraduates) involved in this exercise in my most recent classes have spontaneously offered to continue the work as a more formal research project by systematically examining several journals. This work has now begun and several small grants have been secured to facilitate the project. It is difficult to imagine a more rewarding conclusion to a class project.

References

Barnwell, G. M. (1984). The multiple benefits of a research literature exercise. *Teaching of Statistics in the Health Sciences, 38,* 5-7.

Cooper, H. M. (1984). *The integrative research interview: A systematic approach.* Beverly Hills, CA: Sage.

Fienberg, S. E., Martin, M. E., & Straf, M. L. (Eds.). (1985). *Sharing research data.* Washington, DC: National Academy Press.

Gordon, L. V. (1973). One-way analysis of variance using means and standard deviations. *Educational and Psychological Measurement, 33,* 815-816.

Huck, S. W., & Malgady, R. G. (1978). Two-way analysis of variance using means and standard deviations. *Educational and Psychological Measurement, 38,* 235-237.

Hunter, J. E., Schmidt, F. L., & Jackson, G. B. (1982). *Meta-analysis: Cumulating research findings across studies.* Beverly Hills, CA: Sage.

Jacob, H. (1984). *Using published data: Errors and remedies.* Beverly Hills, CA: Sage.

Kielcolt, K. J., & Nathan, L. E. (1985). *Secondary analysis of survey data.* Beverly Hills, CA: Sage.

Light, R. J., & Pillemer, D.B. (1984). Summing up: *The science of reviewing research.* Cambridge, MA: Harvard University Press.

Rosenthal, R. (1978). How often are our numbers wrong? *American Psychologist, 33,* 1005-1008.

Rosenthal, R. (1984). *Meta-analytic procedures for social research.* Beverly Hills, CA: Sage.

Rossi, J. S. (in press). One-way ANOVA from summary statistics. *Educational and Psychological Measurement.*

Wolf, F. M. (1986). *Meta-analysis: Quantitative methods for research synthesis.* Beverly Hills, CA: Sage.

Notes

1. Portions of this article were presented at the 94th annual convention of the American Psychological Association, Washington, DC, August 1986.
2. Preparation of this article was supported in part by National Cancer Institute Grant CA27821 to James O. Prochaska. I thank the editor and reviewers for helpful suggestions and Terri Hodson and Elaine Taylor for manuscript preparation.

A Funny Thing Happened to Me One Day in Statistics Class

Kathleen Hynek Dillon
Western New England College

I had been in the habit of lecturing somewhat cursorily on the difference between statistical significance and psychological significance and had usually asked students on examinations to take an article from a psychology journal and discuss whether the results were psychologically significant as well as statistically so, and why. Choosing an article from a psychology journal unfortunately increased the probability the article would be both statistically and psychologically significant.

One final examination, however, I decided to inject a little satirical humor and so I chose an article from the *Worm Runners Digest* entitled "Classical Conditioning of the Thinking Response in College Sophomores" (Reynolds, 1972). I invite you to read the article in its entirety to get the full effect; however, a short quotation should give you the flavor:

> The present study is an attempt to extend our control to an area never before influenced by man—the thinking behavior of college sophomores! Only the extreme 10% of those students screened were used in this study to assure no prior thinking had occurred. The CS, which must be neutral and not evoke thinking, consisted of presentation of selected excerpts from my psychological statistics course lectures. The UCS consisted of presentations of selected passages from *Beyond Freedom and Dignity* which, of course, reliably evoked a UCR of thinking. Reference: Signiphikance, I.C. *Thoughtful data analysis. NY:* Regressive Books, 1873.

The students were given a xerox copy of the entire article which reported statistical significance and were asked to evaluate whether the results were also psychologically significant. Much to my initial surprise and later chagrin, only a handful of students from my two sections concluded that the article was not psychologically significant, and only some of those recognized the article as a satire. The vast majority of remaining students concluded the article had importance and extolled the virtues of classical conditioning and research in the area of cognition as reasons.

Admittedly, it is not easy if even possible to teach the art of evaluation; nonetheless, students should at least be able to recognize the most blatant negative

instances. Needless to say, I have since substantially elaborated on my discussion of significance. I now point out and illustrate that results could come out to be statistically significant yet not be important because, for example, the results were trivial (or satirical), small meaningless differences between groups appeared significant because of large sample sizes, or the design of the experiment was faulty (inappropriate design, confounding, etc.).

Alternatively, I discuss how it is possible for results to be statistically insignificant yet psychologically meaningful; for example, not rejecting the null hypothesis might be important in showing that a drug had no effect on a particular behavior, or the results may not have been amenable to statistical analysis (one case study) yet clinically important.

I recommend students read the following references:

Bakan, D. Psychology can now kick the science habit. *Psychology Today*, March, 1972, 26-28, 86-88.

Loether, H. J. and McTavish, D. G. *Inferential Statistics for Sociologists,* Chap. 10, Boston: Allyn and Bacon, 1974.

Signorelli, A. Statistics, tool or master of the psychologist, *American Psychologist,* October, 1974, 774-777. (A number of other good references are given in this article.)

Finally, I have students take home an exam in which they are asked to make up or find examples of studies that are statistically significant but not psychologically important and discuss why, and to make up or find results that are not statistically significant but are important and discuss why.

Reference

Reynolds, T. W. Classical conditioning of a thinking response in college sophomores. *Worm Runners Digest,* December 1972, 102.

SECTION III:
RESEARCH METHODS

Reviewing the Literature

Louis Gardner described his method for introducing students to the literature search. After summarizing the usual library resources, he provided students with a list of platitudes, such as "birds of a feather flock together" and "opposites attract." Each student selected at least two of these bromides and went to the library to find empirical evidence to support or reject the hypothesis implicit in each one.

James Mathews developed his own version of the psychological scavenger hunt. After summarizing general references and types of psychological literature in class, he met his students at the library for the next session. Students were randomly assigned to teams but worked individually to find answers to questions that required them to locate specific references. A scoring system determined the winning team. Mathews reported that his students learned from this enjoyable "game."

Virginia Parr, a librarian, described how she and some psychology faculty members cooperated to introduce students to basic library research strategies and appropriate reference materials. They designed one approach to course-related library instruction for the introductory course and another for advanced courses, including research methods. Parr insisted that more coordination between teachers and library staff members should help to improve students' bibliographic skills.

In her second article, Virginia Parr highlighted the advantages and disadvantages of on-line computer searches for the bibliographic needs of undergraduates. She also indicated how computer and traditional searches can be effectively combined. The recommended references at the end of the article may be quite informative.

Richard Feinberg and his colleagues wondered if on-line information retrieval might have advantages other than being faster and more efficient. Half of the students in a small environmental psychology class received training in the Dialog retrieval system and the other half received training in traditional bibliographic techniques. Using anonymous and blind procedures, the researchers found that students who used Dialog made significantly higher grades on their literature review than did students in the traditional group. The Dialog group also expressed more positive attitudes about the library and the literature search process.

Linda Lewis, a librarian, outlined the advantages and disadvantages of bibliographic computerized searching and described the databases in psychology. Given the rapid growth in the number of databases and the increased availability of equipment, she predicted accelerated expansion in the use of computer searches, but concluded that they cannot answer all bibliographic needs.

Teaching Experimental Design and Methods of Observation

Have you ever thought about using radishes to teach experimental design? William Stallings had his graduate students design and perform an experiment to assess the effects of fertilizers on the growth of radish seedlings. The goal of this project was to provide students practice in making design decisions, collecting and analyzing real data, and writing up results. The results of an informal evaluation suggested that this approach was a promising technique for teaching experimental design.

Dominic Zerbolio and James Walker described a factorial experiment that they used as a laboratory exercise in a research methods course. Using the Howard-Dolman depth perception apparatus, the authors manipulated the factors of viewing condition (binocular and monocular) and rod orientation (vertical and horizontal). The exercise illustrated the nature of an interaction and the necessity of an additional analysis of simple main effects. This simple technique may be particularly useful for departments having limited financial resources.

Kenneth Kerber wanted his students to have direct experience with different research strategies. His first article described a two-part project for a laboratory course in social psychology. Using the rewards-cost model for evaluating helping behavior, students conducted and analyzed results from a correlational and an experimental study. They learned how these approaches complement each other when used to investigate the same variables. The project served as a springboard for discussing several essential elements of empirical inquiry.

Kerber's second article summarized projects used in his research methods course to familiarize students with four investigative strategies: experimental, observational, survey, and archival. Students conducted and analyzed results from one study of each kind. Kerber's two articles demonstrate the advantages of having students do research rather than merely reading about how to do research; they also provide a treasure trove of ideas for other teachers.

Andrea Zeren and Vivian Makosky described an in-class activity that permits systematic observations of spontaneous human behavior as portrayed on television. The activity involves: a lecture about observational techniques; a demonstration of time sampling, event sampling, and trait ratings; and a class demonstration that compares and contrasts the three methods. Students reacted favorably to the exercise and claimed that it helped them to understand observational techniques and other facets of research.

Many instructors rarely teach techniques of naturalistic observation in their undergraduate research methods classes. Harold Herzog described exercises he designed to give students experience in using methods of naturalistic observation to quantify behavior. The illustrations using animal behavior can also be applied to human behavior.

Teaching Research Ethics

Bernard Beins generated the Barnum effect to teach his students about the ethics of and the feelings associated with deception in research. Students in research methods classes received feedback based on a bogus personality inventory and rated the perceived validity of the interpretations. The class discussed the ethics of deception based on their own reactions to the knowledge that they were deceived. Students agreed that the approach was effective in helping them learn first-hand about the costs and benefits of deception in research.

Ralph Rosnow described a role-play technique he developed to involve students actively in evaluating research ethics. Students scanned the literature for research that used techniques judged as unethical. After giving an oral report on the articles, students role-played the author of the article attempting to justify the study to an institutional review board. Finally, all students in the classmade judgments about the studies' ethical value, and the instructor graphed the results on a matrix that represented the costs and benefits of studies.

David Strohmetz and Ann Skleder used Rosnow's (1990) role-play for teaching research ethics to undergraduates in research methods classes. Results indicated that the exercise can be a valuable tool for sensitizing students to the factors involved in judging the research ethics.

Harold Herzog devised a method that encouraged students to confront the ethical issues involved in animal research. Students played the role of institutional animal care committee members and discussed several research proposals presented by the instructor. The proposals were based on actual animal research. Many scientific and philosophical issues highlighted the discussion. The author presented several helpful suggestions for tailoring the activity to the needs of the course.

Teaching Principles, Concepts, and Skills

Joe Hatcher promoted critical thinking in his research methods classes by giving students riddles to solve. After solving several riddles, the instructor outlined seven ways that scientific thinking paralleled riddle solving. Students rated the activity as interesting and useful.

Larry Vandervert used the analogy of baking a cake to illustrate important aspects of experimentation. Calling a recipe the operational definition of the concept *cake,* he discussed empirical referents, quantification, and replication as seen in the process of producing a cake. He also used the analogy to demonstrate the psychological concept of fear. Students enjoyed and learned from this clever and effective tactic.

Art Kohn used a simple stay-switch probability game to demonstrate the importance of testing our beliefs empirically. Despite students' and faculty's beliefs to the contrary, a simple inclass experiment illustrated that switching wins twice as often as staying. This demonstration pointed out the value of validating our beliefs empirically. A follow-up questionnaire showed that participating in this experiment may increase students' trust in the empirical method.

Jan Yoder described a simple procedure and identified resource materials for teaching students interviewing skills. The procedure consisted of having students work in 3-person groups; alternately each student took a turn as interviewer, interviewee, and observer. Yoder pointed out how such interviewing skills were important for applied and laboratory investigators.

Virginia Falkenberg described her unusual way of implementing research projects. Each shldent submitted a research proposal to a funding agency (the teacher). Nine of 15 students requested funding to support their proposals, which were evaluated by three faculty members. The agency funded four proposals, and the students/authors became research directors. Funding consisted of points with which project directors could purchase help on a variety of tasks from their unfunded classmates. Among other advantages, the teacher supervised 4 instead of 15 separate projects.

Have you tried to improve your students' performance in laboratory courses? David Carroll had his students work in small, interdependent groups in which each person contributed a unique piece to a research project. The technique encouraged students to cooperate during the research enterprise. Results indicated that shudents evaluated the approach favorably and that their academic performance improved. Carroll also discussed some applications and potential problems of the technique.

The students in Blaine Peden's research methods class discovered a technique for recognizing and preparing references for four types of works commonly used in research reports. Subsequent performance on the reference section of their research reports earned either an A or F grade (after Cronan-Hillix, 1988). The technique helped students learn to prepare accurate reference lists and appeared to sensitize them to other aspects of APA style.

Paul Gore and Cameron Camp used a poster session as an integral part of an undergraduate experimental design course. Undergraduates designed and conducted original experiments using radishes as subjects. The students presented the results of these experiments in a poster session. The authors described the benefits of using radishes as subjects. Radishes? Yes, radishes.

Have you tried using a technique based on the popular TV show Jeopardy? Bryan Gibson used the game in study sessions to help students organize the course material in a research methods course. Students reported that the format was educational and entertaining.

Using Computers

In one of the earliest and most comprehensive summaries of computer data generators, Robert Gregory described the range of complexity and the pres and cons of a variety of such generators. Among the pedagogical advantages are that students can acquire experience in designing experiments and analyzing data without the boring and time consuming activity of conducting trivial experiments.

Alan Hartley and his associates described two exercises based on EXPERSIM, the computer simulation package from the University of Michigan's Center for Research on Learning and Teaching. MARYJANE simulates the effects of marijuana on motor behavior and MOON allows students to explore the relationship between phases of the moon and number of murders committed. Preliminary evaluation indicated that the simulations increased students' understanding of experimental design.

Alan Hartley and Daryl Smith summarized their use of a computer simulation to investigate the effects of vitamin C on the incidence and severity of colds. Students designed an experiment to manipulate three independent variables and to measure three dependent variables. The authors mentioned several benefits of simulations and concluded that they can be economical and effective supplements to actual research projects.

James Benedict and Beverly Butts conducted a study to evaluate the relative effectiveness of computer simulations and real experiments. Both approaches enhanced students' understanding of experimental methods. After citing advantages and disadvantages of each strategy, the authors concluded that simulations were more efficacious when combined with actual experiments and that, when the two were

used in the same course, simulations should probably come first.

Blaine Peden described (a) student use of the microcomputer before, during, and after an experiment; and (b) the benefits that students derive from learning about microcomputers, in particular, and from conducting research, in general.

Undergraduates conducted a micro-computer- controlled investigation in John Hovancik's research methods course. The author designed a study to determine the relationship between forced-choice reaction times to different colors generated on a video monitor and subjects' affective reactions to their choices. Advantages of computer-controlled research projects included students' excitement about first-hand experience with modern equipment.

Blaine Peden and Gene Steinhauer described an exercise concerning the reliability of behavioral observations. In a computer graphics laboratory, students learned to identify facial expressions of emotion. The authors then paired trained and untrained students and had them rate subjects in natural settings on facial expression, gender, and age. Students analyzed interobserver agreement scores and collaborated to write a paper. The authors were enthusiastic about using microcomputers to complement traditional instruction.

Using Popular Media and Scholarly Publications

Patricia Connor-Greene conducted a classroom exercise and gave individual assignment designed to teach critical evaluation of research reports in the popular press. The classroom exercise used active and collaborative learning to apply the principles of scientific investigation, particularly the distinction between correlation and causation, in analyzing the limitations of a newspaper account of a research study. The individual assignment required students to locate and critique a newspaper or magazine summary of research. Students strongly agreed that the exercises gave them a clearer understanding of correlational research and helped them critically evaluate media reports of research.

Students in S. Viterbo McCarthy's laboratory course experienced a novel approach that challenged them to evaluate the results of an interview with a political hostage. Students discovered that a single behavior did not possess only one index and that several factors influenced the transition from observation to interpretation. The author pointed out how students' skills learned by the experience transferred to laboratory projects.

Is White Cloud the softest bathroom tissue on earth? Does Ban or Sure antiperspirant keep you drier? Do people prefer the taste of Pepsi-Cola to that of Coca-Cola? Paul Solomon's students conducted sophisticated replications of studies used by manufacturers to support claims for their products in television commercials. Students were enthusiastic about this real-world research and sometimes came up with insightful methodological extensions and refinements. Solomon concluded that his approach increased students' interest and diligence without watering down content.

Kerry Chamberlain devised realistic laboratory projects to enhance research training for undergraduates. An appropriate core article served as the basis for each project; projects were full or partial replication of an experiment from the core article. Chamberlain discussed the advantages and limitations of the technique.

Newton Suter and Paula Frank stressed the value of having undergraduates read classic research articles from primary journals. They mentioned three criteria for selecting such articles, suggested how 12 particular ones illustrate some core concepts, and included examples of questions to ask students about those studies.

George Howard and Jean Engelhardt used Huck and Sandler's *Rival Hypotheses* (1979, New York: Harper & Row) as a teaching device and as the basis for an experiment. The investigators pretested students on their ability to critique research and then randomly assigned them to one of two treatment conditions. Posttests evaluated students' ability to critique problems selected from *Rival Hypotheses.* Results were not clear-cut, but the study demonstrated some important research issues and provided students with valuable experience.

1. REVIEWING THE LITERATURE

A Relatively Painless Method of Introduction To the Psychological Literature Search

Louis E. Gardner
Creighton University

It would seem that one of the earliest considerations in an experimental psychology course ought to revolve around the literature search. This seems particularly important in the experimental or methodology courses where original individual or group research projects are a part of the requirements. Where this is the case, the most obvious method of introducing the idea of a literature search involves waiting until the students have developed hypotheses and then direct them to the various available sources of information on that particular topic. Another frequently used method is found in assigning various traditional topics and requiring students to write term papers gleaned from the literature. Although both of these procedures ensure some exposure to the literature and the mechanisms for search, they do have some drawbacks.

First, on the subjective side, students report that they find the exercise of writing just another term paper to be distasteful and boring. Objectively, from the instructor's point of view, this kind of activity usually fails to produce a very extensive or creative literature search. As a result, the students really don't gain much additional knowledge of the literature or search techniques from another term paper. Having students use their self-developed hypotheses as starting points for literature searches works somewhat better than the term paper because they have some investment in the problem. However, the development of hypotheses for individual projects usually means that the literature search takes place in a hurried fashion sometime near the end of the course, or even in some cases after the data have been collected. As a result, at a time in the course when students should be concentrating on the development of methodological and reporting skills, they are still stumbling around in an unrewarding literature search. A much more satisfactory approach is to get them involved with the literature and help them develop search skills early in an experimental or methodology course so that this tool is available when needed. In addition, it seems desirable to do this in an atmosphere which fosters ingenuity, creativity, and breadth in carrying out their search for existing knowledge. The method described below appears to do these things.

Description of the Method. The concept of a literature search is introduced on the first day of class as are the early steps in the development of a psychological experiment. By way of introduction, the usual sources are explained to the students with particular reference to the way in which the *Psychological Abstracts* are organized and used. At the second class meeting, the students are given an assignment requiring that they experience a literature search.

At the basis of this assignment is a list of clichés and old sayings. Part of that list is reproduced here, and of course, there are many others available. Like father like son. Chip off the old block. One bad apple spoils the barrel . Can't teach an old dog new tricks. Where there is a will there is a way. Let sleeping dogs lie. You can't fight city hall. Birds of a feather flock together. Opposites attract. You can't change a leopard's spots. Politics make strange bedfellows. Better late than never. The early bird catches the worm. Out of sight out of mind. Absence makes the heart grow fonder. Sly as a fox. More fun than a barrelfull of monkeys. Blood is thicker than water. Once a thief always a thief. Too many cooks spoil the broth. Laughing on the outside, crying on the inside. To err is human, to forgive, divine. After his own heart. As mad as a March hare. Tired Nature's sweet restorer, sleep. The course of true love never runs smooth. While there is life there is hope. Virtue is her own reward. Old as the hills. Music hath charms to soothe a savage beast. Men talk only to conceal their minds. Good breeding is the blossom of good sense. Coming events cast their shadows before. Brevity is the soul of wit.

One notes that most of these phrases have a component related to behavior and the students are instructed to treat these sayings as hypotheses. Next, after selecting at least two of the sayings from the list, each student is required to find empirical evidence which would contribute to either the support or rejection of the hypothesis implied by the saying. Finally, they are required to submit abstracts of the studies indicating how they support or refute a saying and to defend their position before the class.

Results. The responses of the students over several years have reinforced the use of this method of initial exposure to the psychological literature. The students appear to be challenged by the assignment and go about the successful completion of it with a high degree of enthusiasm.

Quantitative assessments of the method have been made only over the last three years the course has been taught. During this period, the method was employed in teaching 26 Junior and Senior students in an Advanced Experimental Psychology course, and the following data are based upon measures taken with these students. One estimate of the utility of a method such as this can be gained by simply asking if-students can successfully complete the assignment. The answer is found in looking at the successful completion rate. That is, the proportion of studies reported by students that do realistically serve as evidence for or against the sayings. The result of this analysis indicated that 85% of the reported studies were relevant to the hypothesis implicit in the sayings chosen by the students. This result would seem to indicate that the students were able to use the psychological literature successfully and thus achieve the primary objective of this exercise. A second major objective in designing this particular method was to present a challenging assignment which students would enjoy. Assessment of the attainment of this objective was possible through analysis of the students' responses on the course evaluation. Again, using data based upon the responses of 26 students over the last three years that the course was taught, it was indicated that 77% of the students found the work to be challenging and yet maintained a positive attitude in regard to the assignment.

Part of the instructor's verve for using this method stems from the frequent instances of ingenuity and creativity displayed by the students in translating the sayings into behavioral terms and then fitting those to the empirical studies in the literature. Some insight into their behaviors can be gained by looking at some selected titles of studies presented along with the related sayings:

> Maruthi (1966) "The impact of genetic propensity and environmental modifiability of human behavior"; Wohlford (1970) "Initiation of cigarette smoking: Is it related to parental smoking behavior?" (Like father, like son.)
>
> Davids, et al. (1961) "Anxiety, pregnancy, and childbirth abnormalities." (Coming events cast their shadow before.)
>
> Darley and Latane (1968) "When will people help in a crisis?" (Too many cooks spoil the broth.)
>
> Kogan and Wallach (1969) "Risk taking behavior in small decision groups."; Connoly (1969) "The social facilitation of preening behavior in

> *Drosophila melanogaster.*" (Two heads are better than one.)
>
> Byrne et al. (1967) "Attraction and similarity of personality characteristics". (Opposites attract.)

These kinds of responses to the assignment, together with the interaction and debate initiated by the defense of the evidence have proved valuable as more than just an introduction to the literature search. That is, the process and outcomes of this procedure serve as natural leads to the discussion of central concepts in experimental psychology such as operational definitions and conflicting evidence. In addition, many students find that their ideas for their individual projects later in the semester are germinated during this assignment.

In conclusion, this method achieves its primary objective of introducing students to the idea and process of a literature search in a novel and effective manner. Also, there are secondary gains which are important to other portions of the course. These conclusions are based upon student reports, specific student behaviors in doing the work, and the instructor's subjective evaluation over the past six years. The end result is that both students and instructor find the procedure to be a practical, enjoyable, and challenging learning experience.

References

Byrne, D., Griffitt, W., & Stefaniek, D. Attraction and similarity of personality characteristics. *Journal of Personality and Social Psychology,* 1967, *51,* 82-90.

Connoly, K. The social facilitation of preening behavior in *Drosophila melanogaster. Animal Behavior,* 1968, *16,* 11-19.

Darley, J., & Latane, B. When will people help in a crisis? *Psychology Today,* June 1968, *2,* 54-57; 70-71.

Davids, A., DeVault, S., & Talmadge, M. Anxiety, pregnancy and childbirth abnormalities. *Journal of Consulting Psychology,* 1961, *25,* 74-77.

Kogan, N., & Wallach, M. Risk taking behavior in small decision groups. *Bulletin du C.E.R.P.,* 1967, *16,* 363-375.

Maruthi, G. The impact of genetic propensity and environmental modifiability of human behavior. *Psychology Annual,* 1966-67, *1,* 54-58.

Wohlford, P. Initiation of cigarette smoking: Is it related to parental smoking behavior? *Journal of Consulting and Clinical Psychology,* 1970, *34,* 148-151.

Hunting for Psychological Literature: A Methodology for the Introductory Research Course

James B. Mathews
University of Hartford

Developing an awareness of the sources of psychological literature is an important early step in teaching the research process. I have discovered and rediscovered that students at all levels of the undergraduate program and even many entering graduate students show surprise that there are places other than their textbooks where they can obtain information about research which has been done in the past. As an apparent remedy to this problem, which has plagued many, some authors of textbooks for the Introduction of Psychological Research course, or its equivalent, are now including a section concerning journals and other sources of psychological literature. Similarly, many instructors have included in their courses a section dealing with this material. These passive solutions to the problem, however, do not effect much short- or long-term success. Later on in these courses, introductions of laboratory reports written by students are often of poor quality because they suffer from: (a) a lack of depth of information because the literature has not been covered thoroughly; (b) an omission of controls that might be found in past experiments; (c) a sparseness of alternative theoretical frameworks which might be utilized to generate meaningful hypotheses; and (d) a paucity of evidence which might suggest alternative hypotheses. Similar concern is often reported by colleagues who find that term papers for their content-oriented courses are prepared from only a few sources, and these instructors are beginning to ask "What is being taught in the methods courses?"

Through dealing with this recurring problem I have developed a technique designed as a quasi-laboratory experience that is modeled after the old school or camp treasure hunt." Similar to a technique recently described by Gardner (1977), it provides students with an active learning experience. This approach has two short-term goals; familiarization with a broad range of different sources of psychological literature and knowledge of the specific location of these sources within the library as well as a long-term goal of increased later utilization of these sources. While this technique has been developed for the Introduction to Psychological Research course it can be employed in any course where the problem exists.

Procedure. Students are first exposed to the general reference sources and types of psychological literature that are available at the library in a regular class meeting and then told to meet for the "treasure hunt" at the entrance to the library at the beginning of the next class hour. We use our two-hour laboratory session but the activity can be adjusted to the available time.

Students are randomly assigned to teams in order to increase face validity of the "game" and "experiment," but work individually since each member of the team is responsible for collecting different information. Each team is given its packet of data recording sheets a different sheet for each member of the team and told that the sheets must be returned to the lobby by the end of the session and that the penalty for late return is equal to one item for each two minutes of lateness. Examples of items that have been used on a recent hunt include: (1) What is the title for Abstract 5001 Vol. 49 (1973) of the *Psychological Abstracts?; (2)* Who was the author of the chapter on Personality in the 1971 edition of the *Annual Review of Psychology?;* (3) What is the library call number of the *Journal of Psychology?;* (4) What is the title of the first abstract on page 6093-B in the 1973 volume (33) of *Dissertation Abstracts International?;* (5) On what page, in what journals and in which volume does the article by Kahn and Tice written in 1973 appear? Copies of the full exercise are available from the author.

Students are instructed that completeness and accuracy are as important as speed and that the emphasis is on learning not running. Because the "hunt" is done during library hours, the hunters are urged to follow full library decorum. The individual score that each student earns is recorded as their individual unit assessment grade and the team with the highest combined score is the declared "winner." Each member of the winning team is allowed to choose a paperback from a list of psychology titles. In preparing alternative forms of the data sheet, each item remains equivalent with respect to the content but differs with respect to such requested information as year, volume, edition, author, journal, etc.

The location of the specific reference material in our laboratory was considered when the order of the items was constructed to insure that the student would have to be aware of and make decisions as to location of sources (cognitive map development) as well as having to make many repeated responses, such as use of the card catalog for location of items and use of the index of the *Psychological Abstracts* (response practice). The assumption that these response activities will recur when needed at a later time is encouraged in part by the motivation built into the "hunt" and the double reinforcement opportunity that is present in terms of the unit assessment score, which is equal in value to all other semester units, and the team win with its associated reward.

Results. Two measures of the short term effects of this exercise were taken. In the first, a bibliography generation exercise on a topic of the student's choice, there were significantly more items listed ($t(36)$ = 2.92, $p < .01$) and a significantly greater number of different sources used ($t(36)$ = 3.11, $p < .01$) than for the similar class taught prior to the introduction of the Treasure Hunt. In the second, the development of an introduction section for an original project, there were again significantly more references cited ($t(36)$ = 2.85, $p < .01$) and significantly more sources used ($t(36)$ = 3.76, $p < .01$). Long-term effects will have to wait until these students have reached later courses, although it will be very difficult to assess these effects of this activity because so many students either leave the major or transfer to other schools.

Concluding Remarks. Although it may seem folly to some to create "games" to induce learning in a post-secondary school population, it is our responsibility as teachers to have our students meet our own course objectives as well as the greater objectives demanded by the profession. Thus, if we are to create psychologists of the future who will be able to extend the knowledge already gained through the research process, it falls upon us who teach the future psychologists to develop whatever techniques will accomplish this goal. And besides, what's wrong with playing a game that accomplishes a learning objective?

Reference

Gardner, L. E. A relatively painless method of introduction to the psychological literature search. *Teaching of Psychology, 1977, 4,* 89-91.

Course-Related Library Instruction for Psychology Students

Virginia H. Parr
University of Oregon

I was pleased to see Gardner's and LeUnes' articles in the April 1977 issue of *ToP* as there has been very little in the psychology literature concerning the integration of library instruction into psychology curricula. I would like, however, to suggest some other effective ways to introduce beginning students and undergraduate majors to a wider range of print and non-print bibliographic materials available within psychology and related disciplines.

These suggestions are not meant to dispute that the library scavenger hunt assignment described by LeUnes and the hypothesis-verification assignment used by Gardner can challenge many students. I have used both techniques myself, but only after employing two preparatory steps. First, the teaching faculty is urged to include a subject specialist librarian in the planning of library assignments. Second, students are given an introduction to bibliographic research strategies and provided with annotated bibliographies of salient library sources.

Similar course-related library instruction techniques are discussed in articles by Farber (1974), Frick (1975), and MacGregor and McInnis (1977). Farber and Frick document methods used at Earlham College to integrate library instruction into its psychology curriculum. More recently, MacGregor and McInnis have made a strong intellectual as well as practical case for integrating course-related library research instruction with classroom instruction.

For the past four years several psychology faculty at the University of Oregon and I have experimented with various methods of introducing students to basic library research strategies and to psychology reference materials. Two course-related approaches have evolved from this experimentation.

The first approach is used primarily for introductory level classes, often quite large, in which the vast majority of students will not become psychology majors, but in which a term paper or library assignment is required. After consultation with the course professor regarding the sophistication of the class, the nature of the library-related assignment, and the potential for follow-up with students desiring additional bibliographic assistance, I prepare a one- to two-hour general presentation.

In preparing this presentation I assume that many of the students have not used a large academic research library, and thus I cover the library's organization, hours, and policies. The students are given a librarian-prepared mini-bibliography of resources they may find helpful in researching their assignment. I introduce the rudiments of efficient library research principles, and using sample term paper topics, illustrate these by outlining strategies a student might use to find suitable materials. Emphasis is put on locating and using bibliographic resources that will be relevant to a student's topic as well as to the level of knowledge with which the student begins a given project.

For instance, I may track a cross-disciplinary topic through a wide range of relevant resources: subject encyclopedias or major encyclopedia yearbooks, authoritative handbooks and literature reviews, specialized bibliographies, *Psychological Abstracts, as* well as other relevant indexes such as *Current Index* to *Journals in Education* and *PAIS Bulletin* (Public Affairs Information Service). Evaluations from classes exposed to this approach indicate that the students have found the library instruction to be beneficial not only for the assignments that followed the presentation but also for other course work. All students surveyed said they would use the librarian-prepared bibliographies for related courses.

A different approach has been adopted for advanced students. A new course, Research Methods in Psychology, is now required of all psychology majors at the University of Oregon. A description of this course was presented at the 1977 APA Convention (Posner, Note 1). The first of six modules in this course is directly related to library research. Early in the module, a lecture/discussion on bibliographic research strategy is conducted by the faculty members teaching the course.

This is followed by a two-hour session in the library in which I introduce the organization of the academic research library, discuss resources listed on an extensive librarian-prepared bibliography, use sample research topics to elaborate on the faculty members' introduction to research strategies, introduce the concept of computerized information retrieval, and answer questions. I am available immediately following this presentation and later at prescribed times to help students with their initial projects.

During the week following the library presentation, each student is expected to develop a list of 20 to 30 bibliographic sources pertinent to a controversial topic relating psychological principles to current social issues, e.g., violence on television, supersonic air travel. In preparing the list each student is expected to use a wide range of general literature, authoritative overviews, current periodical indexes, scholarly articles and technical reports. The completed list is to be accompanied by a report detailing the strategy and resources the student used to find relevant and timely sources. These reports are followed by faculty-led classroom discussion about difficulties and successes the students encountered in completing the projects and about alternative strategies and resources they might have used .

In summary, I would like to stress that as psychology literature and library resources proliferate, course-related library instruction needs to be included in psychology curricula. Psychology faculty are urged to consult with reference or subject specialist librarians in designing library assignments or sequential units. Such cooperation should benefit the students as well as the goals of the immediate course and the total psychology curriculum. Library instruction followed immediately by relevant exercises designed to reinforce the use of efficient library research strategies will furthermore enrich students' total education by preparing them for future bibliographic inquiry.

References

Farber, E. I. Library instruction throughout the curriculum: Earlham College Program. In J. Lubans, Jr. (Ed.), *Educating the library user.* New York: Bowker, 1974.

Frick E. Information structure and bibliographic instruction. *Journal of Academic Librarianship,* 1975, *1,* 12-14.

Gardner, L E. A relatively painless method of introduction to the psychological literature search. *Teaching of Psychology,* 1977, *4,* 89-90.

LeUnes, A. D. The developmental psychology library search: Can a nonsense assignment make *sense? Teaching of Psychology,* 1977, *4,* 86.

MacGregor, J., & McInnis, R. G. Integrating classroom instruction and library research. The cognitive functions of bibliographic network structures. *Journal of Higher Education,* 1977, *48,* 1 7-38.

Note

Posner, M. I. An integrated curriculum for undergraduate study in psychology. Paper presented at the meeting of the American Psychological Association, San Francisco, August, 1977.

Online Information Retrieval and the Undergraduate

Virginia H. Parr
University of Oregon

Online in formation retrieval is one of the most rapidly growing areas of information technology. At present 90 percent of the libraries belonging to the Association of Research Libraries, as well as increasing numbers of other college and university libraries, have access to online information retrieval. Very soon it will be imperative that undergraduates be aware of this bibliographic tool.

Knowledge of online retrieval is particularly important in psychology as data at both the national level (Wax & Vaughn, 1977) and the University of Oregon indicate *Psychological Abstracts is* often the second most heavily used data base in the social sciences. At this time, however, no widely distributed guide to psychological literature or bibliographic research methods intended for psychology undergraduates details the availability or uses of online retrieval through such relevant computerized data bases as *Psychological Abstracts,* ERIC, *Social Science Citation Index, Language and Language Behavior Abstracts, Child Abuse and Neglect Abstracts,* and *Science Citation Index.*

Despite the dearth of formal information about online retrieval written for undergraduates, increasing numbers of them are hearing about "computer searches" from friends, teachers, research classes, and notices in the library. Atherton and Christian (1977) concisely outline what it is that these students are hearing about.

> Seated at a computer terminal, the online searcher [usually a librarian] is in direct contact, via a telecommunication link, with a remotely located computer system. There, machine-readable files called data bases are stored. These data bases are essentially electronic versions of the indexing and abstracting services already familiar to librarians [and students]. Through a structured protocol established by the retrieval system and using subject descriptors, key words. and basic Boolean logic, the searcher can examine the contents of the data bases. (p. 2)

Because online information retrieval can be a simple yet powerful tool, questions arise about its appropriateness for undergraduates. Some consider it inappropriate for undergraduates to use online retrieval for term papers because this seems to allow students to circumvent traditional bibliographic methods.

Rather than being a method to escape involvement in bibliographic work, however, the process through which a librarian and student cooperate to "negotiate" an online search can be a highly educational experience. If carefully carried out, the negotiation will refine students' thinking and sharpen their skills at traditional bibliographic inquiry as well as introduce a new bibliographic resource.

Moreover, an online search provides only a bibliography. The student must still cull through citations obtained online for those most relevant and must then find and use the cited books and journals. Students are also reminded to use bibliographies found in the materials obtained online to lead to further bibliographic sources. An online search is best viewed as one portion of a total literature search.

As a subject specialist librarian who is often requested by undergraduates "to run a computer search", I have evolved a review of bibliographic approaches that I explore with students before we mutually decide if an online search is appropriate:

1. Has the student clearly defined all aspects of the research topic?
2. Are there specialized encyclopedias, bibliographies. reference guides, vertical file materials, or government documents that the student has overlooked?
3. Has the student exhausted the card catalog? If so, using what subject headings?
4. Has the student used relevant periodical indexes in their traditional format? It so, using what subject headings?
5. How much information does the student need? How extensive is the term paper or research topic under consideration?

If responses to the above questions indicate an online search is the best strategy with which to continue bibliographic searching, I proceed to work with the student in developing a search strategy. Very often, however, the above review will be enough to lead students to sufficient bibliographic information to complete their proposed research.

If the student and I do decide to proceed with the online search strategy and the topic is multifaceted, I explain Boolean logic using a Venn diagram to illustrate the set theory we will be using. The student and I then review all bibliographic sources used thus far and determine how much more information is needed and in what depth—a few highly relevant citations, a broad set of citations from *Psychological Abstracts,* or extensive information available through several data bases.

We then search relevant thesauri to find precise subject headings if the agreed upon data base(s) use controlled vocabularies. When no appropriate subject headings exist, the student and I determine what natural language terms are most appropriate. We then search a few selected subject headings in the indexes to determine how many of the items indexed under these appear to be relevant. Again, at this point some students decide an online search is not necessary after all and confidently proceed on their bibliographic way, usually a great deal wiser in the ways of bibliographic searching.

In other situations, I may suggest an online search as a first step in finding bibliographic information. These rare occasions occur when, based on experience with the library's resources on the topic, I realize immediately it is going to take an online search to ferret out elusive citations efficiently.

Examples of undergraduate term paper topics for which online searches have been used to help students obtain bibliographic citations include: *Single concept:* Mensa (the organization); Procrastination; Prosody; Visual cliff (recent research). In each of the above cases, literature is available; but it is embedded in a variety of cumbersome subject headings. The use of one or two natural language terms quickly pulled the exact citations needed from the *Psychological Abstracts* online data base. *Multiple concept:* Relationship between social activities and academic performance among college students; Second language learning in preschool children; Suicide and parasuicide on college campuses; Use of the MMPI with prison populations.

Here again, extensive literature is available for each topic; but obtaining suitable citations for such multifaceted topics would have involved searching through several traditional periodical indexes under many subject headings. Several terms, controlled and natural language, were used to develop each concept; and the online search efficiently pulled citations appropriate to the stated topics.

In summary, as online information retrieval becomes increasingly available on college campuses, undergraduates in all disciplines should be formally introduced to the capabilities and appropriate uses of this new bibliographic tool. Online retrieval is an especially useful resource for psychology students. because of the large number of relevant data bases. Online information retrieval adds a new dimension to bibliographic inquiry while at the same time reinforcing use of traditional bibliographic sources.

References

Atherton, P., & Christian, R. W. *Librarians and online services*. White Plains, New York: Knowledge Industry Publications, 1977.

Wax, D. M., & Vaughan, P. E. *Northeast Academic Science Information Center. Final report*. Wellesley, Mass.: New England Board of Higher Education, 1977. (ERIC Document Reproduction Service No. ED 145 831)

Recommended Reading

Williams, M. E. Data bases—a history of developments and trends from 1966 through 1975. *Journal of the American Society for information Science*, 1977, *28*, 71-78. (34 additional references.)

Williams, M. E. Networks for on-line data base access. *Journal of the American Society* for information Science, 1977, *28*, 247-253.

Yarborough, J. *How to prepare for a computer search of ERIC: A non-technical approach*. Stanford: ERIC Clearinghouse on Information Resources, Stanford University, 1975. (ERIC Document Reproduction Service No. ED 110 096). (This booklet is a simplified explanation of online searching and is an excellent introduction for undergraduates or for any new online user.)

Note

The author wishes to thank Rod Slade, Coordinator of Online Services at the University of Oregon Library, for providing bibliographic and statistical background and for reviewing the manuscript. The author also wishes to thank him for so often picking up the overflow of students wishing to use the Psychological Abstracts online data base.

Positive Side Effects of Online Information Retrieval

Richard A. Feinberg
Purdue University

David Drews
David Eynman
Juniata College

As online information retrieval becomes increasingly available for use by undergraduate students it becomes important to understand the appropriateness and ramifications of the use of this simple yet powerful tool for generating research literature (Atherton & Christian, 1977). In a recent article in this journal, Parr (1979) presents general arguments for the addition of training in online information searching for undergraduates. Parr argues that instead of allowing undergraduates to circumvent traditional bibliographic techniques and skills, use of online systems reinforce such bibliographic skills and adds new dimensions to library usage.

But is the influence of online retrieval of information limited to the acquisition and reinforcement of library skills? It is important to illuminate the scope of influence of these systems. Does the use of such systems influence attitudes toward assignments, class, or library usage? Does its use affect course performance? Exploration of these unintended side effects can illuminate the appropriate use of such online technology in undergraduate education.

Method. Subjects were 11 of 15 undergraduates enrolled in an environmental psychology course at a small liberal arts college. All students were invited to participate in this experiment which was introduced as an effort to evaluate a new library system. This new system was described as being relevant for a portion of their course requirement; a literature review worth 20% of their final course grade. The literature review was described in a handout during this first class session as an opportunity to actively explore research in environmental psychology in depth. It was suggested that the best approach would be to select an interesting section of the course text (Bell, Fisher, & Loomis, 1978) and review studies not included. Students were also given detailed style requirements and references of examples of literature reviews in *Psychological Bulletin,* although it was pointed out that their reviews need not be as extensive.

Two of the 15 students (one male and one female) refused to participate. The remaining 13 students were randomly assigned to either the standard bibliographic skills group (four males and three females) or the online retrieval system group (three males and three females). Two students failed to attend their respective training sessions (one male from the standard skills and one female from the online systems group) and were discarded from the study. Thus only data from the remaining 11 students were collected and assessed for this study.

During the first week of class, students were required to attend a 50 minute training session. Students in both groups were introduced to library hours and procedures. The standard bibliographic group was given an introduction to the use of *Psychological Abstracts*. Emphasis was placed on locating abstracts relevant to a particular subject area or topic. Students in the online information retrieval group received a 50 minute introduction in the use of the use of the Dialog system (A Brief Guide to Dialog Searching, 1978). Dialog is a commercial online data base system offered by Lockheed Information Systems. The system includes approximately 100 data bases, accessible through remote terminals over commercial telephone lines. Emphasis was placed on getting students started at developing a search strategy in association with one of the trained reference librarians. Students in both groups were given a brief questionnaire to assess their grade point averages and attitudes toward the library.

The course lasted ten weeks with the literature review due the last day of class. To eliminate the possibility of experimenter bias in assigning grades to students, literature reviews were handed in without identification and graded blindly to student identity or experimental condition. After handing in the literature review students were given a follow-up questionnaire concerning their attitudes to the library and assignment. To minimize any potential bias of students trying to please the teacher it was emphasized that they were not to identify themselves on this questionnaire.

Results. The online information retrieval group outperformed the standard skills group in grade on the literature review. The average grade on the computer groups' papers (93, which was equivalent to an A) was significantly greater than that of the standard skills group (81.8, which equalled a B-), $t(9)=3.01$, $p <.01$. The online retrieval group believed the library to be significantly more adequate and prepared for literature review assignments, $t(9)=2.59$, $p <.05$, and they derived more satisfaction from completing that assignment, $t(9)=2.94$, $p <.05$. Prior to the training sessions there were no significant differences between groups in grade point average, in prior library use or confidence in library use (t's <1).

A semantic differential-like questionnaire used to assess feelings toward the library showed that the computer information retrieval group was significantly more positive to the library than the standard skills group, $t(9)=2.31$, $p <.05$, feeling the library to be more interesting, satisfying, exhilarating, stimulating, complex, orderly, good, positive, and useful .

Discussion. Developing an awareness of techniques to generate psychological literature is an integral step in teaching the research process. The ineffectiveness of typical approaches has led to the discussion and development of painless methods of acquainting students with the literature review process (e.g., Gardner, 1977; Parr, 1978). The results of the present study indicate that the introduction of the technologically powerful online retrieval search not only leads to better performance but has the unintended consequence of improving feelings and attitudes toward the library and the literature review process.

Online information retrieval represents a potent new addition in training undergraduates. It has been shown to reinforce traditional bibliographic skills (Parr, 1979) and, in the present study, to possibly increase the exercise of such skills by improving attitudes to the library and to the literature search process.

References

A Brief Guide to Dialog Searching. Palo Alto, CA: Lockheed Information Systems, 1978.

Atherton, P., & Christian, R. *Librarians and online services.* White Plains, NY: Knowledge Industry Publications, 1977.

Bell, P., Fisher, J., & Loomis, R. *Environmental Psychology.* Philadelphia, PA: Saunders, 1978.

Gardner L. A relatively painless method of introduction to the psychological literature search. *Teaching of Psychology,* 1977, *4*, 89-90.

Parr V. Course-related library instruction for psychology students. *Teaching of Psychology,* 1978, *5*, 101-102.

Parr, V. Online information retrieval and the undergraduate. *Teaching of Psychology,* 1979, *6*, 61-62.

Bibliographic Computerized Searching in Psychology

Linda K. Lewis
General Library
University of New Mexico

Computerized searching can now locate information or produce bibliographies in many different subject areas. This article presents some of the advantages and disadvantages of computerized searching, and describes the databases in the area of psychology.

Social science researchers have used computers to manipulate quantitative data for many years, but the ability to conduct a survey of the literature or to prepare subject bibliographies is a comparatively recent development. This article introduces some of the resources available and discusses the advantages and disadvantages of computerized searching in psychology.

Most computer searching mentioned in this article involves the processing of a file of information, a *database,* in order to locate specific information. The results may be a bibliography of an author's works or citations concerning a topic. Many of these databases are the computerized counterparts of indexes available in most libraries, such as *Psychological Abstracts,* whereas others, such as *Family Resources,* were developed only as databases.

Advantages

A computer search may be more useful than a manual search of the indexes for several reasons. A computer search can save a researcher considerable time. Because the computer is capable of rapidly processing large amounts of information, it can search several years of information in a few seconds. Although the response time does vary with the equipment and the system, many searches can be completed in less than 20 min.

Some databases are updated weekly or daily, whereas their printed equivalents are issued monthly or less frequently. A search may supply references that will not appear in the printed index for weeks or even years. The *Mental Measurements Yearbook* database includes references that will appear in the ninth edition of the printed equivalent, which is not yet published.

Some databases were created as computerized files; they do not have an equivalent index. Databases such as *Mental Health Abstracts* provide exclusive information, unavailable from any other source.

The computer can search for a specific term or phrase in several places in an entry. A newly developing area may not be assigned a formal subject heading, or the subject may be listed under a different heading than expected, but if the terms are used in the title or the abstract of the article, the computer can retrieve the citations. For example, the phrase *guided imagery* is not used as a descriptor in *Psychological Abstracts,* but when the phrase was entered in the equivalent database, *PsycINFO,* the computer located 84 references.

The computer can search for several different terms, then compare the citations in order to identify only those references in which all the desired terms appear. This is especially valuable when each of the terms has a large number of references because the computer can cross-match them easily. A request for information about stereotypes among and about artists was searched in *PsycINFO.* The terms were searched in the fields for the titles and assigned subject headings only. In addition to *artist,* the terms *painter* and *sculptor* were also entered, all in a truncated form in order to retrieve both singular and plural forms. This portion of the request located 652 references. The terms used in addition to *stereotype* included *prejudice* and *attitudes,* which retrieved 9,261 references. When these two areas were combined, there were only 19 articles concerning both stereotypes and artists.

In addition to checking the subject headings that have been assigned by an index, the computer can search many other areas of the citation. Depending on the database, the date, issuing agency, title, language, author, special feature, or type of document could be searched. A search topic in some databases could be limited to journal articles written in English, with bibliographies, published within the last 2 years. In other databases, the searcher could locate conference proceedings, classroom materials, review articles, or audiovisual materials related to a specific topic.

Disadvantages

There are, of course, some problems with computer searches. The cost may be a consideration. The cost for computer time varies widely among databases; ERIC is $25 per hour, but *Social SciSearch is* $110 per hour. Although the length of time it takes to do a search will vary with the speed of the computer terminal and printer, many searches take only a few minutes. A request for information concerning women's fear of success and motivation for power was run in *PsycINFO* on a Texas Instruments Silent 700 terminal. The search lasted 11 min, and cost $7.61. The cost for printing the 85 references and mailing them to the library was $17. Some libraries subsidize the cost of a search; others charge for computer time, telecommunications costs, and staff time.

The computer retrieves the exact words requested. It cannot distinguish among the various meanings of a word or between homographs. For example, if the computer is asked for references about *pool,* it will retrieve materials about sports and about water unless terms are added to clarify the request. Although these irrelevant results can be reduced by combining terms, some unrelated references may still appear. Such references would also be seen in a manual search, but would not be copied down; the computer cannot make that kind of critical judgment.

Most databases in the social sciences were created in the 1960s and 1970s; for earlier research, the printed sources must still be used. *Psychological Abstracts* began publishing in 1927, but is available on computer only since 1967.

Table 1. Databases in Psychology

Databases and Beginning Dates	Equivalents	Subjects
Child Abuse and Neglect, 1965	None	Child abuse, including programs and bibliographic entries
Druginfo and Alcohol Use and Abuse, 1968	None	All aspects of drug and alcohol use and abuse
ERIC, 1966	*Resources in Education, Current Index to Journals in Education*	All aspects of education
Exceptional Child Education Resources, 1966	*Exceptional Child Education Abstracts*	Education of gifted and handicapped children
Family Resources, 1973	None	All aspects of family relations, including program descriptions and bibliographic entries
Medline, 1966	*Index Medicus, Index to Dental Literature, International Nursing Index*	Biomedicine, nursing, and dentistry
Mental Health Abstracts, 1969	None	All aspects of mental health
Mental Measurements Yearbook, 1977	*Mental Measurements Yearbook*	Descriptions and reviews of psychological tests
National Rehabilitation Information Center, 1950	None	Rehabilitation of physically and mentally disabled persons
PsycINFO, 1967	*Psychological Abstracts* plus material from *Dissertation Abstracts*	Psychology and the behavioral sciences
PsycALERT	None	Psychology; new items are entered here prior to indexing for *PsycINFO*
Social SciSearch, 1972	*Social Science Citation Index*	Social and behavioral sciences
SciSearch, 1974	*Science Citation Index, Current Contents: Clinical Practice, Current Contents: Engineering, Technology, and Applied Science, Current Contents: Agriculture, Biology, and Environmental Sciences*	Pure and applied science and technology
Sociological Abstracts, 1963	*Sociological Abstracts*	Sociology and related social and behavioral sciences

Searching With Microcomputers

Until recently, most bibliographic computer searching had been done through libraries or by information science businesses. As microcomputers have become widely available, it is possible to use them for database searching.

There are several companies that provide microcomputer users with access to most databases. The companies vary in cost, hours, computer compatability, and available databases. Some systems are structured so that the searcher responds to questions from the computer, following a programmed format, as does BRS/AfterDark. Some are designed to enable a beginning searcher to use the system without training (e.g., BRS/BRKTHRU), and others (e.g., Dialog), require searchers to learn a specific command language. Some of the major companies now offering programs for microcomputers are Dialog in Palo Alto, CA; BRS in Latham, NY; Source in McLean, VA; Easynet in Marberth, PA; and CompuServe in Columbus, OH.

Obtaining the Article

If a reference that has been located through a search is not available in an area library, it may still be acquired. Many libraries will borrow a copy from another source through interlibrary loan. Some companies (e.g., the Institute for Scientific Information, which publishes *Science Citation Index* and *Social Science Citation Index),* will provide copies of the articles they index. Some journals, including the *Harvard Business Review* and those published by the American Chemical Society, have the complete text of the article available on the computer database.

Databases for Psychology

There are many databases that include psychology and more are being developed continually. Table 1 lists some of the major ones, giving the beginning dates, print equivalents, and general subjects included. There are other databases in many subject areas that have information related to psychology, such as those in the areas of business, law, political science, health, or technology. There are also databases about grants, foundations, biographical information, and educational tests. Others contain bibliographical records about books, conference papers, dissertations, periodicals, audiovisual materials, and government publications.

Conclusion

For many years, most computerized searching has been done through libraries or businesses. Few psychologists had the terminals that could connect with the small number of available files. Recent years have seen rapid growth in the number of databases and in the availability of the equipment necessary to manipulate the databases. The companies that once assumed their only users were specialists have now created programs for beginning searchers. Although computerized searching cannot answer all needs, a researcher aware of the basic concepts of searching will find it a valuable tool.

2. TEACHING EXPERIMENTAL DESIGN AND METHODS OF OBSERVATION

Return to Our Roots: Raising Radishes to Teach Experimental Design

William M. Stallings
Georgia State University

Students design and perform an experiment to assess effects of fertilizers on the growth of radish seedlings for a graduate class in design and statistics. The goal of this project is to provide students practice in making design decisions, collecting and analyzing real data, and writing up results. An informal evaluation, based on written comments and a content analysis of the individual reports, suggests that this approach is a promising technique for teaching experimental design.

Alternative ways of teaching applied statistics have been described in journals such as the *American Statistician* (e.g., Hogg, 1972; Tanner, 1985), *Chance* (Joiner, 1988), *Teaching of Psychology* (Hettich, 1974), and the *Journal of the Royal Statistical Society Series A* (Jowett & Davies, 1960). This literature emphasizes the importance of having students work with real data. For example, Singer and Willett (1990) argued that "real data sets provide a more meaningful and effective vehicle for the teaching of applied statistics" than do synthetic data, no matter their numerical tractability (p. 223). Perhaps ideally, students should pursue their own research interests, collecting data from studies they design and conduct (see Jowett & Davies, 1960; Tanner, 1985).

Teachers of psychological and educational statistics are concerned that some students can complete the assigned computational exercises without understanding the purpose of the computations. For example, one of my students correctly computed a two-way analysis of variance (ANOVA) but could not distinguish between the number of levels in a factor and the number of independent variables. This incident illustrates the limitations of textbook exercises.

Although students could replicate classic experiments or design and complete simple studies of their own, both options are time-consuming. In addition, one now has to comply with institutional guidelines for research participants. Fortunately, many of these problems can be avoided. Students can work with real data by conducting simple agricultural experiments, what I call "returning to our roots." After all, as Lovie (1979) noted, "the first practical applica-tion of analysis of variance (ANOVA) was on the effects of manure on the rotation of potato crops (Fisher & Mackenzie, 1923)" (p. 151).

The last three times I taught our second course in statistics, an ANOVA-based course using Keppel (1991), I required each student to collect and analyze data from a gardening experiment. Students assess the effect of growth accelerators on radish seedlings that they grow at their homes.

Typically, students enrolled in the course are working toward advanced degrees or certification in education or nursing; they tend to be mature women who are employed. Our students live off campus. Except for the nurses, they tend to have weak science and mathematics backgrounds.

Equipment

The inexpensive equipment consists of plastic ice cube trays or egg cartons, potting soil, fine gravel, mechanical drawing dividers (for measuring the heights of the seedlings), a ruler, radish seeds (or any other fast-germinating vegetable seeds), several jars with lids, and one or more growth accelerators (e.g., Miraclegro® or RA-PID GRO®).

Procedure

Instructions for the procedure and analysis are given in Table 1. Students decide whether to compare different growth accelerators (qualitatively different levels) or different amounts of the same growth accelerator (quantitatively different levels). Other issues that each student considers are experimental mortality, unequal sample sizes, unit of analysis, number of comparison groups, and choice of dependent variables. Most students use seedling height, but germination rate and length of tap root are possible also.

Students have reported that seeds germinate in 3 to 5 days. Most students obtain usable measurements at intervals of 5 to 7 days. I allow several days for students to obtain the equipment and set up the experiment. Two weeks has been a sufficient time for analysis and write-up. Hence, students can complete the project in 5 to 6 weeks.

As an illustration of a typical student project, one student grew three sets of 10 seedlings each with treatments of water and no accelerator, two drops of accelerator, or four drops of accelerator. After 4 weeks, the mean growths were 1.50, 2.74, and 2.96 in., respectively. A completely randomized ANOVA on these data yielded a significant difference, $F(2, 27) = 7.41$, $p < .01$. To obtain equal sample sizes, which is not a requirement of the completely randomized design but helpful in other analyses, students often have thinned seedlings immediately after germination.

Table 1. Instructions for Project: Procedure and Analysis

Procedure

1. Prepare three ice cube trays or egg cartons. To facilitate drainage, punch small holes in the bottom of each tray or carton. Then add gravel, and fill with potting soil.
2. In each mold or receptacle, plant three to four seeds about 1/4 in. deep. Soak seeds in water for 15 min before planting to promote germination.
3. Use the jars to mix and store the various concentrations or brands of growth accelerators.
4. Administer the treatment, either different types of growth accelerators or different concentrations of the same growth accelerator (e.g., no drops, one drop, and two drops).
5. Except for the application of the experimental treatment, treat all containers alike.
6. After germination (3 to 5 days), make three sets of measurements at equally spaced intervals (5 to 7 days).

Analysis

1. Write your report in a fashion similar to writing the Method, Results, and Discussion sections of a journal article.
2. Under Results, present the outcomes in words, graphs or tables, and statistics (both descriptive and inferential). For each data-gathering period, construct a graph showing the mean height of the seedlings plotted against levels of the independent variable.
3. For the final data-gathering period, compute a completely randomized ANOVA, omega squared, and (if you find statistical significance) Scheffé and other post hoc comparisons. If your experiment involved quantitatively different levels and if you obtained statistical significance, analyze the data for trends.
4. Optional analyses (beyond minimal expectations) could include computing a repeated measures design, making a priori comparisons, and estimating post hoc power.

Evaluation

Anecdotal evidence of students' positive reactions to the radish project comes from seven written comments appended to project reports and course evaluations. Examples include the following:

"The radish experiment . . . seemed to tie up many of the principles and techniques we learned in class. "

"My classmates seemed unanimously enthusiastic about the project."

"The concept of experimental learning is an excellent one and very useful in helping students to grasp abstract concepts such as ANOVA. The requirements. . . were not too costly or time-consuming. "

To further evaluate this project, I conducted a content analysis of 31 student reports. I examined the various statistical and design features that students used or could have used, and I judged the appropriateness of their decisions. For example, a post hoc trend analysis following a nonsignificant omnibus F was an inappropriate application; a failure to follow up a significant omnibus F with a post hoc test was an inappropriate nonapplication. By contrast, not following up a nonsignificant omnibus F was an appropriate nonapplication. The content analysis is summarized in Table 2.

The data suggest that, overall, students made appropriate decisions. However, post hoc analyses of means and trends were troublesome. Graphing also appears to have been a problem. This may be attributed to students' weak science and mathematics backgrounds. Only seven students went beyond the minimal statistical requirements. Given Keppel's (1991) emphasis on planned comparisons, it is disturbing that only two students even attempted an a priori test. None considered low power due to small sample size as an explanation for not obtaining statistical significance. Four students reported problems with experimental control (e. g., "The cat walked on the trays"). Still, most met the minimal expectations.

Conclusion

Overall, I am satisfied with the results of the radish project, but I plan several changes. I will provide a more detailed handout of instructions (including suggested schedules); encourage and reward use of more complex designs, associated ancillary tests, and tests of model assumptions; and append a project evaluation to the anonymous course/instructor evaluation.

All of my students have completed this project in an 11-week academic quarter. Nearly all informally agreed that the project made vivid the concepts of experimental design and ANOVA. During class discussion, some reported that the project was fun and even became a topic of family conversation. In my experience, raising radishes is a successful teaching technique.

Table 2. Frequency of Design and Statistical Treatment Decisions

Topic	Appropriate		Inappropriate	
	Application	Nonapplication	Application	Nonapplication
Design selection	29		2	
Post hoc comparisons	15	8	6	2
Effect size/omega squared	23			8
Trend analysis	12	11	3	5
Interpretation of significance	29		2	
Graphs	22		2	7

Note. Thirty-one student reports were analyzed. Each report is listed only once in each row but may appear more than once in each column.

References

Fisher, R. A., & Mackenzie, W. A. (1923). Studies in crop rotation. II. The manurial responses of different potato varieties. *Journal of Agricultural Science, 13*, 311-320.

Hettich, P. (1974). The student as data generator. *Teaching of Psychology, 1*, 35-36.

Hogg, R. V. (1972). On statistical education. *American Statistician, 39*, 168-175.

Joiner, B. L. (1988). Let's change how we teach statistics. *Chance, 1*, 53-54.

Jowett, G. H., & Davies, H. M. (1960). Practical experimentation as a teaching method in statistics. *Journal of the Royal Statistical Society Series A, 123*, 11-35.

Keppel, G. (1991). *Design and analysis: A researcher's handbook* (3rd ed.). Englewood Cliffs, NJ: Prentice Hall.

Lovie, A. D. (1979). The analysis of variance in experimental psychology: 1934-1945. *British Journal of Mathematical and Statistical Psychology, 32*, 151-178.

Singer, J. D., & Willett, J. B. (1990). Improving the teaching of applied statistics: Putting the data back into data analysis. *American Statistician, 44*, 223-230.

Tanner, M. A. (1985). The use of investigations in the introductory statistics course. *American Statistician, 39*, 306-310.

Note

I thank Ruth L. Ault and three anonymous reviewers for comments on earlier drafts of this article.

Factorial Design: Binocular and Monocular Depth Perception in Vertical and Horizontal Stimuli

Dominic J. Zerbolio, Jr.
James T. Walker
University of Missouri—St. Louis

This article describes a factorial experiment that is useful as a laboratory exercise in a research methods course. In the Howard-Dolman depth perception apparatus, two vertical rods are adjusted, using binocular or monocular vision, so they appear equidistant from the observer. The two rods can also be oriented horizontally, which allows a factorial design combining the factors of Viewing Condition (binocular and monocular) and Rod Orientation (vertical and horizontal). The exercise illustrates the nature of an interaction and the necessity of an additional analysis of simple main effects. It also provides a basis for understanding a perceptual problem in the real world— the difficulty of localizing horizontally extended stimuli such as power lines.

145

Factorial designs represent one of our most useful and powerful research tools. Yet the major advantage of factorial designs over simpler designs (i.e., the ability to detect interactions between variables) is also what makes them difficult to teach, because interactions are not always intuitively obvious to students. Teaching students to understand the nature and interpretation of an interaction can be greatly facilitated by an exercise, as long as it reliably produces an interaction, and the results are readily and obviously interpretable. We have tried to manipulate many variables factorially during our collective 4 decades of teaching. None of these efforts was completely satisfactory until recently, when we discovered an exercise that meets these requirements. In addition, this exercise requires minimum equipment and makes a substantive point about a real-world perceptual problem.

The equipment required is some form of the Howard-Dolman depth perception apparatus (Howard, 1919a, 1919b; the Howard-Dolman depth perception apparatus was supplied by Lafayette Instrument Company, P.O. Box 5729, Sagamore Parkway, Lafayette, IN 47903) and masks or goggles to restrict viewing to one eye. The usual application of the Howard-Dolman apparatus requires the subject to adjust two vertical rods in the third dimension so that they appear equidistant from the observer. The dependent variable measure is the separation between the two rods, measured along the subject's line of sight. The average error is typically much smaller when rods are viewed binocularly than when viewed monocularly. If the apparatus is laid on its side, the rod orientation becomes horizontal (see Figure 1); in this orientation, Howard (1919b) found that the average errors for binocular and monocular viewing did not differ.

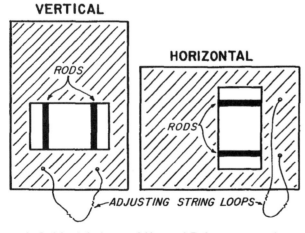

Figure 1. Subjects' views of Howard-Dolman apparatus. Rods are adjusted to appear equidistant in depth using loops of string. A pointer indicates the adjustment error on a scale hidden from the subject. Extraneous cues are reduced by diffused white backlighting.

Orienting the apparatus horizontally or vertically allows a factorial combination of Rod Orientation and Viewing Condition. We expected and found little or no difference between monocular and binocular viewing conditions with the rods in the horizontal orientation, but a substantial superiority of binocular over monocular with the rods in the vertical orientation (i.e., a Viewing Condition x Rod Orientation interaction). The example we report used an independent-groups procedure, but the design lends itself just as well to a repeated-measures design, assuming the instructor wishes to grapple with the problems associated with teaching interactions and repeated measures simultaneously.

Method

Subjects

Thirty subjects participated as a class requirement in an undergraduate research methods course.

Apparatus

The apparatus (see Figure 1) was adjusted by means of a string looped around the back of a chair. Subjects were allowed to use only one hand in making adjustments in order to minimize kinesthetic cues.

Procedure

The experiment used a 2 x 2 independent-groups factorial design. The factors were Viewing Condition (binocular and monocular) and Rod Orientation (vertical and horizontal). Using a table of random numbers, we assigned each of 30 students to one of the four experimental conditions with the constraint that the number of subjects per cell was to be as nearly equal as possible. The dependent variable for each subject was the mean separation between the rods in 10 adjustment trials.

In two of the groups, the largest scores were so deviant that questions were raised regarding whether the subjects were following instructions in adjusting the apparatus or whether the student-experimenters were recording the data accurately. In the interest of reducing error variance, these two scores were discarded.

The apparatus was located approximately 5.5 m from the subject. At the beginning of each trial, the rods were positioned at their extreme departure from equidistance, 20 cm apart. The rod nearest to the subject (left or right in the vertical orientation and top or bottom in the horizontal orientation) was determined randomly using a Gellerman series. The student-experimenter blocked the subject's view of the apparatus with his or her body during the initial positioning of the rods before each trial. In monocular viewing, each subject used the dominant eye, as determined by a measure of sighting dominance.

Results and Discussions

The mean separations for all four groups appear in Figure 2. The main effect of Viewing Condition was significant, $F(1, 24) = 4.91$, $p < .05$. The effect of Rod Orientation approached significance, $F(1, 24) = 3.77$, $p < .10$, and there was a significant interaction between these factors, $F(1, 24) = 9.59$, $p < .01$. Because the main effects are not interpretable when an interaction is present, simple main effects for Viewing Conditions at each Rod Orientation were calculated. With the rods oriented vertically, binocular viewing was significantly superior to monocular viewing, $F(1, 24) = 14.11$, $p < .001$. With the rods oriented horizontally, no difference between binocular and monocular viewing was observed, $F < 1$. These results are clearly illustrated in Figure 2.

The results allowed us to demonstrate the problem of interpreting a main effect in the presence of an interaction and readily led our students to see the necessity of partitioning the data into simple main effects. Figure 2 was particularly helpful in this respect. In this context, the question of whether binocular or monocular vision is better clearly depends on the horizontal or vertical orientation of the target stimuli.

This exercise greatly facilitates the exposition of a factorial design, and it relates to some perceptual problems in the real world. Horizontally extended stimuli, such as wires, are difficult to localize in depth because they provide little or no binocular disparity. Thus, line workers, tree trimmers, and construction workers moving equipment near power lines are at great risk, as accidents frequently occur in such situations. Airplane pilots flying near wires are also at risk, as Howard (1919b) pointed out long ago. Our exercise serves the dual purpose of explicating a factorial design and providing a substantive basis for understanding a real-world perceptual problem.

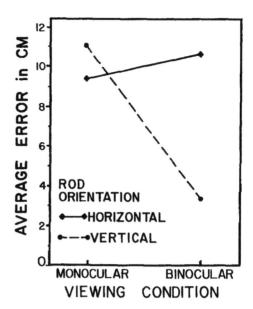

Figure 2. Results. Smallest mean (binocular viewing with vertically oriented rods) differs significantly from all other means, $p < .01$, which do not differ from each other.

References

Howard, H. J. (1919a). *A* six meter stereoscope. *American Journal of Ophthalmology, 2,* 849-853.

Howard, H. J. (1919b). *A* test for the judgment of distance. *American Journal of Ophthalmology, 2,* 656-675.

Rewards, Costs, and Helping: A Demonstration of the Complementary Nature of Experimental and Correlational Research

Kenneth W. Kerber
College of the Holy Cross

Cronbach (1957) maintained that there are two principal research strategies in psychology: the experimental and the correlational. Textbooks in psychology often provide discussions of these two methods. Although many psychologists prefer the greater control of experiments, some researchers believe that it is desirable to use both methods when feasible because the disadvantages of one are frequently offset by the advantages of the other. For example, in their textbook on social psychology, Baron and Byrne (1977, pp. 18-24) give an interesting example of how the same psychological relationship, specifically, the relationship between the exposure of young children to violent television shows and their level of aggression toward peers, has been examined by using both the correlational (Eron, 1963) and the experimental (Liebert & Baron, 1972) methods.

In this article, I will describe a two-part research project which I have used in a social psychology laboratory course. The major purpose of the project is to demonstrate how the correlational and experimental methods can be used to explore the same psychological relationships. The project can be employed in general laboratory courses or in lecture courses where an understanding of the correlational and experimental methods is important.

The project focuses on a set of relationships from Piliavin and Piliavin's (1972) reward-cost model of helping behavior in emergency situations. In a very simplified form, their model suggests that the probability that an observer will provide help to a victim depends upon the relative strength of the costs and rewards for providing help. For example, if the costs for providing help are low and the rewards are high, direct help would be expected in the situation. On the other hand, if the costs are high and the rewards are low, the observer may attempt to escape from the situation rather than provide help.

According to Piliavin and Piliavin (1972), the costs for providing help are a function of the costs for helping and the costs for not helping. Costs for helping may include personal danger, expenditure of effort, lost time, embarassment, disgusting or sickening experiences, and feelings of inadequacy or failure if the help is not effective. Costs for not helping may include self-blame, public censure, loss of rewards for helping, and continued empathic arousal. Similarly, the rewards for providing help are a function of the rewards for helping and the rewards for *not* helping. Rewards for helping may include feelings of competence, self-congratulations, thanks from the victim, praise and admiration from bystanders, money, and fame. Rewards for not helping refer to rewards associated with the activities that would be interrupted were the individual to help and any rewards associated with personal freedom and lack of involvement.

A very important feature of this model is that rewards and costs are in the eye of the beholder (Walster & Piliavin, 1972). Thus, any assessment of rewards and costs must be from the point of view of the person who provides the help.

Although this model explicitly refers to responses in emergency situations, which are, by definition, an important context in which to study helping, one might argue that non-emergency situations are a more common and no less valid context in which to study altruistic behavior. A request for help in a non-emergency situation requires some response on the part of the person who is asked. A person who is asked for help may respond with different degrees of help from no help at all to very much help. The present research project examines the possibility that the amount of help provided in a non-emergency situation may depend upon the strength of the costs and rewards for providing help. Specifically, the research question to be explored in the current project is: What are the relationships between rewards and helping and between costs and helping in a non-emergency situation where help is requested?

On the basis of the model of helping presented by Piliavin and Piliavin (1972), hypotheses were derived for a correlational study and for an experimental study. For the correlational study, it was hypothesized that there would be a positive correlation between rewards and helping and a negative correlation between costs and helping in a non-emergency situation. For the experimental study, it was hypothesized that high rewards would lead to more helping than low rewards and that high costs would lead to less helping than low costs in a similar non-emergency situation.

Method

Correlational Study. Subjects in this study were recruited by the thirteen students in my social psychology laboratory course. Each student obtained data from four subjects who were friends or acquaintances of the students. In order to have the same number of male and female subjects, each student recruited two males and two females. All 52 subjects completed a two page questionnaire that was prepared especially for this study. On the first page of the questionnaire, subjects were told to read the following situation:

> One evening, just as you settle down to study for an important test, an acquaintance from down the hall in your dormitory enters your room. He/she asks for assistance with some homework which is due the next morning. It turns out that you have already taken the same course in which your acquaintance needs assistance.

Subjects then rated how much help they would give to the person who asked for assistance (1 = *No help at all*; 7 = *Very much help*).

On the second page of the questionnaire, subjects gave their estimates of the rewards (1 = *No rewards at all*; 7 = *Very high rewards*) and the costs (1 = *No costs at all*; 7 = *Very high costs*) of helping the person in the situation. Above the appropriate rating scale, subjects were given the following brief definitions of rewards and costs:

> When helping a person, we sometimes experience *rewards* as a result of our behavior. For example, we may feel better about ourselves, we may receive thanks from the person we help, we may receive praise for our behavior, we may receive assistance at a later time from the person we helped.
>
> When helping a person, we sometimes experience costs as a result of our behavior. For example, we may lose valuable time, we may receive no thanks for our help, we may have to expend a lot of effort, we may never receive assistance at a later time from the person we helped.

The data from this study were compiled in class, and each student performed an analysis of the results.

Experimental Study. This study consisted of a 2 X 2 factorial design with costs and rewards as the independent variables. The study was divided into two parts: (a) a check on the manipulation of rewards and costs; and (b) the effect of the manipulation of rewards and costs on helping.

For both parts of this study, subjects were told to read the following situation:

> It is 8 o'clock on a Monday evening, and you have just begun to study for a very important examination. The examination is scheduled for tomorrow morning at 10 o'clock. You need an excellent performance in order to make up for a poor showing on the previous test in this class.
>
> Just as you settle down to work, an acquaintance from down the hall enters your room and asks for some assistance with his/her mathematics homework which is due the next morning. You took the same mathematics course last semester.
>
> Before responding to his/her request you ask if your acquaintance will do a favor for you in return for your help. Your acquaintance says that he/she is willing to do a favor of your choice in return for your assistance with the homework.

The cost manipulation was accomplished by changing the day of the examination from tomorrow morning (High Cost) to Thursday morning (Low Cost). The reward manipulation was accomplished by stating that the acquaintance was willing to do a favor (High Reward) versus was not willing to do a favor (Low Reward) in return for assistance with the homework.

To check the manipulations of the independent variables, 52 subjects gave their estimates of the rewards and the costs of helping the person in the situation. The rating scales and the definitions of rewards and costs were the same as those in the correlational study. Subjects were recruited by the students in the course. Each student recruited four subjects, one in each of the four conditions of the study. In order to have the same number of male and female subjects in each condition, each student recruited only persons of his or her own sex.

To assess the effect of the manipulation of rewards and costs on helping, 52 subjects rated how much help they would give to the person who asked for assistance by using the same rating scale as that in the correlational study. A new group of subjects was recruited for this part of the study. Once again, each student in the class obtained data from four subjects, one in each of the four conditions of the study, and each student recruited all male or all female subjects to control for sex.

The data from both parts of this study were compiled in class, and each student performed the analyses of the results.

Results

Correlational Study. The correlation between rewards and helping in this study was statistically significant in the predicted direction, $r = .57$ $(df = 50, p < .01)$. However, the correlation between costs and helping, although in the predicted direction, did not reach conventional levels of significance, $r = -.24$ $(df = 50, p < .10)$.

Experimental Study. For the manipulation check, separate 2 X 2 analyses of variance were performed for the dependent variables of rewards and costs. In the analysis of rewards, the High Reward condition (4.77) was rated as significantly more rewarding than the Low Reward condition (3.62), $F (1, 48) = 8.78$, $p < .01$, and neither the main effect for costs, $F (1, 48) = 3.16$, nor the interaction of rewards and costs, $F (1, 48) = .98$, were significant. In the analysis of costs, the High Cost condition (5.39) was rated as significantly more costly than the Low Cost condition (3.12), $F (1, 48) = 31.74$, $p < .01$, and neither the main effect for rewards, $F (1, 48) = .01$, nor the interaction of rewards and costs, $F (1, 48) = .74$, were significant. Therefore, the manipulation of rewards and costs was highly successful.

Finally, a 2 X 2 analysis of variance was performed for the dependent variable of helping. Subjects indicated that they would give significantly more help in the High Reward (5.31) as opposed to the Low Reward (3.00) condition, $F (1, 48) = 31.08$, $p < .01$. In addition, there was a trend toward greater helping in the Low Cost (4.54) as opposed to the High Cost (3.77) condition, $F (1, 48) = 3.45$, $p < .10$. The interaction between rewards and costs was not significant, $F (1, 48) = 2.21$.

Discussion

The purpose of this research project was to demonstrate how a correlational study and an experimental study can explore the same psychological relationships. The two studies described here present a correlational and an experimental investigation of the relationships between rewards and helping and between costs and helping in a non-emergency situation. The results of the project show how the findings from these two types of studies may complement one another. The results of the correlational study support the hypothesis that there is a positive relationship between rewards and helping. One advantage of this study was that the subjects themselves estimated the rewards and costs of the situation, as they perceived them, as well as the extent of their helping. Of course, statements about causality in this study are problematic. The experimental study supports the hypothesis that increases in reward cause increases in helping, although in this study the rewards and costs were contrived by the experimenter. Taken together, these studies indicate that in at least one non-emergency situation, helping is strongly related to the rewards in the situation but is not clearly related to the costs in the same situation. With respect to the model proposed by Piliavin and Piliavin (1972), perhaps the relative importance of rewards and costs varies in non-emergency as opposed to emergency situations.

The only materials necessary to use this research project in the classroom are the questionnaires described in the method section. The amount of time that students devote to the project could be reduced if the instructor instead of the students analyzed the data. In addition, with larger classes, the students themselves could be the subjects, thus eliminating the need for data collection outside of class.

This project could initiate the discussion of many important aspects of psychological research: (a) differences between correlational and experimental research; (b) advantages and disadvantages of each of these methods; (c) the generation of hypotheses on the basis of previous research; (d) operational definitions; (e) manipulation checks; (f) the adequacy of subject samples; (g) generalization of research findings; and (h) statistical analysis and inferences from data. In short, this project could be a valuable tool when teaching courses that require an understanding of research methods in psychology.

References

Baron, R. A., & Byrne, D. *Social psychology: Understanding human interaction* (Second edition). Boston: Allyn & Bacon, 1977.

Cronbach, L. J. The two disciplines of scientific psychology. *American Psychologist,* 1957, *12,* 671-684.

Eron, L. D. Relationship of TV viewing habits and aggressive behavior in children. *Journal of Abnormal and Social Psychology,* 1963, *67,* 193-196.

Liebert, R. M., & Baron, R. A. Some immediate effects of televised violence on children's behavior. *Developmental Psychology,* 1972, *6,* 469-475.

Piliavin, J. A., & Piliavin, I. M. Effect of blood on reactions to a victim. *Journal of Personality and Social Psychology,* 1972, *23,* 353-361 .

Walster, E., & Piliavin, J. A. Equity and the innocent bystander. *Journal of Social Issues.* 1972, *28,* 165-189.

Note

The author wishes to thank Dr. Royce Singleton, Jr., for his helpful comments.

Beyond Experimentation: Research Projects for a Laboratory Course in Psychology

Kenneth W. Kerber
College of the Holy Cross

Wachtel (1980) has strongly criticized psychologists for ". . . the often exclusive reliance on experiments as the sole means of empirical inquiry. " Along with other factors, Wachtel suggests that this tendency to rely on experiments has produced a pattern of research activity that has limited progress in psychology, and he calls for a greater diversity of method.

Although the use of diverse methods should be encouraged among established researchers, this strategy also should affect the training of would-be psychologists. A general laboratory course should include projects that familiarize students with the variety of methods available to a researcher. This paper describes four newly developed research projects that have been used in a laboratory course for psychology majors. The four projects address questions about human behavior by means of experimental, observational, survey, and archival research methods.

The projects were conducted in a laboratory course of approximately 20 students. The students served as the experimenters for each project, and the data from the entire class were pooled prior to statistical analysis. This procedure had several advantages: (a) the time required by each student to complete a project was reasonable; (b) the sample size for each project was large enough to achieve satisfactory statistical power; and (c) students received first hand experience as researchers for each of the four methods.

The students in the laboratory course were enrolled concurrently in a research methodology course, and had previously taken psychological statistics. Under the supervision of the laboratory instructor, students statistically analyzed the data for each project with the help of a computer and interpreted the findings in light of assigned readings. Of course, given a different background in statistics and computer usage, the students could calculate the statistics by hand, or the instructor could distribute summaries of the statistical results.

Experimental Method: The Interpretation of Gestures. Munn (1940) discovered that knowledge of the situation in which an affective response occurs often facilitates the accuracy of judgments of emotion from facial expressions. In this project we examined the effect of knowledge of the situational context on interpretation of the meaning of gestures.

As shown in Table 1, ten gestures (e.g.. standing/open hands) and their corresponding interpretations (e.g., sincerity) were taken from a popular book on body language (Nierenberg & Calero, 1971). Male students learned to portray these gestures by referring to drawings from Nierenberg and Calero, and the females were trained as experimenters. Each male-female research team recruited 12 subjects (6 males, 6 females) from among their friends and randomly assigned equal numbers of each sex to an in-context or an out-of context condition. For the out-of-context condition, subjects were asked to identify the meaning of each gesture portrayed by the male "sender" by choosing from the list of ten descriptive terms. For the in-context condition, the subjects' task was the same except that for each gesture, the experimenter briefly described a situation in which the gesture might occur. Table 1 also contains the description of the context for each gesture. The dependent variable was the number of correct identifications out of ten by each subject.

Subjects $(N = 94)$ correctly identified fewer gestures in the out-of-context $(M = 3.67)$ as opposed to the in-context $(M = 4.96)$ condition, $t(92) = 3.33$, $p < .01$, indicating that situational context facilitates the interpretation of gestures. However, the generally poor performance of subjects in both conditions suggested that many of the gestures may not have well-defined meanings. The validity of the gesture interpretations by Nierenberg and Calero (1971) was discussed, along with related research on nonverbal communication (Gitin, 1970; Mehrabian, 1969).

Observational Method: The Environment and Drinking. Rosenbluth, Nathan, and Lawson (1978) found that the social environment in which alcohol consumption takes place is related to the amount consumed. In this project we examined the relationship between the interpersonal environment and the amount and rate of beer consumption by college students.

Table 1. Stimuli Used in the Experimental Study on the Interpretation of Gestures

Gesture	Interpretation	Context
Standing/open hands (45)	Sincerity	A celebrity in a TV commercial tells you about the quality of a new product.
Standing/ crossed arms/ clenched fists (49)	Defensiveness	A person that you just met at a party listens as you talk about your summer job.
Seated/ straddling a chair (53)	Dominance	A stranger in a bar walks over to your table and introduces himself.
Seated/hand-to-cheek (59)	Critical Evaluation	A professor listens to a class presentation that you are giving.
Seated/touching nose/mouth covered (71)	Doubt	Your father listens as you describe where you were until 4AM last night.
Seated/leaning forward/hand on knee (77)	Readiness	A friend waits for you to get dressed so that you can go to a movie together.
Seated/steepling with hands (94)	Confidence	A person responds to a question while being interviewed on a TV talk show.
Seated/leaning back/hands supporting head/crossed legs (103)	Superiority	A professor listens as you ask for a letter of recommendation.
Seated/head-in-hand/drooping eyes (123)	Boredom	A student listens to a class lecture.
Seated/rubbing hands (132)	Expectation	A young man waits for his mother to serve his favorite meal.

Note: The numbers in parentheses indicate the pages in Nierenberg and Calero (1971) on which there is a drawing of each gesture.

Members of the class observed the drinking behavior of students in the college pub. Observers worked in pairs so as to remain unobtrusive. Each class member observed three or four beer drinkers for thirty minutes each $(N = 66)$. Observers recorded the sex of the subject, the number of drinking partners (1 to 3, or 4 and above), the presence of an opposite sex drinking partner (present or absent), the number of beers consumed to the closest quarter cup, and the number of sips per beer. A sip was operationally defined as a tilt of the cup such that its contents at least touched the subject's lips; if the subject tilted the cup, took a sip, and then repeated this motion without putting the cup down, each tilt was counted as a separate sip.

The number of beers and the average number of sips per beer were analyzed separately in 2 x 2 x 2 (sex of subject x group size x presence of the opposite sex) analyses of variance. Males $(M = 1.68)$ consumed more beer than females $(M = 1.14)$, $F(1,58) = 10.33$, $p < .01$, and at a faster rate (males, $M = 12.11$; females, $M = 19.30$), $F(1, 58) = 12.89$, $p < .01$. Of greatest interest, the presence of an opposite sex drinking partner was unrelated to the rate of consumption in large groups (present, $M = 15.80$; absent, $M = 15.93$), but was associated with a reduced rate of consumption in small groups (present, $M = 19.30$; absent, $M = 11.70$), $F(1,58) = 4.82$, $p < .05$. Results were discussed in terms of the effects of the physical and social setting on alcohol consumption (Hendricks, Sobell, & Cooper, 1978; Strickler, Dobbs, & Maxwell, 1979).

Survey Method: ESP and Psychokinesis. Jones, Russell, and Nickel (1977) found that college students are generally quite positive toward extrasensory perception (ESP) and other paranormal phenomena. In this project we examined the attitudes of a sample of college students toward ESP (telepathy, clairvoyance, and precognition) and psychokinesis.

A twelve item questionnaire constructed for this course contained two statements each regarding belief in telepathy, clairvoyance, precognition, psychokinesis, and the existence of scientific "proof" for ESP, along with two statements regarding personal experiences with ESP. The items are listed in Table 2. All responses were on a five-point scale (1 = strongly disagree with statement; 5 = strongly agree with statement). Each class member contacted six or seven individuals taken from a random sample of on-campus students $(N = 129)$. Respondents who agreed to participate $(N = 67)$ completed the survey anonymously and returned it directly to the course instructor via campus mail.

The percentage of respondents who accepted the existence of paranormal phenomena increased as one moved from psychokinesis (32.8%), to precognition (50.7%), to telepathy (55.2%), to clairvoyance (67.2%). Significant correlations ($p < .01$) revealed that if respondents believed in one of these types of paranormal phenomena, they also tended to believe in the others. Approximately fifty-one percent (50.7) of the sample believed that there is scientific proof for ESP, and 38.8 percent acknowledged personal experience with ESP. Belief in the existence of scientific proof for ESP and experience with ESP both were correlated significantly ($p < .01$) with greater acceptance of the specific types of paranormal phenomena. Potential sources of beliefs in the paranormal were discussed (Ayeroff & Abelson, 1976; Layton & Turnbull, 1975).

Archival Method: Stereotypes in Television Commercials. McArthur and Resko (1975) found that women are portrayed in an unfavorable manner relative to men in American television commercials. In this project we examined whether male and female central figures in television commercials are portrayed according to stereotyped sex roles.

Initially, students were trained to code the characteristics of adult males and females playing a major role in a television commercial. During data collection, students worked in pairs as a check on

Table 2. Items Used in the Survey Study on ESP and Psychokinesis

Topic	Items
Scientific Proof	Extrasensory perception (ESP) has been scientifically proven to exist.
	Reports of the scientific proof of extrasensory perception are strictly sensationalism with no factual basis.
Personal Experience	I firmly believe that, at least on a few occasions, I personally possessed extrasensory perception.
	I firmly believe that, at least on a few occasions, people I know possessed extrasensory perception.
Telepathy	Thought transference from one person to another in the absence of known methods of communication is impossible.
	Some people can read another person's mind through special psychic ability.
Clairvoyance	The idea that someone could perceive a physical object without using any of the known senses is unbelievable.
	Some people can perceive events in the absence of any stimulation of the known senses.
Precognition	Some people have a supernatural ability to predict the future.
	It is impossible to predict another person's future thoughts through special psychic ability.
Psychokinesis	Some people can move physical objects by using mysterious mental powers.
	The ability to move material objects through the power of the mind with no physical intervention does not exist.

reliability, with each pair coding approximately 20 commercials. Students agreed on the central figures in each commercial, but their characteristics were coded independently. The characteristics to be coded were: sex of the central figure (maximum of two per commercial), basis for credibility (product-user, authority, other), role (spouse, parent, homemaker, worker, professional, celebrity, narrator, boyfriend/girlfriend, other), location (home, store, outdoor setting, occupational setting, other), arguments given (factual evidence, opinions, no arguments), and type of product (body products, home products, foodstuffs, recreational items, automotive products, other). Detailed descriptions of the coding categories are contained in McArthur and Resko (1975). Research teams were assigned to watch television during different times of the day and evening and for different networks.

Overall agreement across all categories (excluding sex) and across all research teams was 82 percent, indicating adequate reliability. Five chi square statistics were calculated on contingency tables constructed by crossing sex of the central figures with each of the coded characteristics; all five statistics were significant ($p < .001$). In summary, male central figures ($N = 181$) were portrayed more often as authorities on food and auto products, in the roles of worker or narrator, located in stores or occupational settings, and using factual arguments. In contrast, female central figures ($N = 121$) were presented more often as users of body products, in the roles of parent or homemaker, located in the home or outdoors, and giving no arguments. Results were discussed in terms of the potential effects of sex role stereotypes in television commercials (Jennings, Geis, & Brown, 1980; McGhee & Frueh, 1980).

Discussion. In my laboratory course, these four projects provided an excellent context for analyzing the advantages and disadvantages of different methodological techniques (see Selltiz, Wrightsman, & Cook, 1976; Sommer & Sommer, 1980). They also initiated discussion of many important aspects of psychological research. For example, the observed relationship between situational context and the interpretation of gestures fulfills the requirements for a causal inference, whereas the relationship between the presence of an opposite sex drinking partner and beer consumption is simply an instance of covariation. Such comparisons were used to clarify the differences between experimental and correlational research. Regarding research ethics, informed consent is relevant when obtaining opinions about ESP, but is unnecessary when observing public beer drinking. Students were made aware of the ethical considerations relevant to specific research methods. Ways of obtaining subjects vary with the study, from an accidental sample observed in a college pub, to a time sample of television commercials. to a random sample drawn for a survey about ESP. In this case, discussion centered on the choice of a sampling procedure and the resulting implications for the generality of the findings.

Finally, the researcher's expectations regarding the results of a study may be influential, perhaps when observing the behavior of males and females in television commercials or in a college pub. The possibility of experimenter expectancy effects or experimenter bias was discussed in light of the findings of these studies. Of course, many other aspects of psychological research were examined such as the generation of hypotheses, operational definitions, checks on reliability, statistical analysis, and inferences from data. When students have conducted the research themselves, these abstract and, at times, complex research issues appear to be more memorable and to generate more interest than examples taken from the literature because of the direct involvement of the students and their intimate familiarity with the studies.

In a recent laboratory course, student ratings suggested that reactions to these projects were quite favorable. According to the syllabus, the objectives of the course included: (a) development of a scientific attitude toward problem solving; (b) experience with some of the methodological techniques used in psychology; (c) training in the ability to statistically analyze and interpret the results of a research study;

and (d) improvement of the capacity to present the results of such a study in a written report. When asked if the course content covered announced objectives (1 = very well; 7 = very poorly), student responses indicated that the projects were very successful *(M =* 1.88, *SD* = .86, *N* = 16). When asked if the course increased their capacity to think and formulate questions (1 = definitely, yes; 7 = definitely, no), students once again gave favorable responses *(M =* 2.31, *SD* = 1.31, *N* = 16). Finally, students were asked if the material in the course stimulated discussions outside of class (1 = very often; 7 = seldom, if ever); responses suggested a high degree of student interest and involvement in the research *(M =* 2.69, *SD* = 1.49, *N* = 16). In fact, when asked an open-ended question about what aspects of the course as a whole should *not* change, five students indicated that the projects were "interesting" or "fun to do" and should be retained; when asked what aspects of the Course were in greatest need of improvement, no one suggested changes in the projects.

When planning a laboratory Course in psychology, it is no small matter to find projects that can be done by as many as 20 novice experimenters and still generate significant findings! The relationships examined in the projects described here appear to be strong enough to remain significant in spite of the increased error inevitably associated with research done in general laboratory courses. The obtained findings also facilitate the discussion of substantive theoretical issues related to the specific content areas of the research. Therefore, these projects provide an excellent way to move a laboratory course beyond experimentation.

References

Ayeroff, F., & Abelson, R. P. ESP and ESB: Belief in personal success at mental telepathy. *Journal of Personality and Social Psychology*, 1976, *34*, 240-247.

Gitin, S. R. A dimensional analysis of manual expression. *Journal of Personality and Social Psychology,* 1970, *15*, 271-277.

Hendricks, R. D., Sobell, M. B., & Cooper, A. M. Social influences on human ethanol consumption in an analogue situation. *Addictive Behaviors*, 1978, *3*, 253-259.

Jennings (Walstedt), J., Geis, F. L., & Brown, V. Influence of television commercials on women's self-confidence and independent judgment. *Journal of Personality and Social Psychology*, 1980, *38*, 203-210.

Jones, W. H., Russell, D. W., & Nickel, T. W. Belief in the Paranormal Scale: An objective instrument to measure belief in magical phenomena and causes. *JSAS Catalog of Selected Documents in Psychology*, 1977, 7, 100. MS. 1577.

Layton, B. D. & Turnbull, B. Belief, evaluation, and performance on an ESP task. *Journal of Experimental Social Psychology*, 1975, *11*, 166-179.

McArthur, L. Z., & Resko, B. G. The portrayal of men and women in American television commercials . *The Journal of Social Psychology*, 1975, *97*, 209-220.

McGhee, P. E., & Frueh, T. Television viewing and the learning of sex-role stereotypes. *Sex Roles*, 1980, *6*, 179-188.

Mehrabian, A. Significance of posture and position in the communication of attitude and status relationships. *Psychological Bulletin,* 1969, *71*, 359-372.

Munn, N. L. The effect of knowledge of the situation upon judgment of emotion from facial expressions. *Journal of Abnormal and Social Psychology*, 1940, *35*, 324-338.

Nierenberg, G. I., & Calero, H. H. *How to read a person like a book.* New York: Pocket Books, 1971.

Rosenbluth, J., Nathan, P. E., & Lawson, D. M. Environmental influences on drinking by college students in a college pub: Behavioral observation in the natural environment. *Addictive Behaviors,* 1978, *3*, 117-122.

Selltiz, C., Wrightsman, L. S., & Cook, S. W. *Research Methods in social relations* (Third Edition). New York: Holt, Rinehart, and Winston, 1976.

Sommer, R., & Sommer, B. B. *A practical guide to behavioral research: Tools and techniques.* New York: Oxford University Press, 1980.

Strickler, D. P., Dobbs, S. D., & Maxwell, W. A. The influence of setting on drinking behaviors: The laboratory vs. the barroom. *Addictive Behaviors*, 1979, *4*, 339-344.

Wachtel, P. L. Investigation and its discontents: Some constraints on progress in psychological research. *American Psychologist*, 1980, *35*, 399-408.

Note

The author wishes to thank Dr. Royce Singleton. Jr.. and Dr. Charles M Locurto for their helpful comments.

Teaching Observational Methods: Time Sampling, Event Sampling, and Trait Rating Techniques

Andrea S. Zeren
Vivian Parker Makosky
St. Lawrence University

This in-class activity permits the systematic observation of spontaneous human behavior as simulated on television and provides one effective way to demonstrate and compare time sampling, event sampling, and trait rating techniques. Students responded favorably to this activity, and many reported that it increased their understanding of the different observational techniques.

The observation of human behavior plays a central role in many areas of psychology, particularly social psychology, child psychology, and group processes. Several observational techniques are available for scientifically describing human behavior. These techniques can be divided into two general types, unstructured (narrative) methods and structured (checklist) methods. The former approaches involve using narrative types of data to "reproduce behavioral events in much the same fashion and sequence as their original occurrence" (Brandt, 1972, p. 80). In contrast, the latter approaches entail deliberately selecting and defining specific behaviors before the observation process, and developing a format on which to record the observations. Since the early 20th century, the structured methods have been used with increasing frequency to study social behaviors.

Wright (1967) identified time sampling, event sampling, and trait ratings as three of the most frequently used structured approaches for obtaining observational data. These basic observational "tools" are often taught to college and graduate school students in lecture format. Although teachers might prefer an in-class demonstration of these techniques, severe difficulties often block an effective in-class presentation. First, having student observers in the room with the people being observed is intrusive and affects the behaviors of those observed. For example, decreased negative behaviors, increased desired behaviors, and a reduction in overall activity are some specific behavioral changes that result from an awareness of being observed (cf. Selltiz, Wrightsman, & Cook, 1981). A second alternative is to have the class observe through one-way mirrors. However,

even if the facilities are available they only partially eliminate intrusiveness. These settings severely restrict the behaviors it is possible to observe as adults are often conscious of the observations being conducted. A third alternative is to abandon the idea of observing as a class and to send students out to observe on their own. This alternative leads to a loss of structure and comparability across observational techniques. It also raises important ethical concerns that may be too complex to address fully in the time available (e.g., issues of informed consent, veto power over the use of obtained information, and invasion of privacy).

The following activity permits the systematic observation of spontaneous human behavior as simulated on television. Televised behavior has previously been used for demonstrating both observational techniques and individual differences in the perception of social motives (Russo, 1981). Our exercise extends the use of televised behavior by providing one way to demonstrate and compare time sampling, event sampling, and trait rating techniques and avoids the problems previously mentioned. Furthermore, it is an excellent illustration of many aspects of the scientific approach to studying behavior, as the students' observations (a) serve a formulated research purpose, (b) are planned deliberately, (c) are recorded systematically, and (d) are subjected to checks and controls on reliability.

Method

Equipment and Preparation

The only equipment needed is either a videocassette recorder or a facility for closed-circuit television from which to air a prerecorded television show. The only initial laboratory preparation involves videotaping a popular television show that is high in the frequency of target behaviors. A variety of shows may be used, with the choice of depending mainly upon the nature of the questions being asked. For example, *The Love Boat,* a television show depicting aspects of several types of relationships that differ in level of intimacy, was used with social psychology students whose purpose was to study interpersonal attraction and love. However, when this technique was used with students enrolled in a research methods course in which the questions involved a broader array of behaviors and emotions, the soap opera entitled *All My Children* was chosen. Because the show can be chosen according to the behavioral domain being examined (i.e., liking, loving, aggression, prejudice, etc.) the approach permits flexibility to accommodate student and teacher interests.

Procedure

The entire activity involves three steps: (a) a lecture about observational methods; (b) an exercise demonstrating the use of time sampling, event sampling, and trait ratings; and (c) a class discussion comparing the three methods. It is more effective as a 2-hr lab activity but can be condensed into one class period.

Lecture. The activity begins with a brief introduction to direct observation as a research method. Specific points covered might include the role and importance of observation in research and teaching; the main distinguishing features among naturalistic observation, experimental manipulation, and self-report methods; and the difference. between non-structured and structured observational strategies.

The structured observational techniques of time sampling, event sampling, and trait ratings become the specific focus of the lecture. Each method is described in detail (see Irwin & Bushnell, 1980 for background reading) and the following similarities among the three methods are presented: (a) each focuses on specific behaviors or constellations of behaviors, (b) each identifies behavioral categories in advance, (c) each relies heavily on an unambiguous operational definition of the variable(s) being measured, and (d) each requires preconstructed recording formats.

Finally, the class discusses the preparation, development, and completion of each technique (i.e., formulating research questions, defining target behaviors, forming operational definitions, and constructing recording formats).

Class activity. The class is divided into small groups of three to five students, each of which is responsible for the actual development of all components of one of the three observational strategies. This group size was chosen because it seems to maximize time efficiency and student productivity in the preparation, development, and data collection for each technique. The students are presented with the option to consult the instructor on all pertinent decisions, which include the following: the purpose of the observation; the type of information to record; how the variables will be

operationalized; whether to include verbal and/or nonverbal behaviors; constructing an appropriate recording format; (for time sampling) deciding the length, number, and spacing of intervals; and (for trait ratings) the type of rating scale to use.

The class reconvenes for approximately l/2 hr to observe the taped program. Students independently record samples of behavior using the method and data sheets constructed by their subgroup.

Interrater reliability coefficients are computed among all subgroup members, using the formula:

$$\text{Reliability} = \frac{\text{agreements}}{\text{agreements} + \text{disagreements}}.$$

Each group is instructed to identify shortcomings in its use of the strategy, improvements that would overcome these problems, and the relative advantages and disadvantages of the method they used.

Class discussion. We have found that a beneficial way to begin the discussion is by comparing the obtained reliability coefficients among thee three methods. The differences in level of interobserver agreement reveal some of the strengths and weaknesses associated with each technique. Specifically, every time this lab activity has been used, the reliability coefficients were found to be highest for time sampling, next highest for event sampling, and lowest for trait ratings. The instructor discusses this pattern, noting that rating scale reliability coefficients are usually lower because this strategy requires a judgment from the rater and, therefore, is more subjective. Consequently, rater error and biases occur, including the halo effect, errors of leniency, and errors of central tendency. In contrast, time sampling reliability coefficients are typically higher than those for trait rating or event sampling methods. Consistent with this, the observer must focus on easily observable, concrete, and preselected behaviors.

Additional discussion topics might include specific uses of each method, major advantages and disadvantages, possible data analyses, the importance of precise operational definitions and their impact on the precision of interrater agreement, and the defining characteristics of scientific observation.

Students' Evaluation of the Activity

This technique was first used as a laboratory activity in social psychology and students informally praised its instructional value. The technique was later refined and used both in other classes and by another instructor. To evaluate its effectiveness, a survey was distributed to all students in a research methods course at the time of the exercise ($N = 15$). Although the sample was small, the ratings were consistent with the more impressionistic feedback from larger classes. Responses to the four questions are summarized below. Each question is followed by the mean and the standard deviation (in parentheses).

1. "How interesting did you find this activity?" On a scale ranging from *very uninteresting* (1) to *very interesting* (5), students gave a mean rating of 3.47 (1.6).

2. "How well did this activity facilitate your understanding of the different structured observational methods?" On a scale ranging from *it was confusing* (1) to *very helpful* (5), the mean rating was 4.33 (.82).

3. "Overall, how would you compare this activity to other psychological lab activities?" On a scale ranging from *inferior* (1) to *superior* (5), students gave a mean rating of 3.67 (.72).

4. "Would you recommend the use of this lab in future offerings of this course?" On a scale ranging from *no, absolutely not* (1) to *yes, most definitely* (5), the mean rating was 4.47 (1.06).

Students generally agreed that the objectives of this exercise were met. Answers to Questions 2 and 3 indicate that the activity facilitated an understanding of structured observational techniques and was an effective teaching aid. Responses to Question 1 revealed wide variations in interest levels. This appeared to be due to the specific television show viewed, rather than to the actual lab activity involved. This conclusion is supported by the students' recommendation to use this activity in future offerings of the course. Overall, the students responded well to the exercise.

Summary and Conclusions

We believe that this is an educational and flexible teaching tool. It permits an in-class demonstration and comparison of three major structured observational techniques, but its utility is far more comprehensive. It illustrates other important facets of psychological research, such as the scientific approach to gathering observational data, the importance of precise operational definitions on interrater agreement, and the calculation of reliability coefficients. This activity is particularly appropriate for social, developmental, and methodology classes.

References

Brandt, R. M. (1972). *Studying behavior in natural settings.* New York: Holt, Rinehart, & Winston.

Irwin, M., & Bushnell, M. M. (1980). *Observational strategies for child study.* New York: Holt, Rinehart, & Winston.

Russo, N. F. (1981). Observation: A standardized experience. In L. T. Benjamin Jr. & K. D. Lowman (Eds.), *Activities handbook for the teaching of psychology* (pp. 3-4). Washington, DC: American Psychological Association.

Selltiz, C., Wrightsman, L. S., & Cook, T. D. (1981). *Research methods in social relations.* New York: Holt, Rinehart, & Winston.

Wright, H. F. (1967). *Recording and analyzing child behavior.* New York: Harper & Row.

Note

An abbreviated version of this paper was presented at the 1984 meeting of the American Psychological Association, Toronto, Canada.

Naturalistic Observation of Behavior:
A Model System Using Mice in a Colony

Harold A. Herzog, Jr.
Western Carolina University

Despite their importance, techniques of naturalistic observation are rarely taught in undergraduate research methods courses. This article describes exercises designed to give students experience in using methods of naturalistic observation to quantify behavior. Students construct a coding system (ethogram) of the behaviors observed in a small mouse colony. This behavioral catalog is then used to gather data by two techniques: instantaneous and focal animal sampling. The data can be used to calculate interrater reliability and then subjected to sequence analysis. The application of naturalistic observation to the quantification of human behavior is considered.

Among the ethologists' contributions to psychology is the development of methods that allow quantitative analysis of naturally occurring behaviors. As a result, ethology has emerged from its descriptive, natural history phase to become a quantitative science. Even though naturalistic observation can be applied to a wide variety of research problems and requires little equipment, it is typically neglected in undergraduate research methods courses. The exercises described herein were developed to give students experience with naturalistic observation, using mice as subjects. The exercises also offer students an opportunity to work with animals in an ethically sensitive fashion at a time when many psychology departments are eliminating animal colonies because of pressures from animal welfare groups and government regulators.

Mice are ideal animals for these exercises, although other small mammals, such as gerbils, can be substituted. They are readily available from pet shops or from colleagues in biology departments. Mice come in a variety of colors and patterns, which makes for easy identification of individual animals. (If they are available only in white, a dab of hair dye can be used to mark individuals.) Because mice almost never bite and have an interesting repertoire of behaviors, even students who do not like working with larger animals, such as rats, enjoy observing them.

Preparation

Mouse colonies can be made from 10-gallon aquaria with cedar chips for bedding and wire mesh tops. The animals should have soft paper or other materials available for building nests. They can also be provided with objects to climb on or hide in. Between three and five mice should be placed in each aquarium. The use of mixed-sex groups leads to a greater variety of behavior patterns, but can also lead to population problems in 3 to 4 weeks.

Although the techniques are explained during class, students come into the laboratory on their own time to make observations. Observations are made by pairs of students who work as a team throughout the exercise. So that they can experience the widest possible range of behaviors, students are encouraged to observe the animals at several different times a day.

Techniques of Naturalistic Observation

Constructing an Ethogram

The students first spend 1 hr or so simply observing a group of mice. They are instructed to look for, and make notes on, patterns of behavior. This "field note stage" is sometimes referred to as *ad libitum sampling* and is particularly useful in the initial stages of naturalistic observation. A list of the behavior patterns is then constructed. This catalog is called an *ethogram* and forms the basis of a behavioral coding system. Each recurring behavior pattern is given a one- or two-word name, an abbreviation, and a brief description. The exercises are based on the category system, and it is important that students in each pair agree on the categories and have a clear understanding of what constitutes the specific behavior in each category. The ethograms are discussed in class, and I emphasize the importance of avoiding anthropomorphic interpretations of behavior and of specifying the difference between functional and descriptive categories.

Ideally, ethograms should be exhaustive and mutually exclusive; all behaviors a mouse normally exhibits should be included on the list, and the animal's observed behavior should fall into only one category. In reality, these goals can be obtained only by many hours of careful observation.

However, even the first short observation period typically generates an ethogram containing between 15 and 25 of the most common mouse behaviors. Students are encouraged to include a miscellaneous category for new behaviors that they will inevitably encounter.

Quantification of Streams of Behavior

Once each pair of students has developed a category system, they can use it to quantify streams of behavior in a number of ways. The advantages and disadvantages of various techniques are discussed in several sources (e.g., Altmann, 1974; Hutt & Hutt, 1974; Lehner, 1979; Martin & Bateson, 1986). The students typically practice two methods, instantaneous sampling and focal animal sampling.

Instantaneous sample. In instantaneous sampling, observations are made of ongoing behaviors at precise intervals. For example, samplings made every 15 sec for 15 min will yield 60 observations. The technique requires that students in each pair prepare checklists based on their ethogram categories. The checklist we use is a matrix with 60 observation periods numbered across the top (several pages may be needed) and the behavioral categories along the left side. Each pair also needs a timer to signal exactly when the observations are to be made. Although a mechanical timer that produces a tone at preset intervals can be used, a tape recorder is quite adequate. Simply make a tape with either an audible signal or the word *observe* at regular intervals (e.g., 15 sec).

It is important that the students in each pair make simultaneous, independent observations on the same animal, because their data will be used to calculate interrater reliabilities. During the observation period, students independently check the category best describing what that animal is doing when the signal occurs. Care must be exercised to ensure that the check is placed in the column representing the appropriate observation interval. At the end of the period, each student should have a single check in each of the 60 columns. They then count the number of times each behavior was scored. By dividing these numbers by 60, they can calculate the percentage of intervals in which each behavior was observed. This measure estimates the relative amount of time the animal spent performing the various behaviors during the observation period.

Students may then evaluate their observational skills by calculating interrater reliability as estimated by percent agreement. Interrater reliabilities of over 90% are normally interpreted as indicating an acceptable level of agreement, but in this exercise, they often vary widely. The reliabilities obtained depend on several factors, including the number of categories, how well they are defined and understood, and the activity level of the animals when they are observed.

Focal animal sampling. Focal animal sampling involves recording all the ongoing behaviors of individual animals. Data can be used to make a variety of comparisons, such as behavioral differences between sex and age. This method can also be used to generate information amenable to the analysis of behavioral sequences. Students again work in pairs, with one student initially designated observer and the other recorder. Using the ethogram categories, the observer dictates the behavior patterns the animal performs sequentially. After 50 behaviors have been dictated, the observer and recorder change roles for another 50 behavior changes.

The list of 100 behaviors can now be analyzed in a number of ways. The simplest way is to count the relative frequencies of various behavior patterns. Data gathered using this method can also be used for sequence analysis in which the stream of behavior is divided into units consisting of an initial behavior and a following behavior. These units can be entered into a matrix, and transition probabilities can be calculated. After all pairs of behaviors have been entered in the matrix, it is easy to calculate the relative frequencies of the various behaviors. More important, the students also see that patterns emerge; some behaviors frequently follow each other, but others rarely do.

Take, for example, a chain of behaviors in which a mouse engages sequentially in the following behaviors: scratch-sniff-rear up-scratch. This chain contains three pairs of behaviors (scratch-sniff, sniff-rear up, rear up-sniff). These two-behavior units are then entered into a transition matrix. The ethogram categories are listed across the top and along the left side of the matrix. The left-side categories are designated initial behaviors, and the categories across the top are subsequent behaviors. Tally marks for the pairs of behaviors are placed in the matrix as follows: The first pair of behaviors, scratch-sniff, is scored by placing a tally mark in the box that has scratch as the initial behavior and sniff as the subsequent behavior. Sniff now becomes the initial behavior for the next pair (sniff-rear up), which is entered in the matrix with sniff as the initial behavior and rear up as the subsequent behavior. Rear up now becomes the initial behavior for the unit rear up-scratch.

Discussion

These exercises provide students with opportunities to learn how naturally occurring behaviors can be subjected to quantitative analysis. I use them as required labs (graded on a satisfactory/unsatisfactory basis) in courses in experimental psychology and animal behavior. However, they are also appropriate for courses in social or developmental psychology. Course evaluations and informal discussions with students indicate that most of them find the exercises interesting and enlightening. Many students report being surprised at the patterns that emerge as they begin to quantify the animals' behavior.

These techniques can be applied to virtually any species that can be unobtrusively observed, including our own. Indeed, the instructor may want to include an investigation of humans as an exercise. For example, a coding system of the book-carrying behavior of college students can be quickly constructed, and students can be sent out on campus with a checklist of the categories to look for sex differences in book-carrying modes (Hanaway & Burghardt, 1976; Jenni & Jenni, 1976). Sex differences will inevitably be found, and a lively discussion of possible reasons for this result will likely ensue.

References

Altmann, J. (1974). Observational study of behavior: Sampling methods. *Behavior, 49,* 227-265.

Hanaway, T. P., & Burghardt, G. M. (1976). The development of sexually dimorphic book-carrying behavior. *Bulletin of the Psychonomic Society, 7,* 276-280.

Hutt, S. J., & Hutt, C. (1974). *Direct observation and measurement of behavior.* Springfield, IL: Charles C Thomas.

Jenni, D. A., & Jenni, M. A. (1976). Carrying behavior in humans: Analysis of sex differences. *Science, 194,* 859-860.

Lehner, P. N. (1979). *Handbook of ethological methods.* New York: Garland STPM Press.

Martin, P., & Bateson, P. (1986). *Measuring behavior: An introductory guide.* Cambridge, England: Cambridge University Press.

Note

I thank Gordon Burghardt, Mary Jean Herzog, and Jerry Baumgartner for their comments on this rticle.

3. TEACHING RESEARCH ETHICS

Using the Barnum Effect to Teach About Ethics and Deception in Research

Bernard C. Beins
Ithaca College

The Barnum effect was generated to teach students about the ethics of deception in research and the feelings of subjects who are lied to. Students in research methods classes received feedback based on a bogus personality inventory and rated the perceived validity of the interpretations. Students accepted the feedback, although seniors were more skeptical than juniors or sophomores. The class discussed the ethics of deception based on their own reactions to the knowledge that they were deceived. Students agreed that the approach was effective in helping them learn firsthand about the costs and benefits of deception in research.

Psychologists are intensely interested in establishing ethical guidelines that help direct their professional relationships. The American Psychological Association exerts ongoing efforts to revise its guidelines (e.g., "APA Continues to Refine," 1992), and a growing corpus of relevant articles and publications exists (e.g., Tabachnick, Keith-Spiegel, & Pope, 1991).

Although professionals are acutely aware of the importance of this issue, students do not systematically learn about it at more than a cursory level (Korn, 1984). Fortunately, individual instructors have recognized the traditional gap in teaching ethics. McMinn (1988) developed a computerized approach to ethical decision making; Rosnow (1990) described an approach involving role-playing, discussion, and debate.

The approach to teaching ethics described here puts students in the role of the deceived in a classroom project. There are two main students why lectures and discussions about the ethics of deceit need to be supplemented by a more direct demonstration.

First, Milgram (1963) found that people are not very accurate in predicting how subjects will react when confronted with an ethically ambiguous situation. If people cannot reliably predict subjects' behavior, perhaps students might think that they know how a deceived subject would feel, but the actual experience may be much more compelling.

Second, students may not empathize initially with research subjects who are deceived. For example, student researchers who participated in some conformity studies (Beins & Porter, 1989) showed no distress about using deception in the research (the Institutional Review Board that approved the research also showed no distress). Similarly, Harcum and Friedman (1991), who expressed reservations about the ethics of using some fairly common classroom demonstrations, noted that about 93% of their subjects accepted deception as part of a legitimate research design.

The vehicle for creating this teaching activity is the *Barnum effect,* in which individuals are gulled into believing invalid results of psychological tests. This effect was originally used to teach students about testing (Forer, 1949); as a phenomenon, it is well documented (e.g., Baillargeon & Danis, 1984; Furnham & Schofield, 1987; Holmes, Buchannan, Dungan, & Reed, 1986). It can also introduce students to the pitfall of blind acceptance of test results (Palladino, 1991).

The goals of the activity described herein are to foster an appreciation of the feelings of research subjects who are lied to and an awareness of the need to avoid deception when possible. This approach complements those used by McMinn (1988) and Rosnow (1990). The demonstration combines an initial discussion of crucial ethical issues that I take from Reynolds (1982), a firsthand account of being deceived, and a final discussion.

Generating the Barnum Effect

Procedure

Students in a research methods class participated in the project as part of the course requirement. There were 28 women and 11 men; 10 were sophomores, 23 were juniors, and 6 were seniors.

Students completed a 20-item bogus personality inventory, the Quacksalber Personality Inventory for Normal Populations (Beins, 1987). They subsequently received interpretations that were identical for all students. All feedback statements were intended to be neutral or mildly positive.

One class (n = 19) completed the test with a version designed for Apple 11 computers; feedback was provided immediately. The second class (n = 20) took a version printed on paper and responded on a computer scoring sheet. A confederate of the teacher left the room and returned about 10 min later with printouts that had been prepared in advance with each student's name written across the top. There was no obvious reason to expect the two groups to differ in their reactions; a comparison between the two would only indicate how robust the effect might be.

Both groups then completed a form designed to access the perceived validity of the test. One question asked how well students thought the feedback described themselves. Students responded using a scale ranging from *this is the real me* (1) to *this is not like me* (10). In addition, they indicated how useful the test would be in five situations: personal adjustment, employment screening, assessment of honesty, identification of a person's minor problems, and identification of a person's major problems. Students responded using a scale ranging from *very useful* (1) to *not very useful* (10).

Assessing the Barnum Effect

Students were predictably accepting of the test results as descriptive of themselves. The mean rating was 3.6. This represented a significant departure from a neutral value of 5.5, $t(38) = 6.24$, $p < .001$. However, students felt that the test would not be particularly effective in assessing personal adjustment, employee honesty and stability, or major or minor emotional problems. Thus, students did not blindly accept the test as being a universally valid instrument.

To test the robustness of the effect, a 2 (Medium: Computer vs. Paper) x 2 (Sex) x 3 (Year in School) analysis of variance was conducted on the acceptance ratings. Only the main effect of year was significant, $F(2, 36) = 5.09$, $p = .011$. Sophomores ($M = 3.00$) and juniors ($M = 3.43$) did not differ reliably, but they were significantly less skeptical than seniors ($M = 5.67$). The small number of seniors renders the difference between them and the sophomores and juniors somewhat suspect. I have tried to generate acceptance of the results of the Quacksalber inventory for other seniors and for graduate students without much success. Even so, these students experience the deceit, their skepticism in the results of the test notwithstanding.

Generating Postdemonstration Discussion

Students discussed their feelings when I told them that they had been deceived. Their initial reaction to the deceit was to feel gullible and stupid. In general, they were mildly distressed at first. I also noted what seemed to be nervous laughter from several students during the initial stages of the discussion.

Discussion focused on the fact that they had taken the Quacksalber inventory seriously, on their feelings about being deceived, and on the idea that their reactions to being deceived were common. I also pointed out that if they used deception in research, their subjects would feel the same way. Finally, I used this situation to illustrate the importance of debriefing.

During the next class meeting, they wrote answers to questions about the suitability of this exercise to illustrate relevant points about deception in research and whether this demonstration should be repeated in future classes. We spent nearly an entire class period discussing what they had written. I made it clear that I would consider their responses seriously before deciding whether to repeat this activity with another class. I pointed out that deception was as much a problem in the classroom as in the context of experimental research.

Assessing Student Reactions to the Deception

Of the 31 students who commented anonymously about whether this demonstration was effective in teaching about both the Barnum effect and deception, *30* students responded affirmatively. Their comments generally asserted that the costs of doing the demonstration (failure to acquire prior informed consent, invasion of their privacy in asking questions about their likes and dislikes, and lying to them about the nature of the test) were outweighed by the benefits of learning that deception is not free of cost and of knowing firsthand how subjects feel when lied to. Other notable and potentially serious effects of this exercise are that students may question the instructor's credibility, they may think that psychological research is without validity or integrity, and they may develop negative feelings about psychological research. None of these unwanted eventualities emerged.

The sole dissenter suggested that it was not worth making students feel stupid and that the point about deception in research could be made simply by giving facts and examples. Several students noted that some students may be distressed (e.g., freshmen who lacked confidence in themselves) and that I should be aware of this. We had not discussed the question of individual differences regarding negative reactions, but some students spontaneously mentioned it.

Discussion

This project seems to have been effective on two levels. On one hand, the students became acquainted with the Barnum effect. More important, they also seemed quite touched at the personal level by the experience. It was clear to me that they did not enjoy the trickery when it was inflicted on them. On the other hand, they agreed that it provided a compelling message. The class discussion was tinged with a sense of empathy with research subjects who are deceived. The degree to which students objected to the procedure was as low as that reported elsewhere (Britton, Richardson, Smith, & Hamilton, 1983; Harcum & Freedman, 1991): Students may have felt some distress, but it was mild and short-lived.

The students also learned that, in some cases, deception can be tolerated. For example, in my classes, the students agreed that I should not regularly lie to them; however, the mild and short-lived discomfort about knowing that they had been lied to served to teach them an important lesson about deception in research. Thus, they asserted that the project was worth repeating with subsequent classes.

This demonstration has several advantages. It teaches about deception in the context of a social psychology phenomenon. It is more accessible than Forer's (1949) original demonstration of the Barnum effect, which was based on his Diagnostic Interest Blank and some astrological personality descriptions. This version is also quicker than Forer's, which extended over a period of 1 week. Also, the Quacksalber inventory provides the same kind of feedback Forer provided, although the personality descriptions used here are more neutral.

Furthermore, when the computer version is used, no responses are actually recorded, thus ensuring confidentiality. (The computerized version is available only for Apple 11 computers, but is written in BASIC, so it should be easily convertible to GW BASIC for IBM-type computers.) The project seems amenable either to computerized or paper application. Men and women reacted in the same way, both in generating the effect and in their responses to deception. Seniors seemed more skeptical of the feedback (as did master's level students in education in a similar situation). Even when students failed to accept the output as descriptive of themselves, they still seemed to have accepted the test as legitimate. This demonstration seems robust and pedagogically useful for a wide range of students.

References

APA continues to refine its ethics code. (1992, May). *APA Monitor,* pp. 38-42.

Baillargeon, J., & Danis, C. (1984). Barnum meets the computer: A critical test. *Journal of Personality Assessment, 48,* 415-419.

Beins, B. C. (1987). Psychological testing and interpretation. In V. P. Makosky, L. G. Whittemore, & A. M. Rogers (Eds.), *Activities handbook for the teaching of psychology* (Vol. 2, pp. 266-274).

Washington, DC: American Psychological Association.

Beins, B. C., & Porter, J. W. (1989). A ratio scale measurement of conformity. *Educational and Psychological Measurement, 49,* 75-80.

Britton, B. K., Richardson, D., Smith, S. S., & Hamilton, T. (1983). Ethical aspects of participating in psychology experiments: Effects of anonymity on evaluation, and complaints of distressed subjects. *Teaching of Psychology, 10,* 146-149.

Forer, B. R. (1949). The fallacy of personal validation: A classroom demonstration of testing. *Journal of Abnormal and Social Psychology, 44,* 118-123.

Furnham, A., & Schofield, S. (1987). Accepting personality test feedback: A review of the Barnum effect. *Current Psychological Research & Reviews, 6,* 162-178.

Harcum, E. R., & Friedman, H. (1991). Students' ethics ratings of demonstrations in introductory psychology. *Teaching of Psychology, 18,* 215-218.

Holmes, C. B., Buchannan, J. A., Dungan, D. S., & Reed, T. (1986). The Barnum effect in Luscher color test interpretation. *Journal of Clinical Psychology, 2,* 186-190.

Korn, J. H. (1984). Coverage of research ethics in introductory and social psychology textbooks. *Teaching of Psychology, 11,* 146-149.

McMinn, M. R. (1988). Ethics case-study simulation: A generic tool for psychology teachers. *Teaching of Psychology, 15,* 100-101.

Milgram, S. (1963). Behavioral study of obedience. *Journal of Abnormal and Social Psychology, 67,* 371-378.

Palladino, J. J. (1991, August). *The BRPI—The Blatantly Ridiculous Personality Inventory.* Paper presented at the annual convention of the American Psychological Association, San Francisco.

Reynolds, P. D. (1982). *Ethics and social science research.* Englewood Cliffs, NJ: Prentice-Hall.

Rosnow, R. L. (1990). Teaching research ethics through role-play and discussion. *Teaching of Psychology 17,* 179-181.

Tabachnick, B. G., Keith-Spiegel, P., & Pope, K. S. (1991). Ethics of teaching: Beliefs and behaviors of psychologists as educators. *American Psychologist, 46,* 506-515.

Note

I thank Ruth Ault for her comments on a previous draft of this article.

Teaching Research Ethics Through Role-Play and Discussion

Ralph L. Rosnow
Temple University

Failing to conduct a research study because it involves deception or invasion of privacy is as much an act to be evaluated on ethical grounds as is conducting such a study. A classroom exercise was designed to teach that there are several vantage points from which the ethical evaluation of a study can be made. Role-play and discussion are used to sharpen critical thinking and develop an appreciation of the subtleties of research ethics.

When lecturing on research ethics, instructors tend to consider only the costs and benefits of conducting particular studies, as if from the perspective of an institutional review board (IRB). Seldom is due consideration given to the ethical implications of the failure to conduct ethically ambiguous studies that might reduce violence, prejudice, mental illness, and so forth. The failure to conduct such a study because it involves deception or invasion of privacy, however, is as much an act to be evaluated on ethical grounds as is the act of conducting a study (Rosenthal & Rosnow, 1984). This idea is important to communicate to psychology students, because it teaches that there is more than one vantage point from which the ethical evaluation of a study can be made. This article describes a classroom exercise that, through role-play and discussion, leads students to develop an appreciation of the subtleties of research ethics.

The technique considers at least three vantage points. The first is that of the research discipline itself, as represented by the ethical principles of the American Psychological Association (1982). A second frame of reference is that of the community in which the research is being sanctioned (e.g., the class in which the person is a student or an IRB). The third is the point of view of the individual investigator (e.g., the student-researcher), who may not have thought much about his or her own ethical assumptions and biases.

This article proceeds in two parts. First, I suggest some readings and ideas to stimulate discussion. The discussion, which takes place either before the role-play (i.e., to set the stage) or afterward (i.e., to tie things together), is intended to provide a real-world context for the students. Next, I describe the role-play technique, which I have condensed into a five-step

exercise. In this exercise, students defend a position they have recently attacked by role-playing an author who is defending the value of a study. This exercise helps sharpen critical thinking and reduces the initial tendencies of many students to "play it safe" by eschewing any study that appears to involve deception or intervention. The technique can be modified to fit scheduling constraints or larger classes.

Readings and Discussion

If the exercise is to be part of a research methods class, the textbook will usually contain relevant material. For graduate and advanced undergraduate students, such material can be supplemented by outside readings (e.g., Doob, 1987; Kelman, 1968; Kimmel, 1981, 1988; Schuler, 1982; Sieber, 1982; Smith, 1969), chosen with the course objectives in mind. Because some students tend to approach such readings uncritically, it is helpful to provide a background to focus their attention. For example, students could be assigned to read selected chapters in Miller's (1986) book on Stanley Milgram's classic studies. The ethics of Milgram's research were widely debated; this debate is captured in an absorbing way in Miller's book.

A comparison between the ethical dilemmas faced by Milgram and those faced by action researchers can be made by using the quality-of-work-life experiment that was conducted in 1973 at the Rushton Mining Company in Pennsylvania (Blumberg & Pringle, 1983). Developed on the basis of earlier research in the United Kingdom, the purpose of this project was to improve employee skills, safety, and job satisfaction, which raised the level of performance and as a result, company earnings. After months of research preparation, volunteers were sought for a work group that would have direct responsibility for production in one section of the mining operations. After exhaustive training in safety laws, good mining practices, and job safety analysis, the volunteers were paid at the top rate as the highest skilled job classification on that section and left to coordinate their own activities. They became enthusiastic proponents of "our way of working." Other workers (i.e., those in the control

166

condition), however, expressed resentment and anger at the volunteers' haughtiness. The resulting negativity in the atmosphere surrounding the experiment led the investigators to end it abruptly.

Action research can frequently have its own set of ethical problems, quite apart from the ones encountered by Milgram in his laboratory research. There was no deception in this study, but there is the problem of "fairness" because a sizable number of workers (nonvolunteers) did not receive the benefits enjoyed by those in the experimental group. By analogy, the ethical cost of using placebo control subjects in biomedical research could be examined, because they also fail to receive the benefits (if any) received by the experimental group. What if instead of receiving a placebo, the controls received the best available usual or common treatment to serve as a comparison with the effects of the experimental treatment?

Still other ethical risks may be incurred in participant-observer research. For example, what about the moral cost that is possible simply in the reporting of results (cf. Johnson, 1982)? What if, despite the author's use of pseudonyms, some persons or communities can be identified (or can identify themselves) in the publication? Would those that are identifiable be vulnerable to embarrassment or to unwanted publicity? On the other hand, what is the social and scientific cost of not publishing the findings (i.e ., not disseminating research results) ?

Deception, fairness, and the invasion of privacy also come into play outside the research situation. Broome (1984) discussed the ethical issue of fairness in selecting people for chronic hemodialysis, a medical procedure that can save the life of a person whose kidneys have failed. The procedure is expensive, and in many communities there are not enough facilities to treat everyone who could benefit, yet without treatment a patient quickly dies. How should candidates for hemodialysis be selected? The inventor of hemodialysis was said to have used the following guidelines to select people: under 40 years old, free from cardiovascular disease, pillars of the community, contributors to the community's economics, married, and attends church. Is this ethical and fair? Another procedure would be randomness. Broome noted that selecting people randomly—such as using a lottery to choose conscripts to fight in a war—is justified as the "fairest" procedure, because everyone has an equal chance at being selected for life or death. But suppose conscripts for the military were not selected randomly, but on the grounds of who was the biggest and strongest. Which procedure is more ethical—randomness or selection on the grounds of who is more likely to survive?

These are the kinds of ideas and questions that instructors might pose to stimulate discussion. Students need to understand that research is not conducted in isolation from the surrounding community. For example, when researchers study prejudice, mental illness, or AIDS, they are touching on highly charged social problems. Even when they study topics that appear to be neutral (e.g., marriage and the family, the genetics of intelligence, or learning behavior), they must realize the implications for others. Thus, it is important to understand that psychological research forces investigators to "tread on thin moral ice" (Atwell, 1981, p. 89).

The Role-Play Exercise

Step 1 is to familiarize the class with the "Ten Commandments" of the APA's ethical recommendations (American Psychological Association, 1982, pp. 5-7). The ethical standards were developed to check the possible tendency of some researchers to be carried away by the judged importance of doing the research. The class might, therefore, be asked to think about the possibility that there are ethical boundaries that should not be crossed, as put forth in the APA code. Then each student peruses the past year's issues of any primary research journal of interest. The assignment is to find an article that reports a research study that the student personally feels used an "unethical" manipulation or other "reprehensible" procedure. The student is instructed to read the article carefully and thoroughly, to be prepared if called on in class to give a detailed report and be able to answer questions about it, and to turn in a brief paper that focuses on the ethics of the study. The sampling bias in this assignment would seem implicit, inasmuch as the students are reading only studies that supposedly have passed ethical scrutiny. Students have an uncanny ability, however, to ferret out ethically ambiguous studies, even in recent APA journal articles.

Step 2 is to have the students give oral reports of the results of their assignment for the entire class. I then pose questions regarding potentially troublesome aspects of the procedure (e. g., invasion of privacy, deception, use of confederates, or concealed observation). The objective of the questions is to draw the group as a "community" into the discussion.

In Step 3, after all the studies have been discussed, the class examines them from a different perspective. Instead of acting as critics, the students role-play the author of the study and defend their study in the face of criticisms by the rest of the group. If the most articulate and confident students begin this phase, they can provide a good example for the students who follow.

Step 4 is to have each person in the group evaluate the studies on their moral or ethical cost and their theoretical or practical utility. Taking each study in turn, the students evaluate the moral or ethical cost on a 101-point scale ranging from *no ethical or moral cost* (O) to *the highest ethical or moral cost* (100) . Students evaluate the studies individually, based not on how they think that others in the group will vote but on their own personal perspective. Next, students evaluate each study's utility on a 101-point scale ranging from *no theoretical or practical utility* (0) to *the highest theoretical or practical utility* (100). I then draw two matrices on the blackboard, one for the "cost of doing" and the other for the "utility of doing" ratings. The students' names begin the rows, and one- or two-word descriptors of the studies head the columns. While the group copies down the results, I calculate the row and column means and the grand mean and insert this information. The results tell the students at a glance whether they were tough or easy relative to one another (row means), to the group as a whole (grand mean), and to the collective perception of each study. I also point out outliers and clusters of ratings and ask the students to speculate on their implications.

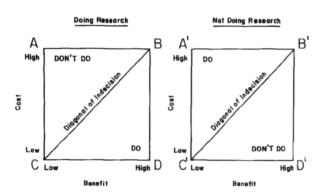

Figure 1. Decision planes representing the costs and utilities of doing and not doing research. *Note.* From "Applying Hamlet's Question to the Ethical Conduct of Research: A Conceptual Addendum" by Robert Rosenthal and Ralph L. Rosnow, 1984, *American Psychologist, 39,* p. 562. Copyright 1984 by the American Psychological Association, Inc. Adapted by permission.

Step 5 concludes the exercise. Using Figure 1 (Rosenthal & Rosnow, 1984), I then develop the idea that the decision-plane model on the left represents the costs and utilities of doing research. Studies falling at A are not carried out, studies falling at D are carried out, and studies falling at B-C cannot be determined. Results in the previous matrices (Step 4) can be used to illustrate the various possibilities. The model represents the way that most IRBs seemingly operate, but this "IRB" (the class)—through role-play in Step 3—also thought about (but did not rate) the other side of the ethical equation, the costs (and utilities) of not doing research (represented by the model on the right). I point out the ethical value of considering both models to arrive at a balanced analysis of the costs and utilities of doing and not doing a study. Examples from the previous role-play are used to underscore the idea that ethical decision making calls for such a balancing of considerations, even though it makes the decision process more complex. Note that IRBs review research proposals, not research results, but we had

knowledge of the results. Did it make a difference in the ratings, and what are the implications?

If the class is large and there are section meetings in which the students are divided into small groups, then it is better to run the exercise in the latter context. Small groups establish a tone that makes it easier for students to be less inhibited and to throw themselves into the exercise. Student reactions have been consistently positive. Making social comparisons is intrinsically motivating, thus adding to the appeal of the exercise. The exercise provides students with a way of looking to others for information while looking within themselves to cope with their uncertainties.

References

American Psychological Association. (1982). *Ethical principles in the conduct of research with human participants.* Washington, DC: Author.

Atwell, J. E. (1981). Human rights in human subjects research. In A. J. Kimmel (Ed.), *Ethics of human subject research* (pp. 81-90). San Francisco: Jossey-Bass.

Blumberg, M., & Pringle, C. D. (1983). How control groups can cause loss of control in action research: The case of Rushton coal mine. *Journal of Applied Behavioral Science, 19,* 409-425.

Broome, J. (1984). Selecting people randomly. *Ethics, 95,* 38-55.

Doob, L. W. (1987). *Slightly beyond skepticism: Social science and the search for morality.* New Haven: Yale University Press.

Johnson, C. G. (1982). Risks in the publication of fieldwork. In J. E. Sieber (Ed.), *The ethics of social research: Fieldwork, regulation, and publication* (Vol. 1, pp. 71-91). New York: Springer-Verlag.

Kelman, H. C. (1968). *A time to speak: On human values and social research.* San Francisco: Jossey-Bass.

Kimmel, A. J. (Ed.). (1981). *Ethics of human subject research.* San Francisco: Jossey-Bass.

Kimmel, A. J. (1988). *Ethics and values in applied social research.* Beverly Hills: Sage.

Miller, A. G. (1986). *The obedience experiments: A case study of controversy in social science.* New York: Praeger.

Rosenthal, R., & Rosnow, R. L. (1984). Applying Hamlet's question to the ethical conduct of research: A conceptual addendum. *American Psychologist, 39,* 561-563.

Schuler, H. (1982). *Ethical problems in psychological research.* New York: Academic.

Sieber, J. E. (Ed.). (1982). *The ethics of social research* (Vol. 1 & Vol. 2). New York: Springer-Verlag.

Smith, M. B. (1969). *Social psychology and human values.* Chicago: Aldine.

Notes

1. Preparation of this article was supported by Temple University through the Bolton Endowment and an NIH Biomedical Research Support Grant.

2. I thank Robert Rosenthal, Joseph Palladino, and three anonymous reviewers for their helpful comments on a draft of this article.

The Use of Role-Play in Teaching Research Ethics: A Validation Study

David B. Strohmetz
Anne A. Skleder
Temple University

Rosnow's (1990) role-play exercise for teaching research ethics was used in undergraduate research methods courses, and its effectiveness was evaluated. Results indicate that the exercise can be a valuable tool for sensitizing students to the factors involved in judging the ethics of research.

Rosnow (1990) argued that, in order to make students aware of the ethical complexities of psychological research, the moral or ethical costs and benefits of doing research might be evaluated in a role-play context. He described a classroom exercise designed to teach students the necessity of viewing the importance of both cost and benefit considerations in the evaluation of research studies. We incorporated this procedure into our lectures on research ethics and evaluated its effectiveness using questionnaires administered before and after the study.

Following Rosnow's suggestion, the procedure begins with a lecture on research ethics based on the ethical principles of the American Psychological Association (1981). The discussion includes a consideration of why proposed research must be evaluated in terms of the ethical costs and benefits of doing the study as well as the costs and benefits of not doing the study. Students are then given a homework assignment to find a recently published study that they consider to be unethical. They are told to read the study carefully and to be prepared to present it during the next class.

During the next class, students present their studies in a discussion led by the instructor. Afterward, they are asked to rate the cost and utility (benefit) of each study. Students are then asked to role-play a "devil's advocate" and defend the scientific value of their "unethical" study before the rest of the class. Following this role-play, each student rerates the cost and the utility of the studies. Finally, the reevaluations are discussed to uncover how and why cost and utility ratings may have changed as a result of the students advocating studies that they originally viewed as unethical.

How effective is this role-play exercise in communicating the ethical complexity of psychological research? We were able to compare the changes in the cost and utility ratings from classes that used the role-play activity with similar ratings from a class that heard the lecture on research ethics but did not use the role-play activity. We predicted that participating in the role-play exercise would increase students' perceptions of the utility of their "unethical" studies. Similarly, we hypothesized that ratings of the perceived ethical costs of these studies would be lower after the role-play. Finally, we predicted that the magnitude of any obtained effects would be larger in these six classes than in the comparison class, which did not use the role-play exercise.

Method

Subjects

Students in both the role-play and nonrole-play classes were junior and senior psychology majors enrolled in a required research methods course. Six classes incorporated the role play exercise into the lecture on research ethics; a seventh class had the same research ethics lecture and unethical article assignment but did not use the role-play exercise.

Each of the authors taught two of these classes; the remaining two role-play classes and the nonrole-play class were taught by three other instructors. Approximately 18 students were enrolled in each class.

Procedure

We used the role-play exercise as described earlier, with one modification. Because of class size and time constraints, only a limited number of the students' "unethical" studies were selected for the role-play. The number of studies selected was left to the instructor's discretion, so the number of rated articles was inconsistent among the classes, ranging from 5 to 11 studies. Before engaging in the role-play, each class rated the cost and utility of the selected studies on a scale ranging from *no cost or utility* (0) to *highest cost or utility* (100).

After this first set of ratings, we asked each student who had initially critiqued one of the selected articles to imagine himself or herself as the article's primary author or researcher. The rest of the class role-played a peer review board that called upon the student to defend the ethics of his or her study. After the selected articles were defended, students rerated the perceived cost and utility of the articles on the same scale.

The instructor in the comparison class followed the same procedure except that he did not conduct the role-play segment after the initial set of ratings. Instead, the instructor turned to another research topic. After about 30 min, the instructor again asked the students to rate the perceived cost and utility of the selected articles. The changes in cost and utility ratings for each class provided the basis for our analyses.

Results and Discussion

Correlated *t* tests were computed to evaluate whether there were significant changes in the cost and utility ratings from Time 1 to Time 2. Because each class rated different articles, we treated each class separately in our analyses. We used meta-analytic procedures (Rosenthal, 1984) to compare and contrast the results from each of the classes.

The direction of the changes in utility ratings for all the role-play groups was consistent with our prediction (see Table 1). The magnitude of the effect varied slightly among instructors, with effect sizes (calculated as a Pearson *r*) ranging from .33 to .75. For the nonrole-play class, the change in the perceived utility ratings was not significant and in the opposite direction of that in the role-play classes.

A meta-analytic comparison revealed that the utility results from the role-play classes were homogeneous with regard to significance levels, $\chi^2(5) = 3.30$, $p = .65$, and effect sizes, $\chi^2(5) = 4.55$, $p = .47$. Combining the significance levels for the role-play classes' utility

ratings yielded a *Z* score of 6.05, $p < .0000001$. We calculated that it would take an additional 76 nonsignificant studies to achieve such an effect, thereby suggesting that our combined significance level was not due to sampling bias (Rosenthal, 1984; Rosenthal & Rosnow, 1991). Combining the effect sizes for the role-play classes resulted in an average effect size of .57 for the change in utility ratings, which is considered to be a large magnitude of effect in psychology (Cohen, 1977).

The results for the utility change ratings were homogeneous among the role-play classes. Therefore, significance levels and effect sizes were contrasted between the role-play and nonrole-play classes. Both the contrasts for significance levels, $Z = 3.089$, $p = .001$, and effect sizes, $Z = 3.264$, $p = .0006$, suggest that the role-play exercise affected students' utility ratings.

Table 1. Changes in Utility Ratings

Class	Utility Change[a]	Correlated *t* Test[b]	*r*
Instructor A			
Semester 1	10.76	$t(15) = 3.31$, $p = .002$	.65
Semester 2	4.22	$t(21) = 1.61$, $p = .06$	.33
Instructor B			
Semester 1	8.02	$t(15) = 2.75$, $p = .007$	.58
Semester 2	8.34	$t(15) = 4.43$, $p = .0002$	.75
Instructor C	7.37	$t(18) = 3.54$, $p = .001$	.64
Instructor D	3.13	$t(14) = 1.58$, $p = .069$	.40
No role-play[c]	−1.18	$t(18) = -.89$, $p = .39$[d]	−.20

[a]Mean change, Time 2 minus Time 1. [b]One-tailed *p*-values for role-play groups. [c]The utility ratings for one student were incomplete. [d]Two-tailed *p*-value.

The separate class results for changes in the perceived cost ratings were also in the expected direction (see Table 2). However, none of Instructor B's results were statistically significant. Instructors A, C, and D's results were homogeneous for significance levels, $\chi^2(3) = 4.17$, $p = .24$, and effect sizes, $\chi^2(3) = 3.95$, $p = .27$. They were significantly different from Instructor B's significance levels, $Z = 3.75$, $p = .0001$, and effect sizes, $Z = 3.74$, p = .0001.

We have no single explanation for this result, but note that Instructor B's cost results were not significantly different from the nonrole-play class. Clearly, the role-play exercise had little impact on student reevaluations of the studies in Instructor B's classes, whereas the other role-play classes differed from the nonrole-play class with respect to significance levels, $Z = 3.83$, $p = .0001$, and effect sizes, $Z = 4.10$, $p = .00002$. If we consider Instructor B as an outlier for the purposes of this analysis, then the average effect size for Instructors A, C, and D was .72. For these classes, the role-play exercise produced the hypothesized significant effect on cost ratings.

We thought of two plausible explanations for why Instructor B's changes in cost ratings were significantly different from the other role-play classes. First, Instructor B may have placed less emphasis on defending the perceived costs of the studies during the role-play part of the exercise than the other instructors. As a result, there would be little reason for Instructor B's students to change their initial cost ratings.

Another plausible explanation stems from a consideration of the number of studies discussed by each class. Both of Instructor B's classes discussed approximately five more articles than did the other role-play classes. Perhaps Instructor B's students rated too many articles and were unable to concentrate on

Table 2. Changes in Cost Ratings

Class	Cost Change[a]	Correlated t Test[b]	r
Instructor A			
Semester 1	−8.98	$t(15) = 5.11, p = .0001$	.80
Semester 2	−6.91	$t(21) = 6.91, p = .00001$	.83
Instructor B			
Semester 1	−.22	$t(15) = .05, p = .50$	.01
Semester 2	−.85	$t(15) = .35, p = .40$	.09
Instructor C	−5.63	$t(18) = 3.08, p = .003$	.59
Instructor D	−8.67	$t(14) = 2.60, p = .011$	.57
No role-play	1.14	$t(19) = −.85, p = .41$[c]	−.19

[a] Mean change, Time 2 minus Time 1. [b] One-tailed p-values for role-play groups. [c] Two-tailed p-value.

both the cost and utility issues for each study. Instructor B's students may have focused on the utility issue because it was a new concept introduced during the previous lecture. Anecdotal evidence seems to support this latter interpretation. In written evaluations of the exercise, Instructor B's students were more likely to suggest that they "needed more time for each study" and that there were "too many studies to consider."

This argument could be extended to explain at least the change in cost results for the nonrole-play class, because this class rated approximately the same number of articles as did Instructor B's classes. However, closer examination of Table 2 reveals that the mean cost ratings from Time I to Time 2 for the nonrole-play class appeared to increase, which is in the opposite direction of that of the role-play classes, including Instructor B's classes. Such a pattern

suggests that this class may have been evaluating the articles differently than were the role-play classes.

Nevertheless, our results generally support the effectiveness of Rosnow's (1990) exercise in sensitizing students to the complexity of research ethics. However, instructors should be aware of the constraints that class size and time limitations may create when selecting articles for the exercise. The question that future researchers may want to address is whether the role-play has a lasting impact on students' treatment of ethical issues in research.

References

American Psychological Association. (1981). Ethical principles of psychologists (revised). *American Psychologist, 36*, 633-688.

Cohen, J. (1977). *Statistical power analysis for the behavioral sciences* (2nd ed.). New York: Academic.

Rosenthal, R. (1984). *Meta-analytic procedures for social research.* Beverly Hills: Sage.

Rosenthal, R., & Rosnow, R. L. (1991). *Essentials of behavioral research: Methods and data analysis* (2nd ed.). New York: McGraw-Hill.

Rosnow, R. L. (1990). Teaching research ethics through role-play and discussion. *Teaching of Psychology, 17,* 179-181.

Note

This research was supported by Temple University fellowships awarded to both authors. We thank Dixon Bramblett, Richard Shifman, and Donna Shires for assistance in data collection; our students for participating in this study; and Ralph L. Rosnow and the anonymous reviewers for their helpful comments on earlier drafts of this article.

Discussing Animal Rights and Animal Research in the Classroom

Harold A. Herzog
Western Carolina University

There is growing controversy over the ethics of using animals in biomedical and behavioral research. This article reviews two prominent philosophical justifications for animal liberation and describes an exercise that facilitates class discussion of animal research issues. Students simulate participation on an institutional animal care committee and decide whether a series of hypothetical experiments will be allowed. Students reported that the exercise sharpened their awareness of this issue and of the complexity of making ethical decisions.

Since Singer's influential book *Animal Liberation* was published in 1975, public concern over the ethical treatment of animals has increased dramatically. Animal rights groups have criticized a variety of human uses of animals, including sport hunting, rodeos, intensive agricultural practices, consumption of animal flesh, and the wearing of furs. The use of animals in behavioral and biomedical research, however, has become the primary focus of public attention in recent years. Experimental psychology has been singled out as particularly offensive by animal rights activists who consider much behavioral research frivolous and cruel. For example, Rollin (1981) called experimental psychology, "the field most consistently guilty of mindless activity that results in great suffering" (p. 124).

Although psychologists have responded to such criticisms (e.g., Feeney, 1987; N. E. Miller, 1985), the animal rights movement has had a significant effect on animal research. In addition, teachers of psychology courses are being confronted with students who question the ethics and validity of behavioral research using animals (Gallup & Beckstead, 1988). There are three reasons why discussion of animal rights is relevant to students taking psychology courses. First, students should be aware of political and social issues related to psychology that affect their lives. In this context, the animal rights controversy joins other social issues, such as the effects of day care, television violence, and pornography, as topics relevant to psychology courses. Second, the animal

rights issue raises questions that are basic to psychological inquiry: What are the essential differences between humans and other animals? Can animals think? What psychological factors influence judgments about what constitutes moral behavior? Finally, the use of animals in laboratory courses has come under special criticism (e.g., Regan, 1983). Many animal liberationists believe that the routine dissection of animals in biology laboratories and the equivalent use of animals in psychology courses (e.g., physiological psychology students learning stereotaxic surgery on rats) are particularly onerous practices.

Although the animal rights movement affects research and teaching, few psychologists are informed about its intellectual underpinnings. Animal activists are often dismissed as intellectual lightweights whose arguments are based on emotional responses to pictures of kittens with electrodes in their skulls. Although this stereotype is accurate in some cases, there are also some first-rate philosophers behind the movement whose arguments are quite rigorous. This article briefly reviews two major philosophical positions used by animal activists in their arguments against the scientific use of animals and then describes a classroom exercise that stimulates discussion about this debate.

Philosophical Positions

The animal defense movement is divided into two groups. *Reformers* admit the necessity of using animals in biomedical research but want to eliminate as much suffering as possible. The more radical faction, *animal liberators,* view animal research as immoral in almost all cases and want to abolish it. It is not the purpose of this article to review all of the philosophical positions on animal rights. Interested readers should consult sources such as H. B. Miller and Williams (1983) for representative statements. Rather, I briefly summarize two of the most influential perspectives used by animal rights activists in their argument against using animals in research.

The Utilitarian Argument

The utilitarian argument is most clearly presented by the Australian philosopher, Peter Singer. In *Animal Liberation*, Singer (1975) effectively invoked emotional appeal and a consistent ethical philosophy to argue the case for abolishing animal research. The *principle of equality* (or *equal consideration of interests*) is the crux of Singer's argument. It holds that all sentient creatures (he draws the "line" at the phylogenetic level of oysters) have the same stake in their own existence ("interests"). Singer argued that this principle leads to the conclusion that there is no basis for elevating the interests of one species, *Homo sapiens*, above any other. Differences in intelligence, race, and gender are not valid criteria to exploit other humans; to Singer, a creature's species is equally irrelevant. He claimed that "From an ethical point of view, we all stand on an equal footing—whether we stand on two feet, or four, or none at all" (Singer, 1985, p. 6). The only relevant moral criterion for discrimination for or against a species is the capacity to suffer. Singer argued that, by definition, all sentient animals have the capacity to suffer and, therefore, are the subject of equal moral consideration. He claimed that to elevate the human species above all others on the basis of criteria other than suffering is arbitrary and a form of *speciesism*. Singer defined this term as "a prejudice or attitude of bias toward the interest of members of one's own species and against those of members of another species" (p. 7). He believed that speciesism is as illogical and morally repugnant as racism or sexism. Note that Singer would permit research with animals in some circumstances, but only if it is so important that we would also consider conducting the experiments using human subjects.

The Rights Argument

The rights argument is forcefully argued by Regan (1983, 1985) and Rollin (1981). Rights positions typically take the form that at least some creatures have certain fundamental rights (e.g., the right to moral consideration and the right not to be harmed). The question then becomes, Who is entitled to hold rights? Many philosophers restrict rights holders to beings that meet certain criteria, such as language, self-consciousness, or the ability to enter into reciprocal contractual obligations that they believe would eliminate non-human animals. There are several problems, however, that confront such philosophical positions. One problem concerns the moral status of humans who do not meet the criteria (i.e., the severely retarded, infants, and the insane). A second problem is how to deal with animals that appear to meet some of the criteria (e.g., members of large-brained species such as some primates, cetaceans, etc.)?

Animal rights theorists broaden the criteria so that animals are included as rights holders. To Regan

(1983, 1985), the fundamental criterion for having rights is "inherent value." He argued that sentient creatures, including humans, have inherent value in equal measure and thus are entitled to certain fundamental rights, including the right to be treated with respect and the right not to be harmed. For Regan, there are a number of reasons for abolishing research with animals, even research that will directly benefit humans. First and foremost, science treats animals as renewable resources rather than as "subjects of a life"—creatures with inherent value—thus violating what he called the "respect principle." In addition, he argued for the "worst off principle"—that the rights view does not permit the sacrifice of an innocent few even though such sacrifice may benefit many more individuals. For Regan, there is no justification for any animal research; the fact that the experiments could benefit hundreds of thousands of human lives is morally irrelevant.

Comparisons and Comments

There are clear differences between advocates of the utilitarian and rights positions as to why animal research is immoral. Singer suggested that there are philosophical problems with arguments based on the proposition that animals have rights, and Regan insisted that the utilitarian position is fatally flawed. There are, however, commonalties in the two positions. The most important is that Regan and Singer ended at about the same place, even though they took quite different paths. The logical extension of both arguments leads to vegetarianism, and both would eliminate research with animals as it is now conducted. In addition, the two positions are based on the notion that fundamental similarities between humans and other species are ethically significant (i.e., all sentient creatures have "interests") but that differences between humans and other species (i.e., language and greater intelligence) are morally irrelevant. Finally, both positions view speciesism as deplorable and the animal liberation movement as the logical extension of other social movements, such as civil rights and women's movements.

It is not my purpose to critique these views. The interested reader will want to consult sources such as Fox (1985), Frey (1980, 1983), and Narveson (1983) for critiques of the animal liberation philosophers. It is safe to say that most Americans would disagree with one of the basic tenets of activists, that human life per se is not more important than that of other species. If it were possible to transplant an organ from a healthy sheep into a dying infant, most of us would readily approve of the operation; Singer and Regan would not.

Though one may disagree with their thinking, philosophers, such as Regan and Singer, have raised some troubling issues that can be addressed in psychology courses. The following exercise was designed to facilitate discussion of the ethics of animal research in the classroom.

Discussing the Animal Research Controversy

The exercise described here is designed to facilitate thinking on these issues by having students make decisions about whether a series of hypothetical research and educational projects should be conducted. It is appropriate in a wide variety of courses, including general psychology, experimental psychology, animal behavior, and physiological psychology. It would also be useful in biology and bioethics courses.

Method

Institutions receiving federal funds for scientific research must have a standing Animal Care and Use Committee (ACUC) to review and approve all animal research conducted at the institution. In the exercise, students role-play participation on an ACUC. I divide the class into groups of between five and seven students. If class time permits, each group must make a decision on each of four research proposals. Otherwise, each group can discuss and make a decision about one of the proposals and present their decision and rationale to the class. The proposals are based on actual experiments or situations, and they are designed to exemplify different factors related to making ethical decisions. I remind students that the purpose of the exercise is to generate discussion and critical thinking. Thus, groups should be encouraged to reach a consensus rather than simply take a straw poll on each proposal.

Instructions to Students

Your group is the Animal Care Committee for your university. It is the committee's responsibility to evaluate and either approve or reject research proposals submitted by faculty members who want to use animals for research or instructional purposes in psychology, biology, or medicine. The proposals describe the experiments, including the goals and potential benefits of the research as well as any discomfort or injury that they may cause the animal subjects. You must either approve the research or deny permission for the experiments. It is not your job to suggest improvements on technical aspects of the projects, such as the experimental design. You should make your decision based on the information given in the proposal.

Proposals

Case 1. Professor King is a psychobiologist working on the frontiers of a new and exciting research area of neuroscience, brain grafting. Research has shown that neural tissue can be removed from the brains of monkey fetuses and implanted into the brains of monkeys that have suffered brain damage. The neurons seem to make the proper connections and are sometimes effective in improving performance in brain-damaged animals. These experiments offer important animal models for human degenerative diseases such as Parkinson's and Alzheimer's. Dr. King wants to transplant tissue from fetal monkey brains into the entorhinal cortex of adult monkeys; this is the area of the human brain that is involved with Alzheimer's disease.

The experiment will use 20 adult rhesus monkeys. First, the monkeys will be subjected to ablation surgery in the entorhinal cortex. This procedure will involve anesthetizing the animals, opening their skulls, and making lesions using a surgical instrument. After they recover, the monkeys will be tested on a learning task to make sure their memory is impaired. Three months later, half of the animals will be given transplant surgery. Tissue taken from the cortex of monkey fetuses will be implanted into the area of the brain damage. Control animals will be subjected to sham surgery, and all animals will be allowed to recover for 2 months. They will then learn a task to test the hypothesis that the animals having brain grafts will show better memory than the control group.

Dr. King argues that this research is in the exploratory stages and can only be done using animals. She further states that by the year 2000 about 2 million Americans will have Alzheimer's disease and that her research could lead to a treatment for the devastating memory loss that Alzheimer's victims suffer.

Case 2. Dr. Fine is a developmental psychobiologist. His research concerns the genetic control of complex behaviors. One of the major debates in his field concerns how behavior develops when an animal has no opportunity to learn a response. He hypothesizes that the complex grooming sequence of mice might be a behavior pattern that is built into the brain at birth, even though it is not expressed until weeks later. To investigate whether the motor patterns involved in grooming are acquired or innate, he wants to raise animals with no opportunity to learn the response. Rearing animals in social isolation is insufficient because the mice could teach themselves the response. Certain random movements could accidentally result in the removal of debris. These would then be repeated and could be coordinated into the complex sequence that would appear to be instinctive but would actually be learned. To show that the behaviors are truly innate, he needs to demonstrate that animals raised with no opportunity to perform any grooming-like movements make the proper movements when they are old enough to exhibit the behavior.

Dr. Fine proposes to conduct the experiment on 10 newborn mice. As soon at-the animals are born, they will be anesthetized and their front limbs amputated. This procedure will ensure that they will not be reinforced for making random grooming movements that remove debris from their bodies. The mice will then be returned to their mothers. The animals will be observed on a regular schedule using standard observation techniques. Limb movements will be filmed and analyzed. If grooming is a learned behavior, then the mice should not make grooming movements with their stumps as the movements will not remove dirt. If, however grooming movements are innately organized in the brain, then the animals should eventually show grooming-like movement with the stumps.

In his proposal, Dr. Fine notes that experimental results cannot be directly applied to human behavior. He argues, however, that the experiment will shed light on an important theoretical debate in the field of developmental psychobiology. He also stresses that the amputations are painless and the animals will be well treated after the operation.

Case 3. Your university includes a college of veterinary medicine. In the past, the veterinary students have practiced surgical techniques on dogs procured from a local animal shelter. However, there have been some objections to this practice, and the veterinary school wants the approval of your committee to continue this practice. They make the following points.

1. Almost all of these animals will eventually be killed at the animal shelter. It is wasteful of life to breed animals for the vet school when there is an ample supply of animals that are going to be killed anyway, either because their owners do not want them or they are homeless.

2. It costs at least 10 times as much to raise purebred animals for research purposes; this money could be better used to fund research that would benefit many animals.

3. Research with dogs from animal shelters and the practice surgeries will, in the long run, aid the lives of animals by training veterinarians and producing treatments for diseases that afflict animals.

A local group of animal welfare activists has urged your committee to deny the veterinary school's request. They argue that the majority of these animals are lost or stolen pets, and it is tragic to think that the dog you have grown to love will wind up on a surgical table or in an experiment. Furthermore, they claim that as people become aware that animals taken to shelters may end up in research laboratories they will stop using the shelters. Finally, the activists point out that in countries such as England, veterinary students do not perform practice surgery; they learn surgical techniques in an extensive apprenticeship.

Case 4. The Psychology Department is requesting permission from your committee to use 10 rats per semester for demonstration experiments in a physiological psychology course. The students will work in groups of three; each group will be given a rat. The students will first perform surgery on the rats. Each animal will be anethestized. Following standard surgical procedures, an incision will be made in the scalp and two holes drilled in the animal's skull. Electrodes will be lowered into the brain to create lesions on each side. The animals will then be allowed to recover. Several weeks later, the effects of destroying this part of the animal's brain will be tested in a shuttle avoidance task in which the animals will learn when to cross over an electrified grid.

The instructor acknowledges that the procedure is a common demonstration and that no new scientific information will be gained from the experiment. He argues, however, that students taking a course in physiological psychology must have the opportunity to engage in small animal surgery and to see firsthand the effects of brain lesions.

Notes to the Instructor

Case 1 forces consideration of whether injury to another species, which is fairly closely related to humans, is justified if the results will be applicable to human beings. Case 2 asks students to think about the use of animals in pure research in which there is no direct connection to future human application. Based on a study of Fentress (1973), this case offers an excellent opportunity for the instructor to discuss the importance of pure research in the progress of science. Incidentally, in the Fentress experiment, amputated mice exhibited "remarkably normal" grooming movements with their stumps, demonstrating that the movements were innate. Case 3 involves the use of pound animals in research and is one of the more controversial issues in biomedical and veterinary research. Several state legislatures have passed laws banning the use of pound-seizure animals for biomedical research or student surgeries in veterinary schools. (See Giannelli, 1988, for a discussion of this issue from an activist viewpoint.) The use of animals in student laboratories (Case 4) has been singled out by animal welfare groups as being particularly unnecessary. They argue that videotapes and computer simulations are adequate substitutes for live animals in classroom behavioral studies and dissections.

Numerous modifications can be made with these scenarios to tailor them to the needs of particular topics or courses. For example, Case 1 could be changed so that some groups are given the case using monkeys as subjects and some are given the same case using rats. This would lead to a discussion of factors that come into play in making ethical decisions (e.g., why might it be acceptable to use rodents in the study but not primates?). Other cases could be added for different courses. Thus, a proposal in which an ethnologist wants to confront mice with snakes to study antipredator behavior (Herzog, 1988) could be included for a course in animal behavior.

Student Responses

I have used this exercise with 150 students in five classes. After the exercise, each student was asked to write an anonymous evaluation of the exercise and indicate whether it should be used in the future. The responses were extremely positive; except for two of the students, the remainder recommended that I continue using the exercise. The following statements were typical: "I feel that this was a valuable experience as part of my psychology class, and it was beneficial in developing my thoughts on this topic. I had never really considered such issues," and "I believe this exercise was valuable to the students in the class because it made us think about which is more important—an animal's life or a human life."

Discussion

The Christian writer C. S. Lewis (1988) stated, "It is the rarest thing in the world to hear a rational discussion of vivisection" (p. 160). These exercises are designed to elevate discussion of one of the most controversial topics in science to a rational forum. However, attitudes about the appropriate use of animals in research are not only a function of logic. Judgments about animals are influenced by many factors, such as their physiognomic similarity to humans, their "cuteness" and perceived intelligence, and the labels we assign them (Burghardt & Herzog, 1980; Herzog, 1988). In addition to raising sensitivity about an important ethical issue, these exercises promote discussions of how moral judgments are made.

The animal rights movement will continue to grow in numbers and visibility. The goal of many animal rights activists is the abolition of animal research. As Regan (1988) proclaimed, "It is not bigger cages we want, but empty cages. Anything less than total victory will not satisfy-us!" (p. 12). Psychologists must be prepared to confront this challenge in their roles as scientists and teachers. Inevitably, there will be

disagreements within the profession. Some will side with the animal rights faction and become active in organizations like Psychologists for the Ethical Treatment of Animals; others will support the rights of researchers to use animal subjects. Increasingly, psychology teachers will be confronted by activist students who demand justification for research practices they find disagreeable. (I can also envision pressures on authors and publishers of introductory psychology textbooks to reduce or eliminate coverage of controversial experiments, such as Harlow's studies of social deprivation in monkeys and Seligman's learned helplessness research.) The issue of animal rights is philosophically and psychologically complex. It is mired in a milieu of rationality, emotion, convention, ethical intuition, and self-interest. We owe it to ourselves and our students to become familiar with both sides of this issue so that more light than heat will emerge from the debate.

References

Burghardt, G. M., & Herzog, H. A., Jr. (1980). Beyond conspecifics: Is "Brer Rabbit" our brother? *BioScience, 30,* 763-767.

Feeney, D. M. (1987) . Human rights and animal welfare. *American Psychologist, 42, 593-599.*

Fentress, J. C. (1973). Development of grooming in mice with amputated forelimbs. *Science, 179,* 704-705.

Fox, M. A. (1985). *The case for animal experimentation.* Berkeley: University of California.

Frey, R. (1980). *Interests and rights: The case against animal rights.* Oxford, England: Clarendon.

Frey, R. (1983). On why we would do better to jettison moral rights. In H. B. Miller & W. H. Williams (Eds.), *Ethics and animals* (pp. 285-301). Clifton, NJ: Humana.

Gallup, G. G., Jr., & Beckstead, J. W. (1988). Attitudes toward animal research. *American Psychologist, 44,* 474-475.

Giannelli, M. A. (1988, Fall). Shelter animals as research models: Scientific anachronism, social ignominy. *PsyETA Bulletin,* pp. 6-12.

Herzog, H. A. Jr. (1988). *The moral status of mice. American Psychologist, 43,* 473-474.

Lewis, C. S. (1988). A case for abolition. In A. Linzey & T. Regan (Eds.), *Animals and Christianity: A book of readings* (pp. 160-164). New York: Crossroad. (Original work published 1947)

Miller, H. B., & Williams, W. H. (Eds.). (1983). *Ethics and animals.* Clifton, NJ: Humana.

Miller, N. E. (1985). The value of behavioral research on animals. *American Psychologist, 40,* 423-440.

Narveson J. (1983). Animal rights revisited. In H. B. Miller & W. H. Wiliiams (Eds.), *Ethics and animals* (pp. 45-59). Clifton, NJ: Humana.

Regan, T. (1983). *The case for animal rights.* Berkeley: University of California.

Regan, T. (1985). The case for animal rights. In P. Singer (Ed.), *In defense of animals* (pp. 13-26). Oxford, England: Basil Blackwell.

Regan, T. (1988, September/October). The torch of reason, the sword of justice. *The Animal's Voice Magazine,* pp. 12-17.

Rollin, B. E. (1981). *Animal rights and human morality.* New York: Prometheus.

Singer, P. (1975). *Animal liberation.* New York: Avon.

Singer, P. (1985). Prologue: Ethics and the new animal liberation movement. In P. Singer (Ed.), *In defense of animals* (pp. 1-10). Oxford, England: Basil Blackwell.

Note

My thanks to Mary Jean Herzog, Sandra Skinner, Glen Erikson, Gordon Burghardt, and Lisa Finley for helpful comments on a draft of this article and my treatment of the animal rights movement and to my students at Western Carolina University and Warren Wilson College for discussing and evaluating the exercises

4. TEACHING PRINCIPLES, CONCEPTS, AND SKILLS

Using Riddles to Introduce the Process and Experience of Scientific Thinking

Joe W. Hatcher, Jr.
Ripon College

Science has been described as puzzle solving. This article describes an exercise that uses riddles to expose students to important aspects of the process and experience of scientific thinking.

Science has been described as a process of puzzle solving (Kuhn, 1970). The use of riddles described in this article is useful in demonstrating to students, especially those in introductory or experimental design classes, key points concerning scientific thinking as well as the process and experience of being a scientist.

Students are told that they will participate in an exercise involving scientific thinking. They are given the following information.

> You are walking in the desert and find a man lying face down with a pack on his back, dead.
> How did he die?

Students are told that the instructor will respond to any yes/no questions. After several false starts, the class arrives at the correct answer: The man is a parachutist whose chute failed to open. Students are divided into small groups and given the following series of riddles, one at a time, with one member of each group receiving the answer and serving as moderator.

A. A man walks into a bar and asks the bartender for a glass of water. The bartender reaches under the bar, pulls out a large pistol, and points it right in the man's face. The man says "thank you" and turns and walks out of the bar. Why did the man say "thank you"? (He had the hiccups.)

B. A man is at work and wants to go home. However, he will not go home because a man wearing a mask is waiting there for him. What does the first man do for a living? (He's a baseball player standing on third base.)

C. A man is found shot to death in a room with a table, four chairs, and 53 bicycles. Why was he shot? (He was cheating at cards by having an extra ace; there are 52 Bicycle playing cards in a normal deck.)

After the riddles have been solved, I point out that both scientific thinking and riddle solving attempt to make sense of data that may appear contradictory. More specifically, the following lessons in scientific thinking may be derived from solving the riddles.

1. It is often important to view a problem from more than one perspective.

The ability to alter perspective, termed *lateral thinking* by De Bono (1967, 1968, 1985), is fundamental to any science and is demonstrated in the paradigm shifts discussed by Kuhn (1970). From this exercise, students learn that determined questioning from a wrong perspective leads to little or no progress, but once the correct perspective is found, the solution to the riddle is often easily determined.

2. Prior assumptions concerning data are dangerous.

In the parachute riddle, students typically assume that the man is wearing a common backpack, leading to fruitless questioning. Similarly, in viewing scientific data, interpretations can be guided by assumptions to the point of overlooking the unexpected. For this reason, questioning basic assumptions is often productive.

3. Yes/no questions, properly formed, yield highly useful data.

The yes/no questions of the riddles are paralleled in science by the alternative and null hypotheses of the typical experiment. In each case, when precisely formed, the question (or experiment) allows one to choose between two mutually exclusive views.

4. Details that do not fit expected patterns are often of crucial importance.

In the parachute riddle, discovering that there are no footprints around the body is inconsistent with most interpretations of the problem, leading to a swift reappraisal of the situation and usually a quick solution. Similarly, details inconsistent with general assumptions often spur scientific advances.

5. Persistence is a key quality in problem solving.

Students often terminate a promising line of questioning, unaware that the answer is close at hand. Although persistence can lead to the accumulation of mounds of useless data (e.g., alchemy), some degree of persistence is often necessary to solve a problem.

6. By expecting complicated answers, simple ones may be overlooked.

Students often comment that the riddles, although they appear complex, have simple solutions. This observation can be developed in several fruitful directions, such as: (a) discussing the law of parsimony; (b) noting that a conceptually simple approach may account for vast amounts of data (e.g., Darwin's theory of natural selection); and (c) extending the second point to the possibility that we may be able someday to understand behavior from relatively simple principles, a position I find especially interesting (Hatcher, 1987).

7. Science is an enterprise that is frustrating, exciting, and requires considerable courage.

This exercise also serves to introduce students to the "human" side of scientific thought. While solving riddles, students become alternately frustrated and excited, and by exposing their own thought processes to the scrutiny to others, students gain a glimpse of the courage that it takes to subject one's ideas to possible falsification. At the conclusion of the exercise, I note that, whatever the similarities between riddles and the scientific process, there is a crucial difference.

Although riddles have solutions that perseverance will discover, science makes no such guarantee; scientists must pursue their goals with no assurance of success which requires a special kind of commitment.

Three laboratory exercises used in the class were evaluated on 5-point scales by two classes of experimental design students ($N = 40$), on the dimensions of *uninteresting-interesting* ($M = 4.62$ for the present exercise vs. 3.87 for the other two labs combined), *not useful-useful* (4.09 vs. 4.05), and *definitely drop-definitely keep* (4.58 vs. 4.06). Written comments indicate that students often remember the riddles when attempting to solve a difficult experimental design problem and that the riddle exercise is a good icebreaker for the class.

Based on student responses and my observations, I believe that this simple exercise helps students to understand the process and experience of science. The technique may be useful in a variety of classes involving scientific thinking.

References

De Bono, E. (1967). *The five day course in thinking.* New York: Basic Books.

De Bono, E. (1968). *New think: The use of lateral thinking in the generation of new ideas.* New York: Basic Books.

De Bono, E. (1985). *De Bono's thinking course.* New York: Facts on File.

Hatcher, J. W., Jr. (1987). Arguments for the existence of a general theory of behavior. *Behavioral Science, 32,* 179-189.

Kuhn, T. S. (1970). *The structure of scientific revolutions* (2nd ed.). Chicago: University of Chicago Press.

Note

I thank Mark Nussbaum, Robert Wallace, Patricia White, three anonymous reviewers, and the editor for comments and suggestions on earlier drafts of this article.

Operational Definitions Made Simple, Lasting, and Useful

Larry R. Vandervert
Spokane Falls Community College

One of the most difficult things to get across to beginning psychology students is a reasonable understanding of the usefulness and limitations of operational definitions. To be sure, there are always students who quickly grasp these ideas and see their significance, but those students always seem to be in the minority. Should we go to a lot of trouble for operational definitions? I believe we should. One of the deeper appreciation's for modern psychology, in my estimation, comes from the way psychologists have dealt with "mind" while attempting to maintain a scientific framework of activity. This is a perspective on psychology that students cannot afford to miss, and psychology probably cannot afford to have them miss it.

My goal, when dealing with difficult concepts, is to *find something that is in the background of all of my students* that will recognize the new as something already well understood. One way to help break down ideas involved in operational definitions has been to relate the entire process by story-like analogy to something all of the students are familiar with. I have used the household kitchen and kitchen recipes as analogies to the scientific laboratory and the operational definition. The analogy becomes so thoroughgoing, and the students' understanding so great, that many students become able to write fairly good definitions for certain psychological concepts. Some students, perhaps the more creative ones, are even able to originate fictitious psychological concepts and write operational definitions for them. I will give an example of these student efforts later.

Kitchen Analogy. The purpose of the kitchen-analogy is to show students that they are already familiar with the important ideas related to operational definitions of psychological concepts. The main ideas covered are: Constructs, Empirical Referents, Quantification, Conditions of Control, and Scientific Agreement.

Most people don't think about it, but we all grow up (in this country anyway) in homes that contain highly sophisticated *scientific* laboratories—the household kitchen. Stretching the point, you say? Let's take inventory: (a) Hot and cold running water—into a temperature and corrosive resistant basin; (b) An adjustable cooling chamber; (c) An adjustable heating chamber; (d) A motorized, variable-speed mixing device; (e) A high-speed blending device; (f) A long list of reasonably accurate measuring devices and containers; (g) Containers for use in the heating and cooling chambers; (h) A great collection of substances which may be combined in accordance with empirically established (often internationally) methods and rules; (i) Handling and cutting tools.

Now, we begin to have a little more appreciation for the old kitchen. Have we left anything out? (Students will supply the entire list if you simply ask them how a kitchen is like a scientific laboratory.) Oh yes, one of the most important things, a shelf of specialized texts, handbooks, and manuals of methods. There might even be a procedures book written by a team of French experts, perhaps one by a Japanese expert. Yes, we seem to have a complete scientific laboratory. (Ask students if they think the term "scientific" is really appropriate here.)

Most of the things we prepare in the kitchen require a combination of activities or *building operations* in the combining of ingredients. Therefore, we might easily refer to the things we prepare as things we construct— or simply refer to them as *constructs*. For example, we might refer to a cake prepared in our scientific kitchen as a physical construction, much like a building is a physical construction. More simply, we may refer to a cake(or a building) as *a physical construct*. We usually follow a precise recipe in constructing a cake. The recipe lists specific activities or *operations* we must perform to obtain the desired physical cake. The recipe can be referred as a definition of the cake in terms of operations. More simply, the recipe is an *operational definition* of the cake. Now, we have two ways of saying the same thing: "recipe for a cake," OR "operational definition for a physical construct."

As we all know, the operational definition (recipe) for a cake consists of written instructions including specification of the substances to be mixed in relation to one another (empirical referents), the apparatus to be used (conditions of control), the various amounts of substances and apparatus used (quantification), and the operations one must perform to mix things in the proper relationship. If the operational definition is followed carefully, the result will be the specific, desired cake. Perhaps the operations have defined a chocolate cake with vanilla frosting—first defined by that team of French experts in 1938.

The perfect cake obtained by sticking closely to the *operational definition* for the *physical construct,* "cake," should be identical to the one the French creators had in mind in 1938. We might conclude that the motive behind writing operational definitions for cakes is to insure that anyone, anywhere who wished to follow the operations could produce and observe the same cake. This result is a type of scientific agreement. Personally, I would say it *is* scientific agreement. One may not like this particular cake, or think anyone ought to eat it, but he certainly could produce what the French experts had in mind.

These ideas about converting the making of a cake into a set of operations to be carried out in scientific laboratore are: (a) *Physical Construct*—"Cake"; (b) *Operational Definition*—Recipe; (c) *Empirical Referents*—Ingredients, aspects of apparatus; (d) *Quantifications of Control Conditions*—Cups, teaspoons, ounces, etc. Specification of apparatus conditions, e.g., 350° for 45 minutes; (e) *Scientific Agreement*—Identical cakes produced in France and United States 39 years apart. (This all assumes very close control over specifications of ingredients and apparatus. Surely, if all possible factors were controlled, there would be no reason for the cakes not to be identical.)

At this point in the analogy two very important points should be made. Both of them refer to the limitations of operational definitions, and the limitations apply to both the constructing of cakes and to the construction of psychological concepts. We normally would not think about these points in relation to recipes and cakes, but they are of crucial importance when discussing operational definitions and psychological constructs. *First,* it is worth noting that cakes never occur naturally, they must be constructed. The same may be said of psychological constructs. At least three ideas (in analogy form) are important here: (a) Cakes can only be constructed by the following the appropriate operational definition (recipe), (b) In reality, then, the recipe can not be separated from the cake—the operational definition cannot be separated from the construct, and (c) It would be a mistake to assume that the recipe carried some "real" meaning beyond the cake it produced. *Second*, the writing of recipes for the constructing of cakes may tend to fix the way cakes are generally constructed, as well as the way we think about them, *but it certainly does not fix the way they can be made in the future.* Actually, if one realizes that the set of operations is always open to alteration, it can be seen that the operational definition can serve as a basis for the continual refinement of the construct in question. We can always attempt to produce a better cake by adding a little extra of this or that. Also, it sometimes happens that we follow the recipe perfectly, except for one mistake or accident, and we stumble onto a new

treat. A new construct has come into being, and if we are smart, we'll immediately write a set of operations that will reproduce it.

Psychological Concepts (Ideational Constructs). In the same way we talk about a cake as a *physical construct,* we can talk about certain psychological concepts such as "fear" or "intelligence" as *ideational constructions.* With the appropriate operational definition a particular version of the psychological concept can be produced for observation.

Through the kitchen-analogy we have been brought very close to what P. W. Bridgeman was expressing in his *The Logic of Modern Physics (1927),* "We mean by any concept nothing more than a set of operations: *the concept is synonymous with the corresponding set of physical operations."* Students do not find it too difficult to interpret Bridgeman's statement in terms of cakes and recipes.

A summary which point-by point matches the ideas presented in the physical construction of a cake with the ideational construction of a version of the psychological concept of "fear" is as follows: (a) *Ideational Construct*—"fear"; (b) *Operational Definition*—written statement of operations to perform to observe; (c) *Empirical Referents*—stimuli, responses, and organismic variables; apparatus. (One may wish to equate S, R, and O with machine versions of them.); (d) *Quantifications of Control Conditions*—amplitude, frequencies, duration, latency, type; specification of apparatus conditions; (e) *Scientific Agreement*—Identical observations of "fear," and possible identical notions of fear in observers. At this point, for the explication of the relation between operational definition and psychological constructs I begin to move from lecture-discussion to a classroom exercise.

In a scientific psychology's ideational constructions such as "fear" are constructed from such empirical "ingredients" as stimulus, response, and organism variables. These variables are expressed in a particular relationship to one another (mixed and baked) to stand for, for examples, "fear." Notice that the S, O, and R variables serve as the building blocks in the derivation of the construct of fear. The point that these variables can be taken as the counterparts of the ingredients of the cake is critical in helping students understand what is necessary in the writing of new operational definitions for new psychological conceptions.

Classroom Exercise. I have found that student enjoy this classroom exercise on operational definitions tremendously. Not only do they enjoy its but the exercise illustrates in a simple way the necessity of reaching agreement as to what set of operations will be used to define the psychological concept in question.

Having been exposed to the kitchen-analogy, students are asked to write an operational definition for the construct "fear," (since they have not yet been given a complete definition of it). If they are cautioned to think through the analogy and to carefully restrict themselves to statements about stimuli, responses and organismic variables they will find that they can do quite well. They might even find they have improved upon the definition for "fear" provided by William S. Verplanck in his "A Glossary of Some Terms Used in the Objective Science of Behavior" (1957):

> FEAR: 1. *(empirical behavior theory)* the behavior produced either by sudden and intense stimulation or by specific classes of stimuli that must be identified empirically for each species studied. Responses include alterations of sphincter control, flight behavior, respiratory changes, and the suppression of behavior occurring at the onset of stimulation. (p.15).

The fear definition has been used because it illustrates the S-O-R construct so well. Also students can identify in a humorous way with *alterations of sphincter control,* and *suppression of behavior occurring at the onset of stimulation* (just says BOO!). Students become particularly fascinated when given a chance to try their hand at writing operational definitions for such concepts as love or religions etc. They also now have a clear mental-set to ask critical questions about what sub-sets of S's are mixed with what sub-sets of R's and O's to produce what psychologists are talking about.

The most exciting things the kitchen-analogy has produced for me have been occasions when students have gone beyond the classroom activity of writing operational definitions for already defined pieces of "mind" and have attempted to produce new operational expressions of "mind" that have never

before been written (as far as they know). For examples one student decided (after a discussion of how intelligence might be operationalized) that *belief* was an ability, and, further, was normally distributed. He suggested that some people had a greater *ability* to believe than others, and the variations in the ability to believe accounted for a number of everyday observations on human behavior. He felt he could eventually define belief as an ability and develop a test for it. I don't know whether or not he ever did. But I have the satisfaction of knowing that his belief about *belief* was originally cultured into existence by a discussion of intelligence within the context of the kitchen-analogy. I also know that the student came to grips with one of the deeper appreciation of modern scientific psychology.

References

Bridgeman, P. W. *The logic of modern physics.* New York: Macmillan, 1927.
Verplanck, W. S. A glossary of some terms used in the objective science of behavior. *Supplement to the Psychological Review,* 1957, *64* (6, Part 2, November).

Note

Reprinted from *Understanding* Student *Behavior: A newsletter for Teachers Using UNDERSTANDING HUMAN BEHAVIOR,* by James V. McConnell, Vol. 2; No. 1. , Spring 1978, published by Holt, Rinehart and Winston. By permission of the publisher.

Defying Intuition: Demonstrating the Importance of the Empirical Technique

Art Kohn
North Carolina Central University

A simple stay-switch probability game demonstrates the importance of empirically testing our beliefs. Based on intuition, most undergraduate subjects believe that a stay *strategy leads to a higher percentage of winning, and most faculty subjects believe that the* staying *and* switching *strategies yield equal probabilities of winning. However, a simple in-class experiment proves that switching wins twice as often as staying. Rather than teaching specific probability principles, this demonstration emphasizes reliance on empirically validating our beliefs. A follow-up questionnaire shows that participating in this experiment may increase students' trust in the empirical method.*

In about 350 BC, Aristotle argued that the speed with which an object falls to earth is directly proportional to its weight (i.e., that heavier objects would fall to earth faster than lighter ones). Aristotle was wrong. But owing to the sheer force of his rhetoric, his axiom remained unchallenged for more than 2,000 years. Indeed, it was not until the Renaissance that Galileo performed his famous experiment proving gravity works with equal force on all objects. This refutation of Aristotelian physics shook the intellectual community of the time because it highlighted the limits of human intuition and emphasized the importance of inductive reasoning. This insight, in turn, helped to usher in the era of empirical exploration.

The following classroom demonstration, which is based on a puzzle that appeared in *Parade* magazine, dramatically illustrates both the limitations of intuitive judgments and the power of empirical investigation. The activity takes about 15 min of class time, and the only materials required are three identical envelopes and a $1 bill. I conduct this activity on the first day of my introductory and experimental psychology courses to set an empirical tone for the semester.

The Demonstration

The demonstration consists of three parts: presenting the probability puzzle, polling the class's intuitive judgments about the optimum solution to the puzzle, and conducting an experiment to test the accuracy of these intuitive judgments. To begin, tell your students that you plan to present a simple probability question involving three choices. Place the $1 bill into one envelope, seal all three envelopes, and then shuffle them so that no one, yourself included, knows which one contains the $1 bill. (You may want to put some folded paper into each envelope so that the students cannot see or feel the bill through the envelope.)

Now ask a volunteer to select an envelope, promising that the person will be able to keep the $1 bill if she or he guesses correctly. After the volunteer selects the envelope, announce that you plan to reveal that one of the unchosen envelopes is empty. Examine the contents of the two unchosen envelopes and, with a bit of fanfare, reveal to the class that one of them does not contain the $1 bill. (Indeed, at least one remaining envelope must be empty.) Finally, holding up the remaining unchosen envelope, present the class with the critical question: "As you can see, the volunteer and I each have an envelope. However, at this time I will offer the volunteer a chance to switch with me. In your opinion, for the greatest chance of

winning, should the volunteer stay with the initial choice or switch to my envelope?"

Following the discussion, poll the class's opinions. In my sections, typically 50% to 60% of the students favor staying, 20% to 30% favor switching, and 10% to 20% argue that, in terms of probability, it makes no difference whether the volunteer stays or switches.

Point out to the class that they are basing their opinions on intuition rather than on empirical data. Invite them to test their intuitive beliefs by conducting an experiment that will identify the best strategy.

Instruct the students to pair up, with one member acting as the experimenter and the other as the subject. Each experimenter should make a data sheet by labeling four columns "Correct Answer," "Subject's Choice," "Stay/Switch," and "Win/Lose" and by numbering the rows 1 to 20. Finally, the experimenters should fill in the correct-answer cells with a random assortment of the letters *A, B,* and *C.*

To conduct the experiment, each experimenter simply imitates the procedure I used with the class volunteer. The experimenter should (a) prompt the subject to guess either *A, B,* or *C*; (b) reveal that one of the unchosen options is incorrect; and (c) offer the subject the option of switching to the other unchosen option. On Trial 1, for example, if the correct answer is *A* and the subject chooses *C,* then the experimenter would inform the subject that *B* is an incorrect choice and offer the subject a chance to switch to *A.* On Trial 2, if the correct answer is *A* and the subject chooses *A,* then the experimenter would reveal that *B* (or *C*) is incorrect and offer the subject the chance to switch. For each of the 20 trials, the experimenter should record the subject's initial choice, whether the subject switched, and whether the subject ultimately selected the right choice. After everyone has completed the procedure, experimenters calculate the number of times that switching led to a win and the number of times that staying led to a win. Finally, the instructor should combine the results for the entire class and draw a graph comparing the percentage of wins that result from switching and from staying.

Evaluation

I evaluated this demonstration in three ways. First, I asked 140 undergraduates and 73 university faculty members which strategy they thought was most likely to result in winning. Each subject read a 150-word summary of the situation and then circled one of the following responses: "Your chances are best if you stay with your initial choice," "Your chances are best if you switch to the other choice," or "It will not matter whether you stay or switch; your chances of winning will be the same."

Fifty-five percent of the undergraduates believed that staying provided the greatest chance of winning, whereas 66% of the faculty believed that staying and switching yielded the same chance of winning. Only

28% of the undergraduates and 7% of the faculty believed that switching envelopes provided the best chance of winning.

Second, I conducted the in-class experiment with 84 introductory psychology students. I tallied the number of times the 42 subjects chose to stay or switch and the consequences of each choice.

Subjects significantly preferred the staying strategy, staying on 60% of the trials (binomial test, $N = 840$), $p < .001$. Although the subject preferred to stay, switching actually resulted in a significantly greater proportion of wins, χ^2 (1, $N = 840$) = 95.9, $p < .001$. Subjects won in 69% of the trials when they switched, whereas they won in only 34% of the trails when they stayed. I recently replicated this study with as few as 6 subjects, so the demonstration should work for all class sizes.

Finally, I asked all the students to complete the Trust in Research Survey (Kohn, in press) that measures reliance on intuition versus empirical investigation. The questionnaire consists of 10 questions such as "Your religion tells you that an event occurred, but research clearly shows that it did not happen. What will you base your opinion on?" and "You need to buy a reliable car, and your intuition tells you to buy *Brand X*. However, all the research shows that *Brand Z is* better. How will you decide which car to buy?" For each question, the subjects rated whether they would base their actions on *intuition only* (1) to *research only* (9). The students filled out the Trust in Research Survey along with several other unrelated surveys. Half the students filled out the survey immediately before participating in the demonstration, and half of them completed it 2 hr afterward.

Results of the Trust in Research Survey indicate that students who participated in the demonstration had higher trust in the empirical technique than students before the demonstration; however, this effect did not reach statistical significance. The mean for students who took the survey before the demonstration was 4.5, whereas the mean for those who took it afterward was 6.1, $t(166) = 1.53$, $p < . 1$.

Discussion

This activity provides a dramatic example of the limitations of intuitive judgments and the importance of empirical testing. Although the puzzle is simple, involving only three possible answers, most subjects fail to solve it; ironically, subjects with doctorates err more often than undergraduates.

After the demonstration, you may want to explain the mathematical rationale for these counterintuitive results. In this explanation, the critical premise is that the instructor's act of eliminating an unchosen envelope does not affect the chances that the student's envelope is a winner. To illustrate this, I begin with an analogous, realistic situation. I tell my class to imagine that four teams have qualified for an upcoming Final Four basketball tournament. In the first round, Kentucky is scheduled to play Duke and Indiana is scheduled to play UCLA. Given equal quality of the teams, the chances that Kentucky, for example, will win the tournament are one in four. However, assume that the Indiana team decides to withdraw from the tournament. How will this affect Kentucky's chances? In fact, the odds of Kentucky winning do not change at all. Indiana was outside Kentucky's qualifying bracket in the first round, so Kentucky still must win two games. As a result, the chances that Kentucky will win the tournament remain one in four. For UCLA, however, the chances of winning improve to one in two. A betting person should shift from backing Kentucky to backing UCLA.

This situation is analogous to the three envelope problem. The initial probability that the instructor has the $1 bill is two chances in three, and the initial probability that the student has the $1 bill is one chance in three. Importantly, once the student selects an envelope, that envelope becomes a set that is entirely independent of the instructor's set; in effect, the envelope is placed into a separate qualifying bracket. Thus, when the instructor acts as an omniscient agent and eliminates a certain loser from within his or her set, that act in no way affects the probabilities that the student's set contains the winner. The chances that the instructor has the winner remain two out of three; the chances that the student has the winner remain one out of three. As a result, the student is better off switching envelopes.

Consider a different situation, however, in which the student selects envelope A and then accidentally peeks into envelope C and realizes that it is empty. Should the student switch from A to *B?* The answer is no because, under these conditions, A was not segregated into a separate category; the student's insight simply eliminated an option from the set A, *B,* and C. Thus, the student's insight leaves two alternatives with equal probabilities of being correct. This latter situation is analogous to a student guessing A on a three-item multiple-choice exam. If the student later realizes that answer C is certainly wrong, the student gains no advantage by switching from A to *B.*

Your students might appreciate knowing that when mathematicians were confronted with an analogous puzzle, their intuition misled them as well. In 1990, a similar question was submitted to Marilyn vos Savant, a newspaper columnist who, according to the *Guinness Book of World Records*, has the world's highest IQ. When Ms. vos Savant answered (correctly) that switching provided the greatest chance of winning, she received a storm of protests from mathematicians around the country. See Posner (1991) for an interesting history of this controversy.

Following the discussion, you can again ask your volunteer whether he or she wants to stay with the original choice or switch to the remaining envelope. About 90% of the time, my volunteers seem convinced by the data and switch envelopes. However, if your experience is like mine, some of your students (and even some of your colleagues) will continue to insist that switching envelopes does not increase their chances of winning. Under these conditions, your only option may be to encourage them to conduct the experiment on their own, and then you may want to remind them that truth is not obliged to be consistent with intuition.

References

Kohn, A., (in press). *Communicating psychology: An instructor's resource guide to accompany Kalat's Introduction to Psychology* (3rd ed.). Belmont, CA: Wadsworth.

Posner, G. P. (1991). Nation's mathematicians guilty of 'innumeracy.' *Skeptical Inquirer, 15,* 342-345.

Note

I thank the students in Experimental Psychology and in History and Systems at North Carolina Central University for their assistance with this study. I also thank Wendy Kohn, Richard Burke, Jim Kalat, Ruth Ault, and anonymous reviewers for their help in improving this article.

Teaching Students To Do Interviewing

Jan Yoder
State University of New York at Buffalo

Most undergraduate research methods classes emphasize experimental design. Survey methods are quickly reviewed, if they are mentioned at all. Yet, surveying techniques, most notably instrument construction and interviewing, are important skills for the applied researcher, program evaluator, and even the laboratory experimentalist. For example, careful debriefing procedures, that is, interviewing by the researcher, are important in order to discover subjects' reactions to an experimental procedure, especially those procedures that may produce suspicious or upset participants. Although it is not my intent to demean the importance of teaching experimental design, it is my contention that this process would benefit and be expanded if survey methods were included as part of a methods class. Interviewing is probably best taught to students by having them actually do it. The following describes a simple procedure for experientially teaching these skills.

My design for the research methods class includes an in-class study, a research project, and a proposal (Yoder, 1979). Briefly, the in-class study is the first assignment which teaches students to write a journal article. A study is conducted using the students as subjects. The research project is a replication of a piece of research conducted by 3-4 person groups. The proposal is a proposed piece of research designed by each student at the end of the class. This design takes the goals of a methods class—teaching students to design, conduct, analyze and interpret, and write up research—and distributes the learning process over a sequence of class assignments. Data collected from students who participated in the class showed that the project and proposal were well received, but the in-class study appeared to serve simply as a way to first expose students to writing. The following design for an in-class study expands the role this assignment plays in fulfilling the goals of the class.

Design. First I show the film, "Interviewing" (Video Works, 1974), a film used by our Survey Research Center to train interviewers. It discusses issues such as tactful probing, leading questions, and dealing with deviations of interviewees from the task. Students are then given an interview instrument, and its design is described. Students learn about closed—and open-ended items, coding systems, dealing with missing data, filter questions, and instructions for the interviewer embedded within items. The class is then divided into 3-person groups with each person taking a turn at interviewing, being interviewed, and observing. The observer is instructed to give constructive feedback to the interviewer at the conclusion of the interview (see Exercise 24, *Interviewing Trios,* in Hall, Bowen, Lewicki, & Hall, 1975). The film is 1½ hours long, and the lecture and interviewing require a period of at least one hour.

After the data have been collected, they are analyzed and fed back to the students. The analyses are simple, usually just means, frequency distributions, and correlations, so that they are easily understood by the students. Each student is required to write a journal report describing the procedure and results of this study. Because the content of my instrument dealt with adult learning programs, students were told to make recommendations for our evening college program in their discussion section.

Students' Reactions. Students' reactions (n = 15) to the specific design were assessed through a questionnaire distributed the day that the written assignment was due. Since 7-point scales were used (7-*learned a lot*; 7-*liked it*), responses of five or greater were interpreted as indicating support for the item. A majority of students (84%) rated the film as a positive learning experience. Most students (64%) also found that exposure to an interviewing instrument was a good learning experience. In addition, the majority of students (53%) liked doing the interviewing. Students did not like the specific content of my interview schedule (adult learning), so that these ratings would probably be enhanced if instructors would devise more interesting instruments. An additional class period might be devoted to selecting a topic and having small groups of students devise items and coding schema.

In conclusion, interviewing and instrument design are important skills for the researcher in whatever area he or she may pursue. Teaching these skills should be an important part of a research methods class. The design presented here describes a way to have students learn these skills in a short time period and by actually experiencing them.

References

Hall, D. T., Bowen, D. D. Lewicki, R. J., & Hall, F. S. *Experiences in management and organizational behavior.* Chicago: St. Clair Press, 1975.

Video Works (Producer). *Interviewing.* Princeton, NJ: Urban Opinion Surveys, Division of Mathematica, 1974. (Film)

Yoder, J. D. Teaching students to do research. *Teaching* of *Psychology,* 1979, *6*, 85-88.

Note

The author would like to thank Jack Loftis for using her general design in his methods class and for letting her 'borrow'" his class to conduct this in-class study.

A Funding Simulation for Use in an Advanced Experimental Laboratory Class

Virginia P. Falkenberg
Eastern Kentucky University

Keep the number of student projects limited to your time available, but increase the reality of the experience. This paper tells you how.

For a number of years, it has been our practice to require each student enrolled in our Advanced Experimental Psychology laboratory course to propose, design, carry out, analyze and report on an original research problem. These independent research projects require a great deal of time from both the student and the professor supervising the laboratory class. However, the benefits to the students, both in the development of basic skills and in the development of a professional attitude, have made the time expenditure well worth while.

Last year the enrollment in the advanced lab exceeded our wildest dreams. With over fifteen students in one section, the amount of time needed to carefully supervise fifteen independent projects became a serious concern. Also, the probability of receiving fifteen proposals, all worthy of passing the departmental ethics committee seemed too low. Several options to the independent projects occurred to us from past experience. One way to handle more students in less time is for the instructor to plan a uniform series of experiments for the students to carry out, usually using the students themselves as subjects. Another option is the use of a packaged series of computer simulated experiments, such as the Wabash Research Investigation Simulation Teacher (WRIST) program. We have used both of these options before, and they failed to provide the quality of experience that is provided in the independent project.

At this point I decided to look more closely at the independent project in an effort to determine why it was deemed so valuable by us and the students. What emerged was the conclusion that a large part of the effectiveness of the independent project was provided by it's approximation of the real life experience of a scientist. It was at this time that I began to think of an even closer approximation to the current "science game." I decided to incorporate a governmental funding simulation into the individual project format.

Description of Funding Procedure. Each student enrolled in the course was required to develop an original research problem, design a research program and write a proposal. Every proposal was graded and contributed to the student's grade (50 of 300 points); however, it was up to the student to decide if he/she wished to carry out the proposed project. If the student chose to attempt the project she/he could submit it to the professor (the "funding agency") as a grant proposal. The author of a project that was approved for funding would become a project director, and be funded with grade points with which to "purchase" help from unfunded classmates in completing the project. The project director's grade came totally from the acceptable completion of the project. The grade of the remainder of the students came entirely from the points they could earn by working for a project director on one of the funded projects and from the required proposal (which all students wrote).

Nine students wished to carry out their projects, and therefore submitted their proposal for funding. The remaining students preferred for various reasons to work on someone else's project rather than direct their own. Three faculty members in the department evaluated the nine proposals submitted for funding. The evaluators took into account such things as the feasibility of the project (could it be completed in the allotted time), the value of the project to students and subjects, the quality of the proposal in terms of presentation, the ethics of the proposed study, and the experimental design and originality of the project. The instructor took the comments and ratings of the evaluators and selected the projects to be funded. Four proposals were finally approved for funding. The number of grade points distributed was arrived at by multiplying the number of points possible in this portion of lab (250 points) times the number of students who did not receive funding plus 250 points. This made more points available than students could receive credit for earning, and allowed working students some necessary flexibility in selecting jobs. The directors were required to submit a list of jobs and job descriptions for approval before jobs could be advertised. At this time, the instructor (as the funding agency) equalized payment scales for identical jobs. Directors then advertised positions available, accepted applications, and hired. Positions which could not be filled left extra jobs for the director. Upon satisfactory completion of jobs, project directors filed a request for payment and points were paid by the funding agency. Labor disputes were submitted to the instructor for arbitration, but management was the responsibility of the project director.

Discussion. To my pleasure, the types of jobs available to nonfunded students were primarily of a professional nature. The most common help requested by directors involved data collection, data analysis, professional writing of the final paper, additional research of the literature, and formal presentation of the final paper. At the same time that I (as the funding agency) equalized payment scales for identical jobs, I also placed some restrictions on the assignment of jobs, and adjusted the job descriptions when necessary. For example, no one was allowed to receive points for writing the results section unless they had also been primarily responsible for data reduction and statistical analysis. For the one paper which needed it, rewriting the introductory section of the proposal for the final paper was tied to additional review of the literature. Three out of four project directors wished to have someone else present the final paper to the class. I viewed this as a marginal activity for funding, therefore it was assigned a very low payment level. In addition, those presenting were not al lowed to read the paper, therefore they had to be familiar enough with the study to review the literature, understand the results, and handle questions. It was suggested that they observe data collection as well as study the paper. Because of the low level of payment for presentation, no students could earn all their points by presenting papers. In fact, in every case presenters had been actively involved in some other phase of the research they were presenting.

Most of the students had to select a variety of jobs to earn their maximum possible 250 points. This provided a variety of learning experience for the students who did not direct funded projects. Only one student earned all 250 points by doing data collection, and this was for a project for which the data collection was a very complicated, time consuming and sensitive job. To be sure, the directors had the greatest sense of accomplishment when the course was over, but unfunded students also reported a high degree of satisfaction with this procedure. As a teacher, I found the funding simulation to provide significantly better educational benefits for students than other alternatives to individual research projects.

In the Fall semester of the following year, two of the student projects completed under the funding procedure were presented to the Kentucky Academy of Science at its 66th annual meeting. One of these papers won the third place Griffith Award for creative psychological research (see Baker, 1970).

Reference

Baker, R. A. Contributions to the history of psychology: XIII. Richard Marion Griffith: 1921-1969. *Psychological Reports,* 1970, 27, 317-318.

Use of the Jigsaw Technique in Laboratory and Discussion Classes

David W. Carroll
University of Wisconsin—Superior

A method for improving student performance in laboratory courses is described. Students work in small, interdependent groups in which each person contributes a unique piece of a research project. The technique is designed to encourage student cooperation during the research enterprise. Results indicate that students evaluate the approach favorably and that their academic performance improves. Some applications and potential problems of the technique are discussed.

Although undergraduate courses in research design are invaluable for giving students a perspective on how research is done, many students find such classes difficult. Many are more interested in the nonresearch aspects of psychology, and even those who see its importance are sometimes afraid of a class that requires them to develop, perform, and report an original study.

For 8 years I have taught a one-credit, upper-division, laboratory course in the psychology of learning and memory. Each student is required to carry out a sample experiment provided by the instructor and then develop, perform, and report an original experiment. During the first 4 years of teaching this course, I noticed several distressing trends, including:

1. Approximately one third of the students failed to complete the course in a single quarter.

2. Those who did complete the work on time often chose simple topics and finished them in a perfunctory fashion.

3. Nearly all of the students regarded the course as more than one credit of work.

4. Student evaluations were generally poor.

In the last 4 years, I have been using an adaptation of the "jigsaw classroom" (Aronson & Bridgeman, 1981) as a means of teaching this course. This technique is designed to encourage cooperation by making individuals dependent on each other in pursuit of a common goal. Each person is assigned or chooses one piece of a larger task, and group members depend on each individual to complete the assigned function. Aronson and Bridgeman found that positive changes occurred in group members' attitudes toward one another. My more immediate concern was with the potential of this structure to enable students to tackle more substantial challenges and complete them in a single term.

Method

The jigsaw technique is first introduced in the sample experiment, in which the class replicates a published study. The assumption is that the group process can be learned in the sample experiment and

191

then applied to the subsequent original experiment. In the sample experiment, students are assigned to one of four tasks (construction of study materials, construction of test materials, randomization of study and test lists, and writing instructions). They spend 3 weeks developing the materials, performing the study, and then discussing it.

Each student is then required to develop a proposal for an independent experiment. The goal of the proposal assignment is to get students to think through an idea to the point of presenting it to the entire group. After the students present their ideas, they are given the options of (a) choosing one idea for a group project, (b) combining or consolidating ideas into a group project, or (c) doing an individual project. Ideas are presented one week, with decisions due the next week.

Students who select a group project sign a contract that specifies the members of the group (maximum: four), the tasks each person will perform (for example, pilot study, instructions, running subjects, statistical analysis), and the division of Labor in the writing of the final report (introduction, method, and so on). Those who do a group project are given the further option of writing a group report or writing separate reports. If a group report is chosen, all group members receive the same grade on the report (which is the major but not the total basis for the course grade). Decisions regarding the various aspects of the contract are placed at different parts of the term: Students must form groups by the 5th week, but have until the 6th week to divide the tasks, and until the 9th week to decide on writing assignments. This schedule gives them time to learn more about the work habits of group members and make more informed decisions about how much to entrust their course grade to another person.

Results

There are three sources of evidence of the effectiveness of the jigsaw approach: student evaluations of the class, the percentage of students who complete the course in a single term, and subjective impressions of the choices students make for projects.

Student evaluations are available for the last 3 of the 4 years the jigsaw approach has been in effect, and they indicate a positive student response. Student evaluation was assessed by a 13-item form. Each item was rated on a 5-point scale ranging from a highly negative response (I) to a highly favorable response (5). The means of the individual item means were 4.19, 4.04, and 4.41, respectively, for the last 3 years. Individual items included the knowledge gained from the course (4.12), the fairness of the grading system (4.19), and the degree of intellectual motivation in the class (4.63). On the negative side, comments on the evaluation form revealed that students still regarded the course as more than one credit of work.

The question of whether students were better able to complete coursework in a single term was examined by comparing course records for the 4 years before and the 4 years after the introduction of the jigsaw approach. Of the 55 students who took the course prior to the jigsaw approach, 35 (64%) completed the course, 16 (29%) took incompletes, and 4 (7%) dropped the course or received an F; comparable numbers over the last 4 years were 40 out of 46 (87%), 1 (2%), and 5 (11%).

Whether or not students tackle more challenging assignments is difficult to say, but there are some indications that this is the case. There is much evidence of serial revision throughout the term whereas students in the earlier years, partly due to time pressure, tended to pursue the first idea that came to them. There has been an increase in studies of children as opposed to college students, despite the additional difficulties in securing child participation. Moreover, there has been an increase in students' commitment to their research. For example, one group chose to do a study on mice even though our school has no animal laboratory. The students bought the animals, secured a room, and continued their work the next term as an independent study project. Further evidence of such commitment has been the increased participation in student research conferences.

Discussion

Some of the most significant advantages of this technique relate to the attitudes of students. They seemed to be convinced of the usefulness of the approach. In addition to learning about research design, they learned some valuable lessons in how to organize a complex task and how to structure an interpersonally ambiguous situation. They also seemed to be having more fun.

Some care, however, must be taken in how the technique is presented and used. There is some potential for resentment toward individuals perceived as not doing their share of the work. The structure of the course (allowing students to choose the jigsaw approach, and giving them time to make important decisions) helps to alleviate some of these concerns, but it does not eliminate them. Ultimately, students must decide how much they trust one another. One year, two different groups had to decide on writing assignments at a time when one member of each group was absent without explanation. I encouraged each group to wait as long as possible to allow the student to rejoin the group, but told them it was ultimately their decision. Both waited and, in one case, the missing group member returned after a brief absence to help finish the project successfully. In the other case, the student remained missing for too long, and the other three members reluctantly decided to write the report on their own, forcing the fourth student to do a great deal of work near the end of the term.

The jigsaw technique thus forces students to do some hard thinking about their judgments of their peers and to take responsibility for their decisions .

Though I have used this technique in only this one course, it might work very well in discussion and seminar classes. It is an excellent motivational device and has the pedagogical value of calling on the distinctive backgrounds, experiences, and abilities of different students. To sum up, the technique enables students to learn course material efficiently, while dealing with social situations that contribute to their overall education.

Reference

Aronson, E., & Bridgeman, D. (1981). Jigsaw groups and the desegregated classroom: In pursuit of common goals. In E. M. Hetherington & R. D. Parke (Eds.), *Contemporary readings in child psychology* (2nd ed., pp. 339-345). New York: McGraw Hill.

Teaching the Importance of Accuracy in Preparing References

Blaine F. Peden
University of Wisconsin-Eau Claire

This article outlines and evaluates a technique for teaching students to recognize and prepare references for four types of works commonly used in research reports. Subsequent performance on the reference section of their research reports earns either an A or F grade (after Cronan-Hillix, 1988). This technique helps students learn to prepare accurate reference lists and appears to sensitize them to other aspects of APA style.

My experience teaching research methods and reviewing manuscripts for *Teaching of Psychology* indicates that correctly citing and referencing works in APA style is a difficult task for inexperienced and veteran authors. Nonetheless, instructors should teach and students should learn precision in preparing reference lists. One reason is that "accurately prepared references help establish your credibility as a careful researcher" (American Psychological Association, 1983, p. 112). Another reason is that inaccurate citations and references produce and perpetuate mistakes and misconceptions (e.g., Griggs, 1988; Soper & Rosenthal, 1988).

This article summarizes and assesses a method for teaching students to identify and list four types of references frequently cited in research reports. Later in the term, students receive a grade of A or F on the reference section of their own research reports (after Cronan-Hillix, 1988). The method improves accuracy in preparing reference lists and seems to increase students' attention to other facets of APA style.

Method

Subjects

Subjects were 63 women and 27 men enrolled in an undergraduate research methods course in the 1989-90 fall or spring semesters.

Materials

A handout summarized the first page of the table from the *Publication Manual of the American Psychological Association* (APA, 1983, p. 118) listing types of work referenced and presented three examples of references for each of four works typically used by students in research reports: journal articles, magazine articles, books, and chapters in an edited book. Other pages in the handout illustrated citations and quotations.

Students' knowledge about references was measured two ways. Three recognition tests each presented five correct references (the four types just mentioned and another type of work, e.g., an unpublished paper or a conference presentation) that students matched with the correct label (e.g., journal article, magazine article . . . none of these). Three production tests each provided information about a journal article, a magazine article, a book, and a chapter in an edited book that students used to prepare a reference list in APA style.

Instruction was the same in both semesters. Early in the term, I distributed and discussed the handout. I stressed the importance of correctly citing and referencing works, illustrated the types of works used in research reports, discussed examples of references for the four common sources, demonstrated citations in text, and announced that students would take a multiple-choice recognition test on 3 successive days. At the beginning of the next three classes, students completed a recognition test, exchanged tests for scoring on the basis of 1 point for each correct answer, and then submitted them to me for verification and recording of the grades. On the day of the third recognition test, I dispensed the first production test. Students completed it outside of class, exchanged papers in the next class for grading on the basis of 1 point for each correct reference and one fifth of a point for listing references in the proper order, submitted the papers for verification and recording, and then received another production test. After collecting the third production test, I handed out copies of Cronan-Hillix's (1988) article. In the next period, we briefly discussed the article and the policy of A or F grading for the reference section of their research reports. After further discussion during the next class, students completed one or two posttest questionnaires.

The evaluation was somewhat different in the two semesters. Although students in both terms completed the same 10-item posttest questionnaire and a two-part follow-up question, students in the spring class also completed a 10-item reference recognition pretest and a 12-item pre- and posttest questionnaire. They completed the recognition pretest and the 12-item pretest questionnaire during the first week of class. Students answered the posttest questionnaires and follow-up question in successive periods after finishing the instructional sequence and before the due date for the first research report.

Results

Recognition Test

Forty-four students in the spring semester completed the 10-item reference recognition pretest. The mean percentage of accurately identified references was 93.2% for magazines, 84.1% for books, 72.7% for chapters in an edited book, and 53.4% for journal articles; overall, the mean score was 75.7% correct. The mean scores on the recognition tests were comparable in the two semesters and justified computing an overall mean score. In order, the grand means on the three recognition tests were 90.4%, 98.6%, and 99.4% correct. Thus, the handout and instruction appeared to improve students' ability to recognize types of references above their baseline level.

Production Test

The mean scores on the three production tests were comparable in the two semesters and also justified computing an overall mean score. In order, the grand means were 33.6%, 65.4%, and 78.9% correct. Errors on the final production test were not distributed equally across the five types of answers. The grand mean percentage of errors on the final test was 44.3% for chapters in an edited book, 34.1% for magazine articles, 12.5% for books, 8.0% for journal articles, and 1.1% for listing references in the correct order. Thus, this technique seemed to help students prepare accurate reference lists, although students' production skills lagged behind their recognition skills.

Student Evaluation

Eighty-six of the 90 students completed the 10-item posttest questionnaire. The virtually identical mean scores in the two terms on a scale ranging from *strong disagreement* (1) to *strong agreement* (5) justified reporting an overall mean score. Students agreed that they learned how to recognize different kinds of references ($M = 4.48$, $SD = .41$) and how to prepare the reference section of a research report ($M = 4.55$, $SD = .55$). Students agreed that the number of tests was appropriate ($M = 3.67$, $SD = .69$), the purpose of the activity became increasingly clear ($M = 4.10$, $SD = .28$), and grading of the recognition and production tests was fair ($M = 3.86$, $SD = .63$). Students endorsed Cronan-Hillix's (1988) contention about their need to learn the importance of accuracy in research ($M = 4.21$, $SD = .58$), agreed that it was equally important for them to learn accuracy in referencing ($M = 4.26$, $SD = .54$), and recommended use of this technique in the future ($M = 4.33$, $SD = .75$). Students agreed that feedback was adequate ($M = 3.72$, $SD = 1.25$), but suggested that making and keeping a copy of the production tests might help them understand and correct their mistakes, especially in the absence of the originals submitted for grading. Opinion was divided on whether it was fair to apply an A or F grading system to the reference section of their research reports ($M = 3.33$, $SD = 1.29$).

The lack of consensus prompted me to assess student opinion on the grading issue in two additional ways. First, 81 of 90 students in the two semesters answered a two-part follow-up question by indicating whether or not and why the system was fair. Sixty-two percent asserted that this procedure was fair and typically explained that they had learned and mastered the skill of preparing accurate reference lists and that errors resulted from carelessness (see Cronan-Hillix, 1988). The remaining 38% argued that the procedure was unfair and typically said that the absolute scale produced distress and ignored effort (see McDonald &

Peterson, this issue). The sentiment of these students was that "trying hard" should result in intermediate rather than failing grades. Second, 37 students in the spring completed a 12-item pre- and posttest questionnaire that included a question comparable to one on the 10-item posttest questionnaire. On the most pertinent item (space limitations preclude a report of all the data), students significantly changed their opinion away from *disagreement* (2) on the pretest (M = 2.21) toward *neutrality* (3) on the posttest (M = 2.89) for a question concerning the fairness of the A or F grading system, $t(37)$ = 3.25, p = .003. Thus, the two additional measures of student opinion indicate movement toward greater acceptance of an A or F grading system, but students do not unanimously endorse it.

Compared with the first papers in previous semesters, the first research reports seemed to contain fewer citation and reference errors and to conform better to other aspects of APA style.

Discussion

This instructional technique illustrates sound educational principles. The procedure provides repeated practice with feedback to shape accurately prepared reference lists. Moreover, the sequence of events is consistent with the principle that distributed practice is more effective than massed practice .

This technique reveals unexpected problems for students. For example, students learn that journals and magazines require different formats in the reference list, but find it difficult to distinguish between the two. This problem arises and persists because there are no clear criteria that distinguish these two types of periodicals.

This technique benefits students. First, they learn to recognize the format for different kinds of references, an important but often forgotten prerequisite to locating resources by "treeing" backward through the literature. Second, they learn to prepare a reference section for a research report and appear to be more sensitive to other aspects of APA style. Finally, they better appreciate the professional attitude that accuracy is important in conducting and reporting research. These benefits prompt students to endorse this teaching and learning technique; however, they do not unanimously support an A or F grading system.

This technique also benefits instructors. First, an instructor can perform each step in the learning sequence in only a few minutes of class time. Second, an instructor can use the technique to teach other subtleties about preparing a reference list. Third, although instructors spend time producing and administering tests, they can save time during the grading process because students produce stylistically more accurate reports that are more easily and quickly graded. This benefit multiplies during courses that require several research reports.

Coda

Developing and using this technique enhanced my own referencing skills because I had to verify many details about which I thought I was certain, only to learn that I labored under misconceptions. Developing and using this technique promoted my mastery of APA style because students asked more frequent and more challenging questions about APA style than ever before. In my opinion, developing and using this technique increased my awareness and understanding of other aspects of writing beyond referencing (e.g., Gray, 1988; Woodford, 1967), abilities that serve all of us well in our roles as authors, reviewers, and teachers.

References

American Psychological Association. (1983) *Publication manual of the American Psychological Association* (3rd ed.). Washington, DC: Author.

Cronan-Hillix, T. (1988). Teaching students the importance of accuracy in research. *Teaching of Psychology, 15,* 205-207.

Gray, D. J. (1988). Writing across the college curriculum. *Phi Delta Kappan, 69*, 729-733.

Griggs, R. A. (1988). Who is Mrs. Cantlie and why are they doing those terrible things to her homunculi? *Teaching of Psychology, 15,* 105-106.

McDonald, C. S., & Peterson, K. A. (this issue). Teaching commitment to accuracy in research: Comment on Cronan-Hillix (1988). *Teaching of Psychology, 18*, 100-101.

Soper, B., & Rosenthal, G. (1988). The number of neurons in the brain: How we report what we do not know. *Teaching of Psychology, 15*, 153-156.

Woodford, F. P. (1967). Sounder thinking through clever writing. *Science, 156*, 743-745.

Notes

1. I thank Allen Keniston, Ken McIntire, Mary Meisser, Karen Welch, and three anonymous reviewers for helpful comments on this article.
2. This article exemplifies the teaching of Mitri Shanab and Eliot Hearst. By word and deed, they taught students to strive for perfection in writing research reports, an attitude I tried to foster in my students.
3. A preliminary report of these results was presented at the Mid-America Conference for Teachers of psychology, Evansville, IN, October 1989.

A Radical Poster Session

Paul A. Gore, Jr.
Cameron J. Camp
University of New Orleans

In the field of psychology, poster sessions have a history of being an easy and efficient way to present data. Recently, the poster session has been introduced in the classroom. For the last 2 years, we have used a poster session as an integral part of an undergraduate experimental design course. Principles of experimental design are demonstrated when undergraduates design and conduct original experiments using radishes as subjects. Results of these experiments are then presented in a poster session. The benefits of using radishes as subjects are described.

Poster sessions have been described as teaching aids for advanced undergraduate seminars (Chute & Bank, 1983) and graduate student/faculty colloquia (Ventis, 1986). Since the spring of 1985, we have used a poster session as an integral part of a sophomore-level course in experimental design; it accounts for 20% of the course grade.

In this course, each student must design and conduct an original experiment and report the results in a poster session entitled "Spring/Fall Radish Festival." The title of the festival is derived from the fact that the subjects in these experiments are radishes. Aside from the long and noble history of radishes in experimental psychology (Lenington, 1979), these plant subjects have much to offer for our purposes. Radishes have a 30- to 40-day growth cycle; hence, in the course of a quarter or semester, almost any experimental design known to psychology (including sequential analyses from developmental psychology) can be executed. Radishes also do best with a spring or fall planting, grow quickly (in case disaster strikes and a fast replication is needed), and their seeds are bought rather than recruited. It is neither surprising nor fortuitous that the statistics of Student and Fisher have their roots in agricultural research.

Most important, the exercise provides students with hands-on experience in applying the principles of experimental design. Because they are working with a different species (indeed, phylum), the students often must be flexible and creative in using operational definitions. For example, two experiments were conducted to test the popularly-held idea that talking to plants influences their growth. One student studied the effects of playing motivational tapes on radish height. As a control measure, she played a tape of mumbling to her comparison group. One student studied the effects of speaking Spanish to her plants, with English being spoken to her control group. Students doing such exercises quickly learn why saline injections or placebos are used as control procedures in more traditional experimental settings.

All posters are required to have an abstract of no more than 300 words, and a listing of hypotheses and operational definitions. In addition, the independent and dependent variables must be clearly listed and defined. Threats to both internal and external validity must be listed, and an explanation of control procedures must be presented. The Results section must include the statistical tests used, as well as tables and charts when appropriate. In drawing conclusions, the students are urged to pay close attention to the question presented in the hypothesis, and the answer as given by the statistical analysis. Finally, a statement about what level of construct was contained in the study must be included (theoretical constructs must be free of mono-method and mono-operational bias, Cook & Campbell, 1979).

The poster session is held in a festival atmosphere, with 1st, 2nd, and 3rd prizes awarded. Students are, however, expected to answer questions presented to them on design decisions, statistics, or other information pertinent to the course. Previous prize winners include studies that examined the effects of the following variables on the growth of radishes: radiation, diazepam with shock, motivational tapes, carbon dioxide enriched atmosphere, and river water versus bottled water. The "Angel of Death" prize for the student suffering the highest level of experimental mortality and the "Square Radish" prize for the most bizarre independent variable are also rewarded.

Students also learn the relationships among statistics, experimental design, and subjects' behavior. Students are required to bring their radishes to the poster session so that the effects of their independent variables can literally be observed. One student reported a highly significant F statistic as a result of comparing the height of two groups when visually the groups were indistinguishable. When forced by the instructor to recalculate the between-groups sum of squares on the spot, the student realized the error of his ways (statistically speaking), and also learned a lesson in the relationship between statistical tests and common sense. The presence of the subjects in this case provided a valuable, concrete lesson in what within-groups and between-groups variance looks like.

Students also are required to bring printouts of data analyses using the SPSSX MANOVA program. Because many students use more than one dependent measure, they stumble on multivariate statistics included on their printouts, and curiosity leads them to learn more about multivariate analyses. We have found this approach to be a valuable introduction for students. In addition, students learn that interventions can have multiple effects, some positive and some negative. For example, a student who watered plants with milk found that the experimental plants had less root growth but larger leaf size in comparison to a control group of water-watered plants.

Finally, our students develop a sense of pride in their craft from this exercise. This festival is open to the entire college community, is featured in the campus newspaper, and is a topic of conversation for weeks afterward. Previous festival participants return each year to observe the growth of "radish psychology." Demonstrating their expertise in experimental design solidifies the lessons of the course in ways that are highly enjoyable for our students.

References

Chute, D. L., & Bank, B. (1983). Undergraduate seminars: The poster session solution. *Teaching of Psychology, 10,* 99-100.

Cook, T. D., & Campbell, D. T. (1979). *Quasi-experimentation.* Chicago: Rand McNally.

Lenington, S. (1979). Effects of holy water on the growth of radish plants. *Psychological Reports, 45,* 381-382.

Ventis, D. G. (1986). Recycling poster sessions for colloquium series. *Teaching of Psychology, 13,* 222.

Research Methods Jeopardy: A Tool for Involving Students and Organizing the Study Session

Bryan Gibson
University of Utah

A game based on the popular TV show Jeopardy is described. The game involves students in study sessions and helps them organize the course material. Students say that the format is educational and entertaining.

The research methods course is viewed by most psychology instructors as an important core course because it introduces students to the scientific method and how it is used to advance psychological knowledge. However, many students consider course completion a mere formality that is necessary for enrollment in more "interesting" courses. Thus, it is sometimes more difficult to involve students in this course as compared with upper level content courses in psychology.

One area in which students' involvement may be lacking is in the typical pretest study session. In many cases, these sessions consist of simple question-and-answer periods that are of little benefit to a majority of students. However, Aamodt (1982a, 1982b) demonstrated that study sessions do help students perform better on exams, particularly when the study session organizes the material, rather than simply giving students an opportunity to ask questions.

In an attempt to get students involved in and excited about a pretest study session and to provide a format for organizing the class material, I devised a game based on the TV game show Jeopardy. Students were assigned to one of three teams a week before the game and were told that members of the winning team would be awarded an extra point on the exam. To prepare for the game, I identified six categories that ranged from general topics, such as "the scientific method," to specific topics, such as "reliability," and devised five questions for each of the six categories. The easiest question in each category was assigned a value of 100 points, with each subsequent question increasing by 100 points.

To begin play, the teams are randomly ordered, and a member of the first team chooses a category and point value. The instructor reads the selected statement, and the student must respond with the correct question (in true Jeopardy format). For example, an item in the "ethics" category might be: "The right to be informed of all information that might influence a decision to participate in a research project." The correct response to this statement would be "What is informed consent?" If a correct response is given, the next player on that team selects a category and point value. When a student responds incorrectly, the second team has an opportunity to "steal" the points by providing the correct response. When attempting to steal, team members are allowed to discuss potential responses. If members of that team successfully steal the question, they are allowed to choose a category and point value. If they are unsuccessful, the third team may attempt to steal. If the third team is unable to answer correctly, Team 2 will then choose the next category and point value. If no one is able to provide the correct response, the instructor explains the answer and tries to stimulate discussion about the item.

A "daily double" is hidden among the items on the Jeopardy board. The student who chooses this item decides (with input from teammates) how many team points to wager. This item is presented to the student privately. If the student responds incorrectly, the wagered points are removed from that team's score, and the next team can choose an amount to wager without knowing what the item is.

After the last item on the Jeopardy board is completed, a topic for the final Jeopardy question is revealed. Team members decide how many points to wager, the final Jeopardy item is presented, and each team discusses potential responses and writes its response on a sheet of paper. Each team reveals its answer, and points are added or subtracted to determine the winning team.

My goal was to create an entertaining and competitive procedure that would actively involve all students and highlight the current course material. Anecdotal reports from students indicate that these goals were achieved. Several students reported that the advanced notice made them study harder than they normally would have. In addition, students displayed much team spirit through hearty congratulations for a correct response and words of encouragement for an incorrect response. Finally, when asked whether a second Jeopardy game should be planned before the next test, students were enthusiastic in their support.

The game also seemed to provide an organization of the material for students. By selecting six major topics, the instructor provided an overarching framework to help students organize their study. Students who were unable to answer questions in a given category could then focus their study on that topic. Although the nature of the game does not provide a review of the more complex theoretical concepts covered, these issues can be dealt with through writing and research critiquing assignments presented at other points in the course. In summary, research methods Jeopardy stimulated enthusiasm in the topic and helped students identify where to focus their study for the exam.

References

Aamodt, M. G. (1982a). A closer look at the study session. *Teaching of Psychology, 9,* 234-235.

Aamodt, M. G. (1982b). The effect of the study session on test performance. *Teaching of Psychology, 9,* 118-120.

5 . USING COMPUTERS

Introduction to Computer Data Generators

Robert J. Gregory
University of Idaho

Being an outline of the nature of computer programs which facilitate the teaching of research design and data analysis.

Computer data generators are computer programs which facilitate the teaching of research design and data analysis by simulating the results of research. In a course where computer data generators are used, the student designs hypothetical experiments in a specific topic area and submits the designs as input to the computer program or data generator. The computer program, which is based on a model of how a particular phenomenon works, gives as output hypothetical but realistic data, "as if" the actual experiments had been conducted in the real world. In psychology, the use of computer data generators has been prompted by the observation that whereas nearly all undergraduates can learn to train rats, tabulate responses, make up lists of nonsense syllables, get equipment to work properly, and the like, proportionately fewer of them learnt he basic principles of research design and data analysis. One reason for this state of affairs is that often the student needs a great amount of time to set up and conduct an experiment, with the consequence that proportionately little time can be devoted to questions of research design and data analysis.

An appropriate computer program which simulates the outcome of research allows the student to rehearse the important design and decision making roles of the researcher while simultaneously forgoing the very time consuming data collection step. Another advantage of computer models is that the range of research topics is greatly extended. Interesting research which would take too long, cost too much, involve great risk to subjects, or require unusual expertise, can be simulated with a computer program. In fact, almost any topical area in psychology is amenable to computer modeling, although great effort and ingenuity are required to obtain a *realistic* simulation.

An example of a computer data generator will help illustrate the central characteristics, from the user's standpoint, of this education innovation. Shown in Figure 1 is a session with an interactive program accessed from a terminal. Some computer data generators use the traditional card deck for input. It is important to note that the computer data generator is only part of the overall simulation and that simply turning the student loose with access to the computer program would be a serious mistake. The overall sequence of activities in a scientific community must be simulated as well. A typical process (after Main, 1975) is summarized below:

1. Orientation to the research program

   a) activities the student or research team will engage in
   b) minimum familiarity with the computer aspects of the simulation
   c) discussion of theoretical issues in the particular area of research
   d) explanation of costs, budget, and time limits
2. First proposal. Usually reviewed by the instructor.
3. Data received, analyzed, and reported. This can be routed directly to the instructor, or made available to the entire class for discussion.
4. Second proposal, based upon results of first proposal. Data received, analyzed, and reported.
5. Third proposal. Data received, analyzed, and reported. The above activities should carry most students well into the intricacies of research design and data analysis. Experience indicates that beyond the third proposal, the student becomes overloaded with data and cannot make constructive use of further experimental results in a given area.

The above process could be considered the *beginning* mode of research simulation and represents only the most rudimentary application of computer data generators to the psychology research course. More advanced use of computer data generators is possible, although certain differences in the pedagogical scheme need to be implemented. Main, Stout and Rajecki (Note 1) describe some of the additional possibilities which they call modes of instruction. Mode 1 is what is described above as the beginning mode. In mode 2 the student is informed of only a subset of the manipulable variables and must infer the existence of one or more X-variables, that is, unknown variables, which may be contributing to the results. Once he has inferred these, they can be manipulated or held constant in future simulations. In mode 3 the student develops his own data-generating model and compares its results to other models in the same area. The final mode is one in which the student compares his simulated data to that which has been collected in real laboratory experiments.

There are two classes of computer data generators: large, flexible, sophisticated programs, and small, structured, special purpose programs. Both types of simulation have their place, and the advantages of each must be traded off against unavoidable shortcomings. In general, the large programs are more elegant, realistic, and generalizable, but they are difficult to implement at new sites because of their size and complexity. Even small incompatibilities between computer systems can result in a fatal "crash." The services of an expert programmer who is also familiar with the specific data-generating program are then mandatory if it is to be made operational. In the case of the larger programs, this is no laughing matter. The Michigan Experimental Simulation Supervisor (MESS), described below, is a computer program whose listing runs to well over 100 *pages* of standard computer paper. The intimidating size of the general purpose programs is a serious problem for those attempting to adopt them at a new site.

The smaller special purpose programs do not have this fragility. On the other hand, they are often less realistic/ and their narrow scope can lead to student boredom quite quickly. Probably the best option available to instructors of undergraduate research courses is to use a battery of small to medium size specialized computer data generators until such time as a large and flexible program set can be developed or imported and made operational.

Large Computer Data Generators. The Michigan Experimental Simulation Supervisor, called MESS by the graduate student who programmed it (Stout, 1974) and EXPER SIM by the faculty member who has advertised it (Main, 1975), is a program whose basic purpose is to facilitate the construction and study of models in the behavioral and social sciences. One or another of its versions is currently in use in several dozen universities and colleges.

The genius of MESS is that it is actually a combination of a supervisory program, which remains essentially static, and various FORTRAN subroutines which can be added to the library, changed, or deleted at any time. A professor or advanced student can write his own model in whatever area he chooses, and need not concern himself with the problem of interfacing the

```
ENTER NO. OF EXPERIMENTAL CONDITIONS
2
DEFINE EXPERIMENTAL CONDITION(S)
TARG=CYL ARO=3,5 WALK=mat @ END
    2 CONDITION(S) DEFINED
THE FOLLOWING VARIABLE SETTINGS ARE CONSTANT ACROSS
ALL CONDITIONS:
    REARING=SOCIAL      INDUCT=MECH      WALK=MATCHED
    AGE=RANDOM
    TEST=1.000
VARIABLE SETTINGS FOR CONDITION A
    TARGET=CYLINDER
    AROUSAL=3.000

    VARIABLE SETTINGS FOR CONDITION B
    TARGET=CYLINDER
    AROUSAL=5.000
ENTER NO. OF SUBJECTS IN EACH GROUP
15
A. EINSTEIN SECT. 029 TARG/ARO EXPT
16:59.08 APR 23, 1973
GROUP NUMBER 1
CONDITION(S): A
NUMBER OF SUBJECTS:  15

    TEST1 SCORES
        2.00        2.80        0.600       1.30        1.30
        0.500       0.700       3.70        1.70        2.50
        1.10        0.900       1.40        6.40        5.20
    NO. OF SS WITH COMPLETE DATA:  15

VARIABLE: TEST1
MEAN: 2.140
VARIANCE: 3.031
STD. DEVIATION: 1.741

A. EINSTEIN SECT. 029 TARG-ARO EXPT
16:59.09 APR 23, 1973
GROUP NUMBER   2
CONDITION(S):  B
NUMBER OF SUBJECTS:  15

    TEST1 SCORES
        4.30        1.50        3.30        1.50        3.10
        0.700       1.90        4.00        4.00        0.200
        5.10        0.0         0.600       1.50        2.60
    NO. OF SS WITH COMPLETE DATA:  15

VARIABLE: TEST1
MEAN:  2.287
VARIANCE: 2.613
STD. DEVIATION:  1.616

EXPERIMENT COMPLETED.
```

Figure 1. **Example of an interactive computer data generator. This is excerpted from the Michigan Experimental Simulation Supervisor, discussed in the article. Illustrated here is a two group experiment on imprinting, where the test scores represent amount of time a duckling spends on target as a function of arousal level. The italicized entries are those provided by the student (after Main, 1975).**

student with the data-generating model. He simply adds the model as a FORTRAN subroutine. Of course, the model most be specific, logically consistent, and specify lawful outcomes for all possible treatment conditions. Beyond this, the supervisory program handles the introduction of input, the definition of experimental situations, and the delivery of experimental results.

The modeling of experimental results can be carried out in a large and continually growing variety of areas which include such topics as motivation, imprinting, schizophrenia, and drug effects. The example shown in Figure 1 is from the MESS simulation of imprinting.

The LABSIM simulation program (Kissler, 1974) was developed at Washington State University in 1971. The model itself is a general purpose multiple regression equation of the form:

$$DV = B_1 \times IV_1 + B_2 \times IV_n + B_{n+1} \times IV_1 \times IV_2... + E$$

where DV is the dependent variable, the IV's are the potential independent variables, the B's are positive or negative weights reflecting the relative importance of each term, and E is an error term produced by a random number generator which guarantees probabilistic outcomes even for the same input.

The general purpose multiple regression equation remains the same, so that new models for simulating different experiments can be developed by merely changing the in put data cards. In this respect, LABSIM resembles MESS: the central supervisory part of the program remains static while peripheral aspects can be added or changed. LABSIM has the additional advantage that model builders need to know little or nothing about computer programming in order to add a new model to the program set. In effect, the model builder needs to supply only two things: for the students, a written introduction or "scenario" for research in the area of the model; and for the computer, actual values for *main* effects and *interaction* effects in the simulated experiments.

The essential aspects of the LABSIM approach to computer generation of data can be illustrated with an hypothetical example. Imagine that an instructor wishes to devise a model for the effects of a drug on operant response rate in the white rat. The dependent variable could be bar presses per minute; potential independent variables would be numerous, but would certainly include dosage level of the drug. If the instructor is well versed in this research area, a specific drug might be chosen, although this is not crucial. Next, additional independent variables would have to be added, and it is here that some expert judgments would need to be made. What is an important independent variable? The expertise of the model builder would be trusted to make this decision. To simplify the example, let us assume that dosage level of the drug (drg), age of the rat (age), and *hours* since last feeding (hrs) are chosen.

The response rate of a particular rat could then be conceptualized in the following manner:

$$Rate = B_1 \times drg + B_2 \times age + B_3 \times hrs + B_4 \times age + B_5 \times drg \times hrs + B_6 \times age \times hrs + B_7 \times drg \times age \times hrs + E$$

In order to make the size of the several B's reflect the relative importance of each term, response rate, dosage level, age, and hours would be normalized, that is, rescaled so their average value would be an arbitrary 0.00 and standard deviation 1.00. The value of the B's, which the model builder would supply, would then reflect the relative importance of each factor in determining response rate. B_1 B_2 and B_3 would be main effect weights, B_4 B_5 and B_6 would be weights for two-way interactions, and B_7 would be the weight for a three-way interaction. In designing an experiment, the student would supply the values for dosage, age, and hours while the computer model would supply the values for the remaining B's and a new E or error term to give each subject a unique outcome; that is, response rate.

The KUSIM simulation used at the University of Kansas (Hallenbeck & Welch, 1974) is the epitome of the large scale computer data generator, replete with both the advantages and the potential pitfalls of such large program sets. It is an extremely versatile system which generates data for several existing problem areas, as well as allowing an instructor unskilled in computer programming to devise his own simulations.

One of the more attractive features of KUSIM is the ease with which an instructor can define a new experimental paradigm for use by students. For example, a simple two factor problem which allows students to investigate test-taking anxiety as a function of age and sex is entered into KUSIM by the following instructions:

```
DEFINITION TEST-TAKING
   PROFESSOR A. L. JONES
FACTOR A  AGE 3  YOUNG MIDDLE-AGED ELDERLY
FACTOR B  SEX 2 MALE FEMALE
EFFECT AB 20,20,25,25,30,20
FINISH
```

The line which begins "EFFECT..." contains the information from which effects in the experimental situation are reconstructed. The numbers represent the mean value of the DV for the complete Cartesian product of factor levels and are stored as a simple FORTRAN array in a large "file," that is, separately demarcated repository of data. The computer programming which makes it possible to define complex experimental paradigms with as little as six lines of input is probably intricate and lengthy. It is likely that KUSIM suffers from the shortcoming so common to the large computer data generators, namely, it will not be implemented easily at new sites.

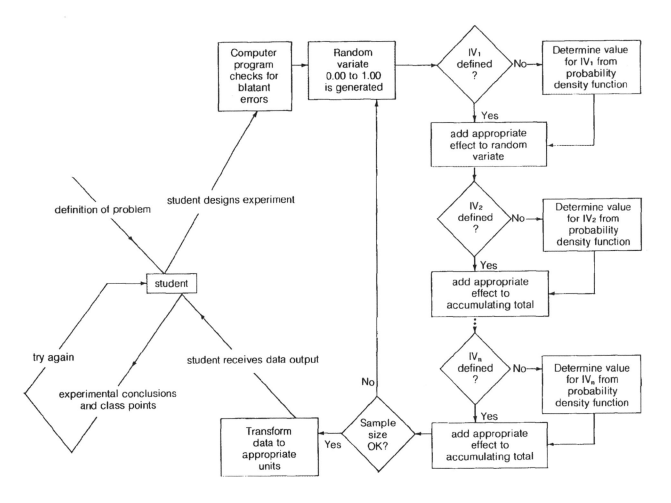

Figure 2. Flow diagram from a DATACALL game. Adopted from Johnson (1971).

The DATACALL simulation (Johnson, 1971) is a program which sets up in the computer a system of six to ten variables which combine additively to produce data from hypothetical experiments. The instructor may adopt pre-existing simulations in a wide variety of areas, or develop his own. In either case, students are given a description of a problem, called the scenario. For example, a scenario might suggest that the computer was going to simulate the teaching of calculus to university freshmen by graduate teaching assistants. The scenario might then go on to describe the results of prior research in this area and then list the variables which are available for experimental manipulation. These might include various teaching techniques, choice of textbook, warmth of the instructors, experience of the instructors, preparation of the students, and the like. The student reads the introductory scenario and designs an experiment which consists of his choices of some subset of these variables. Next, the computer model generates data—in this case scores on a hypothetical final exam in calculus—one subject at a time. The manner in which DATACALL accomplishes this is outlined in Figure 2. For each subject requested by the student, the computer first generates a random value representing the uniqueness of the individual. Then the effects of each experimental variable on the subject are determined and added to this initial value. For variables specified by the student, the appropriate effect is added. If a variable is unspecified, the program consults a pre-determined probability distribution to determine the value for that variable so that the appropriate effect can be added. For example, if the student has not specified the experience of the instructor, where instructors are either experienced or not in a 60-40 ratio, then the computer "draws" randomly and enters the effect of whatever choice is drawn. The overall task of the student is to determine whether and to what extent the experimental variables had any effect on the outcome. DATACALL is typically used in the context of an ongoing game where the student wins points for gaining information, but must enter an "ante" in order to conduct further experiments.

Small Computer Data Generators. The primary virtue of small computer data generators, as mentioned previously, is that they can be implemented quickly without need of specialized computer consulting services. Of course, they are more limited and typically allow the student to conduct hypothetical research in only a single area. An example of a small computer data generator is the program OUTCOME (Gregory 1975), which gives a plausible simulation of the outcome of psychotherapy. With the aid of a detailed scenario, it can be used in the beginning psychology research course to teach elements of research strategy. A scenario, it should be recalled, is a framework within which the hypothetical research is to take place. For the program OUTCOME, the student is informed that he is a researcher at a clinic where many patients apply for outpatient psychotherapy. The clinic director feels that psychotherapy and drug therapy are unproven treatments and therefore has no ethical qualms about assigning certain patients to specific treatments according to the needs of a research design .

In particular, the student-researcher has control over the following variables:

diagnosis; the not unreasonable simplifying assumption is made that clients are either neurotic, schizophrenic or manifesting a specific non-serious complaint such as snake phobia.

therapeutic approach; the therapists at the clinic can be identified as practicing one of three approaches—psychoanalytic, Rogerian, behavioral

treatment length; clients can be assigned to short term (about 15 sessions) or long term (about 30 sessions) therapy.

Drugs; major tranquilizers with anti-psychotic properties, minor tranquilizers with muscle relaxing properties, or no medication, can be specified explicitly by the experimenter.

social class; the social class of the client is arbitrarily dichotomized as high or low.

therapist warmth; therapists are either neutral or warm.

sex of client and therapist

sample size

By carefully selecting subjects and assigning them to treatment regimes, the student can conduct experiments on the effects of psychotherapy. The dependent variable, or outcome, is a choice of any or all of three follow-up measures obtained 1 year after psychotherapy. Like DATACALL, OUTCOME is conducted in a "game" atmosphere. However, in the case of OUTCOME, realistic constraints such as increased costs for greater experimental control and outcome information, and a fluctuating maximum sample size, are used. In general, the student cannot afford to keep constant or control all variables, in which case the computer model generates them probabilistically. The overall goal is to arrive at valid conclusions about the effects of psychotherapy with a small number of carefully designed experiments. Figure 3 illustrates a sample run of OUTCOME.

Summary and Final Comments. Computer data generators are essentially instructional aids for use in courses in research design and data analysis. They allow a student to obtain experience in the design of

```
ENTER AN ODD INTEGER
?11
ENTER THESE PARAMETERS FOR ONE PATIENT GROUP:
SSIZE, GRPTYPE, P-SEX, DIAGNOSIS, THER-TYPE, LENGTH, DRUGS, SES
THER-WM, THER-SEX, SELFR, OBJTEST, GAS, STATS
?4,1,0,2,1,0,0,0,0,0,1,1,1,0
        4 SUBJECTS REQUESTED 4 SUBJECTS WITH APPROPRIATE CHARACTERISTICS COULD BE LOCATED
                  GROUP TYPE 1 (1=TREATMENT,2=CONTROL,3=DRUG ONLY)
                  PATIENT-TREATMENT CHARACTERISTICS AND OUTCOMES
```

								OUTCOME MEASURES		
P-SEX	DIAGNO E IV	THERAPY E IV	LENGTH	DRUGS	P-SES	T-WARM	T-SEX	SELF REPORT	OBJECTIVE TEST	GOAL SCALING
1	2	1	1	1	1	2	1	91.08	78.60	55.85
2	2	1	1	2	2	2	2	91.81	51.17	67.71
1	2	1	2	3	1	1	1	79.13	132.46	102.34
1	2	1	2	2	1	1	2	80.40	41.87	79.93
						MEANS		85.60	76.02	76.46
						SUM OF SQRD DEVS		137.63	4976.41	1183.02
						STANDARD DEVS		6.77	40.73	19.86

```
?
STOP
RAN 5 SECS.
```

Figure 3. Illustrated here is the output for a single group of neurotics treated with Rogerian counseling, all other factors left to vary at random. The student-researcher has a manual which explains the output. Of course, most experimental designs would involve more than one subject group.

experiments and the analysis of data, but do not subject the student to the too often boring and time consuming ritual of conducting a trivial experiment. While it is too early to assess whether their use results in a greater degree of student mastery of principles and concepts in experimental psychology, at least one study (Nusslock, Kaplan & Main; 1974) supports this contention. At any rate, the *prima facie* case for the use of computer data generators is quite strong. In the years ahead, teachers of psychology should witness a dramatic increase in the number of computer data generators, as well as improvements in the quality and ease of transport of these teaching innovations.

References

Gregory, R. J. Outcome: A computer simulation of the results of psycho-therapy and its use in the psychology research course. *Proceedings of the Conference on Computers in the Undergraduate Curricula,* 1975, *6,* 213-218.

Hallenbeck, C. E., & Welch, R. B. Generalizing the problem definition step in the computer simulation of factorial experiments. *Behavior Research Methods and Instrumentation,* 1974, *6* (2), 111-121.

Johnson, R. DATACALL: A computer-based simulation game for teaching strategy in scientific research. *Proceedings of the Conference on Computers in the Undergraduate Curricula,* 1971, *2,* 419-423.

Kissler, G. R. Evaluation of computer-based laboratory simulation models to teach scientific research strategies. *Behavior Research Methods and Instrumentation,* 1974 *6* (2), 124-126.

Main, D. B. EXPER SIM: Experimental simulation. *Creative Computing,* 1975, *1* (3), 43-46.

Nusslock, R. H., Kaplan R. J., & Main, D. B. Casual critiques or active arguments? A comparison of the use of computer data generators and journal article criticism in the science classroom. *Proceedings of the Conference on Computers in the Undergraduate Curricula,* 1974, *5,* 41-48.

Stout, R. L. Modeling and the Michigan Experimental Simulation Supervisor: An overview and some prospects. *Behavior Research Methods and Instrumentation,* 1974, *6* (2), 121-123.

Notes

1. Main, D. B., Stout, R. L., and Rajecki, D. W. A pedagogical scheme for the development and use of computer simulation technology. Paper presented to the combined 12th Annual Symposium of the National Gaming Council and 4th Annual Conference of the International Simulation and Gaming Association, September 1973.

2. Funds to adopt EXPERSIM are available under the Exxon Education Foundation's *Impact* program. A 16 mm, 20 min. film on EXPERSIM is available from the Foundation, 111 W. 48th Street., New York, NY 10020.

Teaching the Arts of Psychological Research

Alan A. Hartley, Lynn A. Fisher, and Joellen T. Hartley
Florida International University

In the standard laboratory course the student is taught to identify and label major components of the experiment such as dependent and independent variables, sample sizes, and experimental controls. The science of experimental research is emphasized. It is much more difficult to convey the arts of experimental research—those decisions that the student learns as rote catechism and that the professional researcher has acquired through slowly accreting clinical experience. These decisions are at the heart of psychological research as a problem solving process; they include the type of design, the naiveté of the subjects, the sample size, etc.

In an attempt to accomplish the objective of teaching some of these arts, we have developed a method which allows students to carry out simulated research investigations. Working from a scenario which describes the topic, the student designs a study by selecting values of available variables. Once the student has specified an acceptable design, data are provided which might have been obtained had such a study actually been carried out. The instructor may produce the data in three ways (Note 1): (a) A data table may be consulted. Random error may be added to the table value if it is desirable that results differ slightly from one simulated subject to another and from one student to another. (b) The data-generating algorithm may be programmed into a suitable electronic calculator. Many calculators will also generate a random variate which may be used to introduce variability. (c) The data generating models have been prepared as FORTRAN subroutines for the Experiment Simulator (EXPER SIM) computer-assisted instruction package (Note 2).

MARYJANE: Marijuana Ingestion and Motor Behavior.

The first model simulates the effect of marijuana on motor behavior. The model is simplified and somewhat stylized since it is designed less to convey what has been discovered by the scientific community than to give first hand experience with certain fundamental problems faced by the behavioral researcher. The first problem is that of contamination or *carry-over effects.* In the model, different "grades" of marijuana may be selected by the student-experimenter. Depending on the grade, the drug causes residual elevation of reaction times which lasts from three to nine days. A second problem is that of *variability.* One of the tasks which may be selected, a standard simple reaction time task carried out under laboratory conditions, yields scores with very low variance; the other, reaction time to traffic signals in a driving simulator, yields scores with a great deal of variance.

Although each of these potential problems has been discussed in class, we have found that most students charge confidently ahead and arrive at conclusions that differ drastically from the pure effect of marijuana on behavior postulated in the model. At this stage, we have given students a handout describing the "True State of the World" and allowed them to explore experimentally the discrepancies between what they found and the model. Some students suggest that the results just go to show that the world is more complex than any model, whereas others take the exercise as conclusive proof of the instructor's status as a fiend. The majority, however, discover the carry-over effects and find that they can be remedied either by sufficiently long intertrial intervals or by relying on between- rather than within-subjects experiments.

Because both between- and within-subjects designs are allowed, it is possible for the student to discover that the sensitivity of a within-subjects design makes it ideal for extracting the effect of a factor in the presence of the masking "noise" of high variance. Our experience has been that this discovery is rarer and requires considerably more guidance from the instructor than the discovery of carry-over effects.

To evaluate the impact of MARYJANE, two sections of the research methods course were given a final examination item containing several brief descriptions of research hypotheses. One section had worked with MARYJANE while the other had not. The same instructor taught both sections, and the course content, except for MARYJANE, was comparable. For each hypothesis, the students were asked to determine whether a between-subjects, a within-subjects, or a mixed design would be most appropriate. Students who had worked with MARYJANE assigned the correct design to more hypotheses ($\overline{X}$ = 2.51) than did students in the other group ($\overline{X}$ = 2.26), $t(60)$ = 1.97, $p <$ .05.

MOON: Phases of the Moon and Murder.

The second simulation, which was prepared recently, is directed to the misconception, common among neophytes in psychology, that a significant correlation establishes a cause and effect relationship. Even students who can recite the catechism by answering correctly examination questions on this topic will often make the wrong inferences when confronted with real world correlations. (During a recent class, 63 of 158 students incorrectly interpreted the following statement as showing cause and effect: "There is a .98 correlation between the number of men over 65 in a city and the number of forcible rapes." Perhaps the cultural stereotype of the Dirty Old Man is simply irresistible.) In this simulation, MOON, the student is allowed to explore the relation between the phase of the moon and the number of murders committed. The student's first step is to rediscover the empirical relationship, which has been reported by Lieber and Sherin (1972): Murders increase at the new and full moon. The purely hypothetical cause and effect relationship used by the simulation to determine the number of murders is this: The number of murders is only indirectly related to the phases of the moon. Murders are "really" of two types, crimes of passion committed at periods of the brightest moonlight and crimes related to property (such as murders occurring during burglaries) which are committed at the darkest periods. Variables such as season and geographical location, which would affect the likelihood that the populace will be out and about, also have small effects on the number of murders. Variables such as the moon's position in orbit, which determines the tidal pull, may also be selected but, following Lieber's evidence, have no relation to the number of murders. In addition to the manipulable variables, several covariates may be provided to the student, but only if directly requested. These include level of moonlight, level of terrestrial magnetism, strength of tidal pull, average daily temperature, and others. Thus, at the next step, the student may be given the hint that there may be other variables, not mentioned in the descriptive material, that may be investigated. The student may be told that several of these have been included in the simulation and, if the student can describe a hunch sufficiently close to an available variable, the instructor will provide measurements of the covariate. The pedagogical uses of such "X-variables" have been discussed by Cromer and Thurmond (1972) and Main, Stout, and Rajecki (Note 3).

At the most basic level, MOON should serve as an introduction to the concept of a variable and its levels and. related notions. Because of its aura of mysterious celestial intervention, the topic provokes interest and because many students can provide personal confirmation of the moon's influence (their own experience, or that of a friend, from working in a mental hospital or on a police force or in a delivery room), there is a strong set to accept the relationship as causal. At a deeper level, MOON provides a challenge to go beyond the apparent and intuitively obvious, to search imaginatively for covariates revealing the causal factors underlying behavior.

MOON was first used in the classroom in Spring, 1976. Data are presently being collected for a formal evaluation of the simulation.

General Evaluation. In contrast to the common "canned" laboratory experiment whose composition is predetermined, the simulations allow the student to select the components of the investigation, manipulate them, evaluate them, and discard them. It is hoped that this will lead to an improved ability to design research. To examine this hypothesis, students who either had or had not been exposed to the simulations (a total of five, including those described in this report) were asked to design an experiment to evaluate a stated hypothesis. The students who had not been exposed to the simulations were those enrolled in the research methods course during the term just preceding the implementation of the simulations; those who had been exposed were enrolled during the second term in which the simulations were used. The designs were blind-scored by two raters for adequateness, completeness, and viability. The two ratings were averaged to provide a score for each student. Students who had worked with the simulations received significantly higher scores ($\overline{X}$ = 4.9) than those who had not ($\overline{X}$ = 3.2), $t(60)$ = 5.02, p < .01.

The present results do not establish that the use of simulations is a universally valuable tool in the laboratory course. They do, however, provide *prima facie* evidence that simulations can increase both the range of topics which may be investigated in the undergraduate research methods course and the student's comprehension of the research process.

References

Cromer. A. O., & Thurmond, J. B. Toward the optimal use of computer simulations in teaching scientific research strategy. *Proceedings of the 1972 Conference on Computers in Undergraduate Curricula,* June, 1972.

Lieber, A. L., & Sherin, C. R. Homicides and the lunar cycle: Toward a theory of lunar influence on human emotional disturbance. *American Journal of Psychiatry,* 1972, *129*, 101-106.

Notes

1. Materials for the use of the simulations in each of the three modes are available from the first author, without charge, at the address given below.
2. EXPER SIM is a package of programs which mediate between the student and data-generating algorithms. It is available in a variety of languages and for a variety of computer configurations. Information on the implementation and use of EXPER SIM is available from the Center for Research on Learning and Teaching, University of Michigan, 109 E. Madison, Ann Arbor, Michigan, 48104. The idea of using simulations to teach research methods is due to Dana Main, Robert Stout, and the others who have contributed to the development of EXPER SIM.
3. Main, D. B., Stout, R., & Rajecki, D. W. *A pedagogical schema for the development and use of computer simulation technology.* Paper presented to the combined Twelfth Annual Symposium of the National Gaming Council and the Fourth Annual Conference of the Intentional Simulation and Gaming Association, September, 1973.
4. Support for the work reported here was provided by a grant from the Exxon Education Foundation IMPACT program. Instruction materials (including FORTRAN IV/EXPER SIM program listings) for MOON and MARYJANE are available without charge from the first author.
5. Lynn A. Fisher is now at the Department of Psychology, University of North Carolina at Chapel Hill. Joellen T. Hartley is now at the School of Social Sciences, University of California, Irvine, California 92717.

Vitamin C and the Common Cold: A Simulation for Teaching Methods of Research

Alan A. Hartley and Daryl G. Smith
Scripps College

It would be desirable if research methods could be taught in the context of topics in which student interest is already high. Unfortunately, there is little overlap between the interests of students new to the research enterprise and the areas that can be studied feasibly and economically in the student laboratory. If questions of current interest could be studied there would be several advantages: First, motivation for undertaking the investigations should be strong, and the student should be less likely to view them as simply exercises. Second, the approach would emphasize the applicability of scientific inquiry to questions of personal interest. And third, it should be possible to tap strong, pre-existing opinions about how the results will turn out. This should facilitate the process of hypothesis formation. It should also increase the chances that the student will think critically about the results, especially if they are counter to an *a priori* opinion. The student may be more likely to search for uncontrolled sources of variation and to design follow-up studies.

In order to achieve our goal of combining "relevance" with the application of basic principles of research design and analysis, we have made use of a simulation that allows students to investigate the effect of vitamin C on the common cold. The simulation was designed primarily to give "hands-on" experience at the logic of manipulating independent variables, the method of concomitant variation, and measuring dependent variables. We have also used the simulation as a basis for discussing controlled and uncontrolled variables, placebo conditions, dose-response relations and response-surface explorations, and other, more advanced concepts.

The claim that vitamin C can reduce the frequency or severity of colds, popularized by Pauling (1970, 1976), has elicited considerable attention and controversy (e.g., King & Burns, 1975). Most college students have an opinion about the value of vitamin C, evidenced either by their spoken remarks or by their behavior—the pattern of ascorbic acid intake. Only 25% of the students we have queried disagreed with the hypothesis that vitamin C beyond the recommended daily allowance would have beneficial effects. All of them supplemented their diets with additional vitamin C. Student opinions about the optimal dose, translated into research hypotheses, vary widely. Some advocate a regimen similar to that Pauling finds most effective—large daily doses of the vitamin (termed the prophylactic dose) and massive doses whenever cold symptoms are present (the therapeutic dose). Others take moderate to large doses daily whether symptoms are present or not or take massive therapeutic doses but no prophylactic doses.

The findings on which the simulation is based are contrary to student beliefs; they show negligible effects of vitamin C supplements on either the incidence or the duration of the common cold (Anderson, 1975; Lewis, Karlowski, Kapikian, Lynch, Shaffer, & George, 1975). However, with a non-zero prophylactic dose and a large therapeutic dose (greater than 2 g/da) there is a modest (25-30%) reduction in morbidity due to cold infections (Anderson, 1975; Coulehan, Kapner, & Eberhard, 1975). A disease's morbidity is the time it "lays you up," the time spent indoors, away from work or school. There is, however, an important qualification. Lewis et al. (1975) found that subjects had a propensity for tasting the tablets they were given and could reliably discriminate between vitamin C and a placebo. Further, those who thought they were receiving the vitamin, whether they were or not, were the only group that showed a significant effect. Those unaware of what they were getting showed no effect.

The simulation mediates between the student and the research findings described above. The student designs an experiment, specifying the prophylactic dose (0, a placebo, to 2 g/da), the therapeutic dose (0 to 8 g/da), and the number of months the study is to run (1 to 20). One of three dependent variables must be specified: number of colds, total duration of symptoms, or total number of days away from work or school. In addition, it is also possible to control variables that are not specified in advance. In this way, the student who hypothesizes an important role for the subject's knowledge of the condition in which he is serving can investigate its effect The student who wishes to explore other variables may do so, but will find they have no effect since they are ignored in the simulation. Once the student has specified the design and the number of subjects, the simulation generates data by consulting tables drawn from the studies summarized above. Individual differences are simulated by representing each subject by a score selected at random from a standard normal distribution. The standard score is multiplied by the tabled standard deviation and the mean is added to arrive at the value of the dependent variable for that simulated subject. The simulation also provides an estimate of the cost of the study had it actually been conducted.

Our experience has been that the question of the value of vitamin C is of considerable interest to students. It is clear that the limited time and budget of a research methods class would normally make it impossible to investigate such a question. Not only does the simulation make this possible, but it also allows the student to carry out large experiments or a sequence of studies in a very short time at a very low cost. Our situation was that we had neither laboratory space nor equipment. Our single asset was unlimited computer time. By developing the simulation in the form of a computer program, we were able to allow our students to design and carry out research projects and to introduce them to the computer terminal and interactive computing at no additional cost and without intensive supervision by the instructors.

Although it has virtues of novelty and convenience, implementing simulations on the computer is not necessary. The vitamin C simulation can be used without difficulty by consulting a list of random samples from a standard normal distribution and the tabled means and standard deviations.

In sum, our experience has led us to believe that the use of simulations in teaching research methods can be an economical and pedagogically sound supplement to actual research projects (see also Hartley, Fisher, & Hartley, 1977).

References

Anderson, T. W. Large scale trials of vitamin C. In C. G. King & J. J. Burns (Eds.), *Second conference on vitamin C: Annals of the New York Academy of Sciences* (Vol. 250). New York: New York Academy of Sciences, 1975.

Coulehan, J. L., Kapner, L., & Eberhard, S. Vitamin C and upper respiratory illness in Navaho children: Preliminary observations (1974). In C. G. King & J. J. Burns (Eds.), *Second conference on vitamin C: Annals of the New York Academy of Sciences* (Vol. 250). New York: New York Academy of Sciences, 1975.

Hartley, A. A., Fisher, L. A., & Hartley, J. T. Teaching the arts of psychological research. *Teaching of Psychology,* 1977, 4, 202-204.

King, C. G., & Burns, J. J. (Eds.). *Second conference on vitamin C: Annals of the New York Academy of Sciences* (Vol. 250). New York: New York Academy of Sciences, 1975.

Lewis, T. L., Karlowski, T. R., Zapikian, A. Z., Lynch, J. M., Shaffer, G. W., & George, D. A. A controlled clinical trial of ascorbic acid for the common cold. In C. G. King & J. J. Burns (Eds.), *Second conference on vitamin C: Annals of the New York Academy of Sciences* (Vol. 250). New York: New York Academy of Sciences, 1975.

Pauling, L. *Vitamin C and the common cold.* San Francisco: Freeman, 1970

Pauling, L. *Vitamin C, the common cold, and the flu.* San Francisco: Freeman, 1976.

Note

A listing of the BASIC program together with a copy of the student handout we have used is available from the first author. Copies of the materials necessary to use the simulation without the computer are also available.

Computer Simulation or Real Experimentation: Is One Better for Teaching Experimental Design?

James O. Benedict
and Beverly D. Butts
James Madison University

An experimental approach to the question yields support for both methods, and an order preference.

The traditional psychology lab course has usually been patterned after the laboratory courses found in the natural sciences. These labs require the student to follow a lab manual, as one might follow a recipe book. The experiments described in the lab manual were probably chosen because they were simple enough to be completed in one or two laboratory periods and have been successfully replicated many times, therefore almost guaranteeing a consistent outcome among all the students. This approach allows the laboratory instructor to conveniently evaluate student work but it makes the student a passive data collector or more simply a technician. It does not stimulate the student to think scientifically nor does it teach the problem solving skills that are essential for good scientific inquiry.

Underwood (1975), an opponent of the lab manual approach, contends that "canned" experiments bore both the student and the instructor. Underwood believes that laboratory courses should maximize the possibility of discovering something new, so that students will feel the possibility that they might make a contribution to the field of psychology. Thus, Underwood favors an approach which emphasizes the conducting of novel experiments. In his experimental psychology labs, he helps the students design and run experiments that have probably never been done before. This exciting approach motivates students and introduces them to the processes of real scientific research.

Since designing and running a novel experiment takes a great deal of time, only a few of them can be run in a semester. A different approach using computer simulation has recently been suggested that allows students to design and run a series of experiments during a one semester experimental psychology course.

There are several computer simulation models that have been written for this purpose. Some of them are DATACALL (Johnson, 1971), LABSIM (Kissler, 1974), EXPERSIM (Main, 1974), LESS (Thurmond & Cromer, 1975) and CLASCONSIM (Benedict, in press). In a typical simulation experiment students are given a written description of a problem area and the published research relevant to that problem. They are provided with a set of manipulable variables and are then permitted to design the experiment of their choice. The computer program executes the experiment and incorporates sampling error into the process of generating data so that the data closely resemble the random variation of real data. Students then perform the appropriate statistical analysis on their data and interpret their results in terms of the initial hypotheses. In essence, experimental simulation allows students to rehearse all of the roles of the research scientist without having to contend with the time-consuming process of data collection (Main, 1974).

There are, then, at least two approaches for getting students involved in the running and evaluating of experiments of the students own designs. The question is which of the two approaches teaches the knowledge and procedures of experimental design better? In a recent review of the use of computer simulation for teaching experimental design, especially of the use of EXPERSIM, Forback (1979) stated that little if any rigorous evidence has appeared that compares the learning effectiveness of computer simulation and the more traditional laboratory approach. He argued that attempts should be made to evaluate exactly what and how much is learned using these different methods. This study is one such attempt.

Our study compared the performance of two sections of the Experimental Psychology course taught at a regional state university. We chose to use the LESS simulation (based on EXPERSIM) because it was written in the BASIC language and it was easily adapted to our computer system. In general the procedure was the following: After both classes received an introduction to research design through the use of a standard text, lectures and discussion of some case studies, one class worked on the LESS simulation for 4 weeks and then worked on an independent experiment for 4 weeks. Each student or pair of students designed and executed their own experiments both during the LESS phase and the independent experiment phase. The other class received the two laboratory experiences in reverse. They worked on the independent project first for 4 weeks and then the LESS simulation for 4 weeks. With this procedure it was possible to compare the effectiveness and contribution of each method and to assess which order of approach might be most effective.

Inasmuch as the simulation approach would allow the students to run several experiments during the 4 weeks on an unlimited number of subjects while the independent project would be only one experiment and probably on a small number of subjects, it was hypothesized that the exposure to the simulation approach could be more effective at teaching the procedures of designing well-controlled experiments and statistically evaluating the results of them. It was also hypothesized that the independent project would better sensitize students to some of the practical problems of running experiments that are often not mentioned in the textbooks, e.g. finding or making equipment, getting equipment to work, and finding subjects that would be willing to be in an experiment, etc. Finally, since the computer simulation approach simplified the variable manipulation and data gathering procedures, it was also hypothesized that students would prefer a gradual introduction to experimental design by working with computer simulation first before the independent project was attempted.

Method. Twenty-eight students in two sections of the experimental psychology course at a state university of about 9000 students served as subjects. The average student was a second semester junior who had taken an average of 3.9 previous courses in psychology.

Both sections of the course received a 6 week introduction to research design through reading a standard textbook, lectures and discussion of a few case studies. After the 6 week introduction, Section 1 with 10 students received the LESS computer simulation program (Thurmond & Cromer, 1975) for 4 weeks, followed by the independent research project (IRP) for 4 weeks. Section 2 worked on the IRP for the first 4 weeks and received the LESS simulation during the last 4 weeks of the course.

During the LESS simulation treatment, students were introduced to four of the simulations in the package, presented in the following order: Reaction Time, Rotorod, Fear and Obesity. The students were presented an outline of the problem area in question and a list of variables that could be manipulated in each model. The students were then assigned to design, execute and write up a short report of the results of the experiments including the statistical analysis of the data. Class discussion focused on the designs used and the appropriate t-tests or analysis of variance that should have been applied to the data. Each student completed five experiments, two of these using the Obesity simulation.

During the independent research project, students were given several different topical areas for possible experiments. From this list each student or pair of students chose one area and did some reading in that area and designed an original experiment. This design was discussed with and modified, if necessary, by the instructor. The students then perfected their design, developed or were assigned the needed materials and acquired the appropriate number of animal or human subjects. After running the experiment they applied the appropriate statistical analysis on their data and wrote up the report following the APA format. The actual experiments varied from studies of cooperation between like and opposite sexes, and attitude change on juries, to studies of conditioned taste aversion and the effects of punishment and omission training on the elimination of lever-pressing in rats.

As part of the assessment process, both sections were administered two exams. A multiple-choice pretest given the first day of class (not returned to the students) was designed to assess the students' factual knowledge of experimental design. An exam given after the first 4 week treatment, containing the same items as the pretest plus additional questions requiring application of knowledge of design to research problems, was used to assess the possible differences in knowledge gained from either LESS or IRP. Also at this same time students in both sections were asked to complete a survey. They were asked to rank-order the problems they encountered during their experimentation, having just completed 4 weeks of either LESS or IRP. The possible problems were (a) getting an idea, (b) deciding on an appropriate design, (c) getting subjects, (d) perfecting the procedure for running subjects, (e) deciding on the proper statistics, and (f) writing up the final report. This survey was used to assess whether IRP or LESS better sensitized students to some of the practical problems of doing experimentation.

At the end of the course students in both sections filled out an attitude survey which was designed to measure their general and specific reactions to the LESS and the IRP approach, to the possible use of these approaches in future experimental psychology classes, and to the preferred order of the two approaches.

Results. A t-test performed on the pretest multiple-choice exam scores showed no significant difference between the two sections $t(24) = 0.79$, $p < .40$. Although both sections showed a significant improvement in their multiple-choice scores after having received the lectures and either LESS or IRP ($ps < .001$), the two sections were not significantly different from each other, $t(26) = 0.92$, $p < .36$. Knowledge of the content of experimental psychology as tested by the multiple choice exam did not seem to be differentially affected by the laboratory experience. However, when both sections were asked in a discussion question to identify the likely hypotheses from a set of data in a 3 x 3 factorial experiment on imprinting in chickens, and to suggest further experiments, the LESS section performed better, but the difference was not significant ($t(26)=1.58$, p < .06, 1-tailed).

When the students in both sections were asked to rank-order the problems that usually occur in doing original research after they had either done LESS or IRP, both sections saw getting an idea as the most troublesome problem. Sixty percent of the LESS section ranked that item first or second and 47 percent of the IRP did so. The sections differed with respect to how they ranked the least troublesome problems. The LESS section ranked writing the final report and deciding on the appropriate statistics to use as the easiest. Sixty and 40 percent respectively of this section ranked these two items the lowest or next to the lowest. The IRP section ranked getting subjects and perfecting the procedure for running subjects as the easiest. The sums of the percentage of these two items were 44 and 55 percent respectively for the lowest two rankings. Both groups ranked as least troublesome those aspects of the experimentation with which they had more experience.

At the end of the semester after the students in both sections had received the LESS and IRP experiences, they were asked to evaluate their reactions to the two approaches on a series of Likert-scaled items. When asked whether LESS or IRP contributed more to their understanding of experimental design, students in both sections agreed with the statement that the independent research project had contributed more, $t(27) = 1.20$, $p < .06$, 2-tailed. When asked whether LESS or IRP led to a greater understanding of which statistics to use in evaluating experiments, students agreed more with the statement that LESS provided the greater understanding, $t(27) = 1.84$, $p < .04$, 1-tailed. When asked whether LESS or IRP should be used in future Experimental Psychology courses, students equally agreed that both LESS with an average of 4.39 on a scale of 5, and IRP with an average of 4.29 should be used. There was no significant difference between these averages, $t(27) =.57$, $p < .40$. When asked in separate statements whether LESS should be given early and IRP later in the course or whether they should be given in the reverse order, both sections agreed with the former statement. The section that received LESS first showed a strong agreement $t(9) = 2.23$, $p < .05$, 2-tailed. The section that received the IRP approach first showed even stronger agreement, $t(17) = 6.06$, $p < .001$, 2-tailed.

Discussion. The present findings indicate that the computer simulation approach using LESS and an independent project approach both contribute to the teaching and understanding of experimental methods as presented in a course on experimental psychology.

The simulation experience allowed students to run five experiments during a 4-week period. Those students who received LESS first were somewhat better able to understand the meaning of data generated from a complex analysis of variance design than those who had worked on an independent research project first. When asked to evaluate their lab experience in the course, students from both sections felt that LESS helped them better understand how to apply statistical procedures to their experimental data. Both felt they learned more about experimental design from the independent research project. But both felt that LESS and IRP should both be used in future experimental psychology courses with the simulation experience occurring first.

If laboratory experiences in psychology are to teach the procedures of experimentation and if Underwood (1975) is correct that laboratory experiences should maximize the possibility of finding something new, then the combination of computer simulation and independently-designed research projects should be an effective combination. Kissler (1974) has argued that simulation is probably most effective when used with other types of instruction. These data support his contention.

Computer simulation allows the students to design and run several experiments on interesting topics in a short period of time. Neither the student nor the instructor has to be concerned about waiting for the approval of a committee whose responsibility is to guarantee the use of ethical procedures. Neither do they have to be concerned about getting research equipment to work nor finding agreeable subjects. And enough data are generated by computer simulated experiments to allow the student to really use some of those statistical procedures they spent many hours learning in their Statistics course.

The independent research project, on the other hand, is perhaps a more realistic research experience for them. The students work by themselves or in small research teams, design their experiments from articles they have read, and their subjects react in a natural way to their experiments. Following this experience, students soon realize the great difference between textbook presentations of experimentation and the real thing.

This investigation is one of the first attempts to compare in a research study the effects of computer simulation and real experimentation in teaching experimental design in psychology. The results do not show any great differences between the techniques. Both contribute to the understanding of experimental design but if both are to be used in a given course, the simulation experience probably should be given first.

References

Benedict, J. O. CLASCONSIM: A computer program to simulate experiments in classical conditioning. *Behavior Research Methods & Instrumentation,* In Press .

Forback, G. B. EXPER SIM: Review and update. *Behavior Research Methods & Instrumentation,* 1979, *11*, 519-522.

Johnson, R. DATACALL. A computer-based simulation game for teaching strategy in scientific research. In *Proceedings of the conference on computers in the undergraduate curricula.* Hanover, NH: Dartmouth College, 1971.

Kissler, G. R. Evaluation of computer-based laboratory simulation models to teach scientific research strategies. *Behavior Research Methods & Instrumentation,* 1974, *6*, 124-126.

Main, D. B. EXPER SIM: Experimental simulation. *Creative Computing,* 1974, 18-21 .

Thurmond, J. B., & Cromer, A. O. Models and modeling with the Louisville experiment simulation system (LESS). *Behavior Research Methods & Instrumentation,* 1975, 7, 229-232.

Underwood, B. J. The first course in experimental psychology: Goals and methods. *Teaching of Psychology,* 1975, *2*, 163-165.

Learning About Microcomputers and Research

Blaine F. Peden
University of Wisconsin—Eau Claire

This article describes (a) student use of the microcomputer before, during, and after an experiment; and (b) the benefits that students derive from learning about microcomputers, in particular, and from conducting research, in general.

In regard to psychologists' use of computers for instruction, interest is growing and resistance is diminishing (Butler, 1986). Bare (1982), Goolkasian (1985), and Hovancik (1986) described innovative uses for microcomputers in undergraduate laboratory courses. All three articles described the use of computers for data collection and analysis. Only Goolkasian discussed using the computer for instruction, although there are other uses for computers in teaching, such as computer-assisted instruction, modeling, and simulation (e.g., Atnip, 1985; Collyer, 1984).

This article outlines an approach that integrates the microcomputer into the entire research process. The method evolved over a period of several years as I worked individually with advanced undergraduates on research for presentation and publication. Nonetheless, this article should provide ideas and impetus for the classroom teacher by illustrating uses for the microcomputer throughout the research process-from the development of researchable hypotheses to the preparation of a manuscript for submission. In this process, students: (a) learn organizational skills, (b) acquire creative problem-solving and forecasting skills, (c) learn to think logically, and (d) develop and refine analytical and writing skills. Students also acquire knowledge about how to structure and program experiments and an appreciation for hardware and software.

Each semester one to three undergraduates begin work in my operant conditioning laboratory. They remain for one to four semesters, starting as assistants and later becoming collaborators. We conduct experiments dealing with conditioning and learning (e.g., Peden & Liddell, 1983), foraging and feeding (e.g., Peden & Rohe, 1984), and cognition and memory. We present the results at undergraduate research conferences or professional meetings, and sometimes they are published.

A typical student entering my laboratory has completed courses in statistics and research methods and has expressed an interest in performing research and attending graduate school. Although highly motivated, these students have little experience with research or microcomputers. My primary concern is to further their goals by involving them in research. This article discusses (a) student use of the Apple II microcomputer before, during, and after an experiment; and (b) some advantages of learning about microcomputers, in particular, and of conducting research, in general.

Prior to an experiment, students read pertinent articles to develop the background and expertise required to understand or generate testable hypotheses for a particular experiment. Although my lab is not now equipped to search on-line data bases for new references (Lewis, 1986), students use the microcomputer to organize previously obtained references from articles, books, and chapters on a specific topic. For example, it is possible to use a file card box for references, but the microcomputer with a specialized data base for references entitled, "Quick Search Librarian" (Interactive Microware), is better than a file card box (Collyer, 1984). This program uses a separate diskette for each different data base rather than different file card boxes. It also permits entering and editing all references in a particular data base, searching and sorting references according to key words, and printing a reference list. Students quickly learn to appreciate such an organizational boon, and experience with this data base prompts them to identify and use other, more generalized data-base programs for academic and personal applications.

Students working on questions about foraging and feeding soon encounter quantitative models. A second application of the microcomputer prior to an experiment involves the use of spreadsheets to perform "What-If" simulations. For example, we use an inexpensive and simple spreadsheet "Magicalc JR" (Main Street Publishing). This program allows us to compute a variety of hypothetical cost/benefit functions in order to select appropriate parameters for a new experiment, and to compare predictions for different quantitative models. Such activity develops problem-solving and forecasting skills that are applicable in many situations. Proficient students sometimes learn to use more advanced spreadsheets such as Visi-Calc.

In combination with ancillary hardware, students use the microcomputer during an experiment to present stimuli, such as lights and tones, and to record responses by pigeons and rats working in an experimental chamber. In my lab, each Apple II microcomputer is connected to one, two, or four different experimental chambers by a MED Associates interface that makes it easy to present stimuli, record responses, and time events. According to students, conducting an experiment with a microcomputer markedly enhances their appreciation for hardware and software.

All programs controlling our experiments are written in APPLESOFT, a version of interpreted BASIC. We use several Beagle Brothers diskettes containing "utility programs" that facilitate writing and editing an APPLESOFT program. They are: (a) "ProntoDOS," which minimizes the time required to load a program into memory and to save a program to a diskette; (b) "Global Program Line Editor" (GPLE), which provides quick and efficient means to correct errors in lines of code; (c) "Double-Take," which requires just a few keystrokes to perform various functions, such as listing the program, cataloging a disk, appending files, renumbering a program, and clearing the screen; and (d) "D-Code," which promptly identifies an error upon entering a line. This function is helpful to student programmers because it identifies statements with typographical errors and illegal commands immediately rather than later during program execution.

"D-Code" also contains a program called COMPACT that eliminates reminders (REM statements) and compresses a program into fewer lines of code. Although it is easier to understand and modify a documented program with many REM statements, a "compacted" (as compared to a fully documented) version of the program executes more rapidly during an experiment. A substantial increment in the speed of execution can also be demonstrated for "compiled" rather than "interpreted" programs. Two familiar and easily used compilers for APPLESOFT programs are the "Einstein" compiler (Einstein Corporation) and "The APPLESOFT Compiler or TASC" (Microsoft). In brief, the fastest program is one that is both compacted and compiled.

All students use the microcomputer to conduct an experiment; however, only the more advanced students and I actually write APPLESOFT programs for an experiment. We are, of course, more interested in conducting experiments than in computer programming per se. Students with majors or minors in computer science typically must learn to program in BASIC because their training begins with PASCAL. Students who have taken only an introductory computing course possess rudimentary programming skills in BASIC. In either case, it is useful for students to improve their programming skills. The computer science students learn a new language and respond enthusiastically to the opportunity to program in a real-time as opposed to a batch mode. A modicum of programming experience helps computer novices understand how the previously described utilities help to overcome the tiresome aspects of writing an APPLESOFT program. The students also learn how long it takes to write a program. Moreover, some programming experience helps computer novices understand the need to write logically organized, or structured programs, and to document programs thoroughly—ideas well-entrenched for more sophisticated programmers. To this end, our programs contain many subroutines, each of which performs one function and includes many REM statements.

Learning about structured programs with internal documentation provides at least three benefits to students. One advantage is that new students can study previous programs and quickly learn the commands required to time events, activate outputs (e.g., lights), and measure inputs (e.g., responses). This experience helps a student to feel more confident about programming an experiment, and to appreciate hardware and software. A second advantage is that the experimenter must use organizational skills to specify each step in the sequence of experimental events before trying to write a program. Attempting to write a program prematurely often reveals logical and procedural problems, whereas the careful planning required to write a program for an experiment may suggest parametric manipulations and variations in the procedure that might not otherwise be obvious. A third advantage of this approach is that a subroutine solving a particular problem may be "transported" from one experiment to another, thereby decreasing the amount of time required for programming from experiment to experiment. For example, a subroutine we named "Activate the Peripheral Devices" provides instructions to the student experimenter about the order in which different peripheral devices, such as the MED Associates interface and the power supply, should be activated. This structured and documented subroutine is easily "transported" from a program for rats to one for pigeons by using "Double-Take" (Beagle Brothers) to append files. In sum, students learn to program experiments, understand procedures, and transfer solutions for one experiment to another. The extent to which an individual student's sophistication grows varies directly as a function of time spent in the lab and the number of projects completed.

After an experiment, the primary goal for the student is to write a report that is correct in form and content. At this point in the research process, the microcomputer is an invaluable tool for statistical analysis, data plotting, and word processing.

My students use statistical programs such as "Key Stat" (Oakleaf Systems) or the "Introductory Statistics Software Package" (Addison-Wesley) for simple statistical analysis and the "HSD Statistics" (Human Systems Dynamics) programs for complex analysis. Easy-to-use statistics programs make a student more willing to analyze data and to perform different analyses on a set of data. Programs such as "Scientific Plotter" (Interactive Microware) or "Alphachart" and "Curve Plotter" (Spectral Graphics Software) make it easy to plot data. These programs encourage a student to consider alternative ways to represent the data.

Finally, all students learn to use "Applewriter II or IIe," a word processor, to prepare successive drafts of their laboratory reports. Word processing encourages students to revise manuscripts. Students are more willing to explore problem-solving strategies for writing, such as generating and organizing ideas, and editing for style and organization (Flower, 1981), when using a word processor than when writing by hand or typing. An outline processor (Rogers, 1986) is another program that will promote student use of problem-solving strategies for writing initial drafts of a paper. Ultimately, I favor use of "Manuscript Manager" (Pergamon Press), perhaps the word processor of choice because it is specifically designed for preparing manuscripts according to the APA style manual. Once students approach a final draft, they use "The Sensible Speller" (Sensible Software) to eliminate misspelled words and typographical errors.

In conclusion, a crucial component to the success of this endeavor is individualized instruction during one or more semesters (see also, Atnip, 1985, for a similar emphasis). This component is more important than either the particular microcomputer or the programs used, because programs comparable to those I have described are available for other machines as well.

Undergraduates working in my lab become skilled in only some of the microcomputer applications to which they are exposed—in large part, by choice. Students tell me that how much they learn about a particular application depends largely on the availability of the microcomputer and the software, and on personal needs. For example, in comparison to the university microcomputer lab, in which pertinent software is unavailable and computer access is limited, students have virtually unlimited access to the software and microcomputers in my lab, except during the hours reserved for experiments. This opportunity allows students to exploit some applications and to explore others according to their needs and interests.

Student use of the microcomputer before, during, and after an experiment produces benefits from learning about microcomputers and from conducting research. Undergraduates working with microcomputers in my laboratory derive, to varying degrees, several benefits, which help them to compete in graduate programs or the job world. With respect to learning about computers and computer applications, students: (a) learn creative problem-solving and forecasting skills, (b) learn organizational skills, (c) develop an appreciation for hardware and software, (d) learn to think logically and to write structured programs for real-time experiments, and (e) improve their analytical and writing skills. Students also gain laboratory experience and have an opportunity to present their experiments at undergraduate research conferences. Students report that these experiences foster self-discipline, responsibility, social skills, a spirit of cooperation, self-confidence, and a sense of personal achievement.

The ideas expressed in this article should also be useful for teachers who use microcomputers in laboratory courses. For example, students exposed to data-base and spreadsheet applications will develop their own uses for these tools, especially as simple and easy-to-use programs become increasingly available in the public domain or at low cost. In a similar fashion, students learn quickly that expertise in using hardware and software programming aids is valuable in academic and applied settings. Finally, experience with outline processors, word processors, and spelling checkers helps students improve the quality of their writing, another important skill in academic and job settings.

References

Atnip, G. W. (1985). Teaching the use of computers: A case study. *Teaching of Psychology, 12,* 171-172.

Bare, J. K. (1982). Microcomputers in the introductory laboratory. *Teaching of Psychology, 9,* 236-237.

Butler, D. L. (1986). Interests in and barriers to using computers in instruction. *Teaching of Psychology, 13,* 20-23.

Collyer, C. E. (1984). Using computers in the teaching of psychology: Five things that seem to work. *Teaching of Psychology, 11,* 206-209.

Flower, L. (1981). *Problem-solving strategies for writing.* New York: Harcourt Brace Jovanovich.

Goolkasian, P. (1985). A microcomputer-based lab for psychology instruction. *Teaching of Psychology, 12,* 223-225.

Hovancik, J. R. (1986). Using microcomputers in the undergraduate laboratory. *Teaching of Psychology, 13,* 94-96.

Lewis, L. K. (1986). Bibliographic computerized searching in psychology. *Teaching of Psychology, 13,* 38-40.

Peden, B. F., & Liddell, B. (1983, May). *The paws that refresh: A preliminary attempt to condition self-grooming and other-grooming by rats.* Paper presented at the meeting of the Association for Behavior Analysis, Milwaukee, WI.

Peden, B. F., & Rohe, M. S. (1984). Effects of search cost on foraging and feeding: A three-component chain analysis. *Journal of the Experimental Analysis of Behavior, 42,* 211-221.

Rogers, R. L. (1986). Preparing course materials with an outline processor. *Teaching of Psychology, 13,* 154-155.

Notes

1. This article is based on a paper presented as part of a symposium, *Preparing Psychology Majors for Careers in Business: Teaching Computer Skills and Applications,* conducted at the meeting of the Midwestern Psychological Association in Chicago, IL, May 2-4,1985.

2. Preparation of this article was supported in part by the University of Wisconsin-Eau Claire Faculty Sabbatical Leave Program and by a supplement to National Science Foundation Grant No. 84-11445 to William Timberlake at Indiana University, Bloomington.

3. I thank Allen Keniston and several anonymous reviewers for their comments on an earlier draft of this article.

Using Microcomputers in the Undergraduate Laboratory

John R. Hovancik
Seton Hall University

A computer-controlled experimental psychology investigation suitable for use in an undergraduate laboratory is described. The investigation examines the relationship between aesthetic preference and speed of reaction in making choices between colors generated on a video monitor. No special interfacing to the computer is required. The techniques have been used successfully and with great reliability to introduce microcomputer use to undergraduate psychology students.

Instructors of courses in experimental psychology and research methods in psychology are always looking for experiments and demonstrations that can be incorporated into their students' laboratory experiences. These procedures should be interesting, easy to instrument for multistudent laboratories, and reliably yield results that illustrate psychological phenomena. The shrinking cost and incredible flexibility of microcomputers make them the psychology laboratory instruments of the future. Teachers need to discover or devise interesting and reliable demonstrations that take advantage of the impressive power of these instruments (cf. Bare, 1982). This article describes a successful incorporation of microcomputer instrumentation into the undergraduate psychology laboratory. The procedures require no interfacing of components to the computer,

217

and thus can be implemented on off-the-shelf computer systems with no need for modification.

My investigation examined the question of whether the time taken to choose between stimulus alternatives is influenced by affective reactions to the choices. The alternatives were different colors generated on a computer video monitor. The correlational design was patterned after the much earlier investigations of Dashiell (1937) and Shipley, Coffin, and Hadsell (1945). The hypothesis tested was that, if a subject has a strong preference (either positive or negative) for a given color, then reaction times to choose between that color and others will be short. Thus, we expect a negative correlation between the strength of the subject's preference for a color and the reaction time for choices involving that color. The strength of subjective preference was gauged by how often the subject chose a given color when it was paired with other colors in a forced-choice situation. If subjects have a strong preference for a particular color we would expect them to choose that color often. A strong negative preference against a particular color would be expected to yield a low frequency of choice.

Either an Apple II + or Apple IIe microcomputer was used to generate a pair of adjacent squares approximately 5 in. On a side displayed on a 13-in. Amdek Model Color-1 video monitor. The two squares varied in color and were either red, orange, yellow, green, blue, or violet. On successive trials, all possible paired combinations of these colors were presented. Each of the resulting pairs was presented twice so that, for a given pair, a color could appear on the right one time and on the left another time. This amounted to a total of 30 test trials per subject. The order of presentation of color pairs was varied randomly by the computer for each subject. A sample pair of colors (used during instructions) and four practice pairs of colors were also presented. None of these trials involved the six test trial colors, however. Each student was responsible for recruiting and running subjects. Data from all students' subjects were later pooled for analysis.

Subjects were seated at the keyboard of the computer and were informed that they were to select their preferred color from the two presented on each trial. Preferences were indicated by pressing designated keys on the computer keyboard. Subjects were specifically advised not to hurry their responses but to take as long as necessary to be sure of their choices. After the instructions were presented, the experimenter left the room and the computer proceeded to present the 4 practice trials and 30 test trials. On test trials, the subject's color preference and choice reaction time were recorded by the computer.

Because each test color was presented exactly 10 times, subjects' preferences produced choice frequencies ranging from 0 (when a color was never picked as preferred) to 10 (always chosen). These frequencies were then transformed into positive and negative values (to reflect positive and negative preferences) by subtracting 5 from the choice frequency. The absolute value of the transformed score is indicative of the strength of the subject's preference. For example, a color chosen 10 times would produce a transformed preference level score of 5, indicating a strong preference. A color never chosen would have a preference level of 5, also a strong preference (in this case a negative one). If our hypothesis is correct, strong preference levels should be accompanied by short reaction times.

Following the final trial, the experimenter revealed on the monitor screen the data collected from the subject and explained the hypothesis. Because six preference levels (1 for each color) and six mean reaction time measures were taken for each subject, it was possible to compute a correlation coefficient for each subject individually. This statistic was also displayed during the debriefing process. The data were then also saved to a disk file for later more extensive statistical analysis.

Data have now been collected independently during four semesters and each time the data have been consistent with predictions derived from the hypothesis. In fact, it is rare when the expected results are not obtained even for individual subjects. Statistical analysis involved computing a coefficient of correlation between each subject's preference level for each color and the mean reaction time for choices on trials that included that color as one of the alternatives. As predicted by the hypothesis, mean reaction times were negatively correlated with the strength of the subject's preference for or against the color, $r(124) = -.337$, $p < .001$. Comparisons involving the most preferred or least preferred colors resulted in faster choices. Results highly similar to these have been obtained each semester this procedure has been used. Also, the results are consistent with those of the original investigation by Dashiell (1937). There appears to be little question of the reliability of the reported phenomenon.

I use this investigation in my research methodology course early in the semester when we consider correlational research. It introduces students to the use of microcomputers and simultaneously shows them a useful application of computers in psychological research. Having the computer present stimuli, control trial pacing, and collect data provides a vivid first-hand experience for the student in how psychological research is being carried out today. This exposure to computer-controlled research early in the semester gives the student an appreciation for how instrumentation can be used to protect against experimenter-induced bias. Using computers in undergraduate research also increases students' motivation. Students get excited about the science of psychology in a way that stopwatches, paper, and pencils never allowed.

Given the reliability of the results, the investigation is a "safe" procedure to use as an early exposure to psychological research when it may not be advantageous to deal with the realities of why expected results were not obtained. In the four semesters that I have used this technique, the data have always conformed to predictions. Because the procedure requires no interfacing to the computer, our students can conduct their research at a number of microcomputer sites around the campus. This possibility sets the stage for discussing proper experimental control procedures, vis-à-vis, control over the environment during data collection.

In summary, this procedure is an effective, reliable technique for introducing microcomputer use in the undergraduate laboratory. It illustrates one way in which the laboratory experience can reflect current methodologies and increase students' interest. Designing laboratory projects to exploit the strengths of the microcomputer as a research tool appears to have great promise in the teaching of psychology.

References

Bare, J. K. (1982). Microcomputers in the introductory laboratory. *Teaching of Psychology, 9,* 236-237.

Dashiell, J. F. (1937). Affective value-distances as a determinant of aesthetic judgment-times. *American Journal of Psychology, 50,* 57-69.

Shipley, W. C., Coffin, J. I., & Hadsell, K. C. (1945). Affective distance and other factors determining reaction time in judgments of color preference. *Journal of Experimental Psychology, 35,* 206-215.

FACES in the Lab and Faces in the Crowd: Integrating Microcomputers Into the Psychology Course

Blaine F. Peden
University of Wisconsin—Eau Claire
Gene D. Steinhauer
University of California—Fresno

This article describes an exercise that teaches students about methodological issues concerned with making reliable observations of behavior. After learning Ekman's (1972) Facial Affect Scoring Technique from a microcomputer program simulating expressions of emotion, students recorded the facial expression, gender, and age of people in natural settings, computed interobserver agreement scores, and submitted a laboratory report. This exercise generated much discussion about research methods, transferred skills from the classroom to a research setting, and illustrated our view that the microcomputer is a new tool that supplements, but does not replace, existing instructional techniques.

Our experimental psychology courses teach students about the use and misuse of naturalistic observation, correlation, and experimentation. Over the semesters we have devised different assignments to acquaint students with methodological issues involved in making reliable observations of behavior.

This article describes an exercise in which students learned to recognize facial expressions in the laboratory and then tested their skills by conducting a naturalistic observation study. We present and evaluate the educational benefits of this assignment, most notably active student discussion of methodological problems. Finally, we comment on the use of microcomputers in teaching interobserver agreement in particular and psychology in general.

The assignment began in a microcomputer lab where students learned to identify facial expressions of emotion. Students were asked to work in pairs. Each pair received a copy of FACES (Steinhauer, 1986), a guessing game written in Applesoft BASIC that uses Ekman's (1972) Facial Affect Scoring Technique and a set of facial features (brows-forehead, eyes-lids, and lower face) to produce six expressions of emotion on the high resolution graphics screen: anger, disgust, fear, happiness, sadness, and surprise. Student pairs worked to complete an "empty" table containing three columns for the facial features and six rows for the emotional expressions (Ekman, 1972, pp. 251-252).

The students observed an image on the screen and described each facial feature for each expression in their own words. For example, the students might write "wide open eyes" as their description under eyes-lids for the expression of "surprise." After about 30 min. the students completed the table, at which time they received a copy of Ekman's table for comparison. The students continued to view facial expressions until they resolved discrepancies between Ekman's and their own descriptions, and identified all six facial expressions without error. From start to finish, the entire laboratory phase required about 45 to 50 min.

During the second phase, students conducted a naturalistic observation study. Each pair recruited a third student who was inexperienced with FACES. The trio selected a location and agreed on a procedure in which all three observers independently made 100 observations. For example, one trio positioned themselves in the entrance to the campus library and observed every second person entering the doorway for 1 sec. Each student also received a data sheet to record each of the 100 subjects' facial expression, gender, and age. Each observer independently classified each subject's facial expression into one of seven categories. For example, each observer indicated either one of Ekman's six categories (e.g., Hager & Ekman, 1979) or a category called "other" by writing the first three letters of the category name in the blank spaces on the data sheet (e.g., ANG—anger, DIS—disgust, FEA—fear, HAP—happiness, SAD—sadness, SUR—surprise, or OTH—other). In this coding scheme, either a neutral expression or a blend of expressions was assigned to the "other" category. Finally, each observer recorded the gender and age range (i.e., 1-10, 11-20, 21-30, . . ., 61-70) of each person.

The students counted each decision for which a pair of observers agreed and computed the percentage of agreement. They performed this analysis separately for each pair of observers on each of the three categories: facial expression, gender, and age. Finally, the students wrote a report, in APA style, that included a table showing the percentage of agreement for the three pairs of observers with respect to gender, age, and expression.

The interobserver agreement scores from each report were subdivided into two categories, depending on whether both members (trained pairs) or only one member (untrained pairs) of the pair of observers was experienced with FACES. Table 1 displays the mean and range of the percentage of agreement scores for trained and untrained pairs of observers. The greater agreement for trained than untrained pairs on facial expression was statistically significant, $t(46) = 2.26$, $p < .05$; however, the differences in the agreement scores were not statistically significant for either gender, $t(46) = .82$, or age, $t(46) = .66$. The range of agreement scores was the least for gender and greatest for age.

This assignment yielded four educational benefits: (a) students were enthusiastic about it; (b) students could immediately assess newly acquired laboratory learning while conducting a study in a natural setting; (c) students learned to work cooperatively and write a paper collaboratively; and (d) students asked questions and willingly discussed methodological issues, a marked contrast from previous semesters in which assignments generated few questions and little discussion.

The assignment produced findings that prompted questions and discussion about methodological issues. First, students were troubled by the higher degree of interobserver agreement in the laboratory and the lower degree of agreement in the field. For example, they asked why they agreed perfectly when judging computer-generated facial expressions but only moderately when judging human facial expressions. The discussion period revealed that the computer program generated full frontal expressions of only six emotions for a single individual, whereas facial expressions were observed from quite different angles for many different individuals in the field. Moreover, in the laboratory the students studied the facial expression at their leisure, whereas in the field they made a decision after just 1 sec. Thus, the greater complexity of viewing conditions, the greater number of categories provided by the additional "other" category, and the restrictions on study time probably contributed to the lower agreement scores obtained in the field as compared to the laboratory. Second, the students observed that the seemingly obvious category of gender produced high, but not perfect, agreement scores, whereas facial expression and age produced only moderate agreement scores. The students asked why all categories were not equally easy to measure reliably. This question led to discussions about the relationship between nominal and actual categories, and how variables (e.g., the

Table 1. Percentage of Interobserver Agreement Scores for Field Observations

Condition		Gender	Age	Expression
Trained Pairs				
	M	99	68	59
	Range	90–100	39–98	41–86
Untrained Pairs				
	M	99	71	50
	Range	95–100	36–100	18–77

number and type of categories) affect the results. For example, even though there were seven nominal categories for age and facial expression, the actual number for age often equaled the number for gender because many trios observed individuals on campus, a location in which ages typically ranged from 18 to 24 years. The classroom discussion revealed that students who observed individuals in the student center and the campus library found it harder to agree on the ages than students who observed individuals at the YMCA or shopping malls. Apparently, it was much harder to distinguish 19- and 20-year-olds from those 21 or older on campus with only two categories than it was to distinguish individuals from a greater age range off campus with seven categories. Third, the benefit of explicit training was obvious because pairs of students previously trained to observe facial expressions produced greater agreement scores than did untrained pairs. This finding prompted more general discussions about the transfer of training, the need to assess interobserver agreement under actual conditions for data collection, and the differences between Ekman's procedure (e.g., Hager & Ekman, 1979) and this assignment. For example, even though the 9-point difference was statistically significant, it appeared small in view of the contention that Ekman can train people to judge expressions proficiently. However, Ekman provided more training than the 45 min. permitted by this assignment, and he trained and tested his subjects with photographs, whereas this assignment trained subjects with simple stimuli in the laboratory and tested them with complex stimuli in the field. Given these procedural differences, the 9% difference appeared more impressive. Finally, the differences in the means and the range of scores for trained and untrained pairs in each of the three categories prompted discussions about the role of statistics in data analysis. The nature of the discussion about descriptive and inferential statistics depended on both the educational intentions of the instructor and the sophistication of the students.

In conclusion, this assignment engendered lively discussions among undergraduate experimental psychology students about methods for naturalistic observation. In addition, features of this assignment may be useful to other instructors. First, the classroom use of a computer graphics program generated considerable student interest. Second, the computer was incorporated without allowing the technology to dominate the exercise (e.g., Leeper, 1985). Thus, this assignment illustrates our view that computers function best for part, but not all, of a learning experience and simple programs that perform one task well provide meaningful learning experiences (e.g., Stowbridge & Kugel, 1983). Third, the two parts of the exercise were integrated to promote the transfer of skills from the classroom to the field. A final and amusing outcome of this exercise was that the instructors learned to produce the different facial expressions of emotion and then used them to provide unambiguous consequences for student behavior during the remainder of the semester.

References

Ekman, P. (1972). Universal and cultural differences in facial expressions of emotion. In J . K. Cole (Ed.), *Nebraska symposium on motivation* (Vol. 19, pp. 207-283). Lincoln, NE: University of Nebraska Press.

Hager, J. C., & Ekman, P. (1979). Long-distance transmission of facial affect signals. *Ethology and Sociobiology, 1,* 77-82.

Leeper, M. R. (1985). Microcomputers in education. *American Psychologist, 40,* 1-18.

Steinhauer, G. D. (1986). *Artificial behavior: Computer simulation of psychological processes.* Englewood Cliffs, NJ: Prentice-Hall.

Stowbridge, M. D., & Kugel, P. (1983, April). Learning to learn by learning to play. *Creative Computing,* pp. 180-188.

Notes

1. We thank various colleagues, notably Dexter Gormley, Erna Kelly, and Allen Keniston, for their comments on a draft of this manuscript.

2. Copies of the assignment and data sheet are available at no charge from the first author. Information about FACES and related programs is available by writing the second author in care of Artificial Behavior, Incorporated, 4974 North Fresno, Suite 326, Fresno, CA 93726 or by calling (209) 229-4703.

6. USING POPULAR MEDIA AND SCHOLARLY PUBLICATIONS

From the Laboratory to the Headlines: Teaching Critical Evaluation of Press Reports of Research

Patricia A. Connor-Greene
Clemson University

This article describes a classroom exercise and an individual assignment designed to teach critical evaluation of research reports in the popular press. The classroom exercise uses active and collaborative learning to apply the principles of scientific investigation, particularly the distinction between correlation and causation, in analyzing the limitations of a newspaper account of a research study. The individual assignment requires students to locate and critique a newspaper or magazine summary of research. The goal of these two exercises is to engage students in active learning about research methods and help them to become critical consumers of media accounts of research findings.

Undergraduate education in psychology should help students understand scientific methodology and improve their critical thinking. These are important skills, given the frequency with which research findings are reported in the mass media. People tend to perceive the press as an objective source of information, despite the fact that subjective decisions determine what is reported (Howitt, 1982). Constrained by space limitations, newspaper and magazine depictions of research findings often omit essential information that would permit the reader to evaluate adequately the strength of the research conclusions. News summaries often distort research findings by sensationalizing the results, minimizing discussion of the research limitations, and confusing correlation with causation (Jacobs & Eccles, 1985).

The distinction between correlation and causation is essential to understanding research methods and statistics (Boneau, 1990). Although a recent analysis indicated that correlational designs are discussed in 87% of introductory psychology textbooks (Hendricks, Marvel, & Barrington, 1990), I often hear upper level students make causal statements when describing correlational studies. The frequency of this error highlights the need to develop teaching strategies that emphasize this important distinction.

The exercise described in this article involves a collaborative, active-learning task in which students use information about the scientific method to analyze a newspaper account of a research study. The technique is designed to increase students' awareness of the distinction between correlation and causation and to encourage them to become critical consumers of research reported in the popular press. I use this exercise in abnormal psychology classes, but it is also appropriate for introductory psychology and other courses that address research methods.

The Class Exercise

Students are given a homework assignment to study the research methods chapter in their textbook and be prepared to discuss these concepts in class. During the next class period, each student is assigned to a small group of 4 or 5 people. One member of each group serves as recorder, and each group member is expected to participate in the small group discussion. Every student is given a copy of an article from USA TODAY titled, "Gay Men Show Cell Distinction" (Snider, 1991; see Appendix) and the following list of questions to be addressed by the group.

1. What conclusion does this article imply? What statements in the article suggest this conclusion?
2. Is this conclusion warranted by the study described? Why or why not?
3. Is the title an accurate summary of the study described? Why or why not?
4. Can this study "prove . . . being gay or lesbian is not a matter of choice," as the task force spokesman suggests? Why or why not?
5. What questions do you have after reading this article ?
6. If you had the power to create guidelines for the press's reporting of a research study, what would you recommend?

Class Discussion

After each group addresses these questions (which takes approximately 40 min.), the entire class reconvenes to discuss the group responses. At this point, I provide excerpts, via overhead projector, from the original research article published in *Science* (LeVay, 1991) that is the subject of the *USA TODAY* article. Students identify omissions and distortions in the newspaper's account of the original research study. By examining both the newspaper article and the original research report, they can now identify flaws or Unanswered questions in the original study and recognize any misrepresentation of the research in the newspaper article.

Usually the small-group responses to the questions are very similar. All groups interpret the newspaper article (Snider, 1991) as implying that male homosexuality is caused by smaller brain cell nuclei. They cite the statements "The debate over the *roots* of *homosexuality has* been going on a long time, but this finding 'suggests a *biological phenomenon*' " (p. 1D) and "It might explain *"why* male homosexuality is present in most human populations'" (p. 1D) [all italics added] as suggesting causality.

In deciding whether this implication of causality is warranted by the research study as described, students discuss the requirements for a true experimental design. They recognize LeVay's (1991) study as a correlational design because it simply identifies a relation between size of brain cell nuclei and sexual orientation. Discussing alternative interpretations of this association (e.g., sexual orientation could affect size of brain cell nuclei, rather than the reverse; the differences may be caused by a third variable) helps to clarify the seriousness of the error of confusing correlation and causation.

Students note two problems with the title of the newspaper article. First, they think the title suggests that all cells are different in gay men, but the news article refers only to brain cell nuclei. (The difference is actually much more specific than implied in the news article; it is only one area of the anterior hypothalamus.) Second, the title suggests that gay men are the "different" ones, but the article reports gay men's brain cell nuclei to be similar in size to those of women. Consequently, the "different" ones are actually the heterosexual men. Then we discuss the political and social context in which *normal* and *deviant* are defined and how subjectivity and bias can occur in the formulation of research questions and in the interpretation and reporting of findings.

The quote from the news article (Snider, 1991) that the study can "prove . . . being a gay or lesbian is not a matter of choice" (p. 1D) provides an excellent opportunity to discuss the nature of scientific experimentation and the inappropriateness of the term *prove* in science.

Students generate questions after reading the news article (Snider, 1991), setting the stage for discussion of the specifics of LeVay's (1991) study. After obtaining information from LeVay's article, students are able to identify limitations in the study itself. (For example, the heterosexual men were "presumed" to be heterosexual; for all but two of them, there was no available information on sexual orientation; there was no comparison of heterosexual and homosexual women; the actual cause of death can vary greatly among AIDS patients; and the brain cell nuclei differences could be a result of the disease process itself.

Students always ask "How did this study get published? How could a respectable scientist confuse correlation and causation?" At this point, I show them several quotes from LeVay's (1991) article in which he pointed out the speculative and preliminary nature of his research, identified limitations of his study, and emphasized that it is correlational and does not permit causal inferences. Then students see that the USA TODAY article (Snider, 1991) sensationalizes LeVay's results and that Snider, not LeVay, confused correlation with causation.

In addition, I show the students the following excerpt from "Is Homosexuality Biological?" (1991), which appeared in the same issue of *Science* as LeVay's (1991) article.

> Lest eager believers jump to too many conclusions, LeVay points out that his finding *contains no direct evidence that the difference he has observed actually causes homosexuality.* He and others in the field acknowledge that the paper *needs replication,* since such studies are difficult and somewhat subjective. "Simon is very good; he's extremely well-equipped to make those observations," said one neuroscientist who is familiar with LeVay's work. *"But we ought to put off big speculation until it is confirmed."* (p. 956) [all italics added]

Clearly, speculation was not put off until LeVay's (1991) findings were replicated; the study was widely reported in the print media and on the network news. Nearly all the students in my class had heard or read about this study and were surprised to learn that the research did not address causality. The extensive media coverage, contrasted with the preliminary nature of the research itself, helps students recognize that factors other than scientific merit may determine degree of media attention and that science and the reporting of science are not value-free.

Students generated recommendations for changing the press's approach to reporting scientific research. These recommendations included discussing limitations of studies, improving accuracy of headlines, distinguishing between correlational and experimental studies, providing a full reference citation to enable the reader to locate the original research article, and making the degree of media attention proportional to the scientific strength of the study.

Individual Assignment

After completing the class exercise, students were individually assigned to find a newspaper or magazine summary of research and compare it to the original journal article. Their written critiques assessed the accuracy of the popular press article and discussed important omissions or distortions in the popular press article (e.g., limitations of the study and accuracy of the title).

Because some popular press articles contain serious distortions and others are accurate summaries, this assignment helps students become critical evaluators rather than simply dismissing all popular press articles as flawed. Several weeks are needed for this assignment. Most students reported that although press summaries of research were easy to find, many of these articles failed to include a citation sufficient to locate the original article.

Evaluation and Conclusions

The day after participating in the class exercise, students (N = 33) anonymously completed a four-item questionnaire using a scale ranging from *very much so* (1) to *not at all* (5). The items and mean ratings are as follows: (a) This exercise gave me a clearer understanding of correlational research *(M* = 1.70), (b) this exercise will help me evaluate media reports of research more critically in the future *(M = 1.55)*, (c) this exercise was interesting *(M* = 1.61), and (d) it was helpful to work in groups for the class exercise *(M =* 1.61). Students' written comments, such as "It gives me a good idea of how to look at articles critically, " "newspaper articles need to be examined much more closely than I've done previously," and "this will help me remember the difference between correlational and experimental studies," suggested positive aspects of the exercise. Students were also asked for written comments after completing their individual assignment. Overall, students perceived the assignment as valuable.

The class exercise and individual assignment encourage students to apply information learned in class to their outside experiences (i.e., reading the newspaper), which makes their learning more personally relevant. The exercises help students understand why the popular press is not an appropriate source of information to be used in writing term papers. The fact that the press typically emphasizes results and not methods convinces students that they can properly evaluate the strengths and weaknesses of a study only after examining the original source. Greater awareness of the importance of precision in reporting research methods and findings should encourage students to be more critical of information

they read in newspapers, journal articles, and textbooks.

References

Boneau, C. A. (1990). Psychological literacy: A first approximation. *American Psychologist, 45,* 891-900.

Hendricks, B., Marvel, M. K., & Barrington, B. L. (1990). The dimensions of psychological research. *Teaching of Psychology, 17,* 76-82.

Howitt, D. (1982). *Mass media and social problems.* New York: Pergamon.

Is homosexuality biological? (1991). *Science, 253,* 956-957.

Jacobs, J., & Eccles, J. (1985). Gender differences in math ability: The impact of media reports on parents. *Educational Researcher, 14*(3), 20-25.

LeVay, S. (1991). A difference in hypothalamic structure between heterosexual and homosexual men. *Science, 253,* 1034-1037.

Snider, M. (1991, August 30). *Gay men show cell distinction.* USA TODAY, p. 1 D.

Note

I thank Charles L. Brewer, Ruth L. Ault, and the anonymous reviewers for their helpful comments.

Appendix

Gay Men Show Cell Distinction
By Mike Snider
USA TODAY

A new study of the brain suggests a biological difference between homosexual and heterosexual men.

The debate over the roots of homosexuality has been going on a long time, but this finding "suggests a biological phenomenon," says neurologist Dennis Landis, Case Western Reserve University, Cleveland, in comments accompanying the study in today's *Science.*

It might explain "why male homosexuality is present in most human populations, despite cultural constraints."

In a study of the brain cells from 41 people, *25* of whom had died from AIDS, certain brain cells of heterosexual men had nuclei that were more than twice as large as those in homosexual men, says researcher Simon LeVay, Salk Institute for Biological Studies.

The difference was apparently not caused by AIDS, because it was constant in a comparison of cells from heterosexual and homosexual male AIDS victims. LeVay also found homosexual men's cells similar in size to women's.

Robert Bray, spokesman for National Gay and Lesbian Task Force, called the study "fascinating."

"If used ethically, (it) can shed light on human sexuality and prove what we've always believed—being a gay or lesbian is not a matter of choice.

"Used unethically, the data could reinforce the political agenda of anti-gay groups that advocate 'curing' or 'repairing' homosexuals—the notion that gay people could be made straight by tweaking a chromosome here or readjusting a cell there."

Note

Interview With a Former Hostage As Class Material

S. Viterbo McCarthy
Regis College

How one arrives at knowledge of psychological principles is usually an objective of any laboratory experience in psychology. The realization of this *how is* affected, in turn, by the way we choose to define the science of psychology. If we think of science as "the observation of uniformities in nature," the behaviors reported by a single individual during an interview may provide material for exploring the meaning of operational definitions. In addition, the content may suggest the usefulness of such interview material for introducing the novice researcher to the value of an *N* = 1 or a case study approach for the purpose of hypothesis-finding, particularly in a unique real-life circumstance that could never be brought under controlled laboratory study. To illustrate, consider the first detailed interview given by the former hostage, Kathryn Knob, to Sandra G. Boodman of the *Washington Post.* There, in nineteen short paragraphs, some of the events, thoughts, feelings, and behaviors of 444 days as a hostage were reported (Boodman, 1981).

Before exposing the class to the content of this interview, I discussed the meaning of an operational definition. To show that the measurement of a concept required its description in concrete terms, several examples of an operational definition were either offered by me or contributed by the students. Then the interview with Kathryn Knob was distributed for study; the class was directed to attend particularly to the observable aspects of behavior. From information revealed through the interview, the students were asked to respond as they thought Kathryn Knob might respond to a Coping Inventory (Horowitz & Wilner, 1980, pp. 373-374); each item could be checked in terms of 0 (does not apply), 1 (does apply), or 2 (does apply and very helpful). The total score, obtained from 33 items, samples three coping strategies: (a) 11 items—turning to other attitudes or other activities; (b) 16 items—working through the event; and (c) 6 items— socialization. To further assess understanding of operational meanings, the students marked each statement (a), (b), or (c), according to their judgment of the coping strategy exemplified by the item.

Students were given the standardized key for the Coping Inventory and they obtained scores for the subtests and overall coping behavior of the former hostage. By use of the key, they obtained feedback on the accuracy of their operational definitions for each coping strategy. These results provoked many questions, lively discussion, and considerable comment, not only when they were gathered early in semester, but also when related problems emerged in remaining laboratory sessions. Consideration of some of these concerns will highlight a few of the theoretical and methodological issues embedded in the unobtrusive study of one former hostage.

First, any expectation that a particular behavior has only one index was shattered as students began to realize the myriad concrete connotations possible for coping behavior, and the complexities in its measurement by single isolated items, by groups of items identifying a constellation of similar behaviors, or, by a composite of several to yield a total score. There are many concrete meanings for socialization items on the Coping Inventory: e.g., item 8 of subtest (c), "I sought increased emotional support from others," was linked with (1) the companionship with Elizabeth Ann Swift, Koob's roommate after her first four months in solitary confinement; (2) bonds with loved ones whose mail from home decorated hostage living space; (3) bonds with captors, Iranian female students who acted as guards; (4) awareness of the presence of other hostages in the embassy compound as a consequence of learning "to read wastebaskets" or "to recognize footsteps."

Second, as students attempted to justify their ratings on inventory items, the perils inherent in moving from observation of behavior to its *interpretation,* and the innumerable factors influencing this leap became apparent. There was only chance probability or an approximately equal number of students at each point of the rating scale for some items: e.g., item 3 of subtest (b) on the Coping Inventory, "I tried to work out how the event related to things in my past." Students rating the statement 0 noted the lack of operational meaning for this item in the content of the interview, whereas those choosing to rate the statement 2 found their explanations in attributions originating within the respondent. On the other hand, there was consensus in assigning a rating of 2 to item 13 of subtest (a), "I sought consolation in philosophy or religion." In assessing the hostage experience, students noted that Koob felt she "grew spiritually very much . . .;" other interview vignettes for her description of a typical day included "Mornings were spent in silent prayers and Bible reading . . . ," "After dinner came more prayer . . ."

As students concentrated on matches that showed high agreement between statements from the Coping Inventory and the interview with Kathryn Knob, they evidenced curiosity about possible parallels between the effective coper and the mature personality. Their inquisitiveness opened the way for additional questions: To what theory do we turn for characteristics of maturity? Will our method of study involve a single individual or a large group?

To illustrate the fruitfulness of an *N* = 1 study for detecting "tracers" capable of being examined for their appositeness to a few theories of personality, we recommended perusal of *Letters from Jenny* (Allport, 1965). Repetition of this laboratory experience with interview material for another former hostage was encouraged. We also noted Figley's extension of this method to include content analysis of items clipped from newspapers and magazines, or gathered from radio or TV broadcasts since "catastrophic events provide some very valuable insight into the general nature of human behavior" (Schaar, 1981, p. 9).

In brief, early exposure to such an unpredictable and globally relevant experience as the hostage crisis helped the newcomer to the laboratory. Thereafter, as students replicated a variety of laboratory projects, this experience served as a point of reference; in the choice of tests or measures, students were sensitive to the need for distinguishing among different kinds of reliability and validity; in the process of drawing generalizations from conclusions obtained from small groups, students reverted to earlier questions about how the coping behavior of a single former hostage compared to that of 51 others; in the search for an explanation of outcomes, students were perceptive of the need to question possible alternatives. Finally, it is my opinion that an early exposure to the laboratory experience described followed by a series of controlled studies will give students an experiential basis for expanding their understanding of the boundaries of psychology while cultivating their appreciation of the complementarity of idiographic and nomothetic approaches.

References

Allport, G. W. (Ed.). *Letters from Jenny.* New York: Harcourt, Brace & World, 1965.

Boodman, S. G. Knob: I knew I'd walk away. *Boston Sunday Globe*, February 1, 1981, p. 16.

Horowitz, M. J. & Wilner, N. Life events, stress and coping. In Peon, L. W. (ed.). *Aging in the 1980s: Psychological issues.* Washington, DC: American Psychological Association, 1980.

Schaar, K. Charles Figley: Working on a theory of what it takes to survive. *APA Monitor,* 1981, *12* (3), 9.

Science and Television Commercials: Adding Relevance to the Research Methodology Course

Paul R. Solomon
Williams College

Teaching experimental methodology can be planned to enhance the probability of transfer to life experiences.

A recent APA survey (Kulik, 1973) indicated that although the specific courses required of psychology majors varies considerably from institution to institution, 94.4% of colleges and universities reporting required at least one course in Statistics-Research Methods. As the APA survey indicates: 'Past conferences on undergraduate education in psychology have affirmed the importance of instruction in statistics and methodology in the major program. Consideration of the role that methodology plays in a frontier science indicates that the emphasis has been appropriate" (Kulik, 1973, p. 55).

Based on the near universal nature of the statistics-methodology requirement as well as its importance as a foundation for subsequent psychology courses, it is not surprising that considerable effort has been put forth to develop innovative techniques to teach these courses. A recent APA Division 2 symposium, for example, was devoted to alternative methods for teaching the first course in experimental psychology (Siege, 1975). Similarly, a recently published summary of innovative teaching techniques in psychology also placed heavy emphasis on the statistics-research methodology area (Maas & Kleiber, 1976).

If for no reason other than sheer quantity, it is not surprising that these innovations encompass a wide variety of techniques. What is surprising, however, is that not one of them is specifically devoted to demonstrating to the student that a command of research skills, and in particular the experimental method, has value outside the laboratory situation. Research methodology courses should be made relevant; that is, such courses should demonstrate that gaining a working knowledge of the experimental method is more than an academic exercise.

The intent of the present paper is to make the case that experimental psychology courses can be relevant to issues outside of psychology proper and then to describe one method which may help accomplish this.

Should Experimental Psychology Be Relevant?
Perhaps the most common plea of the undergraduate psychology student, and the undergraduate student in general, is for relevance. A Carnegie Commission survey revealed that 91% of 70,000 undergraduates questioned would like their courses to be "more relevant to contemporary life problems." Similarly, the concern for relevance is high on the list for professional psychologists. Lipsey (1974) summarized the results of a survey conducted by a group of graduate students at the Johns Hopkins University. The survey, which sampled full-time graduate students and faculty, asked: "What do you feel is the single most important issue confronting psychology today?" Half of the graduate students and 47% of the faculty responding indicated that relevance was the most important issue. The second most mentioned issue, research and theory, ran a distant second with only 12% of the students and 19% of the faculty considering it important.

What Makes Subject Matter Relevant? Although students and faculty appear to agree on the need for relevance, there is considerably less consensus on what constitutes relevant subject matter. A study by Menges and Trumpeter (1972), however, pointed out that the term relevance, although often used idiosyncratically, can be translated into usefulness, both in terms of personal needs and applicability to "real-world" problems.

Even though it is difficult to determine the extent to which undergraduate curricula satisfy personal needs, it seems possible to assess what skills the undergraduate acquires that may be useful in dealing with "real-world" problems.

How Do We Demonstrate That The Experimental Method Is Relevant? If, as previous studies suggest, relevance may be equated with usefulness in solving "real-world" problems, then one way to show the relevance of the experimental method is to show how it is useful in dealing with an everyday problem common to nearly everyone. Fortunately, this is a much simpler task than it seems.

Professional psychologists have recently begun to apply experimental techniques to consumer affairs.

230

Indeed, Perloff (1968) and Jacoby (1975) reviewed an accumulating body of literature showing a growing relationship between social psychology and consumer affairs. Consumer affairs, it seems, fits the criteria of being a real-world problem common to most everyone. Consequently, one way to convince the undergraduates that the experimental method is relevant is to show them the applicability of the method to consumer problems. To accomplish this I have had students use experimental methodology to test the claims made in television commercials.

Science and TV Commercials. Even in the absence of data it seems reasonable to assume that a strong majority of undergraduate psychology students watch television and thus necessarily watch television commercials. Many of these commercials base their advertising claims on the results of "scientific studies" (so named or implied). The television advertiser, it seems, would like the public to believe that since the advertising claims are based on "scientific research," the results are beyond reproach. Advertisers, however, have a concern paramount to the pursuit of scientific knowledge: They want to sell their product. Consequently, many of the commercials represent excellent examples of experimental bias if not of confounding.

It seems, then, that a working knowledge of the experimental method can be applied to evaluating advertising claims. With this in mind, I have given students in my experimental psychology courses the option to replicate the experiments used as the basis for TV commercials. More recently, I have devoted an entire 4-week Winter Studies course to this endeavor. During both the experimental psychology and winter studies courses students are given a firm background in fundamentals of experimental design and analysis. They are then asked to select a commercial which uses 'suspect methodology" and to replicate it using proper experimental design and procedures.

We have replicated research claims of 15 television commercials with mixed results in terms of verification of those claims. In general, these studies attempted to adhere to the procedures used by the advertisers, but in virtually all instances either a modification, intended to eliminate a possible bias or confounding, or an extension was incorporated. Although it is not feasible to present all 15 studies, I would like to present results of three most recent experiments. They are presented with a two-fold purpose. First, to indicate the type of study we have conducted and secondly, to share some interesting consumer information.

Is White Cloud Softer?[1]

Procter and Gamble, the manufacturers of White Cloud bathroom tissue (toilet paper is apparently a taboo word), make the claim that White Cloud is "the softest bathroom tissue on earth." The Consumer Services Division of Procter and Gamble informed us that this television advertising claim was based upon two kinds of softness tests: a technical test made by trained judges, and a consumer softness test made by a group of representative panelists who felt the tissue and made a decision about the softness. Since the consumer softness test forms the basis for the television commercial (and since we had no trained judges) we decided to replicate this test.

Method. The subjects were 50 male and female college students. The bathroom tissues used in this study were: Sofpac (Marcal), Softweave (Scott), Charmin (Procter and Gamble), and Nibroc (the tissue used at Williams).

Procedure. Subjects were randomly assigned to one of five conditions. In four of the conditions, subjects were asked to compare White Cloud to one of the four other tissues. Subjects in the fifth condition were asked to decide between two samples of White Cloud.

Each subject used the nonpreferred hand to judge the softness of the bathroom tissue. To assure that the same part of the hand was used in each comparison, the subjects wore a glove with about one inch of the thumb and forefinger removed. Each roll of tissue was concealed behind a screen which contained two holes, each large enough for a hand to fit through.

Each subject compared the same two brands ten times. Following each comparison the portion of the roll that was handled was discarded. Subjects always sampled the tissue on the left first, and the position of White Cloud and the comparison tissue was alternated over each 10 trial blocks using a Gellerman Sequence. Thus each subject made a total of 10 comparisons and following each comparison indicated which was softer.

Results and Discussion. When subjects compared White Cloud to White Cloud, 51% indicated a preference for the tissue on the left and 49% indicated a preference for the tissue on the right. This suggests that the subjects had no position preference.

Table 1 shows the number of people who selected White Cloud versus the four comparison tissues. The data indicate White Cloud was a strong choice in all comparisons. Chi square tests confirmed these observations by indicating that White Cloud was preferred significantly more frequently than the other brand in each test, $ps < .001$.

Insofar as we can generalize from our sample, the data from this study clearly support the advertising claim that White Cloud is the softest tissue. It is also interesting to note that the increased softness of White Cloud is not reflected in an increased cost. The bathroom tissues used in this study had the following per sheet prices: Softpac, .061¢; White Cloud, .055; and Charmin, .041. The lower price of Charmin may be in part due to the fact that it is a one-ply tissue but the others are two-ply tissues (interestingly, Charmin appears to be the one-ply analogue of White Cloud).

Table 1
Number of People Selecting White Cloud or Comparison Tissue

Comparison Tissue	Tissue Selected			
	White Cloud	Comparison Tissue	No pref- erence	χ^2
Softpac	95	2	3	89.2*
Softweave	81	12	7	51.2*
Nibroc	98	0	2	98.0*
Charmin	78	9	14	54.7*
All combined	352	23	26	288.6*

*$p < .001$

Finally, as the White Cloud Tissue manufacturer points out, the finding that White Cloud is the softest tissue does not necessarily make it the best tissue. other factors such as texture and absorption could also be factors.

Sure or Ban: Which Keeps You Drier?[2]

Both Ban (Bristol Myers) and Sure (Procter and Gamble) claim "to keep you dryer." The two products make a similar advertising claim: that they are the most effective at preventing wetness and thus the most preferable. The purpose of the present experiment was to test these claims by a direct comparison of the two antiperspirants. To accomplish this, both subjective, based on the preference of users, and objective, based on the Galvanic Skin Response (GSR), measures of wetness were used.

Method. The subjects were 44 male and female college students. Twenty-four subjects participated in the subjective portion of the study and the remaining 20 subjects participated in the objective portion.

Four-ounce cans of Sure antiperspirant and Ban antiperspirant were used. Each can was covered with paper and the spray buttons were changed so that they matched. The objective measures- of wetness were taken with two Lafayette Instrument Company (model #7601C) psycho-galvanometers.

Procedure. During the subjective portion of the experiment, subjects were randomly assigned to one of three groups with eight subjects per group. Subjects in Group 1 applied Sure under each arm (Group S-S), subjects in the second group (Group BUS) applied Ban under the right arm and Sure under the left, and subjects in Group 3 (Group S-B) applied Sure under the right arm and Ban under the left. All subjects were instructed to hold the can six inches from their underarm and to apply the deodorant for two seconds. At the end of an 8 hour day, subjects were asked which arm felt drier.

Subjects in the objective portion of the experiment were told they were participating in a study on lie detection. The workings of the Psychogalvanometer were explained and each subject was told that the machine would be used to determine when they had lied. For one-half the subjects Ban was applied to the palm of the right hand while the remaining half had Sure applied to the right palm. The subjects were told that the spray was to facilitate the operation of the psychogalvanometer.

Subjects were wired to the psychogalvanometers (one to the right hand and one to the left) and asked to select a number between 1 and 5 but not to reveal the number to the experimenter. The subjects were then told that the experimenter would try to guess the number, but for each guess the subject was to reply: "No that's not the number." The experimenter then guessed the numbers 1 through 5. Immediately following each response, a GSR reading was taken and the subject's score was determined by the number of times the GSR reading exceeded 60 microamperes above baseline (with a maximum score of 1 deflection per trial). Thus lower scores indicated drier palms.

Results and Discussion. *Subjective Test.* Of the eight subjects in Group S-S, seven indicated that the right arm was drier. Six of the subjects were right-handed and one left-handed. The subject who had a left preference was also right-handed.

Of the subjects in Groups BUS, eight preferred Ban, three Sure, and one was undecided. Identical results were obtained in Group S-B. Since Groups BUS and S-B yielded the same results, their data were pooled for statistical analysis. A chi square test performed on the 22 subjects who expressed a preference revealed that Ban was preferred significantly more than Sure, $\chi^2 (1) = 9.09$, $p < .01$. In addition, this preference was strong enough to overcome the right arm bias suggested by Group S-S. In fact, of the 16 subjects who preferred Ban, eight had applied it under the left arm.

Objective Test. The results of the objective test showed Sure to be slightly, although not significantly so, more effective than Ban. Subjects receiving Sure gave a mean of 6.4 meter deflections on the sprayed hand and 8.6 on the non-sprayed hand. Subjects using Ban gave a mean of 5.9 deflections on the sprayed hand and 7.7 on the non-sprayed hand. A two-way analysis of variance, in which presence or absence of deodorant served as one variable and deodorant type as the other, revealed no significant main effects or interaction, $Fs < 1$, $ps > .05$. This suggests that whereas there is a trend for deodorant sprayed hands to remain drier, this is not affected by deodorant type.

Thus the subjective portion of this study reveals a strong preference for Ban, while the objective test shows no difference. The failure to find that the sprayed hands remained significantly drier in the objective test, however, raises the possibility that this is not a sensitive way to measure dryness.

The Pepsi versus Coke Taste Test[3]

In 1976 the Pepsi-Cola Company launched a comparative advertising campaign which indicated that people preferred the taste of Pepsi-Cola to that of Coca-Cola. Basically, the Pepsi-Cola Company made the following three claims: (a) Nationwide, more people prefer the taste of Pepsi-Cola to that of Coca-Cola, (b) nationwide, more Coca-Cola drinkers prefer the taste of Pepsi-Cola to Coca-Cola, and (c) nationwide, more Pepsi-Cola drinkers prefer the taste of Pepsi-Cola to Coca-Cola. These claims are based on a survey prepared by Marketing Research Incorporated of New York for the Pepsi-Cola Company. The survey was based on a nationwide sample of 3,000 people over the age of 14. In this taste test, each subject was given one taste choice between a glass containing Pepsi and one containing Coke.

The present experiment sought to replicate this study while incorporating several changes in design. In our study each subject was given three trials as opposed to one trial in the Pepsi study. This was done to determine if there was consistency in brand selection. In addition, while the Pepsi study presented each subject with two glasses (one Coke and one Pepsi) on each trial and asked the subject which they preferred, subjects in the present study were presented with three glasses (one Coke and two Pepsi or one Pepsi and two Coke) and asked to indicate which they most preferred and which they least preferred.

Method. The subjects were 24 male and female college students. Pepsi-Cola (12 ounce bottles) and Coca-Cola (10 ounce bottles) were purchased from a local supermarket. Colas were poured immediately before each taste test and between tests they were stored in an ice chest and maintained at 40°F. Subjects were not allowed to observe the pouring of the soda and each person sampled the colas through plastic straws.

Procedure. Each subject was asked to fill out a questionnaire which included a question on Cola preference. The subjects were then presented with nine glasses, each containing one ounce of Cola. The glasses were arranged in groups of three. Within each group, there were two glasses containing Pepsi and one containing Coke or two containing Coke and one containing Pepsi. The order in which the Colas were presented to each subject was counterbalanced. After sampling each group of three Colas, subjects were asked which they most preferred and which they least preferred. The subject then took a sip of water and followed the same procedure on the second and third trials. If the subject selected Coke as most preferred and Pepsi as least preferred, Coke was scored as the preferred Cola; if Pepsi was selected as most preferred and Coke as least preferred, Pepsi was considered the preferred beverage; if the same Cola was selected as both most and least preferred, no preference was scored. After three trials were completed the subjects were informed as to the contents of each glass.

Results and Discussion. Table 2 presents a summary of the taste test data used as the basis for the Pepsi commercial ("Pepsi-Cola, %" entries), and the taste test data from the present study in a similar format. In contrast to Pepsi, our data indicate: (a) More people prefer Coke, and (b) more Coke drinkers prefer Coke. Consistent with Pepsi's data is our finding that more Pepsi drinkers prefer Pepsi.

Although our data are presented in a fashion which allows direct comparison with Pepsi's findings, this may not be the most revealing way to display them. Table 2 also presents the same data in terms of frequencies. What is most revealing here is the small number of subjects, six, who state a preference for Pepsi. Consequently, the finding that nearly twice the percentage of people who stated a preference for Pepsi preferred Pepsi to Coke is attributable to a difference of one trial. Because frequency information is not provided in the Pepsi report, and although they tested 3,000 subjects, it is impossible to determine if their claim regarding a preference for Pepsi among people who have a stated preference for Pepsi is also based on a relatively small number of subjects.

Perhaps the largest discrepancy between our findings and those of Pepsi is the number of subjects who did not show a preference in the taste test. This is probably due to the use of different testing procedures. In the Pepsi study two choices were given: one Pepsi and one Coke. No preference was scored if the subject could not choose one. This occurred in 6.6% of the trials. In our procedure three choices were given, either two Coke and one Pepsi or two Pepsi and one Coke, and the subject had to indicate which they preferred most and which they preferred least. No preference was scored if they selected the same Cola as most and least preferred. Of the 72 trials conducted, there were 27 instances in which the subjects indicated no preference. This suggests that it is difficult to taste the difference between the two Colas. Examination of the three trials for each subject also indicates this is the case. Of the 24 subjects tested only four selected Pepsi as most preferred and Coke as least preferred on all three trials and only five selected Coke as most preferred and Pepsi as least preferred on three consecutive trials. The remaining 15 subjects had at least one instance of a mixed preference.

In summary, our data are not consistent with the Pepsi claim. Since our sample was considerably smaller and more homogeneous than Pepsi's, it is possible that this accounts for the difference. Perhaps more important, our results also suggest that most subjects have difficulty in consistently telling the difference between the two Colas and that the two-choice test used by Pepsi may not be sensitive to this.

General Discussion

From the perspective of using "Science and TV Commercials" as a technique to teach research methodology, this undertaking was quite gratifying. The students demonstrated considerable enthusiasm while collecting data as well as curiosity as to the outcome of the experiments.[4] The scientific curiosity displayed by the students appeared to switch the motive for completing the data collection from one of meeting the requirements of the course to one of finding out which product was superior. In addition, the students not only seemed interested in their own projects, but also in the data other students were collecting. Throughout the term students inquired as to the program and results of other groups. During semesters in which students conducted more traditional independent projects this enthusiasm rarely, if ever, occurred. Finally, many students showed a continued interest at the end of the semester by communicating their results to the advertisers.

The enthusiasm and curiosity displayed by the students engaged in those projects might be perceived as a trade off for "watered down" course content. As Menges and Trumpeter(1972) pointed out, however, the perceived difficulty of a course is independent of its perceived relevance. In the present series of experiments, in fact, we would make the case that they required more work than traditional laboratory experiments. In conducting the literature survey, for example, the students were not given a set of references, nor was it apparent what topics should be reviewed in the various abstracts. Rather, the students were required to gather information from a variety of areas in presenting the background for their experiments. In terms of methodology, the student was not given a design and procedure. Rather, they were required to improve and expand an existing methodology with the intent of conducting a more valid test of the products In several instances this technique produced innovative (especially for the beginning student) methodologies and acquainted the student with the problems encountered in original research.

In as much as the results of the studies ranged from complete affirmation (White Cloud Study) to direct opposition (Pepsi and Coke taste test) of the advertiser's claim, the data suggest that the students were not simply making a series of Type I or II errors, but had actually devised experiments which had the sensitivity to detect differences between products.

References

Jacoby, J. Consumer psychology as a social psychological sphere of action. *American Psychologist,* 1975, *30,* 977-987.

Kulik, J. A. *Undergraduate education in psychology.* Washington, DC: American Psychological Association, 1973.

Lipsey, M. W. Research and relevance: A survey of graduate students and faculty in psychology. *American Psychologist*, 1974, *29,* 541-553.

Maas, J. B., & Kleiber, D. A. *Directory of teaching innovations in psychology.* Washington, D.C.: American Psychological Association, 1976.

Menges, R. J., & Trumpeter, P. W. Toward an empirical definition of relevance in undergraduate instruction. *American Psychologist,* 1972, *27,* 213-217.

Perloff, R. Consumer analysis. *Annual Review of Psychology,* 1968, *19,* 437-466.

Siegal, M. H. Symposium: Teaching the experimental psychology course. *Teaching* of *Psychology,* 1975, *4,* 162-163.

Table 2
Taste Test Preference for Pepsi-Cola and Coca-Cola

Taste Test Preference	Source	Stated Preference			
		Coca-Cola	Pepsi-Cola	No Preference	Total
Pepsi-Cola	Pepsi-Cola, %	49.8	58.2	52.6	51.7
	Our study, %	19.0	12.0	17.0	17.0
	Our study, freq.	7	2	3	12
Coca-Cola	Pepsi-Cola, %	44.2	37.3	41.7	41.7
	Our study, %	59.0	6.0	56.0	46.0
	Our study, freq.	22	1	10	33
No Prefer.	Pepsi-Cola, %	6.0	4.5	5.7	6.6
	Our study, %	22.0	82.0	28.0	38.0
	Our study, freq.	8	14	5	27

Notes

1. This study was done by David L. O'Connell, David D. Sterling, Carl J. Tippit, and K. Elizabeth Wray.
2. This study was done by Fred L. Avery, Jeffrey J. Brinker, Jeffrey C. Hines, Clifford W. Pleatman, and David L. Rashin.
3. This study was done by William G. Antypass, Jr., Lisa F. Halperin, and Stuart W. Reed.
4. Space limitations prohibited the reporting of a fourth study on flashlight batteries by Arthur M. Finch, Thomas L. Keller, Brendan T. O'Neill, and James A. Parsons. It must be noted that these four students contributed to the design of all the studies reported, as did the students acknowledged in notes 1, 2, and 3.
5. The author would like to thank Andrew B. Crider, Bruce W. Godfrey, Alexandra T. Pietrewicz, and Richard 0. Rouse for their helpful comments on an earlier version of this paper.

Devising Relevant and Topical Undergraduate Laboratory Projects: The Core Article Approach

Kerry Chamberlain
Massey University

This article describes an approach to devising realistic laboratory projects to enhance research training for undergraduates. An appropriate core article serves as the basis for each project, which Wolves full or partial replication of an experiment from the core article. Advantages and limitations of the method are discussed.

The value of research experience in the undergraduate curriculum is widely recognized (Edwards, 1981; Palladino, Carsrud, Hulicka, & Benjamin, 1982; VandeCreek & Fleischer, 1984), and various approaches can be taken to provide this experience (e.g., Carroll, 1986; Chamberlain, 1986; Kerber, 1983; Palladino et al., 1982). The most common approach is probably the class laboratory project, which achieves several purpose, ranging from giving students research experience to developing their abilities in statistical analyses.

Several innovative procedures for laboratory assignments have been proposed. Lutsky (1986) outlined a procedure based on the analysis of data sets. Carroll (1986) described a jigsaw approach; students work in small groups and each is responsible for one aspect of the project. Suter and Frank (1986) used classical experiments from the journals as the basis for projects.

This articles outlines an approach to devising laboratory projects that are topical and relevant to the course content and meet a variety of course objectives. The approach is based on choosing a core article that provides the frame work for the research project in terms of scope, method, and reporting. It differs from Suter and Frank's procedure by using recent rather than classical research articles and by having students go beyond critical reading of the article to replication of the research. Because the core article defines the research systematically, projects can be readily generated by the instructor and more easily completed by individual students.

Aims

In my second-year undergraduate course on cognition, I had several aims for my laboratory projects. First, I wanted to have the projects well integrated with the course text. Second, I wanted students to read beyond the text and to use and reference original reports in journal article format. I wanted these articles to be manageable, appropriate for the undergraduate level, and current. Third, I wanted students to function as experimenters rather than as subjects and to collect their own data from "real" subjects rather than their classmates. This data collection needed to be held to manageable proportions to ensure that it was achievable and interesting rather than tedious and time-consuming. Fourth, I wanted to provide opportunities for students to develop their skills at reporting research in APA format. I also wanted to restrict the literature review and data analysis in order to sustain the students' focus on accurate and concise communication. Finally, to avoid the problems of laboratory project reports being passed on from year to year, I wanted to have projects that were easy to generate so that they could be changed annually.

Procedures

Although these aims may appear to be difficult to achieve simultaneously, in practice they were not. The central requirement was to choose a core article as the basis for each project. The core article determined the dimensions of the research and defined the scope of the reports.

Core articles were identified by scanning the course text and recent journals for possibilities, with the constraint that each had to be relevant to a central theme taught in the course, up-to-date, and suitable in length and complexity of design and analysis. Ideal core articles were typically 5 to 7 pages, reported one or two experiments, and warranted at least a brief discussion in the text. Copies of each core article, provided in conformity with current copyright legislation, were issued to students along with the materials and specific requirements for each project.

Each project was organized as a full or partial replication of an experiment in the core article. Procedural details for the research, such as list lengths, number of trials, and stimulus presentation times, were kept as close to the original as possible. Stimulus materials were taken from the core article where possible or generated under the same constraints otherwise. All students in the course completed the same projects but collected data individually. Following data collection, class meetings were held to discuss the research issues arising from each project.

Each student was required to collect data from 4 to 10 subjects, depending on how extensive the procedure was and how many conditions the research design contained. To make the analysis more viable, additional data were provided. Students added their own data and analyzed the total data set. Statistical analyses were limited to techniques already in the students' repertoires, because the course did not include teaching statistical procedures. The provision of additional data also served to ensure that students usually obtained significant results in the direction of the original research and avoided the problem of ambiguous nonsignificant results, which frequently afflicts the group laboratory class. Further, providing data meant that the success of the project did not depend entirely on the students' skills as

experimenters. On the other hand, poor data collection skills could usually be identified by comparing results obtained by other class members. Sources for the additional data were either a subset taken directly from data reported in the core article or hypothetical data generated from the summary statistics given in the core article.

A report of the research in standard APA format was required. Reference sources for the report were limited to the core article and the course text, ensuring that the reports were focused and relevant.

Outcomes

I have been using this approach for 4 years and find it to have several benefits. Although the approach has not been formally evaluated, informal student feedback is positive. The use of a core article produces assignments that are focused specifically. As a result, students report being very clear about the scope of the task and what is expected of them in conducting and reporting their research. Because students are required to collect their data individually, they must rely on their own resources. They comment favorably on the opportunity to conduct research with real subjects and the freedom to complete the laboratory work in their own time. The personal responsibility associated with this approach appears to be highly valued.

From the instructor's viewpoint, the approach produces projects that are relevant to the course content. Studies described briefly in the text can be brought to life when the original material is used as a core article and for a laboratory project. Use of research literature is enhanced, as students must read and understand core articles in detail in order to conduct their projects successfully. Making copies of core articles available ensures ready access to the required material and avoids competition for library resources. Because students find assignments to have a clear and manageable scope and high relevance, compliance with requirements is high. Class laboratory times, scheduled following data collection for each project, provide useful discussion sessions on research issues arising out of the projects. Because students have conducted the research at this point, the discussions are relevant to their experience and provide pertinent learning situations. Finally, the approach allows projects to be developed and changed readily to maintain a topical content and to accommodate course changes, such as the adoption of a new text.

Projects organized on this basis do have some limitations, however. Because the background reading is quite narrowly defined, students gain only limited skills in organizing a body of literature and reporting it in an introduction section. The limited reference set also makes it difficult to develop an in-depth discussion section. Because references are readily available, students need not engage in library search or journal browsing for relevant materials. Suitable core articles are difficult to locate in some areas. Problems also arise when sophisticated equipment is required (e.g., to measure precise reaction times or to control the brief presentation of stimuli).

As with any approach to laboratory project design, this one is a compromise between an ideal and what can be achieved realistically. Certain limitations can be overcome by using other types of assignments to supplement this approach. The advantages of the core article approach outweigh its limitations and help to achieve the course aims just outlined. The approach works well, is highly accepted by students, and should be valuable for other teachers who have similar goals for the laboratory project. Although reported here as part of a cognitive psychology course, the approach should generalize readily to other courses in which laboratory projects are required.

References

Carroll, D. W. (1986). Use of the jigsaw technique in laboratory and discussion classes. *Teaching of Psychology, 13,* 208-210.

Chamberlain, K. (1986). Teaching the practical research course. *Teaching of Psychology, 13,* 204-208.

Edwards, J. D. (1981). A conceptual framework for a core program in psychology. *Teaching of Psychology, 8,* 3-7.

Kerber, K. W. (1983). Beyond experimentation: Research projects for a laboratory course in psychology. *Teaching of Psychology, 10,* 236-239.

Lutsky, N. (1986). Undergraduate research experience through the analysis of data sets in psychology courses. *Teaching of Psychology, 13,* 119-122.

Palladino, J. J., Carsrud, A. L., Hulicka, I. M., & Benjamin, L. T., Jr. (1982). Undergraduate research in psychology: Assessment and directions. *Teaching of Psychology, 9,* 71-74.

Suter, W. N., & Frank, P. (1986). Using scholarly journals in undergraduate experimental methodology courses. *Teaching of Psychology, 13,* 219-221.

VandeCreek, L., & Fleischer, M. (1984). The role of practicum in the undergraduate psychology curriculum. *Teaching of Psychology, 11,* 9-14.

Using Scholarly Journals in Undergraduate Experimental Methodology Courses

W. Newton Suter
Paula Frank
San Francisco State University

Our use of classic psychological experiments from scholarly journals in teaching an undergraduate experimental methodology course is described. We believe that the approach is effective when the experiments are carefully chosen. We include some suggestions for matching journal articles with core topics and some questions that facilitate students' understanding of certain articles.

Considering the number of good undergraduate textbooks in experimental methodology, one may wonder why instructors might use supplementary instructional materials, particularly professional and scholarly journals that report original research. The answer is that judicious use of carefully chosen journal articles may provide students with insight into the application of methodological principles to realistic research endeavors and encourage students' independent exploration of original research. Reading scholarly journals is commonplace for graduate students; encouraging such activity for undergraduates may prompt their interest in pursuing graduate study in psychology. One key element for using scholarly journals in undergraduate classes is the careful selection of articles. In this article, we suggest some ways of increasing the value of using journal articles, based on 6 years of experimentation in the classroom.

Selection Criteria

Three criteria are most important for selecting journal articles to supplement standard text material. Articles must be (a) cited with high frequency in introductory psychology textbooks, (b) prime illustrations of specific methodological principles, and (c) reasonably short and comprehensible to undergraduate students with limited backgrounds.

The criterion of frequent citation is important for several reasons. First, when students know that they are reading well-known research (not merely reading about it), their interest level increases. Second, the research findings of such classic experiments are likely to be known to the upper-division major who has taken previous psychology courses (or at least an introductory course). Consequently, students can concentrate not so much on the findings of the research, but on the methods. There seems to be no better way to demonstrate that experimental outcomes are, at least in part, dependent on the way an experiment is designed and conducted. Third, the use of noteworthy research is likely to have a positive transfer effect in other psychology courses ("Oh, yeah! I read that research in my experimental methods course"). Finally, many students experience a thrill when they uncover minor (or major!) inconsistencies between a description of an experiment in a secondary source and the documented details of the experiment itself. For example, students have proudly reported an incorrect graph of the results from the classic Festinger and Carlsmith (1959) experiment in Atkinson, Atkinson, and Hilgard (1983) and inaccurate procedural details of the same experiment in Lefrançois (1983).

The importance of the relevance criterion is fairly obvious. It makes little sense to read original research that does not relate in a methodological way to the material being covered in a standard text. The criterion of readability is also important in an obvious and not so obvious way. Students must be capable of reading original research with reasonable comprehension; otherwise, the assignment will have limited usefulness and probably will not be completed. Readability is also important because students often experience an attitudinal boost concerning the subject once they understand the major methodological principles used by the experimenters. There is also a sense of accomplishment, mastery, and confidence because the students know that they are doing what graduate students do.

Matching Classic Experiments With Core Topics

A scan of a convenient "on-the-shelf" sample of 26 major introductory psychology texts published in the years 1983-1985, representing all levels of comprehensiveness, reveals that some experimental studies are cited with such frequency that they may be termed classic. Such experiments are more likely to be remembered by students completing the introductory psychology course. Matching classic experiments with important methodological concepts in a way that maximizes the benefit for students poses a challenge for the instructor. Although we offer specific suggestions for concept-experiment matches (ones that have the greatest illustrative power), we must also emphasize a major advantage of this approach for teaching experimental methods: flexibility. Articles tend to come and go over the semesters and be used for specific and changing purposes. We recognize that every instructor is likely to teach an experimental psychology course somewhat differently by emphasizing different components, yet it is reasonable to conclude that there are basic or core elements common to all such courses. We refer to these basic elements as *core topics.*

With this in mind, we present some recommended journal articles and core topics in Table 1. We also indicate the citation frequency of each article (ranked), based on the sampling of 26 contemporary and widely adopted introductory psychology texts. In Table 2, we present some engaging questions that have been used successfully in the past. Because of space limitations, only a sampling of possible homework questions are included to give the flavor of questions that have stimulated interesting discussions.

The citations presented in Table 1 are found in journals published by the American Psychological Association; hence, they are widely available in college and university libraries. These articles, of course, do not exhaust the pool of pedagogically useful articles. For example, the widely cited experiment by Loftus and Palmer (1974) is a gem: It is short, highly readable, enjoyed by students, and well suited for illustrating independent and dependent variables (as well as showing how simple designs may be expanded to more complex and informative factorial designs). Although not frequently cited in introductory psychology texts, Tom and Rucker (1975) catches students' attention and illustrates the partitioning of factorial designs, the presentation of descriptive and inferential (ANOVA) statistics, and the graphing of interactive factors. Additional listings of classic articles can be found in LeUnes (1978), McCollom (1973), and Shima (1977).

We know from formal course evaluations that many original research reports are interesting to students and promote their learning about experimental methodology. We believe that classic experiments in scholarly journals, used along with traditional instructional materials, can add an important dimension

Table 1. Listing of Classic Experiments, Citation Frequency, Core Topics, and Recommended Use

Citation[b]	Frequency[c]	A	B	C	D	E	F	G	H	I
					Core Topics[a]					
Schachter & Singer (1962)	25		X	X			X			X
Milgram (1963)	20	X		X						X
Festinger & Carlsmith (1959)	20		X		X	X	X			
Peterson & Peterson (1959)	19	X				X			X	
Dion, Berscheid, & Walster (1972)	18				X			X		
Bandura, Ross, & Ross (1963)	15			X	X			X		
Darley & Latané (1968)	12				X				X	X
Dutton & Aron (1974)	11	X		X		X	X			
Valins (1966)	11				X		X			
Schachter & Gross (1968)	9				X	X		X	X	
Overmier & Seligman (1967)	4		X		X					X
Miller & DiCara (1967)	4		X		X				X	

Note. One appropriate schedule for the use of these journal articles is designated by an X at the intersection of the reported experiment and core topic.
[a]A = experimentation versus description; B = theory and hypotheses; C = constructs and operational definitions; D = types of variables; E = rival explanations; F = confounding; G = designs; H = graphing and analysis; I = ethical issues.
[b]Published in APA journals and ranked in order of citation frequency.
[c]Based on a sampling of 26 introductory psychology texts copyrighted 1983–1985.

Table 2. Sampling of Questions Based on Classic Journal Articles

Citation	Question
Bandura et al. (1963)	How would you describe the experimental design?
Darley & Latané (1968)	What were the independent and dependent variables?
Dion et al. (1972)	How was jealousy operationally defined?
Dutton & Aron (1974)	Why was a double-blind procedure used?
Festinger & Carlsmith (1959)	What evidence was found in support of the theory?
Milgram (1963)	How would you evaluate this study in light of the ethical principles in the conduct of research with human participants?
Miller & DiCara (1967)	What control techniques were used and why?
Overmier & Seligman (1967)	How did these researchers rule out rival explanations, and how would you evaluate these attempts in relation to the ethics of animal experimentation?
Peterson & Peterson (1959)	What does "significant at the .01 level" mean?
Schachter & Gross (1968)	How could demand characteristics have been an artifact?
Schachter & Singer (1962)	What was the purpose of a placebo group?
Valins (1966)	What was Valins' research hypothesis?

to students' experience. With the proper guidance from the instructor (i.e., what to focus on and what to avoid becoming bogged down with), students are often able to differentiate the content of an article from the methodology within the first few weeks of the course. Scholarly journals help motivate students to pursue the exciting field of experimental psychology by providing the background and confidence needed to explore and understand the ever-expanding stack of published research.

References

Atkinson, R. L., Atkinson, R. C., & Hilgard, E. R. (1983). *Introduction to psychology* (8th ed.). New York: Harcourt Brace Jovanovich.

Bandura, A., Ross, D., & Ross, S. A. (1963). Imitation of film-mediated aggressive models. *Journal of Abnormal and Social Psychology, 66,* 3-11.

Darley, J. M, & Latane, B. (1968). Bystander intervention in emergencies: Diffusion of responsibility. *Journal of Personality and Social Psychology, 8,* 377-383.

Dion, K., Berscheid, E., & Walster, E. (1972). What is beautiful is good. *Journal of Personality and Social Psychology, 24,* 285-290.

Dutton, D. G., & Aron, A. P. (1974). Some evidence of heightened sexual attraction under conditions of high anxiety. *Journal of Personality and Social Psychology, 30,* 510-517.

Festinger, L., & Carlsmith, J. M. (1959). Cognitive consequences of forced compliance. *Journal of Abnormal and Social Psychology, 58,* 203-210.

Lefrançois, G. R. (1983). *Psychology* (2nd ed.). Belmont, CA: Wadsworth.

LeUnes, A. D. (1978). "Classics" in abnormal psychology: A student evaluation. *Teaching of Psychology, 5,* 99-100.

Loftus, E. F., & Palmer, J. C. (1974). Reconstruction of automobile destruction: An example of the interaction between language and memory. *Journal of Verbal Learning and Verbal Behavior, 13,* 585-589.

McCollom, I. N. (1973). Psychological classics: Older journal articles frequently cited today. *American Psychologist, 28,* 363-365.

Milgram, S. (1963). Behavioral study of obedience. *Journal of Abnormal and Social Psychology, 67,* 371-378.

Miller, N. E., & DiCara, L. (1967). Instrumental learning of heart rate changes in curarized rats: Shaping, and specificity to discriminative stimulus. *Journal of Comparative and Physiological Psychology, 63,* 12-19.

Overmier, J. B., & Seligman, M. E. P. (1967). Effects of inescapable shock upon subsequent escape and avoidance responding. *Journal of Comparative and Physiological Psychology, 63,* 28-33.

Peterson, L. R., & Peterson, M. J. (1959). Short-term retention of individual verbal items. *Journal of Experimental Psychology, 58,* 193-198.

Schachter, S., & Gross, L. P. (1968). Manipulated time and eating behavior. *Journal of Personality and Social psychology, 10,* 98-106.

Schachter, S., & Singer, J. E. (1962). Cognitive, social, and physiological determinants of emotional state. *Psychological Review, 69,* 379-399.

Shima, F. (1977). New classics and new classicists in psychology. *Teaching of Psychology, 4,* 46-48.

Tom, G., & Rucker, M. (1975). Fat, full, and happy: Effects of food deprivation, external cues, and obesity on preference ratings, consumption, and buying intentions. *Journal of Personality and Social Psychology, 32,* 761-766.

Valins, S. (1966). Cognitive effects of false heart-rate feedback. *Journal of Personality and Social Psychology, 4,* 400-408.

Note

We gratefully acknowledge Charles L. Brewer for his valuable assistance in the preparation of this manuscript.

Teaching Rival Hypotheses in Experimental Psychology

George S. Howard and
Jean L. Engelhardt
University of Notre Dame

Many instructors of research methods and experimental psychology courses believe that scientific rationality consists of an elaboration and refinement of disciplined inquiry. All people are capable of some degree of common-sense rationality. If students can view scientific reasoning as a natural extension and refinement of their own critical inquiries, their motivation to learn the methods and techniques of experimental psychology might be enhanced. Huck and Sandler (1979) have written a book entitled *Rival Hypotheses* that describes a number of instances where empirical support is claimed as a result of

"research." These studies deal with knowledge claims of practical importance (such as the "Pepsi challenge" or "evidence that saccharine causes cancer") and students find them very interesting to critique.

The class activity offered herein involves the manner in which *Rival Hypotheses* can be used as both a teaching device and an actual experiment whereby students obtain practice performing data analysis, the interpretation of findings, and report writing. The basic strategy is to begin the first day of class by pretesting all students on their ability to critique research and then randomly assigning

240

students to one of two groups (groups A & B). The sequence of activities in the study is presented in the list below.

Lab Session #1: Pretest and assignment to groups
Lab Session #2: Group A—Rival Hypotheses; Group B—Off
Lab Session #3: Group A—Rival Hypotheses; Group B—Off
Lab Session #4: Group A—Rival Hypotheses; Group B—Off
Lecture Session: Posttest #1 to Groups A and B
Lab Session #5: Group A—Off; Group B—Rival Hypotheses
Lab Session #6: Group A—Off; Group B—Rival Hypotheses
Lab Session #7: Group A—Off; Group B—Rival Hypotheses
Lecture Session: Posttest #2 to Groups A and B

Posttests 1 and 2 were administered at the end of lecture classes at the appropriate points in time. Lectures continued throughout the course of the experiment which had implications for the interpretation of within-group changes over time. Students who had "off" lab days were instructed to use the time to complete other lab assignments such as reading material on how to write a research report

Pretest posttest 11 and posttest 2 were constructed by selecting twelve problems from the *Rival Hypotheses book* and randomly assigning four problems to each of the three tests. From the remaining problems in *Rival Hypotheses,* the lab instructor selected a dozen of the most interesting problems and arranged them in what was judged to be an increasing order of difficulty. Students were presented these twelve problems over the three lab periods that constituted the training intervention being evaluated. After students individually critiqued each problem, the group pooled their critiques, discussed the points made, and the lab instructor added any additional points that were not made by the students. (Husk and Sandier provide their critiques of each problem in the book.) The lab immediately following posttest 2 was devoted to describing the design of the study and discussing the strengths and liabilities of the design. Students were encouraged to take copious notes because they each would have to write a research report of the project.

Immediately after the administration of posttest 2, the judgment of the test problems was begun. Ratings were obtained from two students in the class who did not take part in the study. Raters were trained by an author and achieved an acceptable level of agreement before the actual rating of test problems began. A student's critique was scored by rating each comment made on a three-point scale consisting of: 2 (good criticism); 1 (weak criticism); and O (wrong or irrelevant criticism). Subjects' scores were then totaled across the four problems on each test, and then averaged across judges and problems. Students were then given data on all subjects for each of the three test periods and told to analyze the data and write a research report on the study (these students had already taken a semester-long course in statistics and the use of the computer for data analysis). Student

papers were then critiqued by the lab instructor, marked, and returned to the students.

The project served as a basis for several lab and lecture activities throughout the course. Perhaps the most substantial activity involved considering the array of statistical analyses that might have been performed upon the data. It was instructive for the students to realize that many different (potentially acceptable) analyses were possible and that each analysis considered a slightly different research question. Although we advocated an analysis of posttest 1 scores covaried by pretest scores, as the most powerful and appropriate test of treatment effects, the value of additional analyses in affording other insights was highlighted. Further, students were appraised of the conceptual difficulties involved in interpreting other seemingly plausible analyses. For example, one might naively think that a comparison of pretest scores with posttest 2 scores for all subjects would yield an estimate of the effectiveness of the *Rival Hypotheses* lab exercises. Of course, rival hypotheses such as testing and history effects are present and uncontrolled. Furthers students were introduced to the subtleties of integrating design considerations (four rival hypothesis problems were randomly assigned to the pretest and four to each of the posttests) with statistical considerations (how much confidence does one have that these two tests are equally difficult since only four problems were assigned to each test?). Students were also appraised of the difficulties in interpreting subjects' increases in skill in critiquing due to contaminants such as nonspecific treatment effects. Finally, for the remainder of the course students were asked to consider how each new topic being considered did or did not relate to the *Rival Hypotheses* study.

As mentioned earlier the analysis of posttest 1 scores covaried by pretest scores was the most appropriate estimate of treatment (the *Rival Hypotheses* lab exercises) effectiveness. Group A subjects ($N = 13$) scored significantly higher on adjusted posttest 1 scores than their control group ($N = 15$) counterparts ($F(1,25) = 24.62$, $p < .001$). Treatment subjects' scores increased 4.26 points (pretest = 5.16 to posttest 1 = 9.52), but control subjects scores actually decreased by 1.28 points (pretest = 5.68 to posttest 1 = 4.40).

Students find it instructive to consider why any analyses of posttest 2 scores are fraught with difficulties of interpretation. For example, because both groups have studied the rival hypothesis problems, a comparison of posttest 2 scores for the two groups would be expected to show no differences. If, on the other hand, one were to consider pretest to posttest 2 change scores for all subjects as a measure of treatment effectiveness, interpretation is flawed because no control group exists against which to contrast these changes-Finally, one may believe that differences between groups A and B on posttest 1 to posttest 2 change scores might reflect a valid treatment effect. Such a comparison is inappropriate, inasmuch as differences between the two groups existed on posttest 1 precisely because group A had already received the intervention whereas group B had not yet experienced it. Consequently, group differences in change scores are expected even if the treatment was totally ineffectual, which renders interpretation of any findings problematic. By explicating the problems inherent in any consideration of posttest 2 findings, students are once again reminded of the importance of proper design in order to obtain unconfounded results.

In sum, the study accomplished several important goals in a cost-effective manner. Students were encouraged to see the topics of research design as an elaboration of their natural critical thinking abilities.

The actual practice of analyzing and writing this study gave students some exposure to topics (such as, judgment techniques, nonspecific treatment effects, eta) that were considered more thoroughly later in the course. Students were encouraged to integrate and apply their statistics background and skills into the methods course. Finally, students received practice in critiquing studies, which was a skill required for examinations in the course.

Reference

Husk, S. W. & Sandier, H. M . *Rival hypotheses: Alternative interpretations of data based conclusions.* New York: Harper & Row, 1979.

SECTION IV:
HISTORY

Ludy Benjamin described a procedure for involving both faculty and students in the development of a departmental history. The article included valuable information on topics and resources that can be used in such a project. The author advocated this activity as either a course assignment or an independent research project.

Scott Terry described a student research project that involved tracing faculty members' antecedents through psychology's history. Students acquired information about influences on their faculty, reviewed some portions of the history course's contents, and developed library skills. Terry identified cautions with and recommended modifications to the project.

Steve Davis and his colleagues summarized how each student in a history and systems of psychology class took responsibility for a 5-year period and gathered all available information about the university's psychology department. Outcomes included acquiring first hand information about the department, organizing and conducting a symposium, and producing videotapes and printed summaries of the findings. The authors also reported increased student enthusiasm in studying history and pride in their department.

For his history of psychology class, Austin Grigg developed different research projects designed to promote active student participation. Grigg assigned projects, or the student team suggested its own project. Teams of students made oral presentations and wrote reports of their findings. Projects have included: (a) a history of psychology at the students' university, (b) an examination of careers of alumni who became successful psychologists, and (c) an evaluation of psychological journals grouped by decades. The activities in this article contribute additional approaches to promoting active participation in class.

Charles Brooks had students in his history of psychology class portray prominent individuals. Working in teams, students developed a presentation in which they portrayed individuals from different time periods and discussed and debated psychological issues. Students also prepared bibliographies and position papers about those individuals. Brooks also described variations on this technique. Advantages of the exercise included giving students a personal appreciation for historical figures and a greater understanding about the continuity of psychological issues.

Students in David Cole's class experienced mock APA conventions; they presented published research papers as if they were the original author. The audience was limited to questioning the author within the confines of the paper's era. The author also discussed the values and problems with this approach.

Joy Berrenberg and Ann Prosser instructed students to design and construct games that covered a broad range of knowledge about the history of psychology. The authors found that the procedure was a challenging, engaging, and effective supplement or alternative to traditional evaluation methods. Playing the games in class provided an excellent and enjoyable review of course material.

Edward and Sharyn Crossman described the use of crossword puzzles in a history of psychology course to prepare for the matching section on an exam. The analysis of pre- and posttest exam scores showed a significant increase in performance. All of the 14 students reported enjoying the experience, and none expressed any detrimental effects on their interest in the material.

Randall Wight used the social custom of toasting to expand students' knowledge about the range of contributions usually covered in a history of psychology course. Wight identified pitfalls and advantages of this technique. Who said studying history had to be stuffy?

The students in Alfred Raphelson's history of psychology class saw more than 1,000 slides illustrating biographies, concepts, and theories. The author found that scores on an unannotmced, slide recognition test correlated with examination scores given throughout the semester. One conclusion was that the results indicated evidence for incidental learning.

Fairfid Caudle described several activities illustrating early techniques and discoveries in experimental psychology. Activities included psychological demonstrations (e.g., 2-point threshold and just noticeable difference), several introspection demonstrations, learning demonstrations using nonsense syllables and a modified replication of Edward Thorndike's linedrawing experiments, Gestalt phenomena such as the phi phenomenon, and several demonstrations from the writings of William James. Caudle described techniques for demonstrating early experimental laboratory apparatus, including suggestions for building it.

George Diekhoff used factor analysis to develop graphic summaries or cognitive maps of the interrelationships among prominent persons and/or theories. These cognitive maps stimulated class discussions and encouraged students to compare and contrast issues along several dimensions.

Involving Students and Faculty in Preparing a Departmental History

Ludy T. Benjamin, Jr.
Texas A&M University

This article describes researching and writing institutional histories and focuses on preparing a psychology department history. Topics discussed include time requirements for the research, projectformats, sources for historical information, methods for doing historical research, and the benefits to students and faculty derived from these projects.

Scientific psychology in the United States has entered its second century, and centennial celebrations occur each year. Some focus on the founding of psychology laboratories, for example, the University of Wisconsin (1988), University of Nebraska (1989), and Columbia University (1990); others focus on significant publications, such as James's *Principles of Psychology* (1990). These celebrations take various forms (e.g., special conferences and commemorative publications), but they have a common aim of discovering the history of notable events.

Although centennials are an important impetus, historical research can be initiated at any time. A subject of investigation and some knowledge about how to find and use relevant sources of information are required. This article presents ideas about institutional histories and describes sources for data. Such research can unite students and faculty in a cooperative learning venture as a regular course assignment or as a special independent research project. Research related to the college or university or some other local entity or event generates high student interest (Grigg, 1974; Raphelson, 1979). In addition to gaining knowledge, rediscovered or new, students enhance their library skills, learn about important resources in historical research, learn about historical research techniques and issues of interpretation, acquire some group coordination skills, and develop a better appreciation of their institution's past.

Time Requirements of the Project

A first decision concerns the time required to complete a project. If the research is part of a course, then the time frame is obviously dictated. Some projects can be continued from one class to another,
but this procedure precludes the learning and satisfaction that students derive from completing the task. Institutional histories are often too complex to complete in a single term. One solution to this problem is to restrict the subject matter. By dividing it into separate units, the entire project might be completed during several school terms while allowing each group of students to experience closure on its particular unit. A second solution is to restrict the time period (e.g., look only at the first 10 years of an institution's history).

Nature of the Project

Historical research projects on institutions, such as colleges or universities, can range from preparing a departmental scrapbook to writing a comprehensive departmental history. The research can stand alone or be part of a larger institutional history project.

A comprehensive departmental history should answer a number of questions about curriculum, faculty, students, facilities, and departmental events (see Table 1) . Although portions of these histories can be assigned to different groups of students, someone should serve as editor to ensure a coherent product. Publishing these extensive projects can be costly. If institutional or private financial support is unavailable, desktop publishing is an economical alternative for producing an attractive final product.

Less formal histories can take many forms. A *timeline* can be used to portray faculty, curriculum, or psychology major requirements as they change over time. For a faculty timeline, available photographs might be included. Timelines can be reproduced for individual distribution, but they also make excellent displays for bulletin boards. Timelines provide a "time map" on which events are placed in time locations, typically progressing from left to right. Interest in timelines for departments or institutions can be enhanced by adding external events of national or international significance.

The *chronology is* related to the timeline but uses no spatial display. Chronologies simply list items in historical order (e.g., the founding date of a laboratory, the arrival of a particular faculty member, or the introduction of a new course). Chronologies are sometimes constructed in two columns: One lists events of the institution's history (internal history), and the other lists events outside the institution (external history). Sahakian (1981, pp. 445-483) provided an example of a history of psychology chronology. Sahakian's items can be used in conjunction with institutional chronologies to illustrate happenings elsewhere in the psychological world.

Another historical project is the preparation of complete *faculty genealogies* (Weigel & Gottfurcht, 1972). Each student is assigned a particular faculty member, present or past, and is asked to determine that faculty member's academic genealogy (i.e., who was the faculty member's major professor, who was the major professor's major professor, etc.) . These genealogies make nice bulletin board displays. They highlight the youth of scientific psychology and the fact that most lineages are traceable to a few psychologists, principally Wilhelm Wundt, William James, and Carl Stumpf. Hillix and Broyles (1980) provided an excellent example of a psychology depart-

ment genealogy and a description of how to do the necessary research.

Other *display projects* can consist of old photos of faculty, students, buildings, and departmental apparatus; old catalog copies of the curriculum; and old newspaper clippings of departmental activities. These materials make interesting bulletin board displays, departmental scrapbooks, or even slide shows or videotapes. Old equipment can be placed in display cases along with information about the department's use of the equipment. Student or faculty articles (published or unpublished) relevant to that equipment can also be displayed. In fact, student and faculty research articles can be exhibited by themselves (perhaps just title pages) to illustrate projects of earlier years. A good source for locating authors of published articles and books in psychology from 1894 to 1958 is the *Cumulative Author Index to Psychological Index and Psychological Abstracts,* a five-volume work published by G. K. Hall in 1960. These volumes were continued in 5- or 3-year intervals until 1985 and can be found in many university libraries. Subject indexes exist from 1927 to 1985.

Consider also the possibility of *projects other than departmental histories,* such as histories of local institutions (hospitals or mental institutions), local organizations (YMCA, YWCA, Planned Parenthood, AA, or other social service agencies), or local groups (mental health advocacy groups or phrenological societies). Most communities have some psychology-related agencies, past or present. Discovering or recognizing their existence greatly expands the historical research opportunities for your classes.

Sources of Historical Information

After deciding on the time course and nature of your research project, where do you find the information you need? Sources are basically of two kinds: published and unpublished.

Published sources can be found in libraries, rare book rooms, archives, state historical societies, and newspaper publishers. They include faculty and student publications, college yearbooks and catalogs, student newspapers, notes and news listings in journals (see Benjamin et al., 1989), newsletters (e.g., faculty, alumni, and Psi Chi), and local newspapers.

Unpublished materials are more difficult to locate and, for departmental histories, include such items as class and laboratory notes, syllabi, lectures, correspondence, and oral histories. Although these materials are more scattered, the sources listed for published materials may be a good place to begin. Department and/or institutional archives usually contain correspondence, annual reports, self-study documents, alumni records, grant proposals (for instruction, research, or program development), and personal papers of former faculty and students.

Table 1. Questions to Ask in a Departmental History

Curriculum

1. When were the first psychology courses offered? What were their titles? What was their content? What texts did they use?
2. How has the psychology curriculum evolved? When did particular courses first appear? Disappear? How did the catalog course descriptions change over time? What requirements have existed for the psychology major? How have those changed? What psychology courses have been required for nonmajors? What parts of the curriculum might have served other departments?
3. When did laboratory instruction begin in psychology? What was the nature of research in the laboratory? Were students involved in the research? What published research came out of the laboratory?
4. In what department(s) were psychology courses offered? When was the psychology department formally established?

Faculty

1. What faculty members have taught psychology? Where did they receive their training and in what fields? What faculty titles did they hold?
2. Can you locate former faculty members for oral histories?
3. Can you locate published research or other writing by former faculty members?

Students

1. Did student psychology clubs exist? Was there a Psi Chi chapter?
2. What careers did the early graduates of the program pursue?
3. What eminent persons did their undergraduate work in psychology?
4. What was the psychology program like from a student perspective? Can you locate former students in psychology for oral histories? Do they have class notes from their student days?

Facilities

1. What laboratory facilities existed and how long were they used? What equipment was acquired and when?
2. Were off-campus facilities used by the psychology program (e.g., for field work, training, or community service projects)?

Departmental Events

1. Did famous psychologists speak on your campus at some time? Can you locate information about those talks?
2. Were any meetings, symposia, or other special activities related to psychology held on your campus?

Locating former faculty and students provides the opportunity for collecting oral histories. If the department has had a Psi Chi chapter, contact the Psi Chi National Office, which maintains correspondence files for each chapter, some dating back to the 1930s.

The State Department of Education may have files on all state and private colleges and universities within the state. The official state archives is another source to check, and if the college or university is or was affiliated with a particular church, then check the church archives for your district.

Relevant information may exist in other archival collections (e.g., in the extensive collections of the Archives of the History of American Psychology in Akron, OH). More than 650 individuals and organizations have deposited materials at that archive (see Benjamin, 1980; Popplestone & McPherson, 1976). An annotated listing of more than 500 relevant manuscript collections in the United States was compiled by Sokal and Rafail (1982). It is an excellent source for checking the papers of a particular individual or organization.

Many archives have an index system for names of individuals and institutions that appear in their collections. They may even send you copies of pertinent documents, for a nominal sum, if the number is small and their search time short. However, if the holdings related to your project are extensive, then you will need to visit that archive. If you are researching a particular individual, then make some educated guesses about persons with whom your subject might have corresponded. If you locate relevant papers, contact the appropriate archive.

The alumni office can provide addresses of former students. Students who took classes with particular faculty members, and thus have memories of those earlier days (and perhaps even class notes), may be located by advertising for them in a local newspaper. Another way to get information on an earlier faculty member, who is perhaps deceased, is to locate that faculty member's children. Often those children attended the institution where the parent taught, and the alumni office should be able to help you find them. These children may have important materials for your research.

Some sources of information will be obvious. Others will develop from hunches pursued, exhaustive search, and serendipity. Part of the enjoyment of historical research is tracking down obscure, but often important, information.

Doing Historical Research

The projects suggested in this article do not train psychology students or faculty to be competent historians. However, those involved should learn something about the methods of "doing" history as well as the inherent pitfalls and pleasures. Should you need information on historical research methods or approaches to writing history, books by Benjamin (1981, 1988), Brozek and Pongratz (1980), and Hoopes (1979) describe techniques such as citation analysis, content analysis, oral history, and archival research, and provide examples of biographical, descriptive, quantitative, and sociopsychological approaches to writing history. These sources will help you plan your historical research and train your students to do the project.

Before beginning, you might examine several published departmental histories (e.g., Benjamin & Bertelson, 1975; Capshew & Hearst, 1980; Freed & Roberts, 1988; Morawski, 1986; Raphelson, 1980). These will provide some models for your own research and may suggest possibilities that you had not considered. The history of psychology reference book by Viney, Wertheimer, and Wertheimer (1979) lists a number of departmental and organizational histories.

Benefits (and Costs) of Doing Historical Research

Costs for the projects described are quite modest, usually involving only photocopying, photographic work, cassette tapes, and long-distance telephone charges. Travel to archival collections can be expensive but is usually not necessary for most local history projects. Modest funds are often available from the institution for these kinds of projects.

Although costs are small, benefits can be large. Besides the benefits mentioned earlier, the final product can be added to the archival records of the institution. Indeed, at least one copy should be bound and placed in the institution's library. Information gathered in these exercises can be used in future classes, particularly in the history of psychology class. Students and faculty can better understand changes in the department over time and relate those changes to events in the broader context of the institution, national psychology, or the world at large. Finally, these projects involve students and faculty in an exercise that is as much fun as it is educational. My students report a clearer sense of purpose in this kind of written assignment, compared to some of the papers they write for other classes, and they enjoy making a real contribution to their department. Instead of waiting for a centennial, get your students involved now.

References

Benjamin, L. T., Jr. (1980). Research at the Archives of the History of American Psychology: A case history. In J. Brozek & L. J. Pongratz (Eds.), *Historiography of modern psychology* (pp. 241-251). Toronto: Hogrefe.

Benjamin, L. T., Jr. (1981). *Teaching history of psychology: A handbook.* New York: Academic.

Benjamin, L. T., Jr. (Ed.). (1988). *A history of psychology: Original sources and contemporary research.* New York: McGraw-Hill.

Benjamin, L. T., Jr., & Bertelson, A. D. (1975). The early Nebraska psychology laboratory, 1889-1930: Nursery for presidents of the American Psychological Association. *Journal of the History of the Behavioral Sciences, 11,* 142-148.

Benjamin, L. T., Jr., Pratt, R., Watlington, D., Aaron, L., Bonar, T., Fitzgerald, S., Franklin, M., Jimenez, B., & Lester, R. (1989) . *A history of American psychology in notes and news, 1883-1945: An index to journal sources.* New York: Kraus International .

Brozek, J., & Pongratz, L. J. (Eds.). (1980). *Historiography of modern psychology.* Toronto: Hogrefe.

Capshew, J. H., & Hearst, E. (1980). Psychology at Indiana University from Bryan to Skinner. *Psychological Record, 30,* 319-342.

Cumulative author index to Psychological Index (1894-1935) and Psychological Abstracts (1927-1958). (1960). (5 vols.). Boston: Hall.

Freed, D. W., & Roberts, C. L. (1988). Mirror of New England: The early years of psychology at Colorado College. *Journal of the History of the Behavioral Sciences, 24,* 46-50.

Grigg, A. E. (1974). Research projects for a history of psychology. *Teaching of Psychology, 1,* 84-85.

Hillix, W. A., & Broyles, J. W. (1980). The family trees of American psychologists. In W. G. Bringmann & R. D. Tweney (Eds.), *Wundt studies* (pp. 422-434). Toronto: Hogrefe.

Hoopes, J. (1979). *Oral history: An introduction for students.* Chapel Hill: University of North Carolina Press.

Morawski, G. (1986). Organizing knowledge and behavior at Yale's Institute of Human Relations. *ISIS, 77,* 219-242.

Popplestone, J. A., & McPherson, M. W. (1976). Ten years of the Archives of the History of American Psychology. *American Psychologist, 31,* 533-534.

Raphelson, A. C. (1979). The unique role of the history of psychology in undergraduate education. *Teaching of Psychology, 6,* 12-14.

Raphelson, A. C. (1980). Psychology at Michigan: The Pillsbury years. *Journal of the History of the Behavioral Sciences, 16,* 301-312.

Sahakian, W. S. (Ed.). (1981) . *History of psychology: A sourcebook in systematic psychology* (rev. ed.). Itasca, IL: Peacock.

Sokal, M. M., & Rafail, P. A. (1982). *A guide to manuscript collections in the history of psychology and related areas.* New York: Kraus International.

Viney, W., Wertheimer, M., & Wertheimer, M. L. (1979). *History of psychology: A guide to information sources.* Detroit: Gale Research.

Weigel, R. G., & Gottfurcht, J. W. (1972). Faculty genealogies: A stimulus for student involvement in history and systems. *American Psychologist, 27,* 981-983.

Tracing Psychologists' "Roots": A Project for History and Systems Course

W. Scott Terry
University of North Carolina

In this paper I will describe a project my students found to be both valuable and interesting as part of their History and Systems of Psychology course. The basic idea is simple: to select current psychologists from our faculty and trace their various antecedents back through psychological history. Although I have since found that this idea has been reported before (Weigel & Gottfurcht, 1972), the present discussion may be useful in setting out another set of procedures for implementing the project. As will be noted below, the present formulation can be carried out relatively quickly, and provides a broader range of antecedents and influences.

The twofold purpose of the project was to investigate the major psychological influences on our present faculty members, and to review some portions of the history covered during the course. The influences sought could be either direct, as through thesis, graduate, or even undergraduate advisors, or indirect, as through theoretical or research influences. Having obtained some names of influencing psychologists, the students were to proceed to search for the major influences on each of these people. This process was repeated back through as many generations of psychologists as possible.

The procedure used was as follows. The psychology faculty were all informed of the nature of the project, and were asked if they would consent to an interview by some students as a starting point for obtaining information. None voiced any objections, and in fact the reactions were quite favorable. Next, the members of the class were assigned to groups of 2-4 students, one group for each faculty member. The groups were formed on the basis of rank-ordered preferences the students had submitted earlier. A detailed handout of the project procedures and goals was also distributed.

There were two basic phases in collecting information. In the first, an interview with the chosen faculty person, several kinds of data were sol- icited: (a) Does the faculty member fit within one of the major systems of psychology covered in the course (e.g., Behaviorism or Psychoanalysis); in a system derivative from one of the major systems (e.g., neobehaviorism); or in some more contemporary tradition (e.g., information processing or ethological)? In addition, it was suggested that the students probe the faculty person's viewpoints on issues of historical interest in psychology. (b) Faculty members were questioned about undergraduate, graduate and post-doctoral "major advisors." These direct antecedents provided a list of schools attended, degrees awarded, and psychologists they had studied under (c) Faculty members were asked to name any other psychologists they considered to have been important personal influences. These names generally indicated more current influences of the faculty members' research and practice of psychology, and in some cases described their current orientations better than did names of thesis advisors.

The names obtained in (b) and (c) above formed the basis for the second phase of the project. Here, students were to use various library sources to determine the graduate advisors and other antecedents for those psychologists named in the interview. (In many cases, the faculty themselves volunteered this information back through one generation.) This was to be accomplished by looking up published dissertations to find thesis committees, checking History and Systems texts, or using other references such as the *History of Psychology in Autobiography.* Whatever names obtained here were also to be traced for *their* antecedents. Thus, the current faculty's roots were to be traced back several generations. (The students' experiences suggested that the further back one got, the more likely a prominent name would appear, thus getting the students into the standard references for more easily accessible information.)

The method used by Weigel and Gottfurcht (1972) was to have students interview the major advisors by mail, going back as many generations as possible. While this approach probably generated more student involvement, it was also time consuming (requiring the project to begin early in the semester), and the demands made on participants outside the home institution may preclude repeating the project in later semesters.

The two phases of research were summarized in a short paper, which included a summary of the interview, a hierarchical diagram showing the family tree of the faculty member, and a list of references used in obtaining the information.

The results showed that the students traced back an average of three generations (SD = 1.3) beyond each of the 18 faculty members we began with (range: 1-6 generations). Most of these were direct antecedents ("students-of" kinds of relationships). For several faculty, multiple lines of descent were traced, because they had mentioned a number of advisors or influential persons. In virtually every case, names of historically prominent psychologists covered earlier in the course were found (e.g., Lewin, James, Yerkes, Skinner), and a number of surprising relationships appeared when the family trees were collated. For example, two large clusters appeared, one leading back to Carl Rogers and another to Kenneth Spence (with some of our clinical psychologists falling in this latter cluster).

By having the students obtain as many names as possible to start with in tracing back (i.e., undergraduate, Masters and PhD advisors), one could easily obtain a number of different influences on the present generation of faculty members. This also provided a large number of intersections among the family trees, showing interrelationships that would have been missed by tracing only doctoral advisors. This aspect of the present procedure would be especially useful in cases where only a small number of faculty are available, since the likelihood of overlap in antecedents is increased .

The benefits that I perceive this project has to the students are several. They learned about our faculty members, and uncovered basic background information and views the students were not aware of even after nearly four years in out program. The students developed some of their library skills in reseaching the information. They also learned the history of psychology as they took a personal interest in some aspects of it. Finally, the class presentation of the results, done in the last meeting of the semester, served as an excellent review of the entire course.

There are some notes of caution in drawing conclusions from this kind of analysis. First, that current faculty should not be "rated" by the perceived quality of their Ancestry." Second, psychologists change interests and areas during the course of their professional lives, sometimes drastically. This could partially account, for example, for the Hull-Spence antecedents of some of the clinical faculty members. Third, there is the question of the accuracy of the students' findings. It is hoped any errors will comets light either in discussion of the findings with the faculty members, or through repetition of this project in future semesters.

Modifications of this basic project can be readily generated. For example, a genealogical chart could be prepared displaying the roots of the entire department (Weigel & Gottfurcht, 1972). Alternatively, after tracing back to some historical figure, one could work forward again in time tracing the line of descent through other students of the selected psychologist. This could show distant "cousins" of the current faculty members.

In closing, it must be said that the students and faculty reacted very favorably to this project. Discussions with each of the student groups involved showed substantial enthusiasm for the project, and especially for the final results as presented in class.

Reference

Weigel, R G., & Gottfurcht, J. W. Faculty genealogies: A stimulus for student involvement in History and Systems. *American Psychologist,* 1972, 27, 981-983.

Teaching and Learning The History of Psychology Need Not Be Boring

Stephen F. Davis
Walter C. Janzen
Rhon L. Davis
Emporia State University

In the preface to his new book, *Teaching history of psychology: A handbook,* Benjamin (1981) indicates that, "To misquote Henry Fords the notion that history is boring is bunk. History is stimulating! Only certain instructors and certain textbooks are boring" (p. vii). However most, if not all, who have been in the teaching and/or learning roles in this particular course have encountered or may have even expressed reservations. For example, it is not uncommon to hear comments to the effect that the course and/or textbook rank with the telephone directory as intellectual tranquilizers. Benjamin addresses these issues and indicates that, "If you as teacher convey to your students an excitement for the material you are presenting, then many of them will catch that enthusiasm and few, if any, will be disappointed with the course" (p. vii).

We shall describe an ongoing two-year history of psychology project that is being conducted at Emporia State University. We believe that many of these activities and projects are directly transferable to other colleges and universities and that they will help engender the enthusiasm described above.

As is often the case, serendipity played a major role in the development of this project. In the summer of 1979 preparations to move into the new Education and Psychology building were underway. Correspondence, dating to the 1920s, was unearthed saved and stimulated the ambitious project of preparing a comprehensive history of psychology at this university. To involve students as fully as possible, the project was integrated into the regular fall offering of the History and Systems of Psychology class. Initially, the project was received with some skepticism by the students. However, as it began to take shape, enthusiasm and a genuine sense of pride in both the institution and department grew. As part of the course assignment, each student was given a specific five-year time period to research. The general instructions were to "unearth every possible bit of information pertaining to psychology" for the assigned time period. Students were encouraged to exhaust all sources (e.g., old catalogs and historical collections in the library, interview and correspond with former faculty members, etc.). As the semester progressed and the stack of material (and enthusiasm) grew, the students were amazed at the stature and importance of psychologists (both faculty and students) who had been associated with *their* school. For example former faculty included such names as: Norman Triplett (credited by Chaplin and Krawiec, 1979, as having published the first true experiment in social psychology; Triplett, 1897), James Bart Stroud (a Harvey Carr PhD), Robert M. Leeper (noted authority on personality theory), William Gray (author of the Gray Reading Readiness Test), and so forth. Also, it was noted that quite a number of the faculty during the 1920s and 1930s received their doctoral training at either the University of Chicago or Columbia University. Hence a direct link with early Functionalism was readily apparent. Possibly the most noteworthy of the former students was Frank A. Beach. Dr. Beach (1974) is quick to acknowledge his ties, via bachelor's and master's training (especially that of James B. Stroud), to Emporia State.

At this point in the project serendipity once again intervened. As an alumnus, Dr. Beach had received information regarding completion of the new Education and Psychology building. His congratulatory letter encouraged students to propose the staging of a symposium dealing with the history of psychology at Emporia State. The symposium was arranged and held in the spring of 1980. The major participants included: Dr. Frank A. Beach, Dr. John Breukleman (Professor Emeritus of biology and Dr. Beach's first neurobiology instructor), Dr. William Gray (Professor Emeritus of psychology), and Dr. Dal H. Cass (Professor Emeritus and former psychology department chairperson). Prior to the symposium, the history materials that had been gathered were assembled into an eight-page booklet that was duplicated and distributed to all who attended the symposium. (Admittedly, this booklet was incomplete and contained numerous gaps in the listing of faculty and courses. However, it did provide a point of departure for discussion.) If the number of persons in attendance (150) can be used as a barometer of success the event was exceptional. Videotapes were made and later edited to conform to a 50-minute format. Hence, we now have tapes that are being used with considerable impact in a variety of classes.

As anticipated, the symposium provided numerous clues and bits of information about areas that had not been covered in the initial historical documentation. In the fall semester of 1980 the history and systems class once again undertook the history project—their goal was to produce as complete a document as possible. Their efforts, in combination with those of the previous year, resulted in the preparation of a 40-page "History of Psychology at Emporia State University" booklet. This "finished" (surely there will be future additions and revisions) work is divided into three sections: (a) a narrative history of psychology at Emporia State, (b) a chronological listing of courses that have been and/or are being offered, and (c) a chronological listing of

faculty who have taught at the institution. We feel that the booklet is both factually accurate and interesting reading material. For example, the narrative-history section contains such unusual bits of information as the texts (and their prices) that were used in several of the earliest courses. It is hard to imagine the two-volume set of William James' *Principles* of *Psychology* costing $4.80, or Titchener's *Psychology* costing only $1.00. Information reflecting an active 1905 psychology club that was sponsored by, and met in the home of, Dr. Norman Triplett is also presented. Current Psychology Club and Psi Chi members are quick to point this out with an unmistakable tone of prides to prospective members.

What has all of this accomplished, and how does this project relate to other institutions? First, a rather large number of students enrolled in history of psychology courses have experienced the history of their discipline first hand—and they really enjoyed it. Second, the students organized and staged a highly successful history of psychology symposium. The information presented at this event was, without question of considerable interest and importance. However? the student involvement and participation would have to be counted as equally important. Third, the symposium as mentioned yielded several hours of useful videotapes. Fourth we now have a 40-page history of psychology booklet that is being used for many purposes. For examples each new undergraduate major and/or new graduate student is given a copy. We are proud of our heritage and want to share this pride and enthusiasm with our students. As a teaching aid for the history and systems course this booklet is unparalleled. Because the information directly applies to "their" school, it immediately creates a very high interest level in the students. Class discussions, focusing on this works help make the "schools of psychology" concept much more meaningful. After reading and discussing the material in the booklets students have an excellent understanding of their development and how one such school helped mold the diversity that currently exists in their own department. Lastly, the project is not fully completed, nor does it show signs of completion in the near future. Plans are being made by several students to continue researching, "just to make sure that something has not been left out." The addition of a new section for the booklet featuring the chronological listing of graduate students and their thesis titles has also been proposed. The project may never end. We do not think it should.

Our success with this project prompts us to recommend it to others. Certainly, other colleges and universities have equally fascinating psychological histories. The enjoyment and satisfaction (for both faculty and students) that such a project can generate are, in our opinion unsurpassed. The benefits, as noted above, are many and varied. The staging of a history of psychology symposium, in addition to the preparation of a written history, is highly encouraged. Other activities, such as paper sessions and/or pictorial displays, can easily be envisioned. Given the initial excitement and stimulation from a concerned faculty member, the history of psychology can be very stimulating. Once this has occurred then student enthusiasm will help produce the "snowball" effect. One word of caution. Do not hesitate too long to get started. Many of the direct links (e.g., former faculty members) with the founders of psychology in the United States are growing old. What a shame to let their insights die with them.

References

Beach, F. A. F. A. Beach: Autobiography. In G. Lindzey (Ed.), *A history of psychology in autobiography* (Vol. VI.). New York: Prentice-Hall, 1974, pp. 31-58.

Benjamin, L. T. *Teaching history of psychology: A handbook.* New York: Academic Press, 1981.

Chaplin, J. P., & Krawiec, T. S. *Systems and theories of psychology.* (4th Ed.). New York: Holt, Rinehart, and Winston, 1979.

Triplett, N. The dynamogenic factors in pace-making and competition. *American Journal of Psychology,* 1897, *9,* 507-532.

Research Projects for a History of Psychology

Austin E. Grigg
University of Richmond

For a number of years, I have felt that the course in History and Systems of Psychology seemed too much like a lecture course that could be given by an English professor or a History professor if either had known more about psychology. In most of his courses, the psychology major has been given careful indoctrination about the kinds of methodologies a scientist employs so that he can obtain meaningful data and draw proper inferences. But often the course in the History of Psychology has not challenged the student to be a participant investigator. My own identification with History and Systems began when I took a meticulously scholarly course as an undergraduate under a Boring trained professor, then a fine course given in graduate school by John A. McGeoch, and many years later a stimulating intellectual experience under Gustav Bergman. Also, when a young faculty member at the University of Texas, I visited the classes and enjoyed the anecdotal presentations of Karl M. Dallenbach. This background with unusually effective teachers has given me a deep devotion to the course, but even while a graduate student I had been impressed that History of Psychology was a reading and note-taking type of course.

For the past three years, I have attempted to bring the History of Psychology more into line with the stress on research that our psychology majors have experienced in most other courses offered by the department. The results have been gratifying: From a required course for majors that was offered once each academic year, we have moved to a nonrequired course that is offered twice each academic year. Although the course in History and Systems can serve as an advanced course in general psychology as well as a survey of the historical development of our field, the projects described below broaden the goals of the course and make the student more of a participant than a member of a lecture audience.

Students are assigned projects that require research. The traditional term paper has been abandoned and also the usual parallel reading assignments have been dropped. Students are assigned to project teams of two to four students per team. Each team is given a project (or the team may suggest its own project) and after six weeks, a brief oral report is made to the class. Also, a written summary of the major findings and a bibliography of references and other sources of material must be filed.

Several projects will be described below. Projects may be employed again with a new class if appropriate safeguards are employed so that project teams do not present a mere rehash of some earlier team's work. Usually this is accomplished by assigning an extension of an earlier project, or an elaboration from entirely different sources or perspectives.

One of the most effective projects has been a study of the history of psychology at the student's university—in this case, the University of Richmond. One team, for example, studied old University of Richmond catalogues and ascertained when the first course in psychology was given at the university (1881). A study of catalogues and of the faculty meeting minutes was made in an effort to establish the exact date that laboratory work in psychology was begun at the university (1912-13). The team also ascertained that the first animals were introduced into the psychology laboratory in 1937. The team reported the problems in determining exact dates for major developments in the department and this was related to the difficulty in determining whether Wundt actually established his laboratory in 1874 or 1879. Also, the class discussed the several claims for the first psychology laboratory in the United States and the problems of deciding exact dates. This research team also studied the background of the faculty in psychology from the first professor to offer a course at the University of Richmond to the current faculty. Later this was coordinated with a discussion of whether Richmond students had been in the traditions of functionalism, behaviorism, and of the lack of any Gestalt orientation among the succession of faculty.

Another team combed old graduation programs, alumni records and records of the Registrar to learn the names of students who majored in psychology. Then this group searched the Directory of the American Psychological Association and found those graduates of the Richmond program who had become members of A.P.A. (Henry E. Garrett, R. Nevitt Sanford, Fillmore Sanford, Stuart Cook, Lawrence Pinneo, Henry King, MacEldin Trawick and more than 37 others). Three alumni have served as officers of the APA! Needless to say, this remarkable record stimulated excitement and also pride in the students for their department.

In a somewhat more academic library project, a team studied psychological journals for each decade interval beginning with 1910 and concluding with 1970 to determine the characteristic treatment of data. This project resulted in a class discussion of changes in the use of statistics over the years, of shifts from protocols from single subjects, to very small samples, to larger samples. Another team studied four classical experiments, as the Jenkins and Dallenbach study of memory after sleep versus waking, and hypothesized what the attitude of current psychology editors would be to number of subjects, controls employed, statistical treatment and generalization from the data. This project involved a careful analysis of the originally published research and a comparative study of other articles during that period and of changes that have occurred in published research since that time as reflected from current issues of the same journal.

These projects have had a stimulating effect on class discussions and have given students first-hand experience with some of the problems of documenting and evaluating the development of topics in psychology. At the same time, the study of the text and the lectures have insured a good background in the basic essentials of the history of psychology. The course has become an advanced course in general psychology as well as a course that offers some practical experience in investigating the development of local psychology and of topics familiar to the student from general psychology.

A Role-Playing Exercise for the History of Psychology Course

Charles I. Brooks
King's College

A procedure is described in which college students portray individuals studied in the History of Psychology course. The students work in teams, and develop a presentation allowing figures from different time periods (e.g., Locke, Wundt, Thorndike, and Rogers) to discuss and debate psychological issues.

Additionally, each student prepares a bibliography and position summary of the individual portrayed. Variations of this basic procedure, some more successful than others, have been tried in three different classes and are also described. It is concluded that the exercise can be a valuable pedagogical tool that gives students personal appreciation of historical figures, plus a better understanding of continuity in the evolution of psychological issues.

Shaklee (1957) describes an exercise for the History of Psychology course in which students portray renowned psychologists. This format allows for panel discussions and speeches among people such as Pavlov, Watson, Ebbinghaus, and Wundt. Benjamin (1981) has also suggested the possibility of using this role-playing technique as an instructional device. For the past 5 years, I have used this method in three classes that were much larger (30-40 students) than Shaklee's (12-17 students), and have experimented with some variations on the basic technique, some of which seem to work better than others.

In the standard procedure, I divide the class into six teams of six to seven players each. The individuals to be portrayed are specified, and the students decide which role a team member will play.

The general instructions on the course syllabus are as follows:

> Periodically during the semester, a class will be devoted to a team presentation. This presentation will involve each member of the team playing the role of a particular person from the history of psychology. In this way, we should generate some interesting discussions and confrontations (e.g., Skinner and Freud).

> Team assignments will be made during the second class. Each team will be responsible for assigning roles and for developing a 30-minute play, scene, debate, whatever you want to call it, for presentation in class. Each team member should have an equal part in the play and will be graded separately.

> The purpose of this exercise, of course, is to make some important figures in psychology come to life, and to imagine some of the things they might have discussed. Thus, it is very important to match the script to the positions, arguments, and ideas of the individuals being portrayed.

Some sample roles I have used for teams are as follows: (a) Locke, Hartley, Reid, Kant, Brown, J. S. Mill; (b) J. Müller, Gall, Broca, Fechner, Wundt, Helmholtz; (c) Wundt, Locke, Lotze, Brentano, Külpe, Titchener; (d) Wundt, James, Pavlov, Angell, Sechenov, Titchener, Galton; (e) Thorndike, Watson, J. S. Mill, Descartes, Darwin, Morgan; (f) Kohler, Rogers, Kant, Watson, Skinner, Freud, Locke. The presentations are scheduled only after the individuals portrayed have been covered in the course.

Students are expected to research their roles using a minimum of three sources (not including the text), one of which is a primary source. Each student also prepares a 300- to 400-word summary of the position of the individual portrayed, and a discussion of how that position compares with one other character portrayed on the team. The paper serves as a "closing argument" delivered on whatever issue was discussed by the team.

For the actual presentation, members of each team are free to coordinate the different roles in any way they wish. The only requirement is that each team member have approximately equal time in the presentation. Many of the presentations have been ingenious in the coordination of scripts and props to settings meaningful to the students. One skit re-created a local student watering hole, with Wundt the bartender patiently serving and listening to the likes of Brentano and Külpe discussing the nature of thought. Another group used the "This is Your Life" format, with psychologists from the past surprising the course professor, who was the unsuspecting guest. On another occasion, a stuffed dog was rigged with a rubber hose so that when Pavlov rang a cowbell, water literally gushed from the dog's mouth into a bucket. The effect was enhanced when Pavlov rang the bell while Titchener was making a point about the value of introspection. One particularly memorable performance was modeled after "Family Feud." Imagine Darwin as master of ceremonies asking contestants Watson and Descartes to "Give two innate ideas of the mind." (Descartes pressed the buzzer first. Watson's team, however, eventually won the grand prize: a voyage around the world on the *Beagle*).

I have tried some variations on the basic technique and have found some to work better than others. The presentations, for instance, are generally much more effective when students were allowed to form their own teams. When I randomly assigned students to teams, the "chemistry" of some of the teams was often lacking, and they gave somewhat ill prepared presentations. In the classes where the students formed their own teams, the presentations were generally much more sophisticated, lively, and informative. In these cases, the exercise was clearly social as well as academic, and the students learned much about group dynamics, cooperation, and productivity.

Originally, I required only the class presentation and the list of sources used to prepare for the session. This procedure made grading very difficult because it was hard to separate the substance of a student's role from the quality of the performance. I now base the grade (which counts 10% toward the course grade) primarily on the paper, along with how well the student represents a particular position during the class presentation. Evaluation of the latter is helped during class discussion following the team exercise. In fact, sufficient class time should be allowed for such discussion because the other students are usually eager to question the participants .

I have scheduled team sessions periodically throughout the semester, or have delayed them until close to the end of the course. The latter schedule gives more flexibility regarding team make-up. If a session is scheduled around the middle of the term, for instance, inclusion of 20th-century figures not yet covered in the course is precluded.

Students generally view the exercise as a positive experience and a worthwhile addition to the course. The mean rating on a 5-point scale (1 = *not at all worthwhile*, 5 = *extremely worthwhile*) over three classes (*N* = 117) was 4.63. Many students also commented informally that they thought they would remember their role and the importance of their person in the development of psychology long after other aspects of the course material were forgotten.

Overall, I view the exercise positively and plan to repeat it periodically. My experience supports those of Shaklee (1957) and of Balch (1983), who used role-playing in general psychology classes to demonstrate client-centered therapy. The students clearly get involved. Trying to be someone else, rather than merely conveying positions and principles in a term paper, makes students active and independent learners. They are forced to try to get "under the skin" of a Wundt or a Thorndike and, on the basis of their independent research, imagine how they might have responded to a critic or a supporter. The historical

figures in psychology become more than words on a page.

I have also found that the exercise allows students to discover a continuity in the development of psychology. As they are forced to develop interactions among characters of different time periods, they see linkages of thought not previously apparent. Students often have difficulty in uncovering common threads and developmental trends across figures from different time periods. The role-playing exercise brings these figures together and fosters more integrative thinking.

References

Balch, W. R. (1983). The use of role-playing in a classroom demonstration of client-centered therapy. *Teaching of Psychology, 10,* 173-174.

Benjamin, L. T., Jr. (1981). *Teaching history of psychology: A handbook.* New York: Academic Press.

Shaklee, A. B. (1957). Autobiography in teaching history of psychology. *American Psychologist, 12,* 282-283.

The Way We Were: Teaching History of Psychology Through Mock APA Conventions

David L. Cole
Occidental College

From its first year of publication, *Teaching of Psychology* has carried articles concerned with the teaching of history and systems of psychology (Griggs, 1974). The February 1979 issue of *ToP* featured a series of seven articles on this topic, as part of the celebration of the centennial of the founding of psychological laboratories. Those articles, together with all of the others published to date in *ToP* on this topic, are included in the reference list at the end of this article.

As in all teaching, a recurrent concern is how to actively engage students in the learning process. For some this seems a particularly difficult challenge in teaching the history of psychology (Nissim-Sabat, 1980), but others deny special difficulty in this regard (Benjamin, 1979). Independent of the issue of possible student disinterest, many teachers report that they find

it useful to bring the student in contact with original sources in the field (Griggs, 1974; Caudle, 1979; Raphelson, 1979; Benjamin, 1979; Harris, 1979; Kushner, 1980; Smith, 1982).

My own interest in a new approach to original sources began several years ago when a student, after completing the regular undergraduate course in History and Systems of Psychology, asked if she could take an independent study course and read more into original works. I agreed to supervise her in this, with the proviso that one aspect of her reporting to me would be to comment on the perspective she was gaining from her reading against the perspective she had gained from my regular lecture course. She did so, on a regular basis, and what became increasingly clear was that as she had heard and read about past research and experimentation in psychology in my course, she had consistently read into such work the levels of research sophistication and the frames of reference that have characterized our approaches in psychology in the second quarter of the 20th century. She was repeatedly struck by the "naiveté" of past work, and by the ways in which it reflected the era of which it was a part, beginning to recognize in the process that in later years our present work in psychology will surely come to bear the same criticism.

I had used books of readings in my class (Dennis, 1948; Watson, 1979; Sahakian, 1981), but by the very nature of being Classics" these had not brought the same reactions from students in general as I found in this student, who was in part reading the more "commonplace" publications of past psychology. My interest was finally moved to the level of action after hearing an address by Popplestone (Popplestone & McPherson, Note 3) in which he gave many examples of the "homey" nature of the reporting of research from the early laboratories of psychology. Stirred by his illustrations, and the reactions of my former student, I decided to move ahead in holding mock "APA conventions" as part of my class in History and Systems of Psychology. In these conventions, students present past research papers in psychology as if they were the original author, and the audience is confined (in raising questions or challenges) to their understanding of the prevailing state of knowledge and social outlook at the time of the paper's original publication.

Mock Convention Scheme. I have now held the "mock convention" for three years, varying the format each time. In sequence, the requirement for each year has been as follows:

1981: Students were required to select a research article from the period 1890-1910 that was published in a psychological journal of that period. Each student presented a 12 minute "convention" paper as the author of that paper. It was to be presented with conviction, the speaker seeing no flaws in the paper beyond those described by the original author. Members of the audience had to limit their questioning to knowledge available as of the period represented by the publication of the paper. As a follow-up, later in the term, each student prepared a term paper, which traced the research history of the topic covered in the student's oral presentation.

1982: Students were required to select a research article from the period 1940-45 that was published in a psychological journal of that period. The article had to deal with either sex, ethnic, or race differences, or with psychology's involvement in World War II. Each student presented a 12 minute "convention" paper with the same stipulations as used the previous year. Simultaneously with the presentation, the student turned in a term paper which covered the research with which the author of the paper should have been

familiar when he prepared the paper, and also traced the subsequent research history of this topic.

1983: Each student selected a research paper either from the period 1890-1910, or the period 1915-1935, or the period 1945-1955, in the area of child or adolescent psychology. Each time period could only accommodate one third of the class. Papers were presented in chronological order, in the manner of the first two years. A term paper, following the guide lines used the second year, was due on the first day of the convention period.

It will be noted that after the first year, I have required that the term paper incorporate the research body upon which the paper was based, as well as the subsequent research history of the topic. This change resulted from the difficulty and discomfort of students the first year in answering questions from the audience. They had a problem in being too confined to their particular paper in terms of contemporary knowledge as of the date of publication.

I have selected different topics and different time eras each year to avoid a tendency for a student to lean on the work of a previous student, (direct plagiarism would of course be ruled out by my familiarity with the papers given previously), as well as to sustain my own interest Whereas the early dates that we used the first year led to papers that showed how casual some of the early research appears by current standards, other things entered the second year. I had hoped that the selections made would reflect value systems held by psychologists. To a limited extent this was true. However the main impact of the content of the papers was to surprise students when they found out that psychologists had actually been concerned with some of these issues as "early" as the late 1940s! In part, student reaction helped me to understand more clearly that portions of the history of our field which I regard as "recent" in the sense that I lived through those periods, are virtually as distant in the eyes of the students as the work of G. Stanley Hall or James Mark Baldwin is to me.

The idea behind the format for the third year was to be able to show progressions of ideas, and particularly, to show how the systematic positions within psychology impacted on research. A particularly useful pairing in the third year saw the paper presented by "Rosalie Rayner" on the conditioning of little Albert, followed immediately by a paper by "Mary Cover Jones" on the use of conditioning techniques to remove a child's fear.

Values of the System. I have made no formal assessment of outcomes of the approach. Student evaluations of the course express favorable opinions, but the course brought favorable evaluations before I introduced this technique. From the discussions which swirl around the "convention" activities, one can note the following observations by students: (a) Bias and errors do enter into research, and standard text books do not always "tell it like it was" in terms of the conduct of the research. (b) Racism, sexism, and other social attitudes do enter into research in terms of topic selection, assumptions and interpretations. (c) There were many more women active in earlier psychological research than students realized or than their texts lead them to anticipate. (d) Although we are now more sophisticated in terms of methodology even "ancient" research was often interesting, creative, and useful. (e) Psychologists were sucked into the optimism that others felt as to what the world could become after the end of World War II. (f) Most important, perhaps, from the standpoint of understanding the content of the history of psychology, is the students' awareness that the areas of activity for early day psychologists, particularly at the turn of the century were much more diversified than their history of psychology texts invite them to believe. Students express surprise to find so many different topics under early consideration.

Problems. Despite my enthusiasm for the experience, there are unresolved problems. I am never sure how much freedom to allow the students in selection of their papers for oral presentations. Students are attracted, understandably, to "off beat," eccentric papers. Although these may make for very interesting oral presentations, they may leave the student badly disadvantaged when the student seeks to write a term paper tracing the subsequent research history of that topic. I have found myself increasingly warning students away from some of the topics they propose, on grounds that they will find very little bases for their term paper.

Another issue has to do with how early to get the students to make their selections . My predisposition is to ask that these decisions be made very early, to encourage the students to get ahead of the game, and not delay the work on their term papers. At the same time, at the outset of the course many students have very little feeling for which papers will represent major issues, systematic positions, etc., in the history of the field. Early selection often works against the choice of papers of real significance to the course. I have slowly delayed the deadline for topic selection, and will, in 1984 probably not ask for such selection until about halfway through the course—at such time as the basic systematic positions within psychology have been made clearer to the students.

General Observations. As might be expected the conventions provide moments of theater for those willing to enter into the possibilities. A "student of Professor Titchener's" challenged the methodological heresies of an early paper. A young "graduate student at the University of Chicago" expressed vague feelings of discomfort over the anthropomorphizing in a paper he heard on the "psychic development of the young white rat." "Herman Goltz" presented work on cortical localization, which, when he switched to English after

being advised by chairperson "Munsterberg" that many in his audience did not understand German, clearly anticipated the work of Franz and Lashley. "G. Stanley Hall" has talked about his beginning explorations of children's fears, "Florence Goodenough" has discussed what may be gleaned from children's drawings, "Mary Calkins" has talked excitedly about the new program in experimental psychology at Wellesley, etc.

I chair each session, introducing myself as a psychologist of the era involved, who might indeed have been invited to chair a session on the topic at hand. This leaves me free to comment on each paper, perhaps noting its relationship to other work going on "at present," and sometimes to make predictions as to where this particular line of inquiry may lead in psychology's "future." No more trenchant predictions have ever been made in the history of our field.

As noted, the technique is not without its problems. Students are understandably uncertain about the "state of knowledge" as of the time of the presentation of the paper, and this inhibits questioning. Students complain that too many of the papers are poorly presented and hard to follow, and it does not seem to comfort them when I assure them that this is the most ecologically valid aspect of the entire process. Indeed, the ecological validity of the technique is at the same time a source of its weakness. Papers are often read, as they are at conventions, and as at conventions are in fact sometimes hard to follow. Students are nervous, and do not always present the papers well. Time is short, and it is not possible to give as much time to discussion as would be desirable. The time for a session runs out and we have to vacate the room because another group (in this case, another class) needs to get into the room. But after three runs, I intend to continue it, perhaps in modified form, until my own interests dictate a turn to another route. It gets students involved. I hope it teaches history in a way which gives it a dimension of realism that it does not easily achieve in other ways. It suggests that text books construct reality as well as reporting it. And it hints that "progress" is a sometimes thing.

References and Selected Bibliography

Benjamin, L, T., Jr. Instructional strategies in the history of psychology. *Teaching of Psychology,* 1979, *6*, 15-17,

Brown, D. R. The teaching of the history of psychology. *Teaching* of *Psychology,* 1979, *6*, 3.

Caudle, F. M. Using "demonstrations class experiments and the projection lantern" in the history of psychology class. *Teaching* of *Psychology,* 1979, *6*, 7-11.

Davis, S. F., Janzen, W. C., & Davis, R. L. Teaching and learning the history of psychology need not be boring . *Teaching of Psychology,* 1982, *9*, 183-184.

Dennis, W. (Ed.). *Readings in the history of psychology.* New York: Appleton-Century-Crofts, 1948.

Diekhoff, G. M. Cognitive maps as a way of presenting dimensions of comparison within the history of psychology. *Teaching of Psychology,* 1982, *9,* 115-116.

Epstein, R. A. A convenient model for the evolution of early psychology as a scientific discipline. *Teaching of Psychology,* 1981, *8,* 42-44.

Furedy, J. J, Riley, D. M., & Furedy, C. A. Teaching undergraduates the philosophy of psychology: the method of criticized introspection. *Teaching of Psychology,* 1981, *8,* 47-49.

Griggs, A. E. Research projects for a history of psychology. *Teaching of Psychology,* 1974, *1,* 84-85,

Harris, B. Professional seminar in clinical psychology taught from a historical perspective. *Teaching of Psychology,* 1979, *6,* 17-19.

Kushner, R. I. The prescriptive approach to the teaching of the history of psychology course. *Teaching of Psychology,* 1980, 7, 184-185.

Murray, F. S., & Rowe, F. B. Psychology laboratories in the United States prior to 1900. *Teaching of Psychology,* 1979, *6,* 19-21.

Nissim-Sabat, D. Teaching history of psychology through art and music. *Teaching of Psychology,* 1980, 7, 223-226.

Raphelson, A. C. The unique role of the history of psychology in undergraduate education. *Teaching of Psychology,* 1979, *6,* 12-14.

Robinson, D. N. The history of psychology and the ends of instruction. *Teaching of Psychology,* 1979, *6,* 7-11.

Sahakian, W. S. *History of psychology* (Revised Edition). Itasca, IL: Peacock, 1981.

Smith, A. H. Different approaches for teaching the history of psychology course. *Teaching of Psychology,* 1982, *9,* 180-182.

Terry, W. S. Tracing psychology's roots: a project for history and systems courses. *Teaching of Psychology,* 1980, 7, 176-177.

Watson, R. I. *Basic writings in the history of psychology.* New York: Oxford Press, 1979.

Wetmore, K. Notes on graduate training in the history of psychology. *Teaching of Psychology,* 1981, *8,* 50.

The Create-A-Game Exam: A Method to Facilitate Student Interest and Learning

Joy L. Berrenberg
Ann Prosser
University of Colorado at Denver

This article describes the "create-a-game" exam technique for a History of Psychology course. Students design and construct games that incorporate a range of knowledge. The procedure is a challenging, engaging, and effective supplement or alternative to traditional evaluation methods. Playing the games in class provides an excellent and enjoyable review of course material.

Multiple-choice exams, short-answer exams, essay exams, oral exams, term papers, and class projects are traditional methods for assessing a student's mastery of course material. Although all such evaluations should engage the student in the process of reviewing and synthesizing the course material, many students, even the brightest, apply the "least effort principle" in their preparations. Often their review is cursory and involves rote memorization rather than organized analysis.

It is generally assumed that students learn and retain more when they are actively and personally involved with the course material. Although a number of class projects facilitate this type of involvement (e.g., Brozek & Schneider, 1973; Coffield, 1973; Gurman, Holliman, & Camperell, 1988; McAdam, 1987), relatively few examination procedures incorporate this active approach. One example of such an approach allows students to comment on or justify their answers on multiple-choice exams (Dodd & Leal, 1988; Nield & Wintre, 1986). This procedure encourages more thinking and less rote memorization. Another procedure involves innovative and integrative essay questions in a History of Psychology course (Berrenberg, 1990). Presumably, such questions force students to organize and synthesize the material. Benjamin (1979) described an exam "game" in which teams of students compete to identify portraits of famous figures in psychology. He suggested that the element of fun in this kind of exam helps to motivate students to learn more. Ackil (1986) and Carlson (1989) described two teacher-designed games that motivate students to learn factual material and prepare for exams. Note, however, that these last examples are not used to evaluate student performance.

To expand the options for active, personally involving evaluation procedures, we developed an examination technique in which students create a game for a particular subject area. The procedure is designed to engage students' creative talents and to encourage detailed review and synthesis of course material. Unlike assignments that require students to write their own exam questions, the create-a-game exam requires students to develop a structure (e.g., game categories) to present factual material. In many instances, it also requires students to make fine distinctions regarding the difficulty of the material (e.g., how many points to offer for a correct answer). Furthermore, the number of questions students prepare for a game usually exceeds the number requested for a write-your-own exam exercise (most students write 100 or more questions), thus requiring a more thorough review of course material. Finally, the create-a-game exam encourages students to think about and present material in creative and innovative ways that may improve understanding as well as retention.

Our approach can be readily adapted to any course in psychology and used to supplement or replace other evaluation methods. The resulting games may be played with fellow class members, thus providing additional review of course content. What follows is a description of the create-a-game technique developed in a History of Psychology course.

Procedures and Grading

We have used the create-a-game exam as part of a takehome exam in a senior level History of Psychology course. Students answer one or more integrative essay questions and develop a History of Psychology game. Working individually, students have 2 weeks to complete the exam and game. Instructions for the game portion of the exam are:

Create a "History of Psychology Game. " It may be a board game, word game, trivia game, or whatever. It must cover a broad range of information pertinent to the history of psychology. Include rules, game board, game pieces, or whatever is needed to play the game. Have fun and be creative!

Your game will graded on the basis of (a) the accuracy of information, (b) the breadth of coverage (e.g., game covers a variety of historical time periods, events, theories, ideas, figures in the history of psychology), (c) your understanding of course material as evidenced in meaningful organization of game material (e.g., information is grouped into appropriate categories, such as Greek Philosophers, French Positivism, Neo-Behaviorists), (d) neatness of game materials (e.g., readable instructions, game cards), and (e) originality.

We do not provide examples of games because we do not want to limit creativity. Although we have used the procedure as an individual project, it should also work well as a group assignment.

Most students satisfy the criteria so the resulting distribution of exam scores is negatively skewed. The proportion of students who do a substandard job on the game is lower than it is for other assignments. We generally make the game portion of the exam worth 25% of the course grade, which seems appropriate for the amount of time and effort involved.

The completed games, or some sample thereof, can be effective teaching techniques. We have used one full class period before an objective exam to allow students to play the games of their choice as a way of providing painless review of material.

Examples of Games

The most common games include take-offs on Jeopardy, Trivial Pursuit, and Life. Four examples of games developed by students are described next.

1. *Psychological Trivia.* In this game, the players compete for points by correctly answering questions from one of several categories (e.g., functionalism, psychoanalysis, the mind-body problem). The easiest questions in a category are worth 100 points (e.g., Who was the founder of psychoanalysis?); the most difficult questions are worth 500 points (e.g., What is the title and publication date of Dewey's famous "founding" paper on functionalism?).

2. *Freud's Inner Circle.* The object of this game is to move Freudian tokens (e.g., small cigars, toilet seats) around a game board, answer questions correctly, and accumulate enough points to move to Freud's inner circle in the middle of the game board. Once in the circle, players must demonstrate their knowledge of Freud's position or risk getting "kicked out. " Variations of this basic "board and dice" game have been called The Rat Maze, The Therapeutic Couch, The Funny Farm, and Psychomania.

3. *Psych-Out.* This game consists of a board with photographs of famous figures in the history of psychology. Upon landing on a square associated with

a particular face, players must name the figure and as many of his or her contributions to psychology as possible. The more they know, the more points they earn.

4. *Psychogories.* This game is similar to Gin Rummy or Go Fish; the object is to be the first to accumulate complete sets of cards. Players are dealt 10 cards, each of which states a theory, belief, or assumption (e.g., reinforcement plays an important role in learning, higher mental processes cannot be studied experimentally). Cards are drawn and discarded until a player's hand is full of completed sets. A set consists of three or more theoretically compatible cards (e.g., all ideas held in common by behaviorists, gestaltists). Psychogories is a conceptually challenging game because the categories are not indicated on the cards and players must determine for themselves which ideas constitute sets.

Student Response

Students are generally enthusiastic about the create-a-game exam. This enthusiasm is demonstrated by the amount of time and effort they put into their creations: one student sculpted and fired ceramic game pieces, another handprinted 200 question cards in beautiful calligraphy, another found and copied onto the game board old photographs of Wundt's lab and other psychological memorabilia. In a recent term, 63% of the students in a class of 65 found designing the game to be an "extremely useful" method for learning course material, and 77% said using the games for review was an "extremely useful" way to spend class time. Many students spontaneously mentioned the create-a-game procedure in the comment section of the course evaluation. One student said the procedure was a "refreshing change" from traditional exams. Another said designing the game helped him to "learn history inside-out." Others described the exam as "personally involving," "lots of fun," "a really worthwhile exercise," and "a painless way to learn. "

In conclusion, the create-a-game technique is a method for evaluation that actively engages students in the review and organization of course material. It could easily be incorporated into a variety of courses.

References

Ackil, J. E. (1986). PhysioPursuit:A trivia-type game for the classroom. *Teaching of Psychology, 13,* 91.

Benjamin, L. T., Jr. (1979). Instructional strategies in the history of psychology. *Teaching of Psychology, 6,* 15-17.

Berrenberg, J. L. (1990) . Integrative and goal-relevant essay questions for history and systems courses. *Teaching of Psychology, 17,* 113-115.

Brozek, J., & Schneider, L. S. (1973). Second summer institute on the history of psychology. *Journal of the History of the Behavioral Sciences, 9,* 91-101.

Carlson, J. F. (1989). Psychosexual pursuit: Enhancing learning of theoretical psychoanalytic constructs. *Teaching of Psychology, 16,* 82-84.

Coffield, K. E. (1973) . Additional stimulation for students in history and systems. *American Psychologist, 28,* 624-625.

Dodd, D. K., & Leal, L. (1988). Answer justification: Removing the "trick" from multiple-choice questions. *Teaching of Psychology, 15,* 37-38.

Gurman, E. B., Holliman, W. B., & Camperell, K. (1988). Oral application questions as a teaching strategy. *Teaching of Psychology, 15,* 149-151.

McAdam, D. (1987) . Bringing psychology to life. *Teaching of Psychology, 14,* 29-31.

Nield, A. F., & Wintre, M. G. (1986). Multiple-choice questions with an option to comment: Student attitudes and use. *Teaching of Psychology, 13,* 196-199.

Note

Portions of this article were presented at the annual meeting of the American Psychological Association, Boston, MA, August 1990.

The Crossword Puzzle as a Teaching Tool

Edward K. Crossman
and Sharyn M. Crossman
Utah State University

In courses such as the History of Psychology, it is necessary to learn a variety of relationships, events, and sequences in addition to the less-than-pleasant task of having to pair certain key concepts with related names: speed of nervous impulses—Helmholtz; phrenology—Gall; etc.

One tool thought to be useful in assisting in the type of learning mentioned above is the crossword puzzle. Several potential advantages proposed to result from the use of these puzzles were: (a) Many people are already familiar with such puzzles; (b) crossword puzzles are usually perceived as a recreational activity, something not connected with school for most students. Thus, it might be an enjoyable learning experience; (c) might change study habits or skills; (d) could perhaps increase interest in course material; (e) might be a useful technique in other courses; (f) might increase retention of material which in turn might increase exam scores after exposure to puzzles as compared to exam grades before.

Procedure. To evaluate these potential benefits of the crossword puzzle, 15 students in an upper division course in History of Psychology were given three crossword puzzles to fill in during the latter half of the academic quarter One such puzzle, which is shown in Figure 1, contained information from approximately five chapters of the text. The puzzles were used to prepare students for a matching section on subsequent exams. Rather than requiring students to complete the puzzles for a grade, completion of the puzzles was optional .

I used an "availability sample" of students enrolled in the course who were present the day the evaluation was conducted. They showed typical heterogeneity in age, marital status and other variables.

Although creating a crossword puzzle takes a bit of practice, it can be an enjoyable experience. However, in this study a computer was used to construct the puzzle in Figure 1. Initially, a list of matching names and ideas was created. This list was entered into the computer which arranged the names into an appropriate configuration (many permutations per list are possible) and printed out the puzzle shown in Fig-

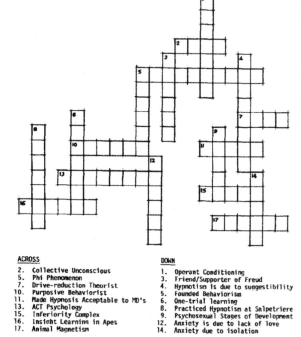

ACROSS
2. Collective Unconscious
5. Phi Phenomenon
7. Drive-reduction Theorist
10. Purposive Behaviorist
11. Made Hypnosis Acceptable to MD's
13. ACT Psychology
15. Inferiority Complex
16. Insight Learning in Apes
17. Animal Magnetism

DOWN
1. Operant Conditioning
3. Friend/Supporter of Freud
4. Hypnotism is due to suggestibility
5. Founded Behaviorism
6. One-trial learning
8. Practiced Hypnotism at Salpetriere
9. Psychosexual Stages of Development
12. Anxiety is due to lack of love
14. Anxiety due to isolation

Figure 1. Crossword Puzzle for a portion of the History and Systems course.

ure 1. The program which accomplished this puzzle construction was written by Wood and Reid[1] for the Commodore series of microcomputers.

Evaluation. After the class had received and completed the three puzzles, which took place over a period of approximately four weeks, a brief 14 item questionnaire, which assessed students' perceptions concerning their experiences in using the crossword puzzles, was constructed. Item construction was guided by the potential advantages outlined above.

Sixty-seven percent of the respondents had former experience with completion of crossword puzzles, and 33% had none. One hundred percent of the respondents found the experience enjoyable. Furthermore, they found it creative, offered variety, and had aided learning. Changes in spelling awareness and working for greater accuracy were noted by 40% of the sample, 40% claimed no changes in spelling and 20% were unsure. Furthermore, 40% indicated a positive change in study habits toward greater care and thoroughness in study, but 60% suggested no change. In a follow-up probe question, students indicated puzzles helped not only in associating the facts, but in lengthening retention and in causing them to form mental pictures to tie names to concepts. As a result of completing the puzzles, some students reported increased levels of confidence in taking tests, were more motivated to study, and had a greater appreciation of the individuals and their theories or findings.

A 5-point Likert-type scale revealed that the puzzles had no detrimental effects on interest; in fact, 40 percent of the respondents indicated they were "somewhat" to a "great deal more" interested in the material and 60% took a neutral position.

Respondents felt a range of 3 to 5 puzzles would be best over the academic quarter with 4 being the optimum number. Fifty percent of the sample thought puzzles would be useful in general education survey courses, 27% in skill courses, 18% in tool courses, and 5% suggested other courses where the puzzles might work well but indicated they did not know how to classify such courses. None selected the "no benefits" category.

Fourteen students had pretest and post-test exam scores. These scores were compared using a t-test for related means $t(13) = 3.81$, $p < .01$. Thus, crossword puzzles appear to have had a positive effect on learning of course material for these students. In fact, only two students showed decreased exam scores at post-test and these losses were negligible in both cases, ranging from one to two and one-half points.

Discussion and Conclusion. Although there are limitations in the data, respondents were distributed across many demographic variables. Thus, their responses are probably suggestive of typical responses for larger samples of students, but generalization of results beyond this small group is not recommended.

These respondents seemed to enjoy the puzzles. They were more motivated to learn and retained the material longer than they did during the first part of the quarter before puzzles were used. Also, post-test scores significantly differed from pretest comparisons at the $p < .01$ level. All-in-all, crossword puzzles seem to be a promising tool for use in a variety of courses where key concepts must be paired with some other piece of information, for example, names and ideas.

There are many possibilities for designing various types of crossword puzzles, limited only by the imagination of the creator. Not only are such puzzles useful in History of Psychology, where important dates, names and concepts must be learned, but such a technique could be used in other psychology, human development, sociology, and anthropology courses, as well as other substantive areas in the social sciences.

Note

This program, "crossword," requires at least 8K of memory and is available on disk TG from the Toronto Pet User's Group, Chris Bennett, 381 Lawrence Avenue West, Toronto, Ontario, M5M 1B9, Canada.

Expanding Coverage in the History Course by Toasting Significant but Often Overlooked Contributors

Randall D. Wight
Ouachita Baptist University

This teaching activity attempts to expand the range of contributions usually covered in a history of psychology course by incorporating the social custom of toasting.

In teaching the history of psychology, one confronts the problem of covering much material in little time.

The following activity attempts to familiarize students with a wider range of contributions to the discipline and to foster a contextual understanding of these contributions in a fashion that compresses both time and information.

I began by converting Zusne's (1984) "Appendix A: Chronological Listing by Birth Date" to a generic calendar of birth and death dates. Individuals recorded in the calendar were ones for whom Zusne recorded at least one precise date. Each week History of Psychology students ($N = 8$) received four to six names from the corresponding week's ensuing list of dates. "Toasting psychology," using coffee and cola, occurred during the first minutes of the following class meeting.

Participation was voluntary, and 1 extra credit point was available for each acceptable toast. An *acceptable toast* was one in which the student demonstrated a creative appreciation of a given individual's contribution; an *unacceptable toast* was one in which the student merely repeated textbook information. Students were to model Franklin Delano Roosevelt's toasting formula: "Be sincere, be brief, be seated." The campus library reserved biographical material (e.g., Gregory & Zangwill, 1987; Zusne, 1984) to help students obtain background information.

Although humorous toasts were encouraged, the guiding principle was to toast, not roast. Students were instructed to honor the accomplishments of contributors. Their toasts included: "Here's to Pinel, who lost his head saving the minds of others"; "Here's to Harlow, who had terry cloth with a monkey on its back"; "Here's to Brill, who got a thrill translating Freud." The students appeared to enjoy the exercise. Results from their semester-end evaluation of the activity confirmed this observation. On a scale ranging from *poor* (1) to *great* (10), students rated this activity as being worthwhile ($M = 7.9$, $SD = 1.36$). On a scale ranging from *ineffective* (1) to *effective* (10), students rated the technique to be efficacious in familiarizing them with the development of psychology ($M = 7.0$, $SD = 2.14$) and in facilitating their ability to verbalize information ($M = 7.8$, $SD = 2.92$).

The aforementioned salute to Brill serves to illustrate comments that an instructor may make following a student's toast. Brill came to New York in 1889 at the age of 15 to escape an intolerable homelife in his native Austria-Hungary. He struggled to put himself through New York University and the Columbia University medical school, often having to interrupt his education to earn money in order to continue that education. In 1907, Brill travelled for further medical study to Zurich where he became acquainted with the work of Freud. Intrigued with what he learned, Brill sojourned to Vienna to meet Freud. Freud's influence changed Brill's life: Brill returned to New York and there became a principal advocate for psychoanalysis (Gay, 1988). It was Brill who first translated Freud's work into English, and therein lies an important point that an instructor may make following a toast to Brill. Brill's enthusiasm for psychoanalysis failed to prompt him to produce a careful translation of Freud's publications. Freud himself was apparently aware of Brill's inaccuracies and wrote, in 1928, to a Hungarian psychoanalyst that, "Of my

Interpretation of Dreams there is, as far as I know, only one *English* [italics added] translation, that of Dr. Brill. It is, I suppose, best, if one wants to read the book at all, to read it in German" (Freud, quoted in Gay, 1988, p. 465). Students need to consider the influence of a translator on the understanding of a theory.

The technique has pitfalls. First, an instructor should provide an appropriate historical context for each individual presented. Failing to do so may perpetuate origin myths (see Samelson, 1974). Second, toasting is a social grace that is unfamiliar to most students. Some training in this custom (see Baldridge, 1978; Martin, 1983; Post, 1940) is often necessary. Third, students need prompting to generate unique toasts; otherwise, they may simply repeat what they read. Fourth, if the activity is voluntary, self-starters may benefit more than reserved students. Fifth, the exercise may be difficult to adapt to a large class.

Despite these drawbacks, there is much to commend this technique. First, and inherently countering the second stated disadvantage, students benefit from practice in public speaking. Second, students become acquainted with contributors to psychology who are often overlooked in the usual history of psychology course. Third, toasts may serve as ready made mnemonic devices. Fourth, and perhaps more subtle, a kindling of the understanding of these historical figures as flesh-and-blood people may occur.

References

Baldridge, L. (1978). *The Amy Vanderbilt complete book of etiquette.* Garden City, NY: Doubleday.

Gay, P. (1988). *Freud: A life for our time.* New York: Doubleday.

Gregory, R. L., & Zangwill, O. L. (1987). *The Oxford companion to the mind.* Oxford: Oxford University Press.

Martin, J. (1983). *Miss Manners' guide for the turn-of-the-millennium.* New York: Pharos.

Post, E. (1940). *Etiquette: The blue book of social usage.* New York: Funk and Wagnalls.

Samelson, E. (1974). History, origin myth and ideology: "Discovery" of social psychology. *Journal for the Theory of Social Behaviour, 4,* 217-231.

Zusne, L. (1984). *Biographical dictionary of psychology.* Westport, CT: Greenwood.

Note

A version of this activity was presented in the Division Two Activities Exchange during the annual meeting of the American Psychological Association, New Orleans, August 1989.

The Use of Slides in Class: A Demonstration of Incidental Learning

Alfred C. Raphelson
University of Michigan—Flint

Two History of Psychology classes were taught utilizing more than 1,000 slides illustrating biographies, concepts, and theories. The students were informed that the slides were ancillary and that they would not be held responsible for them. An unannounced Slide Recognition Test, given at the time of the final exam (but not counted toward any grade) was significantly correlated with all examinations given throughout the course.

Although considerable evidence supports the effectiveness of visual learning/teaching aids for promoting classroom learning, some controversy is still associated with their use. McKeachie (1978), for example, reviewed the research on the use of television, films, and other media and found that the evidence supports their use to achieve certain educational objectives. Their usefulness, however, depends on course objectives, characteristics of the students, and the quality of the materials.

Kulik, Kulik, and Cohen (1980) reviewed over 300 research articles on the classroom use of various types of instructional technology, including personalized, computerbased, and programmed instructions, as well as visual materials (slides, transparencies, and films). The studies they reviewed measured the effects of these technologies on learning outcomes, such as major class examinations, student ratings, and course completion. There was a general trend for such instructional technology to produce positive effects on the previously mentioned types of learning outcomes, but the outcomes varied with the type of instructional technology. Personalized systems of instruction produced the strongest results followed, in order, by computerbased instructions, programmed instruction, the autotutorial approach, and visual materials (slides, transparencies, and films).

The fact that visual aids appear to be the least effective of the instructional technologies is something of a surprise, given their long-standing popularity with many instructors. Benjamin (1981), for example, described ways to use slides in teaching History of Psychology that can add to the interest level and provide a change of pace. He suggested using slides in review sessions, and competitive recognition "game" situations add a dimension of "lively, friendly, fun" to the class (pp. 2-4).

Another study demonstrated that the ratings students gave the instructor and a course in Sensation and Perception increased significantly after slides were added (Beins, 1984). Students appreciated the contribution the slides made to their comprehension of the material and the break they provided from the usual lecture format.

I regularly use a large collection of slides in the History of Psychology course to illustrate biographical and historical events. These slides were made from journals, books, personal papers, as well as from visits to sites that have played a role in the lives of important psychologists and/or the history of the field. Like Benjamin, I believe that the slides add an important dimension to the class, but my evidence has always been anecdotal and intuitive. Many students have remarked that the slides are enjoyable and helped them to learn, but I had no direct evidence that they promote better learning.

An attempt was made to obtain more direct evidence that the slides promote the educational aims of the course rather than serving merely as an affective relief. The plan involved giving an unannounced Slide Recognition Test with the final examination and correlating the scores with each of the content examinations given during the course.

The slides were presented during the course as supplements to the lectures. The purpose was to make biographical, cultural, or theoretical points more concrete. The students understood that they would not be responsible for knowing any of the slides and that they would not be tested on slide recognition in any way that affected their grades. Therefore, any purposeful learning of the slides would not improve their grades.

During the semester, two essay exams were given over portions of the course; a comprehensive final exam consisted of objective questions. A total score was obtained by transforming the three exam scores into standard scores and summing them for each student. In determining the total score, the final exam was weighted 10% more than the scores on the two 1-hr exams.

When students arrived to take the 2½-hr final exam, they were told that after working on the exam for 1 hr. they would be interrupted in order to take the Slide Recognition Test. None of them appeared to be disturbed by this 5-min. interruption. They were also told that, although they would be asked to put their names on the answer sheets, their names would not be seen until after their course grades were determined and recorded.

At the appropriate time, each slide was projected on the screen for 15 sec. Out of almost 1,000 slides shown during the semester, 20 were chosen as representing the content of the course and as being more unusual than the others. Eight slides were selected from material covered on the first exam, eight from the material covered on the second exam, and four from the shorter period between the second exam and the final.

The following is a description of the selected slides: S. Freud; Thorndike's Puzzle Box; Charcot in his clinic; Fechner having his "insight" on October 22, 1850 (a drawing); Clever Hans, the calculating horse; William James walking in the country; Anna O. (Bertha Pappenheim); Socrates' Death (Painting); map of Michigan highlighting Sickles, Michigan (C. Hull's boyhood home); C. Darwin; E. B. Titchener in his academic gown; Pavlov; Margaret Washburn; group picture taken during Freud's visit to Clark University in 1909; Wundt and his assistants; memorial to Pavlov's work; Jeremy Bentham icon; J. B. Watson; house in Fenton, Michigan where J. Dewey was married; urn containing Freud's ashes.

The identical procedure was followed in two different classes separated by 1 year. The first class had 27 students and the second had 50 students. Separate correlational analyses conducted for each class showed identical significant relationships. Because each exam score was transformed into a standard score, similar exams in each class were combined for the analyses reported here. Results are presented in Table 1.

All the correlations are statistically significant (Meredith, 1967). The correlation between the Slide Recognition Test and the final exam (.70) is of the same order as the correlations between the first and second exams and the final exam (.74 and .72, respectively). Therefore, the inference can be drawn that although the slides were presented during the course as incidental to the specific material to be learned, they were not perceived by the students as irrelevant. The better students recognized more slides than did the students who performed less well on the examinations.

The point may be raised that the obtained correlations between the examination scores and the Slide Recognition Scores were mediated by other variables (e.g., class attendance). That observation is

Table 1. Correlations Between Examination Scores and Slide Recognition Test Scores

N = 77	Exam 2	Final Exam	Slide Recognition
Exam 1	.71*	.74*	.60*
Exam 2		.72*	.47*
Final exam			.70*

*$p < .01$.

probably correct. Students could not recognize a slide if they were not present when it was shown. But it is also true that class attendance plays some role in exam performance per se, especially in a lecture class like this one.

The purpose of the study was consistent with our observations. Its intent was to determine if slides presented as part of a class but labeled in presentation as only incidental to grade outcome would be related to such performance in the final analysis. If so, the inference could be drawn that slides can be considered to belong with such variables as intelligence, class attendance, previous course experience, and socioeconomic status, which have been shown to affect academic performance.

This study does not, of course, provide direct evidence that slides helped the students to learn the course material better. It does demonstrate, however, that the better students learn and recognize more of the slides even though they have been presented as only incidental to the course goals. At the very least, this result indicates that using slides does not interfere with the class learning nor is it irrelevant to it. At the very best, it is consistent with the hypothesis that these techniques contribute to learning.

References

Beins, B. (1984). The use of slides in psychology classes: Do they help or are they an invitation to sleep? *Teaching of Psychology, 11*, 229-230.

Benjamin, L. T., Jr. (1981). *Teaching history of psychology: A handbook.* New York: Academic.

Kulik, C. C., Kulik, J. A., & Cohen, P. A. (1980). Instructional technology and college teaching. *Teaching of Psychology, 7*, 199-205.

McKeachie, W. J. (1978). *Teaching tips: A guidebook for the beginning college teacher* (7th ed.). Lexington, MA: Heath.

Meredith, W. M. (1967). *Basic mathematical and statistical tables for psychology and education.* New York: McGraw-Hill.

Note

The research for this project was supported in part by a grant from the Faculty Development Fund of The University of Michigan—Flint.

Using "Demonstrations, Class Experiments and the Projection Lantern" in the History of Psychology Course

Fairfid M. Caudle
The College of Staten Island

A wealth of ideas for making the history course come alive for your students may be found in this report.

In 1903, Titchener wrote:

Now that psychological instruction centres in the laboratory, rather than in the library, it is but natural that the old lecture courses should be replaced by courses in which demonstrations, class experiments and the projection lantern figure as largely as they do in elementary physics or elementary zoology. (p. 175)

Although Titchener's remarks were directed toward the instructor of a "beginners' class," they are particularly applicable to today's history of psychology course. While this course is potentially one of the most exciting in the psychology curriculum, it must be acknowledged that no other basic course has been quite so neglected by publishers and manufacturers of teaching aids.

Such neglect is not a new phenomenon, however, and early teachers of psychology were faced with similar problems. For example, lamenting the lack of demonstration materials, Titchener wrote:

It is really surprising—and it is this sort of lackthat justifiesthe present paper—that no dealer in artists' supplies has lithographed a 'psychological spectrum.' (1903, p. 178)

Today, Titchener would no doubt be delighted with the abundance of materials available forthe introductory course, but he would very likely be extremely dissatisfied with the paucity of resources available for teaching that glorious period in which Structuralism and other schools arose. Just as Titchener advised his readers (1903, p. 179) that "in the meantime, until something of the kind is manufactured, the lecturer will find it worth while to provide himself with" suitable materials, the purpose of this paper is to suggest ideas and sources of materials for using "demonstrations, class experiments and the projection lantern" in the history of psychology course.

My own attempts to develop such demonstrations began when, after a particularly difficult and abstract lecture, a bewildered student came to my office and demanded to know what experimental psychology was really *like* when it began. It was fine to talk about introspection and elements, he said, "but what did those people really do in their laboratories?"

As I teach the course today I am stil l trying to answer that student's question and agree with Edmund Clark Sanford who wrote in 1906 that "many things of the greatest importance cannot be learned without actual experience of them, but that experience can be shortened" (p. 4). What follows are brief descriptions of activities which I have found to be most helpful in teaching the history of psychology. The suggestions range from simple demonstrations requiring no materials to more extensive projects to be completed outside class. However, all the activities share the virtue of demonstrating the experiential or experimental basis of important concepts, and many of them impart, in addition, some of the flavor and atmosphere of the early history of psychology.

The Philosophical Roots of Psychology

One way to involve students in the philosophical origins of psychology is to provide examples of issues d iscussed by philosophers which were later explored empirically in the psychology laboratory.

Aristotle's Experiment. Aristotle has been credited with "the oldest recorded piece of work in experimental psychology" (Warren, 1919, p. 253). In his treatise "De Somniis" (On Dreams) Aristotle wrote:

When the fingers are crossed, the one object [placed between them] is felt [by the touch] as two; but yet we deny that it is two; for sight is more authoritative than touch. Yet, if touch stood alone, we should actually have pronounced the one object to be two. (par. 460b20)

In itself this is a simple and effective demonstration. However, it becomes even more interesting when students learn that one of the exercises which Titchener included in his laboratory manual for students (1901/1971, pp. 190-191) was based upon it. Thus, in addition to illustrating how one early psychologist utilized a philosophical source, students begin to learn a little of what it was like to be a student in Titchener's laboratory. When using this demonstration, it is helpful to provide copies of the original quotation from Aristotle together with Titchener's instructions.

Wundt's Thread Experiment. In his 1709 work *An Essay Toward a New Theory of Vision*, Berkeley proposed that distance perception is learned through associating different distances with the tactile-kinesthetic cues provided by various positions of the eyes. Woodworth (1938) describes. an experiment which Wundt conducted in order to test Berkeley's theory and he provides a diagram of apparatus employed in a later version of the experiment (p. 666). The experiment involves a viewing situation in which all cues to distance perception are eliminated except convergence and/or accommodation. The subject views a hanging thread through a tube. After the experimenter changes the d istance of the thread, the subject must report whether the thread is nearer or farther than before.

Presenting the experimental design and a diagram of the apparatus to the class provides an excellent illustration of how a philosophical statement eventually stimulated empirical research. In my own course, some students became intrigued sufficiently to replicate the experiment and to report the results to the class. In the course of this they explored much of the contemporary work on distance perception. Berkeley's writings became more meaningful and students saw the value of studying philosophical antecedents of contemporary problems.

Demonstrations of Psychophysical Concepts

In teaching the history of psychology, a prominent place is usually given to Weber and Fechner for their contributions to psychophysics. However, unless the student has taken a course in experimental psychology, he or she is frequently left in the dark about what was meant by such terms as "two-point threshold" or "just noticeable difference." This can be remedied to some extent by employing demonstrations adapted from early laboratory manuals.

From 1891 through 1896 Edmund Clark Sanford published a series of articles in the American Journal of Psychology entitled *A Laboratory Course in Experimental Psychology* (see especially 1891a, 1891b, 1892, 1896, as well as 1893, which is not part of the course but which is of interest). Boring (1950) described this course as "the first laboratory manual for the new sciences antedating even Titchener" (p. 542).

The advantage of Sanford's articles is that they provide numerous experiments which can be performed with a minimum of apparatus. In his introduction to the series of articles Sanford notes the following:

The demonstrational character of the work has been kept in mind, and the experiments chosen are generally rather qualitative than quantitative. . . . In selecting apparatus the simplest that promised the desired result has generally been chosen; . . . this. . . may perhaps make [the course] useful to those teachers—unfortunately too many—whose equipment must be brought within the compass of a scanty appropriation. (1891a, p.142)

Two-Point Threshold. Among the many demonstrations in this manuals I will mention onlyone. Sanford provides simple instructions for determining the two-point threshold of Weber (1891a, p. 143, # 6). The apparatus he suggests is the "aesthesiometric compass." However, "scanty appropriations" are still a fact of life for most psychology departments and I have found a far simpler (and cheaper) apparatus for informal classroom use: the lowly box of toothpicks. A few moments working with a partner is enough to discover what is meant by the term "two-point threshold" as well as the fact that it differs widely in different parts of the body (of courses with such an informal demonstrations one should point out that its purpose is merely to il lustrate a phenomenon and not to provide quantitatively precise data.)

The Just Noticeable Difference (JND). Titchener's laboratory manuals (1901/1971, 1905/1971a, 1905/1971b) provide another rich source of demonstrations for classroom use. For example, one can adaptTitchener's instructions for making a series of weighted envelopes (1905/1971a, p. 33). These can be employed in a classroom demonstration in which a volunteer determines the JND in the weights of the envelopes.

Many more demonstrations can be found by consulting Sanford's and Titchener's laboratory manuals. In general the advantage of Sanford's experiments and demonstrations lies in theirvery informality whileTitchener's examples may best be used to illustrate the precision in measurement which the early laboratories attempted to achieve.

The Method of Introspection

Since Titchener's Structuralism and the reactions to it occupy such a prominent place in the history of psychology, it is important that students understand why it ultimately failed. One reason of course was its reliance on the method of introspection. Unfortunately, while a vague understanding of introspection in the sense of examining one's own consciousness is not hard to acquires understanding the introspection of the laboratory is another matter entirely One way to familiarize students with introspection and the many garbs it assumed in the laboratory is to provide opportunities to try it for themselves. Three very different demonstrations can be used to illustrate both good and bad points of introspection.

The Method of Paired Comparisons. This method of ranking stimuli in order of pleasantness is illustrative of introspection in its more precise form ands of courses is still in use today. Titchener gives detailed instructions for this method in his laboratory manual (1901/1971, pp. 92-95). Paper of various colors is the only apparatus needed. While the ever-thorough Titchener proposed that 27 different colors be used (requiring 351 separate comparisons!) it is sufficient to display all possible combinations among five or six sheets of colored paper so that each student can rank the colors in order of individual pleasantness.

An Imagery 'Questionary'. Another form of introspection concerns reporting on the characteristics of one's imagery. One of Titchener's exercises is a "Questionary upon Ideational Type" (1905/1971, pp. 197-200). As Titchener notes "The questionary or'questionnaire' is a series of questions bearing upon the matter to be investigated, and submitted to a large number of persons for introspective answer" (p.197). The first question begins as follows:

> Think of a bunch of white rose-buds, lying among fern leaves in a florist's box (a) Are the colours—the creamy white the green, the shiny white—quite distinct and natural? (b) Do you see the flowers in a good light? Is the image as bright as the objects would be if they lay on the table before you? (p. 198)

Having students complete this 'questionary,' or portions of its illustrates not only one type of problem which Titchener attempted to deal with through introspection; italso provides an example of the general acceptance of imagery in Titchener's psychology ands when compared with methods and problems considered appropriate by other schools (e.g., Behaviorism) provides a basis for discussing ways in which early schools differed.

Introspection on Affective Qualities. A third demonstration of introspection, and the one most useful for illustrating its pitfalls, can be adapted from a study conducted in Titchener's laboratory by Nafe (1924). This study is useful primarily because it provides highly detailed accounts of introspections of the affective qualities of pleasantness and unpleasant-ness. In the original study, a wide variety of stimuli were investigated, including colored strips of paper, the foetus of a dog in a bottle of alcohol, tuning forks, the juice from a can of shrimps, sweet chocolate, a warm egg, and a small strip of very soft fur.

For classroom purposes, two easily accessible stimuli can be used. I chose sweet chocolate and colored strips of paper. Following Nafe's instructions as closely as possible, students made initial introspections in class and later brought in written summariesto compare with those of Nafe's subjects. The following excerpt from the introspection on sweet chocolate by one of Nafe's observers is illustrative:

> The characterization, P [pleasant], applies to the experienced complex, the predominant components of which were the quality of sweet and a brightness or lightness reminiscent of a bright pressure. (p. 515)

In asking students to participate in such an exercise one must, of course, point out that class participants have not been *trained,* as observers in Titchener's laboratory would have been. Even with this qualification, however, the shortcomings of this form of introspection quickly become apparent and lead to discussion of the possible effects of suggestion and experimenter demand on data obtained through this method. (For additional information on exactly *how* to introspect, see English, 1921.)

Early Laboratory Instruments

Early laboratories, particularly Wundt's laboratory at Leipzig and Titchener's laboratory at Cornell, fairly bristled with elaborate equipment, and instrumentation has been of enormous importance in the development of most schools. It stands to reason that, in order to understand the development of experimental psychology, one needs some idea of what the instruments were like! Despite the importance of instruments, however, illustrations of them are rare indeed in history of psychology texts.

Projection Lantern" Presentations. Preparation of one's own "projection lantern" slides provides one reasonably simple way to illustrate early instruments, provided that one has access to photographic equipment or can prevail upon one's media center to make slides. The best sources are the excellent line drawings in Titchener's laboratory manuals (1901/1971,1905/1971a,1905/1971b) and text-book (1910/ 1916). Such slides can be extremely useful, for they communicate many things: the complexity of the equipment, the care taken in its design, the types of problems studied, and the role of the instruments in their study.

Another source, brief but quite useful, is the catalogue prepared by the Archives of the History of American Psychology for an exhibit of instruments in honor of the 75th anniversary of the American Psychological Association (Note 1). This provides brief descriptions of thirty-eight early instruments together with line drawings for twenty of them.

Parenthetically, it should be noted that any photograph or drawing pertinent to the history of psychology is a possible candidate for slide-making (e.g., the illustrations in Davis & Merzbach, 1975; Roback & Kiernan, 1969, and Runes, 1959). Unfortunately, such a "do-it-yourself" approach must suffice until publishers recognize that such materials are needed.

Replicas of Historic Apparatus As Titchener noted,

> it is much better to bring a stereoscope with you into the lecture-room, to pass round slides, and to work out the construction of the instrument by a diagram, than simply to talk about the facts and theories of binocular vision. (1903, p. 176)

If, in fact, one does wish to take a stereoscope into the classroom, one can do just that, since a replica of one has been manufactured (Note 2). In addition, a recent publication (Jones, 1976) reviews the history of the stereoscope and provides a collection of stereoscopic views together with a simple viewer.

Insofar as demonstrating other historic apparatus is concerned, it is once again appropriate to echo Titchener who complained, concerning demonstration apparatus in general, that "there ought to be a full set of ready-made pieces, available to those who desire it at moderate cost" (1903, p. 175). Since such a set is not now available, one must devise other means to obtain replicas of historic apparatus.

One way to obtain replicas is to encourage students to build them. While most of the brass instruments are too complex to duplicate, there are many instruments which are relatively simple to build. So far I have acquired two student-built replicas, a fall tachistoscope (based on information provided by Woodworth, 1938, p. 689) and a Thorndike puzzle box (based on information provided by Burnham, 1972, and Thorndike, 1911/1965). Descriptions of new apparatus are sprinkled throughout early issues of the *American Journal of Psychology,* and many ideas for replicas can be found in early texts.

Although I have only just begun to create a collection of replicas, many students have expressed interest in constructing them, and I expect my collection to grow rapidly. While building replicas and discovering how they were used provides valuable learning experiences, there are other benefits as well: Classroom demonstrations using replicas are exciting as well as instructive, and the instruments can then be employed in replications of important experiments in the history of psychology.

Early Studies of Associative Processes

Lest the reader conclude that the only sources of effective demonstrations, other than replicas, are to be found in early Structural studies, let me hasten to provide additional examples relevant to other schools and points of view.

Ebbinghaus and Nonsense Syllables. Ebbinghaus studied the effects of many variables on the learning of nonsense syllables (1885/1964) and it is helpful for students to attempt one or two such experiments and to compare their findings with those of Ebbinghaus. One good candidate for an outside assignment is for students to determine how the length of the list affects the number of repetitions needed to learn the list. In brief, Ebbinghaus found that a list of seven syllables could be learned with one repetition but increases in the length of the list resulted in disproportionate amounts of effort being required. My students have replicated Ebbinghaus' experimental conditions as closely as possible outside class, learning lists of seven and twelve syllables.

Such an assignment requires very little time and apparatus, but students can learn many things from it: what nonsense syllables were, the kinds of problems studied by Ebbinghaus, and the difficulties inherent in being both subject and experimenter at the same time. In addition, the experience leads to discussion of how such problems stimulated the development of instrumentation such as the memory drum, which one can bring into the class and demonstrate. The attempt to explain the great discrepancy in effort needed to learn seven and twelve syllables leads to more recent theories of information processing. One happy by-product of such discussion is an increased appreciation of historical studies and the degree of continuity between historical and contemporary approaches to psychology.

Trial and Error Learning. Thorndike's studies of learning provide ample sources of potential demonstrations for classroom use. For example, students can experience trial-and-error learning for themselves by attempting to solve a finger maze. (Such mazes can easily be made by drawing on thick cardboard a maze wide enough for the finger to move through. The finger track is cut out and the resulting outline pasted to another sheet of cardboard. A small hole in the bottom sheet indicates when the end of the maze has been reached.) If time is available to construct only one maze, invite a volunteer to attempt the maze, eyes closed, as the class observes.

Thorndike's Line-drawing Experiment. In the history of psychology course, one topic which needs far fuller treatment than it usually receives is the issue of theory revision. All too often, limitations of time require the various theories and systems to be presented more or less as finished products, without showing how they changed in the course of development and research.

Thorndike's theory of learning is an ideal example with which to illustrate this process. One well-known revision made by Thorndike concerned his Law of

Exercise, and his line-drawing experiment was an attempt to determine whether mere repetition of a situation influenced learning. As Thorndike describes the experiment,

> You sit at your desk with a large pad of paper and a pencil, close your eyes, say, "Draw a four-inch line with one quick movement " and again and again draw with one quick shove a line intended to be four inches long. You keep your eyes closed throughout. Day after day you do this until you have drawn 3,000 lines, no one of which you have ever seen. You have then responded to approximately the same situation— "Draw a four-inch line with one quick shove of the same pencil on the same pad in the same position"—3,000 times. (1931/ 1968, p. 8)

The end of the story is well known: Thorndike concluded that sheer repetition without the benefit of seeing the consequences failed to cause learning.

This experiment provides a powerful and reliable demonstration of why Thorndike had to modify his theory. Fortunately it is not necessary to have students draw 3,000 lines—a dozen are sufficient to make the point. It is help fulto provide mimeographed "rulers" to enable students to measure their responses on the spot. (A number of additional ideas for demonstrations can be found in Thorndike's book *Human Learning*, 1931/1968.)

Gestalt Psychology

Demonstrations of some Gestalt concepts are readily available since laws of perceptual organization are easily drawn on the board during a lecture, and almost every text includes some examples. Illustrations for demonstrating figural after-effects are also easily procured (e.g., see Köhler, 1969/1972 p. 101). However, there are additional demonstrations which can greatly enhance understanding how Gestalt psychology differed from other schools.

The Phi Phenomenon. The Phi Phenomenon, or the illusion of apparent movement was particularly important in the development of Gestalt psychology because it provided an example of an experience which could not be analyzed into the elements for which Titchener and Wundt searched so assiduously.

Many schools already possess equipment for studying and demonstrating this phenomenon. However, should such equipment not be available or sufficiently portable to use in the classroom, Köhler (1969/1972, pp. 35-36) has provided a diagram of a relatively simple piece of apparatus, which he describes as follows:

> Two electric lamps are placed behind a translucent screen with a straight vertical rod midway between them, nearer to the screen than the lamps. A double switch makes it possible to turn the two lights on and off in rapid alternation. (p. 35)

Through this demonstration of the apparent movement of the shadow cast by the vertical rod, students can acquire an experiential basis for understanding some of the reasoning behind the Gestalt point of view.

Insight in Problem-solving. Nothing is more effective than first-hand experience in understanding what is meant by "insight." Presenting problems forwhich insightful solutions can be reached provides opportunities for comparison with the trial-and-error solution of the finger maze. Numerous examples of such problems can be found in the collection gathered by Gardner (1978).

The Psychology of William James

In discussing James' psychology, his theory of emotion provides the basis for two interesting demonstrations.

James' Knife-blade Example. In discussing the bodily basis of emotion James suggests the following self-explanatory exercise:

> Imagine two steel knife-blades with their keen edges crossing each other at right angles, and moving to and fro. Our whole nervous organization is 'on-edge' at the thought; and yet what emotion can be there except the unpleasant nervous feeling itself, or the dread that more of it may come? The entire fund and capital of the emotion here is the senseless bodily effect which the blades immediately arouse. (1890/1950, p. 458)

Role-playing an Emotional Situation. One aspect of James' view was the position that, if one goes through the motions of an emotion, one ought to experience the emotion itself. It is said that James asked Broadway actors and actresses if, while acting out emotional scenes on the stage, they experienced any organic changes which brought about the appropriate emotion. James was told that, frequently, such organic changes did occur (Chaplin & Krawiec, 1974, p. 475).

Since professional actors and actresses may not be readily accessible, student volunteers can role-play an emotional situation before the class. Following this (and, of course, without mentioning the purpose of the exercise) the roleplayers should be asked to describe as closely as possible how they felt. Although one should take care to avoid leading questions (thus minimizing "teacher demand"), discussion of this experience can provide an excellent basis for understanding James' theory of emotions, and its shortcomings as well.

In conclusion, allow me to borrow once more from Titchener's words in saying that "I have...written out my own procedure, partly in the hope that some of my colleagues may be able to suggest better demonstrations from their teaching experience" (1903,

p. 190). The suggestions provided here represent only a few of the many possibilities that can be found in the sources already noted. Although limitations of space preclude descriptions of similar activities forother schools of psychology, the interested reader will find that, with a little time, ingenuity, and digging into early source material, they can easily be devised. It somehow seems only fitting that the early texts, journals, laboratory manuals, and apparatus which figured so prominently in the development of psychology should again serve in teaching its history.

References

Aristotle. [De Somniis]. In W. D. Ross (Ed.), *The works of Aristotle translated into English* (Vol. 3). London: Oxford University Press, 1931.

Boring, E. G. *A history of experimental psychology* (2nd ed.). New York: Appleton-Century-Crofts, 1950.

Burnham J. C. Thorndike's puzzle boxes. *Journal of the History of the Behavioral Sciences,* 1972, *8* 159-167.

Chaplin, J. P., & Krawiec,T. S. *Systems and theories of psychology* (3rd ed.). New York: Holt, Rinehart and Winston, 1974.

Davis, A. B., & Merzbach, U. C. *Early auditory studies: Activities in the psychology laboratories of American universities.* Washington, DC: Smithsonian Institution Press, 1 975. (GPO Stock Number: 047-001-00124-9)

Ebbinghaus, E. (*Memory: A contribution to experimental psychology*) (H. A. Ruger & C. E. Bussenius, trans.). New York: Dover Publications, 1964. (Originally published in German, 1885; in English, 1913.)

English, H. B. In aid of introspection. *American Journal of Psychology,* 1921, *32,* 404-414.

Gardner, M. *aha! Insight.* San Francisco: W. H. Freeman, 1978.

James, W. *The principles of psychology* (Vol. 2). New York: Dover Publications, 1950. (Originally published, 1890.)

Jones, J. *Wonders of the stereoscope.* New York: Knopf, 1976.

Köhler, W. *The task of Gestalt psychology.* Princeton, NJ: Princeton University Press, 1972. (Originally published, 1969.)

Nafe, J. P. An experimental study of the affective qualities. *American Journal of Psychology,* 1924, *35,* 507-544.

Roback, A. A., & Kiernan, T. *Pictorial history of psychology and psychiatry.* New York: Philosophical Library, 1969.

Runes, D. D. *Pictorial history of philosophy.* New York: Philosophical Library, 1959.

Sanford, E. C. A laboratory course in physiological psychology: I. The dermal senses; II. Static and kinaesthesic senses. *American Journal of Psychology,* 1891, *4,* 141-155. (a)

Sanford, E. C. A laboratory course in physiological psychology (second paper): III. Taste and smell; IV. Hearing. *American Journal of Psychology,* 1891, *4,* 303-322. (b)

Sanford, E. C. A laboratory course in physiological psychology (third paper): V. Vision. *American Journal of Psychology,* 1892, *4,* 474-490.

Sanford, E. C. Some practical suggestions on the equipment of a psychological laboratory. *American Journal of Psychology,* 1893, *5,* 429-438.

Sanford, E. C. A laboratory course in physiological psychology (sixth paper): Monocular perception of space. *American Journal of Psychology,* 1896, *7,* 412-424.

Sanford, E. C. A sketch of a beginner's course in psychology. *Pedagogical Seminary,* 1906, *13,* 118-124.

Thorndike, E. L. *Animal intelligence: Experimental studies.* New York: Hafner, 1965. (Originally published, 1911.)

Thorndike E. L *Human learning.* New York: Johnson Reprint Corporation, 1968. (Originally published, 1931.)

Titchener, E. B. *Experimental psychology: A manual of laboratory practice* (Vol. 1, Parts 1 & 2). New York: Johnson Reprint Corporation, 1971. (Originally published, 1901.)

Titchener, E. B. Class experiments and demonstration apparatus. *American Journal of Psychology,* 1903, *14,* 175- 191.

Titchener, E. B. *Experimental psychology: A manual of laboratory practice* (Vol . 2, Part 1). New York: Johnson Reprint Corporation, 1971. (Originally published, 1905.) (a)

Titchener, E. B. *Experimental psychology: A manual of laboratory practice* (Vol . 2, Part 2). New York: Johnson Reprint Corporation, 1971. (Originally published, 1905.) (b)

Titchener, E. B. *A text-book of psychology.* New York: Macmillan, 1916. (Originally published, 1910.)

Warren, H. C. *Human psychology.* Cambridge, MA: Houghton Mifflin, 1919.

Woodworth, R. S. *Experimental psychology.* New York: Holt, 1938.

Notes

1. The catalogue, "An exhibit in Honor of the 75th Anniversary, American Psychological Association, Philadelphia—1892, Washington—1967" may be obtained by writing to Dr. John A. Popplestone, Director, Archives of the History of American Psychology, The University of Akron, Akron, Ohio 44325.

2. A replica of a stereoscope used primarily for home entertainment purposes can be obtained from

Stereo Classics Studios, Inc., 145 Algonquin Parkway, Whippany, New Jersey 07981.
3. An earlier version of this paper was presented at the Annual Convention of the New York State Psychological Association, May 1978, as part of a symposium entitled "Innovative Approaches to the Teaching of Psychology."

Cognitive Maps as a Way of Presenting the Dimensions of Comparison Within the History of Psychology

George M. Diekhoff
Midwestern State University

As Benjamin (1981) notes in his handbook for teachers of the history of psychology, there is relatively little published on the teaching of the history of psychology, despite the fact that nearly all psychology departments offer such a course and many require it for majors (Riedel, 1974). In this paper I shall describe an activity which I have developed for use in several courses, including history and systems, that has stimulated much valuable discussion by students and increases test scores in general psychology (Diekhoff & Diekhoff, in press).

Students taking history and systems are typically capable of learning about the accomplishments of individuals through the usual lecture/text combination. However, they frequently lack an appreciation for the dimensions along which psychologists from different schools, theoretical persuasions, and times may be compared and found to be similar or different. This failure undoubtedly results from the linear, sequential way in which lectures and texts cover first one person, then the next and the next, without ever systematically examining any but the most obvious relationships that exist between the individuals.

To facilitate in-class discussions about these structural interrelationships, I have found the following activity to be very useful. Following completion of lectures covering one or more units, I select between 10 and 20 prominent persons and/or theories from the material to be reviewed. I form all possible pairs of these stimuli and rate each pair on a 1 to 9 scale so as to indicate the degree of similarity that exists between the stimuli in each pair (1 = little . . . 9 = great), and the set of ratings is analyzed through principal components analysis as though the ratings were the coefficients of a correlation matrix. The output from the principal components analysis includes a graphic summary (sometimes called a "cognitive map") of the interrelationships between the stimuli judged for similarity. These cognitive maps display stimuli arranged in space in which the proximity of each stimulus to the others is isomorphic to the amount of similarity that was judged to exist between that stimulus and the others. Highly similar or related stimuli thus form clusters in space. Occasionally stimuli are observed to be arranged along identifiable bipolar dimensions. The cognitive maps generated in this fashion may be displayed on a two-dimensional surface, such as a blackboard, or three-dimensionally by using a specially constructed framework to which objects representing the stimuli are attached.

Class discussions of the structural interrelationships in the history of psychology are then guided by the cognitive map. Why are certain stimuli together in a cluster? Why are certain stimuli so far apart? What dimensions can be found within the array and why do various stimuli occupy the positions that they do along these dimensions?

An example of the process described is provided in Figure 1. In this example, a set of 10 key individuals from the early history of psychology has been selected, judged for similarity, and analyzed through principal components analysis. The resulting cognitive map is shown in two dimensions.

In discussing this map, the following comments are representative of those that might occur in class. Three clusters of highly similar individuals appear: (1) Fechner/Wundt/Hobbes/Ebbinghaus; (2) Fritsch & Hitzig/Gall/Descartes; and (3) Mesmer/McDougall. Galton is positioned between Clusters 1 and 3. Cluster 1 contains the names of those of a mentalistic orientation whose contributions are still recognized as important and valid: Fechner's early work in psychophysics; Wundt's founding of a psychology of consciousness; Hobbes' work with associations; and

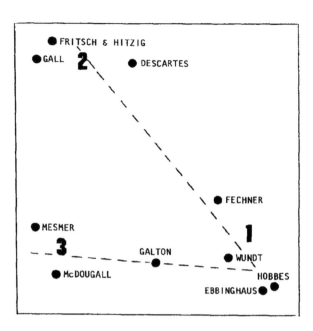

Figure 1. An example of cognitive mapping used in the study of the structural interrelationships between prominent individuals from early in the history of psychology.

Ebbinghaus' studies of memory. Personalities in Cluster 2 all were involved in early attempts to describe physiological bases of behavior and mental processes: Fritsch & Hitzig through early electrical brain stimulation; Gall through phrenology; and Descartes through his hydraulic model of the nervous system. Cluster 3 contains the names of those who offered nonphysiological "false starts" to psychology: Mesmer with his magnetic explanation of hypnosis; and McDougall's overuse of instinct theory. Galton's position between Clusters 1 and 3 reflects that he introduced the important ideas of mental measurement and correlation (Cluster 1), but he mistakenly attempted to use sensory and motor measures of intelligence (Cluster 3).

In addition to these clusters, two bipolar dimensions can be seen. The first extends from Cluster 2 to Cluster 1 and corresponds to a Physiological—Mentalistic orientation or approach. The second dimension extends from Cluster 3 to Cluster 1 and roughly reflects a Credibility dimension along which individuals are arranged according to the current

acceptability of their propositions. Accepted notions are found toward Cluster 1 (with the exception of Wundt, many of whose ideas are no longer accepted, but who holds a revered position in psychology for his work in founding psychology) and ideas which are not now accepted are found toward Cluster 3 (with the exception of Fritsch & Hitzig, whose work in electrical brain stimulation is still viewed as valid). It is interesting to note that with the exceptions noted above, those at the mentalistic end of the dimension are generally seen as having made the most lasting contributions. This tendency to view those who have taken a physiological approach as less credible than those whose theories are more mentalistic is surprising until one notes that physiological theories are usually more testable than are mentalistic theories, and thus, are more easily refuted.

Although there may be disagreement with some aspects of the sample map and with some of the interpretations of that map, these disagreements can themselves serve as stimulation for instructive discussion. I have found, for example, that discussions and comparisons of cognitive maps generated from students' similarity judgments add an enlightening element to review sessions and promote greater participation in these discussions.

In sum, the use of cognitive maps effectively promotes discussions of the structural interrelationships that exist among the personalities and theories in the history of psychology. Given the wide availability of principal components analysis programs in packages such as SPSS, many instructors may find the method described here to be quite useful as an adjunct to their regular lecture materials.

References

Benjamin, L. T. *Teaching history of psychology: A handbook.* New York: Academic Press, 1981.

Diekhoff, G. M., & Diekhoff, K. B. Cognitive maps as a tool in communicating structural knowledge *Educational Technology,* in press.

Riedel, R. G. The current status of the history and systems of psychology courses in American colleges and universities. *Journal of the History of the Behavioral Sciences,* 1974, *10,* 410-412.

Table - Volume 1

Articles	Topics												
	1	2	3	4	5	6	7	8	9	10	11	12	13
Introductory													
Promoting Active Participation													
Gorman, Law, & Lindegren	P												
Kellogg	P	S	S		S	S	S	S	S	S	S	S	S
Wesp	P												
Introducing Research Methods													
Bates	P												
Polyson & Blick	P												
Kohn & Brill	P												
Lutsky	P												
Ward & Grasha	P												
Larkin, Pines, & Julian	P												
Using Computers													
Brothen	P												
Brothen & Schneider	P												
Bare	P												
Integrating Supplementary Literature													
Appleby	P												
Schwartz	P	S	S	S	S	S	S	S	S	S	S	S	S
Winzenz & Winzenz	P	S	S	S	S	S	S	S	S	S	S	S	S
Employing Introductory Laboratories													
Fish & Fraser	P												
Katz	P												
Statistics													
Starting the Semester													
Dillon		P											
Hastings		P											
Jacobs		P											
Making Statistics Relevant													
Beins		P	S										
Shatz		P											
Weaver		P											
Dillbeck		P											
Generating Data													
Cake & Hostetter		P	S										
Hettich		P	S										
McGown & Spencer		P	S										
Dudek		P	S										
Teaching Specific Concepts													
Duke		P											
Huck, Wright, & Park		P											
Johnson		P											
Karylowski		P	S										
Levin		P	S										

Zerbolio			P	S									
Moore			P	S									
Johnson			P	S									
Williams			P										
Buck			P	S									
Allen			P										
Combining Statistics and Research Methods													
Rossi			P	S									
Dillon			P	S									
Research Methods													
Reviewing the Literature													
Gardner		S	P	S	S	S	S	S	S	S	S	S	S
Mathews		S	P	S	S	S	S	S	S	S	S	S	S
Parr		S	P	S	S	S	S	S	S	S	S	S	S
Parr		S	P	S	S	S	S	S	S	S	S	S	S
Feinberg, Drews, & Eynman		S	P	S	S	S	S	S	S	S	S	S	S
Lewis		S	P	S	S	S	S	S	S	S	S	S	S
Teaching Experimental Design and Methods of Observation													
Stallings			P										
Zerbolio & Walker			P		S								
Kerber			P								S		
Kerber			P										
Zeren & Makosky			P								S		
Herzog			P										
Teaching Research Ethics													
Beins		S	P		S	S	S	S	S	S	S	S	S
Rosnow			P										
Strohmetz & Skleder		S	P		S	S	S	S	S	S	S	S	S
Herzog			P										
Teaching Principles, Concepts, and Skills													
Hatcher			P										
Vandervert		S	P		S	S	S	S	S	S	S	S	S
Kohn		S	P		S	S	S	S	S	S	S	S	S
Yoder			P							S	S	S		S
Falkenberg			P										
Carroll			P										
Peden		S	P	S	S	S	S	S	S	S	S	S	S
Gore & Camp			P										
Gibson	S	S	P	S	S	S	S	S	S	S	S	S	S
Using Computers													
Gregory			P										
Hartley, Fisher, & Hartley			P										
Hartley & Smith			P										
Benedict & Butts			P										
Peden			P										
Hovancik			P										
Peden & Steinhauer			P										

Using Popular Media and Scholarly Publications	1	2	3	4	5	6	7	8	9	10	11	12	13
Connor-Greene	S		P		S	S	S	S	S	S	S	S	S
McCarthy	S		P		S	S	S	S	S	S	S	S	S
Solomon			P										
Chamberlain			P										
Suter & Frank	S		P	S	S	S	S	S	S	S	S	S	S
Howard & Engelhardt			P										
History													
Benjamin				P									
Terry				P									
Davis, Janzen, & Davis				P									
Grigg				P									
Brooks				P									
Cole				P									
Berrenberg & Prosser	S	S	S	P	S	S	S	S	S	S	S	S	S
Crossman & Crossman	S	S	S	P	S	S	S	S	S	S	S	S	S
Wight				P									
Raphelson	S	S	S	P	S	S	S	S	S	S	S	S	S
Caudle				P									
Diekhoff				P									

1   Introductory
2   Statistics
3   Research Methods
4   History
5   Physiological-Comparative
6   Perception
7   Learning

8   Cognition
9   Developmental
10 Personality
11 Abnormal
12 Clinical-Counseling
13 Social

P = Primary   S = Secondary

Appendix- Volume 1

Introductory

Promoting Active Participation
Gorman, Law, & Lindegren, 1981, *8*, 164-166.
Kellogg, R. L. 1981, *8*, 178-179.
Wesp, 1992, *19*, 219-221.

Introducing Research Methods
Bates, 1991, *18*, 94-97.
Polyson & Blick, 1985, *12*, 52-53.
Kohn & Brill, 1981, *8*, 133-138.
Lutsky, 1986, *13*, 119-122.
Ward & Grasha, 1986, *13*, 143-145.
Larkin, Pines, & Julian, 1979, *6*, 237-238.

Using Computers
Brothen, 1984, *11*, 105-107.
Brothen & Schneider, 1993, *20*, 186-187.
Bare, 1982, *9*, 236-237.

Integrating Supplementary Literature
Appleby, 1987, *14*, 172-174.
Schwartz, 1980, *7*, 192-193.
Winzenz & Winzenz, 1978, *5*, 159-160.

Employing Introductory Laboratories
Fish & Fraser, 1993, *20*, 231-233.
Katz, 1978, *5*, 91-93.

Statistics

Starting the Semester
Dillon, 1982, *9*, 117.
Hastings, 1982, *9*, 221-222.
Jacobs, 1980, *7*, 241-242.

Making Statistics Relevant
Beins, 1985, *12*, 168-169.
Shatz, 1985, *12*, 85-86.
Weaver, 1992, *19*, 178-179.
Dillbeck, 1983, *10*, 18-20.

Generating Data
Cake & Hostetter, 1986, *13*, 210-212.
Hettich, 1974, *1*, 35-36.
McGown & Spencer, 1980, *7*, 63.
Dudek, 1981, *8*, 51.

Teaching Specific Concepts
Duke, 1978, *5*, 219-221.
Huck, Wright, & Park, 1992, *19*, 45-47.
Johnson, 1986, *13*, 155-156.
Karylowski, 1985, *12*, 229-230.

Levin, 1982, *9*, 237-238.
Zerbolio, 1989, *16*, 207-209.
Moore, 1981, *8*, 163-164.
Johnson, 1989, *16*, 67-68.
Williams, 1975, *2*, 76-78.
Buck, 1991, *18*, 46-47.
Allen, 1981, *8*, 179-180.

Combining Statistics and Research Methods
Rossi, 1987, *14*, 98-101.
Dillon, 1978, *5*, 212-213.

Research Methods

Reviewing the Literature
Gardner, 1977, *4*, 89-91.
Mathews, 1978, *5*, 100-101.
Parr, 1978, *5*, 101-102.
Parr, 1979, *6*, 61-62.
Feinberg, Drews, & Eynman, 1981, *8*, 51-52.
Lewis, 1986, *13*, 38-40.

Teaching Experimental Design and Methods of Observation
Stallings, 1993, *20*, 165-167.
Zerbolio, & Walker, 1989, *16*, 65-66.
Kerber, 1980, *7*, 50-52.
Kerber, 1983, *10*, 236-239.
Zeren & Makosky, 1986, *13*, 80-82.
Herzog, 1988, *15*, 200-202.

Teaching Research Ethics
Beins, 1993, *20*, 33-35.
Rosnow, 1990, *17*, 179-181.
Strohmetz, & Skleder, 1992, *19*, 106-108.
Herzog, 1990, *17*, 90-94.

Teaching Principles, Concepts, and Skills
Hatcher, 1990, *17*, 123-124.
Vandervert, 1980, *7*, 57-59.
Kohn, 1992, *19*, 217-219.
Yoder, 1979, *6*, 170.
Falkenberg, 1981, *8*, 214-215.
Carroll, 1986, *13*, 208-210.
Peden, 1991, *18*, 102-105.
Gore & Camp, 1987, *14*, 243-244.
Gibson, 1991, *18*, 176-177.

Using Computers
Gregory, 1977, *4*, 63-67.
Hartley, Fisher, & Hartley, 1977, *4*, 202-204.

Hartley & Smith, 1979, *6*, 235-237.
Benedict & Butts, 1981, *8*, 35-38.
Peden, 1987, *14*, 217-219.
Hovancik, 1986, *13*, 94-96.
Peden & Steinhauer, 1986, *13*, 85-87.

Using Popular Media and Scholarly Publications
Connor-Greene, 1993, *20*, 167-169.
McCarthy, 1982, *9*, 185-186
Solomon, 1979, *6*, 26-30.
Chamberlain, 1988, *15*, 207-208.
Suter & Frank, 1986, *13*, 219-221.
Howard & Engelhardt, 1984, *11*, 44-45.

History

Benjamin, 1990, *17*, 97-100.
Terry, 1980, *7*, 176-177.
Davis, Janzen, & Davis, 1982, *9*, 183-184.
Grigg, 1974, *1*, 84-85.
Brooks, 1985, *12*, 84-85.
Cole, 1983, *10*, 234-236.
Berrenberg & Prosser, 1991, *18*, 167-169.
Crossman & Crossman, 1983, *10*, 98-99.
Wight, 1993, *20*, 112.
Raphelson, 1987, *14*, 103-105.
Caudle, 1979, *6*, 7-11.
Diekhoff, 1982, *9*, 115-116.

Subject Index